Encyclopedia of
Human Rights Issues
Since 1945

Encyclopedia of Human Rights Issues Since 1945

Winston E. Langley

Greenwood Press
Westport, Connecticut

Library of Congress Cataloging-in-Publication Data

Langley, Winston.
   Encyclopedia of human rights issues since 1945 / Winston E.
Langley.
     p. cm.
   Includes bibliographical references and index.
   ISBN 0–313–30163–8 (alk. paper)
   1. Human rights—Encyclopedias.   I. Title.
Ref JC571.L2747   1999
   323'.03—dc21   98–30498

British Library Cataloguing in Publication Data is available.

Library of Congress Catalog Card Number: 98–30498
ISBN: 0–313–30163–8

First published in 1999

Greenwood Press, 88 Post Road West, Westport, CT 06881
An imprint of Greenwood Publishing Group, Inc.
www.greenwood.com

Printed in the United States of America

∞™

The paper used in this book complies with the
Permanent Paper Standard issued by the National
Information Standards Organization (Z39.48–1984).

10 9 8 7 6 5 4 3 2

To victims of
human rights abuse
everywhere

Contents

Preface

Preparing this volume was both rewarding and difficult. Rewarding, because it gave me a new appreciation for the breadth, richness, and complexity of the human rights movement as it has developed since 1945. Rewarding because it brought home in clear and persuasive terms, the reasons why human rights have provoked such strong and moving passions in people, and why governments have, time and time again, sought to disguise the true meaning of those rights or to employ force and brutality to mute, if not eliminate, their expression. First, international recognition of those rights hold the most profound social and moral promise that people have been offered in modern times. Second, that promise bears with it the potential to revolutionize the entire structure of interpersonal, intersocietal, and international relations. Third, because the state is at once the institution that must guarantee the promotion and protection of those rights as well as the institution most threatened by their full exercise, a large gap has developed between the promise and the reality of people's lives. The gap and the tension the gap occasions are present throughout the book.

Preparing the work was demanding because particular issues had to be placed in the context of the factors mentioned above, on account of the need to cover the complexity of human rights issues in the limited space available, and because of the need to go beyond the narrow confines of the issues generally emphasized by most governments, opinion shapers, and scholars. It was also difficult because, in some instances, the potential for misunderstanding could undermine the good that this volume hopes to serve: to help educate individuals about their moral and legal entitlements, the widespread abuse of those entitlements, and the difference the full enjoyment of those entitlements would make in their daily lives.

I would like to thank the International Studies Library at Harvard University, the staff of the Boston University Law Library, the International

Labor Office, the Secretariat of UNESCO, and the Centre for Human Rights for their help during my work on this volume. Thanks also to non-governmental groups that responded to my request for information, and Professor Robert Weiner for advice on Romania, Dr. Joseph P. Baratta for help in securing an important area of information on Franklin D. Roosevelt, Barbara Rader at Greenwood Press, who urged me to work on the volume and was generous in her suggestions, Amy Grunder, who helped me locate some important documents, and Carol Smythe, who proofread the manuscript.

Introduction

Fifty years ago, the idea of human rights had little significance for most people, including many of those who then considered themselves among the moral leaders of societies. Today, the concept of human rights and the human rights movement have captured the imagination of people, including the unschooled and the socially neglected, throughout the world. And those rights, together with the movement associated with them, have become the most potent moral force in the contemporary world.

The development of the human rights movement can be understood by looking at its political beginnings, conceptual reach, evolution and scope, and the agents of that movement. Understanding may also be gained by reviewing, briefly, challenges to the concept and the movement, and by touching on some controversies surrounding both.

December 10, Human Rights Day, is celebrated worldwide because it is the day in 1948 that Universal Declaration of Human Rights was adopted by the United Nations. This declaration has not only been "a common standard of achievement for all peoples and all nations," but the source of moral inspiration for all other human rights instruments. The United Nations Charter, which came into being in 1945, is, however, the first international mechanism that incorporated human rights as a concept and made the promotion and protection of those rights one of the purposes of the individual and collective obligations of states. In turn, that purpose and its associated international obligations, were informed by four things: a perceived need during World War II to recognize human rights, the Holocaust, a fundamental aim of the UN, and an agreed-on means to realize that aim.

During World War II, the two most prominent Western political leaders—Franklin D. Roosevelt of the United States and Winston S. Churchill of the United Kingdom—concluded that the chances of a military victory against Nazi Germany and its allies, Italy and Japan, could be significantly improved by linking the ongoing military efforts to larger moral goals. Those goals, incorporated in the August 14, 1941, Atlantic Charter, were the respect for the rights of *all* people and ensuring their sovereign right to choose their own governments. Earlier, those goals were expanded by President Roosevelt in his message to Congress about Four Freedoms to include freedom from fear and freedom from want.

The moral depravity of World War II also influenced the evolution of the human rights movement. No area of that depravity was worse than the systematic genocidal slaughter of an estimated 6 million Jews. Although the true nature and extent of the Holocaust was not then fully understood, the existing knowledge contributed to a most important resolve on the part of those who were responsible for planning the post-1945 international political and legal order: to include the protection of human rights as part of its principles and purposes. Article 1 (3) of the UN Charter states that one of the principal aims of the UN is that of "promoting and encouraging respect for human rights and fundamental freedoms for all without distinction as to race, sex, language, or religion." And the UN, itself created out of the material and moral destruction of World War II, was envisioned by its founders as an institution within which nation-states would work together to "codify global human rights principles as well as to promote, monitor, and protect human rights in countries throughout the world." The monitoring and protecting of human rights were seen as according some honor to the many who died from "every corner of the globe," grounding the international system on a moral foundation, aborting the return of a like war, and generating political support for the United Nations.

While the promotion and protection of human rights are important for their own sake, it was understood by the founders of the UN that nations and individuals should be encouraged to work toward making explicit what was implicit in the human rights concept—the moral solidarity of all human beings. It was believed that only through the conscious pursuit and achievement of that solidarity could the previously mentioned aim of the UN, and the full enjoyment of human rights, be realized. But what is the concept of human rights and how did it develop?

The term human rights is relatively new, but aspects of its contemporary meaning are very old. All of the major religions, including Buddhism, Christianity, Hinduism, Islam, and Judaism, for instance (as if to underscore its universality), speak of the inherent dignity of the individual or the sacred nature of the human personality. Our conventional international law of human rights is linked to ideas having roots in natural law (as propounded in many countries, especially those of the West) and Roman law. Political thinkers such as John Locke (1632–1704) and Jean-Jacques Rousseau (1712–1778) and legal scholars such as Francisco Suarez (1549–1617), Hugo Grotius (1583–1648), and Emmerich de Vattel (1714–1767) have also contributed to our current understanding of both natural law and its human rights content. In international practice, historians sometimes point to efforts following World War I, through the League of Nations and what has come to be called "minority treaties," to ensure that states respect the rights of ethnic, linguistic, national, religious, and other minorities among their inhabitants. References are also frequently made to interventionism on the part of states to protect their nationals and coreligionists abroad (as is now being suggested for Christians in China), when they are deemed to have been threatened with injury, injured, or subjected to denial of justice. Thinkers have likewise identified the American and French Revolutions and their emphasis on the idea of liberty and equality and their stance that governments derive their just powers from the consent of the governed, as an important national focus on human rights. As important and as many and varied as the efforts preceding 1945 were in influencing and shaping the human rights movement, the human rights *concept* that was given institutional expression after World War II is more profound in spirit, broader and richer in scope, and morally and socially more groundbreaking in character and promise than anything previously conceived.

First, its emphasis is on human beings. So any focus on nationals and coreligionists is misplaced. This does not mean that a country may not seek to promote and protect the rights of persons who are nationals or coreligionists. Such promotion and protection, however, cannot be on the basis of nationality or religion, but rather on the grounds that the individual is a human being, who just happens to be a national or coreligionist. The country that engages in promotion and protection must also be prepared to act on behalf of other human beings, with whom it shares no ties of religion or nationality, wherever and whenever the need arises. Second, with the *human* rights emphasis, how a country treats individuals under its jurisdiction, even when they are its own citizens, could no longer be only its concern (an issue during World War II, when the Nazis slaughtered its Jewish citizens); that treatment became an *international* concern.

Since the manner in which a country treats people within its borders, including its own citizens, is an issue of concern for all nations, it follows that the pre-1945 stance that would make such treatment a matter of *domestic* jurisdiction is no longer valid. Neither is *national* law the ultimate arbiter of human rights: international standards are. South Africa, with its former system of racial separation called apartheid, discovered that its plea of domestic jurisdiction was invalid as the international community imposed sanctions against it; and the People's Republic of China, despite a similar claim, will one day discover itself facing sanctions if it allows its one-child policy to undermine the equality of men and women.

A fourth area in which the post-1945 concept of human rights has represented a moral and cultural departure is the view that the inherent dignity of all human beings and the rights associated with that dignity not only

bespeak the moral and spiritual sisterhood and brotherhood of human beings, but represent the moral foundations on which friendly relations between and among countries can be fully developed and maintained. Fifth,
if states are obliged to advance the rights of all people, not only those who
happen to be their citizens, and such people have an equal claim to the
promotion and protection of those rights, then it follows that the policies
of states cannot be evaluated on the basis of traditional national interests
but, rather, on the extent to which such policies are grounded in the interests of the community of human beings. Finally, the concept transformed
the standing of individuals in international law from that of object on
whom the law could have an effect to that of subject, who could take the
law into "his or her own hands" (independently of the claims of the state),
in order to advance his or her own rights, even to the extent of suing his
or her own government.

When the above-described concept of human rights was instituted, it
germinated into a worldwide human rights movement, at first led by states,
with the support of individuals and civic groups. Later on, however, the
principal supporters or agents of the movement became individuals and
nongovernmental organizations, with states more or less serving as secondary supporters, sometimes distant followers.

In the case of governments serving as principal agents of the movement,
much of the early support was ideologically motivated, as the West, led by
the United States, sought to advance civil and political rights throughout
the world, in part as an ideal, but more as a political instrument to undermine the authoritarian communist system of the East, then led by the Soviet
Union: if those rights did not undermine communism, they would at least
blunt its revolutionary luster. The communist countries, however, pushed
primarily for the economic, social, and cultural categories of human rights,
which comported with their ideals, but which they also saw as potentially
undermining the capitalist West. So, in accordance with their pledged obligation to "take joint and separate action" to help realize the end for which
the UN was established (including the promotion and protection of human
rights and fundamental freedoms), nation-states began to set themselves the
task of formulating human rights norms or standards.

These norms, first presented in the majestic 1948 Universal Declaration
of Human Rights, found themselves elaborated in many other human rights
instruments (including accords, charters, covenants, conventions, declarations, programs, protocols, recommendations, resolutions, safeguards, and
standard minimum rules). The declaration was itself later refined in two
1966 covenants, the International Covenant on Economic, Social and Cultural Rights, and the International Covenant on Civil and Political Rights.
The first covenant deals with the right to work, to medical care, to education, to food, housing, clothing, social security, and to participate in the
cultural life of the community. The second deals with the right to a fair

trial, to a nationality, to leave and return to one's country, to freedom of speech, to freedom of thought and religion, to associate, and to the prohibition against torture, cruel or degrading treatment or punishment. These two covenants and the declaration have come to constitute what is now known as the International Bill of Human Rights, which house the core of human rights norms. Additional rights, pertaining to special categories of persons such as aliens, children, the disabled, indigenous persons, the mentally retarded, migrant workers, minorities (including ethnic, linguistic, national, and religious), prisoners (including those facing the death penalty), refugees, and women also have been amplified. So, too, are rights relating to certain conditions, including the right to peace, to a health-sustaining environment, and to development.

The standard-setting work of states has not only been confined to the global level. Regionally, important activities have taken place, with western Europe leading the way in its 1950 regional human rights instruments, the European Convention for the Protection of Human Rights and Fundamental Freedoms (called the European Convention on Human Rights), followed by the 1969 American Convention on Human Rights, the 1975 Helsinki Accords for Eastern Europe, and the 1981 African Charter on Human and Peoples' Rights. At both the regional and global levels—but especially at the global—individuals and nongovernmental groups became increasingly involved in influencing the standard-setting role of states, especially in cases on international instruments such as the 1979 Convention on the Elimination of All Forms of Discrimination Against Women, the 1986 Declaration on the Right to Development, the 1989 Convention on the Rights of the Child and the 1997 Declaration on the Human Genome and Human Rights.

The 1979 instrument came in the midst of a period when the human rights movement was spreading to all regions of the world and into almost every area of human activity and concern. In particular, it was formulated as part of the the international momentum of the women's rights movement, through which women's groups effectively influenced national governments and the UN to give support to the convention. Third World countries, many of which had moved from colonial status in 1945 to independent countries by means of the moral and legal force of the human right to self-determination, were among the principal sponsors of the 1986 Declaration on the Right to Development. They were supported by many Western and other civil society groups (nongovernmental organizations), which saw this declaration as potentially beneficial to all countries and individuals. Both the 1989 convention and the 1997 declaration had input and support from groups that have been strong advocates for children, and religious and scientific groups concerned with the dangers of and opportunities in genetic engineering. In the case of children, eighteen years or younger, the idea that they should enjoy rights that are independent of parents, or other adults, superseded the traditional claim that children are merely extensions of their parents' interests.

As important as the work of nongovernmental organizations has been in the standard-setting process during which states have been the major agents in the human rights movement, that work has been outdistanced by the role of those groups in a number of issues and challenges that the human rights movement has faced. These challenges include issues of ratification and implementation, the relationship between classes of rights, disclosures of human rights abuses, sovereignty, including the use of human rights as instruments of national interest, relativism, and business corporations.

On the matter of ratification and implementation, the issues are considerable. The existence of human rights standards by itself does not offer human beings the moral and legal claims to which they are entitled unless states are bound by those standards. And states are not bound, until they ratify the very standards they create. The United States, for example, has not yet ratified the previously mentioned 1979 convention that seeks to ensure equality for women, and so that convention is not legally binding in the United States. Equally important, even after ratification takes place, the claims that individuals can make under the accepted standards cannot be fulfilled unless there are institutional mechanisms to enforce them. Nongovernmental groups have been in the forefront in pressing states to ratify human rights instruments and develop mechanisms for their implementation. At present, one of the most important of such mechanisms is a proposed International Criminal Court, which will have the authority to try individuals, including heads of governments or states, who are alleged to have engaged in particularly serious human rights abuses such as genocide, crimes against humanity (including murder, torture, rape, and extermination), serious violations of the laws of war (including taking civilian hostages and subjecting detainees to medical and scientific experiments), and aggression.

An area of importance that serves to expand the debate on human rights and threatens to undermine the unity of the human rights movement, is that concerning the extent to which some categories of human rights should be accorded priority. If such precedents are allowed, which class of rights should be given the status of first standing? Is the right to freedom of thought, conscience and religion (civil and political rights) more important than the right to food, clothing, and education (economic, social, and cultural rights)? The West, which has championed the civil and political category of rights (often called first generation rights), has taken the position that such a priority exists and that it should be assigned to civil and political rights. The former communist countries, as well as the Global South (countries collectively called the Third World), also agree that such a priority ought to be recognized for certain rights. They, however, seek to give preference to the economic, social, and cultural class of rights. For nearly three decades following the 1966 adoption of the international covenants to the 1993 World Conference on Human Rights, which took place in Vienna, Austria, debate on this issue consumed a considerable amount of the human rights movement's time, energy, and passion. At that conference, under immense pressure from nongovernmental groups, including women's groups and political leaders who sought to preserve the unity of the movement, nation-states collectively affirmed the interdependence and indivisibility of all human rights. The issue is not settled, however, and it is likely to continue far into the future.

Perhaps no area of challenge is more formidable to the human rights movement than the abuse of human rights by governments—abuses that have varied from "disappearances" in Argentina, ethnic cleansing in Bosnia and Nagorno-Karabakh, genocide in Cambodia and Rwanda, torture in Britain, forced labor in Russia, racial discrimination in the Czech Republic, the United States, and Australia, religious persecution in Saudi Arabia, violence against women and homosexuals, as well as child labor, everywhere. First, governments guilty of such abuses deny their own violations of human rights and often overlook comparable abuses on the part of their allies. Second, such denials are invariably accompanied by governmental efforts to disguise (if not destroy) evidence of the abuses. Those efforts, in turn, often lead to other abuses such as illegal imprisonment, "disappearances," and even the death of victims, members of their families, as well as others who are likely to have knowledge of the offenses. Third, uncovering information with which to challenge governments is time-consuming, often expensive, and always risky (sometimes life-risking). Fourth, as international nongovernmental groups, in cooperation with local grassroots organizations, confront governments, they often try to limit access to sources of information they cannot destroy or otherwise disguise. Over the last twenty-five years, individuals and members of nongovernmental organizations have actively increased their roles in fact-finding, gaining access to the United Nations and, through human rights treaties, to regional commissions and courts on human rights. National truth commissions have also been used to uncover human rights violations by governments.

As individuals and groups confront governments and make their cases before the world, they increase awareness of certain human rights (sexual harassment, for example) and make governments, especially authoritarian ones such as those of China, Indonesia, Nigeria, and Serbia, increasingly uncomfortable. Likewise, as people's expectations in the areas of health care, education, food, clothing, working conditions, and the environment are disappointed, citizens groups form transborder alliances to improve their collective lot.

The final areas of challenge are those of sovereignty, relativism, and business corporations. The first assume many forms, including the claim on the part of some states that their supreme authority—sovereignty—entitles them to shape national policy in their national interest, which may exclude, or include to a limited degree only, human rights considerations. At a more fundamental level, governments use the claim of sovereignty to limit the right of individuals, including their own citizens, to hold them accountable, including the right to sue them for human rights abuses or *democratically replacing them.* So countries not only seek to block or limit an individual's access to human rights institutions, such as courts and commissions, but resist the development and expansion of those institutions' authority. Likewise, under the cloak of sovereignty, political groups use the state's coercive machinery to quash or try and deny the right of self-determination to ethnic, linguistic, national, religious, and other minorities. One has only to look at Bangladesh, Chechnya, Kosovo, Kurdistan, and Western Sahara to appreciate this fact. As dark a moral shadow as such practices cast over the human rights movement, they also give new impetus to limit the claims of sovereignty, expand the reach of human rights norms, and reaffirm the sisterhood/brotherhood of humans. Hence, the right to peace, to a life-sustaining environment (as well as the duty to ensure the integrity of the ecological order and the diversity of nature), to development, and duty to future generations.

On the issue of relativism, some states, primarily those of the Global South, and an appreciable number of individuals as well as nongovernmental groups from various areas of the world, including the West, claim that human rights are relative, are primarily rooted in the West, and have little universal validity. This claim, while "flying in the face of historical evidence," the philosophical meaning of the concept of human rights, and the social and spiritual yearnings of people everywhere, has found important support among politically significant groups: some who are disenchanted with certain political and cultural behavior on the part of the West (some are from the West); non-Western political and religious leaders who seek to preserve sources of power threatened by the human rights movement; and well-intentioned persons, who sometimes confuse the concept and content of human rights with certain approaches to the implementation of those rights. For instance, the right of everyone to own property is popularly presented—especially in the West—as the right to *private ownership* of property. Since much of the world pursues varying forms of use and ownership of property, reference to this right, as espoused by the West, often bears a degree of cultural preference. However, if one were to examine Article 17 of the Universal Declaration of Human Rights, one would quickly find that the language of the declaration does not exhibit any cultural preference.

Section 1 of Article 17 proclaims that everyone has the right to *own* property *alone as well as in association with others.* So, while the West may have and push for the cultural preference of private ownership, persons in other areas of the world who also have the right to *own*, may elect to exercise that right in various forms of *association with others*, and in accordance with their respective cultural traditions. The right to ownership is universal, the mode of implementation culturally relative. Capitalism, the dominant economic system in the world, is largely based on private ownership of property. And its expanding influence throughout the world, as well as its links to the cultural traditions of the West, makes that expansion one that generally appears to have a "western cultural content."

Linked to capitalism is a Western democratic system that emphasizes a considerable degree of individualism, in contrast to a more communal focus in most other areas of the globe. And allied to that individualism is the focus on rights, to the frequent exclusion of duties. The communal order tends to emphasize duties. This individualism/communalism divide is also part of the claim of relativism. But the implicit copresence of duties in any system of rights, the strength of the women's movement, which has always assigned importance to duties, and the emerging recognition that the communal order bears with it special attributes of dignity, together have begun to forge a new consensus on the complementary claims of rights and duties, and to blunt the claims of the cultural relativists. At the 1993 World Conference on Human Rights in Vienna, Austria (and earlier that year at a meeting of Asian countries in Bangkok, Thailand), the universalism of all human rights was reaffirmed.

As regards the challenge of business corporations, it may be viewed from many perspectives, but chief among them is the fact that business corporations (especially transnational ones) are often more powerful than states, and therefore enjoy the capacity to promote or undermine the rights and well-being of individuals and groups. Yet, the human rights movement, as it initially developed, did not seek to make business corporations accountable for human rights abuses, such as child labor, business-supported political repression, environmental degradation, and sexual harassment, but, spearheaded by individuals and grassroots organizations, has begun to expand its efforts to find ways to make corporations accountable to the norms of human rights.

No introduction to this volume would be complete without references to specific individuals such as Eleanor Roosevelt, Mohandas K. Gandhi, Andrei Sakharov, and Nelson Mandela. Human virtue, and the concept of human rights, requires its champions and martyrs. In the case of human rights, such champions, vary from those in whose minds the revolutionary ideas associated with these rights have taken shape, to those whose voices have been stilled by the rule of despots such as Joseph Stalin, Mao Zedong, or Augusto Pinochet. The individual is also implicated in the sense that regardless of legal and political institutions, success in making states and other socioeconomic or sociopolitical entities accountable for human rights abuses will at best be limited, unless and until *individuals* are morally transformed and made part of a shared global ethic. A number of religions, in their efforts to expand the reach and affirmative impact of human rights, have called for a global ethic—an ethic that reflects the conviction that rights imply corresponding duties. Equally important—because no government can long contradict the character of the individuals it seeks to govern—the morally transformed individual is seen as the principal source of the morally transformed society and state.

In the final analysis, while the UN and national governments do have institutional responsibilities for human rights promotion, monitoring, and protection, it is individuals and groups who make up the United Nations and national governments. We are the people in whose names they were created, and we are the people in whose names their actions or inactions affect the world. While we are geographically and politically separated, we are morally and spiritually connected. It is that connection that is at the heart of human rights. The separation is often confusing, so much so that it has frequently taken precedence over a common identity. Intuitively, however, it is known that the moral obscenity that informed the human abasement in World War II Germany, or in Rwanda or the former Yugoslavia of the 1990s, threatens and defiles us all. Defilement also threatens when we abandon the elderly, force the hungry to live by the dictates of their bellies, and violate the promise of the young, by failing to afford them an education. We also know that we can turn our backs on such abasement and defilement only at the risk of artificially separating ourselves, and thus living a morally incoherent life. All who read this book, at some time in our lives, will have experienced that disconnection and lived estranged from our moral selves. A commitment to human rights, while a commitment to the others in our midst and our world, is therefore above all an engagement not to some far-off ideal, but a pledge to something at home, a commitment to our moral integrity.

Abbreviations

A/	General Assembly
Add.	Addendum
ADRDM	American Declaration of the Rights and Duties of Man
ACWW	Associated Country Women of the World
AI	Amnesty International
AJIL	American Journal of International Law
ANC	African National Congress
AOHR	Arab Organization for Human Rights
ASI	Anti-Slavery Society International
BBI	B'nai B'rith International
BDPA	Beijing Declaration and Platform for Action
BG	Boston Globe
BJIL	Buffalo Journal of International Law
BPP	Bulletin of Peace Proposals
CAT	Committee Against Torture
CEDAW	Convention on the Elimination of All Forms of Discrimination Against Women
CH	Current History
CHR	Commission on Human Rights
CHRLR	Columbia Human Rights Law Review
CN./4	Commission on Human Rights
CONF	Specially organized conference
CPC	Communist Party of China
CRC	Convention on the Rights of the Child

CSCE	Conference on Security and Co-operation in Europe
CSM	Christian Science Monitor
CSW	Commission on the Status of Women
DCI	Defense for Children International
E/	Economic and Social Council
EAIA	Ethics and International Affairs
ECOSOC	Economic and Social Council
EU	European Union
FIS	Islamic Salvation Front
For. Aff.	Foreign Affairs
FWCC	Friends World Committee for Consultation
HRQ	Human Rights Quarterly
HRW	Human Rights Watch
ICC	International Criminal Court
ICCB	International Catholic Child Bureau
ICCPR	International Covenant on Civil and Political Rights
ICJ	International Court of Justice
ICRC	International Committee of the Red Cross
IHF	International Helsinki Federation
IHT	International Herald Tribune
ILC	International Law Commission
ILGA	International Lesbian and Gay Organization
ILO	International Labor Organization
IMF	International Monetary Fund
IO	International Organization
IPSR	Indian Political Science Review
IRA	Irish Republican Army
JAMA	Journal of American Medical Association
JTWS	Journal of Third World Studies
KLA	Kosovo Liberation Army
MGW	Manchester Guardian Weekly
NAFTA	North American Free Trade Agreement
NATO	North Atlantic Treaty Organization
NGOs	Nongovernmental Organizations
NWICO	New World Information and Communications Order
NYT	New York Times
OAS	Organization of American States

OAU	Organization of African Unity
OSCE	Organization of Security and Co-operation in Europe
PHR	Physicians for Human Rights
PKK	Kurdistan Workers Party
PLO	Palestine Liberation Organization
PRC	People's Republic of China
PRI	Institutional Revolutionary Party
S/	Security Council
SGI	Soka Gakkai International
SJDA	Scandinavian Journal of Development Alternatives
Stat.	Statute (US)
Supp.	Supplement
TNCs	Transnational Business Corporations
TYJIL	Transnational Yale Journal of International Law
UDA	Ulster Defense Association
UDHR	Universal Declaration of Human Rights
UNCED	United Nations Conference on Environment and Development
UNESCO	United Nations Educational, Scientific and Cultural Organization
UNHCR	United Nations Commissioner for Refugees
UNICEF	United Nations Children's Fund
UNTS	United Nations Treaty Series
VDAPA	Vienna Declaration and Programme of Action
WCED	World Commission on Environment and Development
WCU	World Conservation Union
WFM	World Federalist Movement
WFRC	Workers with Family Responsibilities Convention
WHO	World Health Organization
YJIL	Yale Journal of International Law

Users' Guide

The goals of this volume are to help users gain fairly easy access to a wide range of major issues concerning human rights since 1945 and to provide a source for greater understanding of what human rights are and how those rights are central to our lives. These issues, including the adoption of major human rights instruments at the global and regional levels, have been selected because of the impact they have had, are having, or are likely to have on the human condition. The work does not seek to include every human rights issue but does attempt to cover major issues, incidents, events, people, organizations, and instruments. Entries on countries were selected based on the incidence of major human rights issues. Ideas, organizations, as well as authors cited offer a broad range of human rights activities and views.

The entries are presented in alphabetical order, and the human rights instruments are listed under the official titles. Other documents, which do not have the status of "human rights instruments," are also included. At the end of each entry, cross references refer to other entries on related issues. Almost every entry is accompanied by suggestions for further reading.

The citations that accompany the documents included from the UN system generally have symbols that indicate the organs from which they come. For example, (A/) represents the General Assembly; (CN./4) the Commission on Human Rights; (E/) the Economic and Social Council; (S/) Security Council; and (CONF) a specially organized conference, such as the UN Fourth World Conference on Women. Likewise, treaties are officially housed in a UN Treaty Series, and citations for the series follow this pattern: 6 UNTS 25. This abbreviation means that the cited treaty can be found on page 25 of volume 6 of the United Nations Treaty Series. A list of abbreviations appears in the front of the book. The work contains a timeline of significant dates, a glossary, a diagramatic depiction of the UN human rights system and the text of the International Bill of Human Rights.

Significant Dates in the Field of Human Rights

1945   Adoption of the UN Charter; Nuremberg War Criminals Trials began; creation of UNESCO.

1946   Establishment of the UN Commission on Human Rights and the Commission on the Status of Women.

1947   UN General Assembly affirmed the principles of the Charter of the International Military Tribunal (also known as the Nuremberg Tribunal).

1948   Death of Mahatma Gandhi; American Declaration of the Rights and Duties of Man; genocide convention adopted by the UN; proclamation of the Universal Declaration of Human Rights; South Africa officially instituted apartheid.

1949   End of Nuremberg War Crimes trials; UN adopted the Convention for the Suppression of Traffic in Persons and the Exploitation of the Prostitution of Others; Council of Europe created; People's Republic of China established.

1950   European Convention on Human Rights adopted; UN created position of High Commissioner for Refugees.

1951   Convention Relating to the Status of Refugees adopted by the UN.

1952   ILO Convention Concerning Maternity Protection adopted.

1953   Death of Joseph V. Stalin.

1954   UN adoption of the Convention on the Political Rights of Women and the Convention on the Status of Stateless Persons.

1955   Advisory Services in the Field of Human Rights established by UN; European Commission of Human Rights created; Standard Minimum Rules for the Treatment of Prisoners approved.

1956   UN adopted the Supplementary Convention on the Abolition of Slavery, the Slave Trade, and Institutions and Practices Similar to Slavery.

1959   Inter-American Commission on Human Rights created by the OAS.

1960   Declaration on the Granting of Independence to Colonial Countries and Peoples adopted by the the UN; UNESCO approved the Convention Against Discrimination in Education.

1961   The founding of Amnesty International.

1962   Convention on Consent to Marriage, Minimum Age for Marriage and Registration of Marriages.

1964   Founding of the Palestine Liberation Organization.

1965   Adoption of the European Social Charter; International Convention on the Elimination of All Forms of Racial Discrimination adopted by the UN.

1966   Adoption of the two international covenants by the UN; the Great Proletarian Cultural Revolution began in China.

1968   Proclamation of Teheran (International Conference on Human Rights)

1969   Adoption of the American Convention on Human Rights by the OAS.

1971   Civil War between East and West Pakistan begins; the birth of Bangladesh.

1972   Creation of the United Nations University.

1973   Apartheid made a crime against humanity; ILO's Minimum Age Convention.

1974   Universal Declaration on the Eradication of Hunger and Malnutrition.

1975   Helsinki Accords; Indonesia's intervention into East Timor; Khmer Rouge gains control of Cambodia and begins the Cambodian genocide; world conference on women (Mexico City).

1976   Beginning of the "dirty war" in Argentina; death of Mao Zedong; end of the cultural revolution in China.

1977   "Charter 77"; Geneva Protocols I and II; President Jimmy Carter of the United States made human rights a central feature of American foreign policy.

1978   Human Rights Watch founded; UNESCO's Declaration on Race and Racial Prejudice adopted.

1979   Convention on the Elimination of All Forms of Discrimination Against Women adopted by the UN; Idi Amin of Uganda overthrown.

1980   Mothers of the Plaza de Mayo receive the Norwegian Prize of the People; publication of *Many Voices, One World*; second world conference on women held in Copenhagen, Denmark.

1981   African Charter on Human and Peoples' Rights adopted by the OAS Declaration on the Elimination of All Forms of Intolerance and Discrimination Based on Religion or Belief; *Dungeon v. United Kingdom*.

1982   Charter of Rights and Freedoms adopted by Canada; World Charter for Nature adopted by the UN.

1984   Convention Against Torture and Other Cruel, Inhuman or Degrading Treatment or Punishment; Declaration on the Right of Peoples to Peace; publication of *Nunca Mas*.

1985   Mikhail Gorbachev became leader of the Soviet Union; Beijing Rules adopted by the UN; third world conference on women held in Nairobi, Kenya.

1986   Declaration on the Right to Development; overthrow of Ferdinand Marcos; people of the Philippines adopt a Bill of Rights.

1987   Publication of *Our Common Future* by the World Commission on Environment and Development.

1988   Slobodan Milsoevic consolidated his control in the former Yugoslavia.

1989   Convention on the Rights of the Child; Convention Concerning Indigenous and Tribal Peoples adopted by ILO; death of Andrei Sakharov; death of Nicolae Ceauşescu; Second Optional Protocol to the International Convention on Civil and Political Rights adopted; *Solidarity* legalized in Poland; the Tiananmen Square massacre.

1990   Iraq invaded and took control of Kuwait; Nelson Mandela released from prison by South Africa.

1991   Beginning of genocide in the former Yugoslavia; dissolution of the Soviet Union; International Convention on the Protection of the Rights of All Migrant Workers and Members of Their Families; Moscow Human Dimension Mechanism; the Civil Rights Act of 1991 (United States).

1992   Democratic elections cancelled in Algeria by that country's military; United Nations Conference on Environment and Development.

1993   Ad hoc War Crimes Tribunal for the former Yugoslavia approved by the UN; apartheid legally abolished in South Africa; Declaration on the Rights of Persons Belonging to National, Ethnic, Religious and Linguistic Minorities adopted by the UN; post of High Commissioner for Human Rights created by the UN; results of democratic election cancelled by Nigerian military; Bangkok Declaration; World Conference on Human Rights; Vienna Declaration and Programme of Action.

1994   Beginning of Rwandan genocide; Conference on Population and Development, held in Cairo, Egypt; Declaration on the Elimination of Violence Against Women adopted by the UN; European Charter on Sexual Harassment in the Workplace adopted by the European Parliament; Inter-American Convention on Forced Disappearance adopted by the OAS; War Crimes Tribunal for Rwanda approved by the UN.

1995   Delhi Declaration; fourth world conference on women held in Beijing, China; Oslo Accords; World Summit for Social Development.

1996   Board of Immigration of the U.S. Immigration and Nationalization Service (INS) rules that persons fleeing genital mutilation are eligible for political asylum; UN General Assembly, by consensus, votes to support the creation of a permanent International Criminal Court.

1997   Convention on Human Rights and Biomedicine adopted by the Council of Europe; over 100 countries agreed on a treaty to ban land mines; Universal Declaration on the Human Genome and Human Rights adopted by UNESCO.

1998   Anglo-Irish agreement on Northern Ireland on Good Friday.

A _____

ABORIGINAL PEOPLES. See INDIGENOUS PEOPLES.

ABORTION. Abortion is the intentional removal of a fetus or an embryo from a mother's womb for purposes other than that of either producing a live birth or disposing of a dead embryo. Used as one of the principal means by which humans effect population control, protect the health of mothers, and dispose of unwanted pregnancies, the practice of abortion dates as far back as five thousand years in China. The practice has been contested, however, especially since the Middle Ages in the West, on the grounds that the human embryo has the right to life. So when the present emphasis on **human rights** began to take political and legal root in international debates following World War II, matters concerning the right to life of the unborn child and of the mother were repeatedly raised and discussed. For instance, Article 3 of the **Universal Declaration of Human Rights** (UDHR) and Article 6 (1) of the **International Covenant on Civil and Political Rights** (ICCPR) proclaim the right of everyone to life. But when these human rights instruments were debated by their respective drafting committees, no agreement was arrived at on the meaning of that right in relationship to the human fetus, principally because of disagreements on when human life begins. That disagreement continues and is likely to continue into the next century.

Today, abortion is prohibited in some countries, while its availability varies in others. Among the latter, including the **U.S.**, medical termination of a pregnancy is generally permitted under conditions specified by national law: for example, when the continuation of a pregnancy entails risks to the life of the pregnant woman, or when, if the child were born, he or she would suffer from disabling mental or physical abnormalities. In some countries, the issue of abortion is so divisive that it threatens social and international relations. In the United States, for instance, internal social and political divisions have given rise to changes in foreign policy. Congress has placed limits on relations with countries that practice family planning, including abortion. Specifically, Congress has not only cut foreign aid in the general area, but it has prohibited the use of U.S. appropriated funds by countries or organizations participating "in the management" of "coercive" abortion. *Further Reading:* H. Barber, *A Crisis of Conscience* (1993); E. C. Koop, "Why Defend Partial-Birth Abortion?," *NYT* (September 26, 1996); E. R. Rubin, ed., *The Abortion Controversy: A Documentary History* (1994).

ACADEMIC FREEDOM AND HUMAN RIGHTS. The Universal Declaration of Human Rights (UDHR) assigns to "every individual and every organ of society" the responsibility to "strive by teaching and education to promote respect" for **human rights.** Particularly important among those organs are academic institutions and the individuals associated with them. Indeed, it may be confidently asserted that the academy is central to the development and maintenance of national and international civil society. And without a strong civil society, governments, which are the primary violators of human rights, feel little or no moral and political pressure to promote and protect academic freedom and human rights.

When governments target educators, students, and academic institutions for repression, they strike at the heart of human rights promotion and protection. If the human rights movement is to continue its development, and if governments are to be held fully accountable for human rights promotion and protection, harassment, imprisonment of teachers and students, censorship of the right to free expression and inquiry, and the closing of schools, colleges, and universities must be seen as *fundamental* human rights violations. And governments that engage in such violations must be uncompromisingly condemned and punished.

Human Rights Watch (HRW) one of the few **nongovernmental organizations** (NGO) that has emphasized this area of human rights, has developed the Academic Freedom Project, which highlights violations of academic freedom in **China**, Egypt, Guatemala, Israeli occupied territories, **Nigeria,** South Korea, and the Slovak Republic. When one looks at the world at large, however—including Indonesia, **Mexico,** and **Turkey**—one finds widespread limits on academic freedom. See also: Thought, Conscience and Religion; Truth Commissions. *Further Reading:* B. Reardon, *Educating for Human Dignity: Learning About Rights and Responsibilities* (1995); World University Service, *Academic Freedom: A Human Rights Approach*, Vols. 1 and 2 (1990); G. H. Andreopoulos and R. Claude, eds., *Human Rights Education for the Twenty-First Century* (1997).

ADJUDICATION. This is the name given to a legal process used in settling international disputes by submitting them to an established court. There are three distinct stages in the evolution of **human rights**: (1) the **standard-setting** stage, which involves the creation of principles and standards that define those rights; (2) the **ratification** stage, which is the junction at which states undertake to be bound by the standards; and (3) the implementation stage, which concerns enforcement of the standards.

International efforts in the field of human rights have succeeded very well in setting standards, and a significant number of countries have ratified many of the human rights treaties. In the area of implementation, however, there has been less success. At the global level, there is not yet any court to settle disputes arising out of human rights concerns, but on December 17, 1996, the United Nations **General Assembly** adopted a resolution that provides for the convening of a diplomatic conference to finalize the adoption of a treaty on the creation of an **International Criminal Court** (ICC). That conference, which Italy offered to host, took place in June 1998, and the treaty was approved. When the ICC comes into being (and it will after the required number of states ratify the treaty), it will have jurisdiction to try individuals who are charged with a number of crimes that bear on human rights.

At the regional level, two human rights courts have been established—the **European Court of Human Rights** and the **Inter-American Court of Human Rights**. Each, especially the European Court, has had some success in dealing with human rights abuses, but the adjudicative process at the regional level is still in the early stages of development. National courts, even in the most enlightened countries have not been notably active in dealing with human rights issues. Such relative national inaction is understandable and makes the need for global and regional courts all that more important: national courts are extensions of states; states are the principal abusers of human rights and, therefore, the parties against which claims of human rights abuses are likely to be asserted. States are, therefore, not anxious to set in motion processes that can hold them legally and morally accountable. See also: International Court of Justice. *Further Reading:* M. C. Bassiouni, *The Protection of Human Rights in the Administration of Justice* (1994); B. Stephens and M. Ratner, *International Human Rights: Litigation in U.S. Courts* (1996).

ADVISORY SERVICES IN THE FIELD OF HUMAN RIGHTS. Between 1953 and 1954, the United Nations **General Assembly** authorized the secretary-general to assist states, at their request, in promoting **human rights**. That assistance, while general in character, was to be especially concerned with the rights of women, minorities, freedom of information, and racial discrimination. In 1955, those provisions of assistance were consolidated by the General Assembly under a program called Advisory Services in the Field of Human Rights. The program now includes fellowships, regional training courses, seminars, and the advisory service of experts. It also includes a Voluntary Fund for Victims of Torture, which was established by the UN in 1987.

In a 1988 comprehensive report to the **Commission on Human Rights** (CHR), the secretary-general of the UN clearly articulated what the program has been doing to date and aptly outlined what it should be doing in the future: expanding knowledge and understanding of human rights standards; advancing the application of those standards; and offering concrete help in creating and developing national institutions such as law libraries for schools, judges, and lawyers to facilitate the promotion and protection of internationally recognized human rights standards. In states that are parties to human rights instruments, regional training courses, for example, direct their attention to persons who are likely to be directly involved in the implementation of human rights norms—judges, legislators, police, prison officials, health care professionals, community leaders, public and social policy-planners, and others engaged in the administration of justice and social policy. The advisory service of experts focuses on tendering technical and other assistance to governments that need to create and develop the type of legal and other infrastructure (substantive and procedural institutions) to carry out human rights responsibilities.

Since 1988 the program has been expanded, despite financial limitations, and the **Centre for Human Rights** is now coordinating its activities. The Vienna Declaration and Programme of Action (VDAPA), which came out of the 1993 **World Conference on Human Rights**, explicitly calls for increased financing of the center and strengthening of the advisory services. See also: Office of High Commissioner for Human Rights. *Further Reading:* UN Doc., Advisory Services in the Field of Human Rights. *Report of the Secretary General* E/CN.4/1988/40; United Nations Doc., *Vienna Declaration and Programme of Action* A/CONF. 157/23 (July 12, 1993).

AFFIRMATIVE ACTION. Among the fundamental norms of **human rights** are those of equality and nondiscrimination. Human rights instruments, in general, affirm those two norms. In addition many of those instruments, provide for action to be taken by states to remedy, partly or wholly, the effects of past **discrimination** based on language, nationality, religion, race, and sex. The three human rights treaties cited below provide clear and precise statements concerning the norm of nondiscrimination, and the policy of affirmative action (remedy for past discrimination).

Article 27 of the **International Covenant on Civil and Political Rights** (ICCPR) states that "In those States in which ethnic, religious or linguistic minorities exist, persons belonging to such minorities shall not be denied the right in community with the other members of their group, to enjoy their own culture, to profess and practise their own religion, or to use their own language." Article 1(4) of the **International Convention on the Elimination of All Forms of Racial Discrimination** provides that

Special measures taken for the sole purpose of securing adequate advancement for certain racial or ethnic groups or individuals requiring such protection as may be necessary to ensure such groups or individuals equal enjoyment or exercise of human rights shall not be deemed racial discrimination, provided . . . that such measures do not, as a consequence, lead to the maintenance of separate racial groups and that they shall not be continued after the objectives for which they were taken have been achieved.

The 1979 **Convention on the Elimination of All Forms of Discrimination Against Women** (CEDAW) also provides for affirmative action. Article 4 (1) provides that the adoption, by states, of "temporary special measures aimed at accelerating de facto equality between men and women shall not be considered discrimination . . . but shall in no way entail as a consequence the maintenance of unequal or separate standards." It further provides that the special measures (affirmative action) shall be "discontinued when the objectives of equality of opportunity and treatment have been achieved."

In the **United States**, affirmative action programs have been very controversial, with some citizens viewing it as promoting a form of reverse discrimination. In other areas of the world, such as Western Europe and **India**, policies to remedy the effects of past discrimination have, to date, been less controversial. See also: Remedy. *Further Reading:* S. Parikh, *The Politics of Preference: Democratic Institutions and Affirmative Action in the United States and India* (1997); J. A. Sigler, ed., *International Handbook on Race and Race Relations* (1987).

AFGHANISTAN. The Islamic State of Afghanistan, located in southern Asia, shares borders with Pakistan, Iran, Turkmenistan, Uzbekistan, and Tajikistan. It has a population of about 17 million people, which is composed of several ethnic groups, including Hazars, Tajiks, Turkomens, and Uzbeks. The predominant religion is overwhelmingly Islam (Sunni, 76 percent, and Shi'ite, 23 percent). Since its independence from Britain in 1919, successive Afghan governments administered an uneasy internal peace among various political factions until 1978, when the monarchy was overthrown and replaced by a pro–Soviet Union republic on whose behalf Moscow intervened in 1979. This political change not only generated widespread internal unrest but drew Afghans directly into the Cold War. While Soviet and Afghan communists fought Muslim guerrillas called mujahedeen, the **United States** gave considerable military aid to the guerrillas, who succeeded in forcing a Soviet withdrawal from Afghanistan in 1989. The Soviet Union's withdrawal did not end the war. The conflict continued between the guerrillas and the communist regime, which was ousted in 1992. Since that date, despite external efforts at mediation, including the UN's, political control has shifted between rival religious and military groups in different parts of the country. At this writing, the Taliban—an

independent coalition of religious students and certain military command-
ers—appears to have gained political ascendency.

Throughout the conflict since the 1970s, but especially since the Taliban
gained political control, violations of **human rights** have been general, persistent, and egregious. For example, the norm of respect for the integrity
of persons is repeatedly violated through extrajudicial killings (assassinations), disappearances, hostage-taking for ransom or political support, torture, and other degrading treatments to extract information from prisoners.
Arbitrary arrest and detention and exile are also practiced. Likewise, there
are unacceptable limits on freedom of speech, press, and religion. Even
worse, there is no constitutional provision that seeks to offer protection
against those limits.

Perhaps the most significant recent violations of **human rights** are in the
area of discrimination based on race, sex, and religion, among other categories. For example, Tajik women have been targeted for rape, and the
minority Shi'a have consistently been discriminated against by the majority
Sunni. The Taliban has banned the public employment of women and has
prohibited girls from attending school. In April 1996, the UN Office for
Co-ordination of Humanitarian Assistance to Afghanistan had to cancel a
planned donor visit to the province of Kandahar, because the Taliban-
controlled *Shura* (governing council) refused to meet female diplomats and
required them to wear burka (a traditional public facial covering for
women) when they visit project sites. More recently, violence against Iranian citizens in Afghanistan has invited the threat of war with Iran, and
women are being prevented from working outside the home. See also: Declaration on the Protection of All Persons from Enforced Disappearance;
Religion and Human Rights; Sharia. *Further Reading:* A. Arnold, *The Fateful
People* (1993); Human Rights Watch, *The Forgotten War: Human Rights Abuses
and Violations of the Laws of War Since the Soviet Withdrawal* (1991); UN Doc.,
*Report of the situation of human rights in Afghanistan prepared by the Special
Rapporteuer, Mr. Felix Ermacora, in accordance with Commission on Human
Rights Resolution 1989/67, E/CN.4/1990/25*, which deals with promises made by
Afghanistan to the UN concerning the protection of human rights.

AFRICAN CHARTER ON HUMAN AND PEOPLES' RIGHTS. The charter, also known as the Banjul Charter on Human and Peoples' Rights because it was drafted in Banjul, Gambia, was adopted by African states,
with the then exception of South Africa and a few others, in 1981. It represents, among other things, the regional commitment of African states (in
much the same way American and European countries had previously done
in their respective regional human rights instruments) to promote and protect **human rights**. The charter guarantees to individuals the civil, political,
economic, social, and cultural rights that are found in the **International Bill
of Human Rights** as well as other global instruments. In addition, it has
some unique features.

First, it deals with economic, social, cultural, civil, and political rights in a single document, symbolically indicating the equal importance of all classes of human rights. Second, it deals with the right to individual and collective development—a right which, in 1986, the UN recognized in its declaration on development. Third, it recognizes the rights of individuals as well as **peoples**—the latter a form of collective rights, which the West finds unappealing. Fourth, unlike an emerging push at the global level and the present focus in the European and American regions to invoke judicial enforcement of human rights claims, the African Charter emphasizes mediation and conciliation. Fifth, it recognizes in Article 23 (1) the right of all peoples to peace and security—a right that is likely to have increasing appeal. Sixth, it recognizes the right to an environment supportive of one's health, and article 16 of the charter reorganizes the right to "physical and mental health." Seventh, it details rights as well as duties. For example, article 27 states that "every individual shall have duties towards his family and society, the State and other legally recognized communities and the international community." Section 2 of Article 27 goes on to say that the "rights and freedoms of each individual shall be exercised with due regard to the rights of others, collective security, morality and common interest." See also: American Convention on Human Rights; Civil and Political Rights; Economic, Social and Cultural Rights; European Convention on Human Rights. *Further Reading:* W. E. Langley, "The Banjul Charter on Human and Peoples' Rights," *IPSR*, vol. 19 (January-December 1985); U. O. Umoszurike, "The African Charter on Human and Peoples' Rights," *AJIL*, vol. 77 (October 1983). The text of this charter can be found in *ILM*, vol. 21 no. 1 (1982).

AFRICAN COMMISSION ON HUMAN AND PEOPLES' RIGHTS. See HUMAN RIGHTS COMMISSIONS.

AFRICAN NATIONAL CONGRESS. See MANDELA, NELSON; SOUTH AFRICA.

AGE OF CONSENT. The term refers to the chronological age at which persons are deemed legally ready to assume responsibilities prohibited to them (usually for their protection) earlier in life. In international human rights law, Article 2 of the 1962 **Convention on Consent to Marriage, Minimum Age for Marriage and Registration of Marriages** provides that

States parties to the present Convention shall take legislative action to specify a minimum age for marriage. No marriage shall be legally entered into by any person under this age, except where a competent authority has granted a dispensation as to age, for serious reasons, in the interest of the intending spouses.

In 1965, the United Nations General Assembly adopted a Recommendation on Consent to Marriage, Minimum Age for Marriage and Registration of Marriages.

Principle II of that Recommendation *suggests* a minimum age in the following manner:

Member States shall take legislative action to specify a minimum age for marriage, which in any case shall not be less than fifteen years of age. *Further Reading:* For the texts of the Convention and the Recommendation see, respectively, 521 UNTS 231 and General Assembly Resolution 2018 (XX) November 1, 1965.

AIDS AND HUMAN RIGHTS. Acquired immune deficiency syndrome (AIDS), according to the **World Health Organization (WHO),** is a disease caused by one or more naturally occurring retrovirus of unknown geographic origin that has affected over 30 million people throughout the world. Because the disease has assumed pandemic proportions, recognized no national, ethnic, social, religious, gender, geographic, or cultural boundary, and continuously spreads, it threatens WHO's foundational goal of health for all people. Even more significant, there is no known cure for the disease or means by which its spread can be prevented, although the spread can be contained by the use of condoms and safer sexual practices have reduced the number of cases in Australia and the United States. However, in Africa it has been spreading rapidly. And in other regions of the world, such as Eastern Europe, which in the early 1980s had few cases of AIDS, the disease is also spreading.

Current scientific forecasts suggest that a cure is unlikely to be found in the near future, although efforts to moderate the suffering the disease causes, extend the lives of AIDS patients, and even render the virus dormant have met with some success. Furthermore, the infection that causes AIDS, the human immunodeficiency virus (HIV), can remain dormant for many years before AIDS itself develops. Lastly, the known or believed means by which the disease is spread, when combined with its other mentioned characteristics, cause patterns of social and political behavior threatening to **human rights.**

There are three methods by which the disease is known or believed to be transmitted: (1) by contact between the blood of an infected person and that of a healthy individual, either by transfusion, use of needles, or other items that may introduce the virus into the healthy person's bloodstream; (2) by transmission from mother to child, before, during, or after birth; and (3) through sexual relations that entail contact with the body fluids of an infected person. Other means of transmission that have been publicly stated, such as using the same toilet, hand-touching, and hugging, have been persuasively refuted; but because of the fear (and sometimes panic) that accompanies the spread of AIDS many individuals are inclined to believe almost any rumor concerning transmission.

Fear and panic on the part of the public often result in discriminatory behavior against actual or assumed-to-be victims of the disease. AIDS victims become social victims, as they are denied housing, medical care, social security, insurance, education, and even companionship. As victims seek to avoid discrimination, they are often obliged to hide their condition, thus compounding the fear and suspicion as well as the difficulties faced in successfully confronting the public health danger the disease presents.

Discriminatory practices of the types mentioned above, if they are approved or acquiesced to (implicitly or otherwise) by the state, are violations of various human rights standards, among which are the right to life; health; association; privacy; equality before the law; participation in the cultural life of the community; education; freedom and security; not to be subject to cruel, inhuman, and degrading treatment; and the right to marry and establish a family. See also: Health. *Further Reading:* D. L. Kirp and R. Bayer, *AIDS in Industrial Democracies* (1992); M. Leiner, *Sexual Politics in Cuba* (1994); J. M. Mann et al. eds., *AIDS in the Third World* (1992); S. Z. Theodoulou, *AIDS: The Politics and Policy of Disease* (1996).

ALGERIA. The Republic of Algeria, located in North Africa, has a population of approximately 27 million people, with Arabs and Berbers (the original **peoples** of the area) representing the dominant cultural groups. Islam (Sunni), the state religion, is the inherited or chosen religion of about 99 percent of the citizens, with Christianity—principally Roman Catholicism—embraced by the remaining 1 percent. Languages commonly spoken include Arabic (official), French, and Berber.

The country gained its independence from France in 1962 and became a member of the United Nations that year, but not before it fought a bitter war of independence against France, which colonized it from 1830 to 1962. The bitterness of the conflict was due in part to the grassroots strength of the nationalist movement and to the fact that certain Algerian social elites and most of the over one million French citizens who had migrated to and settled in Algeria saw the country as part of France, to which it was legally linked in 1871. The **human rights** violations, including torture, committed by the French government and the Algerian nationalists were many. The social divisions caused by the violations, as well as differences about Algeria's political future, influenced the conduct of succeeding governments from 1962 to 1989. The nature of that conduct was one that allowed limited dissent, espoused a socialist philosophy—although neglecting many of the poor and powerless—and used military support to ensure that those who led the war of independence and their collaborators would maintain control of national life. In 1989, domestic unrest forced the government to adopt a new constitution—one that called for a democratic parliamentary system. But when, in 1992, the democratic process indicated a likely victory by the Islamic Salvation Front (FIS), which cultivated the poor and sought to make Algeria a country whose culture expressed the fundamental norms of Islam, the army intervened and canceled the elections. Since 1992 the government of Algeria has been in a state of civil war with FIS and other groups, and during that time over 70,000 people have been killed. The West, suspicious of Islamic fundamentalism, has not overtly condemned this clear violation of "democratic entitlement."

Following the cancellation of elections, the Algerian government declared a state of emergency, and used disappearances, extrajudicial killings, arbitrary arrests, and torture to destroy members of the FIS. Collaboration between the government and security-force trained and armed paramilitary "self-defense" groups has also resulted in property destruction, extortion, and summary executions of "suspected persons." Because the source of many killings and property destruction are unknown, paralyzing fear gripped the country. Religious and gender discrimination is also considerable: the Family Code prohibits Muslim women from marrying non-Muslims, although Muslim men can marry non-Muslim women. Muslims who converted to Christianity find it necessary to practice their faith in secret. See also: Declaration on the Elimination of All Forms of Intolerance and Discrimination Based on Religion or Belief; Declaration on the Protection of All Persons from Enforced Disappearance; Democratic Entitlement; Sharia. *Further Reading*: Human Rights Watch, *Human Rights Abuse in Algeria: No One Spared* (1994); I. Lustick, *Unsettled States* (1993); H. C. Metz, ed., *Algeria: A Country Study* (1994).

ALIENS. Unlike stateless persons who have no nationality, aliens have the nationality of one or more states. Because of the revolution in the means of travel, however, at any given time many people are not nationals of the country within which they reside. Such persons are called aliens, and whether they are business travelers, students, migrant workers, tourists, or members of religious congregations or professional associations, they enjoy rights as humans beings that states are legally and morally required to protect. That protection is neither automatic nor easy, because cultural differences often fuel suspicions, stereotyping, and even claims of cultural and national superiority. Hence, conduct such as "immigrant bashing" remains part of international relations, even in the face of international human rights standards directed at protecting aliens.

Those standards acknowledge cultural and other differences among people, but they also affirm properties that are common to all human beings: "All human beings," states the first article of the **Universal Declaration of Human Rights** (UDHR), "are born free and equal in dignity and rights." Further, Article 2 asserts that "Everyone is entitled to all the rights and freedoms" associated with the human rights regime (body of norms, principles, and standards), "without distinction of any kind such as race, colour, sex, language, religion . . . national or social origin."

Consistent with "without distinction of any kind," including *national* origin, in 1985 the UN **General Assembly** adopted the **Declaration on the Human Rights of Individuals Who Are Not Nationals of the Country in Which They Live.** Articles 1 and 5 of that declaration are as follows:

Article 1. For purposes of this declaration the term "alien" shall apply . . . to any individual who is not a national of the State in which he or she is present.

Article 5. (1) Aliens shall enjoy . . . the following rights:

a. The right to life and security of person; no alien shall be subject to arbitrary arrest and detention . . . ;

b. The right to protection against arbitrary or unlawful interference with privacy, family, home or correspondence;

c. The right to be equal before the courts, tribunals and all other organs and authorities administering justice and, when necessary, to free assistance of an interpreter in criminal proceedings and, when prescribed by law, other proceedings;

d. The right to choose a spouse, to marry, to found a family;

e. The right to freedom of thought, opinion, conscience and religion . . . ;

f. The rights to retain their own language, culture and tradition;

g. The right to transfer abroad earnings, savings or other personal monetary assets, subject to domestic currency regulations.

The rest of the Article 5 deals with the right of aliens to move within and leave the country in which they reside, freedom of expression, peaceful assembly, and ownership of property. Article 8 provides for the right to safe and healthy working conditions, fair wages and equal remuneration for equal work, join trade unions, medical care, social security, social services, and education. See also: International Convention on the Protection of the Rights of All Migrant Workers and Members of Their Families; Convention Relating to the Status of Refugees. *Further Reading:* F. G. Dawson, *International Law, National Tribunals, and the Rights of Aliens* (1971); R. B. Lilich, *The Human Rights of Aliens in Contemporary International Law* (1984).

AMERICAN CONVENTION ON HUMAN RIGHTS. The convention, also called the Pact of San Jose after the Costa Rican city where it was adopted on November 22, 1969, provides human rights protection for the region covering North, Central, and South America as well as the Caribbean. Like the human rights instruments of Western Europe, the American Convention on Human Rights established two forums to help accomplish this purpose: the **Inter-American Commission on Human Rights** and the **Inter-American Court of Human Rights**. The commission's functions include the investigation of claims of **human rights** violations, preparation and issuance of reports, and making of recommendations to states. The court makes determinations of human rights violations by member states and provides remedies for violations, including awarding damages to victims.

The convention requires member states to respect the rights and freedoms of the pact and ensure that every person under their jurisdiction enjoys the full exercise of those rights, without discrimination on the grounds of race, color, sex, language, political and other opinion, national and social origin, economic status, birth, or any other social condition. The rights recognized include **civil and political rights** such as the right to life, humane treatment, personal liberty, fair trial, privacy, freedom of thought and expression, freedom of conscience and religion, freedom of movement and residence, assembly, nationality, a name, and not to be subject to slavery. **Economic, social and cultural rights** are also recognized, but those rights were only fully formulated through the 1988 additional protocol to the convention.

The rights recognized under the protocol include the right to form trade unions, strike, social security, health, a healthy environment, education, and the benefits of culture. See also: African Charter on Human and Peoples' Rights; European Convention on Human Rights. *Further Reading:* J. S. Davidson, *The Inter-American Human Rights System* (1997); T. Farer, "The Rise of the Inter-American Human Rights Regime," *HRQ*, vol. 19 no. 3 (1997).

AMERICAN DECLARATION OF THE RIGHTS AND DUTIES OF MAN. Although the single most celebrated and cited text in the international **human rights** movement is the **Universal Declaration of Human Rights** (UDHR), it was not the first detailed enumeration of human rights adopted after 1945. That honor belongs to the American Declaration of the Rights and Duties of Man (ADRDM), which was unanimously adopted on May 2, 1948, by the newly formed Organization of American States (OAS). The rights recognized by the ADRDM, however, were unrefined and unelaborated until the 1969 **American Convention on Human Rights**, which has just begun to have the impact it promised when it was adopted.

The ADRDM is unique in many respects. For example, unlike all the earlier, post-1945 human rights instruments, it explicitly deals with *duties* as well as rights. Indeed, it states that the "fulfillment of duty by each individual is a prerequisite to the rights of all. Rights and duties are interrelated in every social and political activity of man. While rights exalt individual liberty, duties express the dignity of that liberty." It also proclaims that the "spiritual development (of the individual) is the supreme end of human existence." As such, rights should be directed toward that end.

Many non-Western countries, which have criticized certain human rights instruments as reflecting a Western bias in their emphasis on *rights* to the neglect of duties, are not aware of the ADRDM. As it becomes better known, it could serve as a link to those who seek a global declaration on duties. Among the rights recognized by the ADRDM are the right to life, asylum, protection for mothers and children, private and family life, inviolability of the home, in addition to many rights cited in the American Convention on Human Rights. See also: Asian Values; Declaration of a Global Ethic. *Further Reading:* T. Farer, "The Rise of the Inter-American Human Rights Regime," *HRQ*, vol. 19, no. 3 (1997); Parliament of the World's Religions, "Towards a Global Ethic (An Initial Declaration)" (1993).

AMNESTY INTERNATIONAL. Amnesty International (AI), a worldwide **nongovernmental organization** (NGO) and **human rights** movement, was founded in 1961 by British lawyer Peter Benenson. Today, it has more than 1 million members, subscribers, and regular donors in over 170 countries and territories, with over 4,000 volunteer groups.

While AI contributes to the overall movement to promote and protect human rights, it is not an all-purpose human rights organization and movement. Rather, it operates under a fairly precise mandate. Its main focus is fivefold: (1) free all prisoners of conscience—people who are detained by governments because of their beliefs or because of their ethnic origin, sex, color, or language and have not used or advocated violence; (2) ensure fair and prompt trials for all political prisoners; (3) abolish the death penalty, torture, and other cruel, inhuman, or degrading treatment of prisoners; (4) end all disappearances and extrajudicial executions; and (5) oppose abuses of political opposition groups, including hostage-taking, torture, and arbitrary killing.

Each year, AI issues its global *Amnesty International Report*, which details human rights violations of a civil and political nature in all regions of the world. It has formal relations with the United Nations **Economic and Social Council (ECOSOC)**, the **United Nations Educational, Scientific and Cultural Organization, (UNESCO)**, the **Council of Europe**, the **Organization of African Unity (OAU)**, the **Organization of American States (OAS)**, and the Inter-Parliamentary Union. Amnesty International works on behalf of thousands of named and unnamed individuals in over ninety-four countries. In 1977, AI received the Nobel Peace Prize for its work in human rights, and in 1978 it was awarded the UN Human Rights Prize. See also: Nongovernmental Organizations. *Further Information:* Amnesty International, International Secretariat, 1 Easton Street, London WC1X 8DJ, UK, Tel.: 011–44–171–413–5500; 322 8th Avenue, New York, N.Y. 10001, Tel.: 212–633–4200.

AMNESTY LAWS. These are legislative and other enactments that seek to nurture the "social forgetting" of past violations of **human rights**, in order to foster the future promotion and protection of those rights. Typically, amnesty is granted to known violators who are made immune from criminal or other prosecution. Such acts of amnesty are often controversial. Critics in Chile, Argentina, South Africa, and elsewhere claim that they do not show enough sympathy for victims, and that they have the effect of undermining the sanctity of human rights.

The means as well as the circumstances through which amnesty laws seek to further the cause of human rights are many. They include:

• *National Emergencies.* Governments, for various reasons, sometimes declare a state of national emergency during which violations of human rights usually take place. The use of amnesty laws in such cases moderates the social tensions that generally follow the lifting of the state of emergency.

• *Transitions to Democracy.* Generally, authoritarian regimes commit many violations of human rights, and the social tensions and conflicts these violations cause make any transition to democracy difficult. Leaders of such regimes fear revenge from the supporters of the incoming government and are, therefore, reluctant to yield political control. The incoming government, however, is anxious to limit social and political conflict so that it can proceed with its political agenda. To facilitate the shift to democracy, amnesty is given to leaders of the authoritarian regime. It may also be given to members of guerrilla and other groups, as a means to encourage combatants to leave their organizations. Beginning in 1982 and continuing through the 1990s, Guatemala used the last tactic to further its antiguerrilla campaign. In **South Africa**, beginning in 1995, a Truth and Reconciliation Commission was created before which violators of human rights could disclose their deeds in return for pardons.

• *Return of Exiles.* In this case, amnesty is granted to induce people to return to their homelands who had been forced to flee their country. Such people are often guilty of nothing more than legitimate opposition to policies of previous governments.

• *Integration of Immigrants.* In this instance, amnesty is given to illegal immigrants to facilitate the removal of unequal social and other conditions under which they otherwise would be forced to continue living.

See also: Derogation; Public Emergency; Truth Commissions. *Further Reading:* S. P. Haynor, "Fifteen Truth Commissions—1974–1994: A Comparative Study," *HRQ*, vol. 16, no. 4 (1994); D. North, *Amnesty, Conferring Legal Status on Illegal Immigrants* (1982); *The Study on Amnesty Laws and Their Role in the Safeguard and Promotion of Human Rights*; UN Doc. E/CN.4/Sub. 2/1985/16.

ANTI-SEMITISM. See RACISM.

ANTI-SLAVERY SOCIETY INTERNATIONAL. This institution is the world's oldest human rights organization. Founded in 1839 as the British and Foreign Anti-Slavery Society, it was the direct successor of the campaign to abolish the slave trade and then slavery in Britain and the British Empire. In 1909, it merged with the Aborigines' Protection Society, which was campaigning for the rights of indigenous peoples. Today, the Anti-Slavery Society International (ASI), has an international membership and enjoys consulative status with the United Nations **Economic and Social Council** (ECOSOC), the **United Nations Educational, Scientific and Cultural Organization**, and the **International Labor Organization** (ILO). As stated in its constitution, its purpose is to eliminate slavery, slave trading, and all forms of unlawful labor, and to promote the advancement of public education on the rights of indigenous peoples and human rights in general, as set forth in the **Universal Declaration of Human Rights**.

Although ASI is a small organization in terms of income and staff, it exercises an influence that belies its size. For example, it was instrumental in establishing the United Nations Working Groups on Slavery (1975) and Indigenous Peoples (1982), as well as the United Nations Voluntary Fund for Indigenous Peoples (1985) and the United Nations Trust Fund on Contemporary Forms of Slavery (1992). In 1994 it led the way in the formation of a United Kingdom Coalition on Child Prostitution and Tourism. It conducts research in many countries and disseminates its findings and recommendations in many worldwide forums. Its newsletter, the *Anti-Slavery Reporter*, is distributed three to four times a year and reports the results of its research, and its documentation center is a very important source of information to researchers on slavery, slavery-like practices, and indigenous peoples. See also: Bonded Labor; Child Labor; Convention for the Suppression of the Traffic in Persons and the Exploitation of the Prostitution of Others; Slavery, the Slave Trade, and Slavery-like Practices. *Further Information:* Anti-Slavery International, The Stableyard, Broomgrove Road, London SW9 9TL, Tel.: 011–44–171–924–9555.

APARTHEID. The term, which means "separation," is a word derived from Afrikaans, the language of the former Dutch colonists in **South Africa**. It is the term for the official racial policy pursued by the former Nationalist government of South Africa from 1948 to 1994, when that government was replaced by **Nelson Mandela** and his African National Congress (ANC). That policy, based on segregation according to the color of one's skin, not only resulted in the complete territorial segregation of Europeans (approximately 18 percent) and non-Europeans (principally those of African and Asian descent), but it effectively ensured Europeans a monopoly of economic, political, and social power. Correspondingly, non-Europeans, especially Africans, were deprived of the rights of citizenship in their own country. They were crowded into relatively barren areas called "homelands," and placed in inferior segregated schools, so that they would be obliged to accept inferior social positions. And when non-Europeans sought to protest this treatment, their organizations were made illegal, laws governing where they could and could not go, and **arbitrary arrest and detention** (often indefinitely and without trial or charges), torture, and murder confronted them.

The policy of apartheid, as practiced, was accompanied by a doctrine that expressed the self-defined mission of the whites in South Africa in terms of three aims: (1) to help preserve the diversity of races that populate the world; (2) to conserve and extend Western Christian civilization; and (3) to discharge a claimed duty to nonwhite races living in South Africa. The first aim is linked to the belief that racial differences are an unbridgeable gulf and that each race must "fulfill itself" according to its own "inner law" of development. Racial integration, therefore, is a morally irresponsible course of conduct. Further, since the European race and its culture are "superior," whites in South Africa, as the heirs of European culture, especially Western civilization, are not only required to preserve their racial purity but to protect and extend that civilization. The extension of Western civilization to non-Europeans does not mean that they would become equals; it merely means carrying out a Christian duty to improve the lot of the less able.

Apartheid violates the **human rights** norm against nondiscrimination based on race and nationality. In practice it also violates other rights, including the right against arbitrary arrest and detention, as well as the right to life, association, and political participation. In 1973, the United Nation **General Assembly** adopted the **International Convention on the Suppression and Punishment of the Crime of Apartheid.** That convention made apartheid a **crime against humanity**, and prepared the way for a worldwide embargo against South Africa.

Article 11 of the convention defines the crime of apartheid to include the following acts committed for purposes of establishing and maintaining domination by one racial group over any other racial group and systematically oppressing them:

a. Denial to a member or members of a racial group or groups of the right to life and liberty of person;

b. Deliberate imposition on a racial group or groups of living conditions calculated to cause its or their physical destruction;

c. Any legislative . . . and other measures calculated to prevent a racial groups or groups from participation in the political, social, economic, and cultural life of the community; . . .

f. Persecution of organizations and persons, by depriving them of fundamental rights and freedoms, because they oppose apartheid.

See also: Racism; South Africa. *Further Reading:* UNGA, *International Convention on the Suppression and Punishment of the Crime of Apartheid,* Resolution 3068 (XXVIII) (November 30, 1973); Nelson Mandela, *Long Walk to Freedom* (1994).

ARAB ORGANIZATION FOR HUMAN RIGHTS. See ARAB WORLD AND HUMAN RIGHTS.

ARAB WORLD AND HUMAN RIGHTS. Human rights issues in the Arab world, geographically encompassing North Africa and west Asia, are often linked to discussions on Islam. Arab countries are predominantly Muslim (people who accept Islam as their religion) and thus share certain human rights issues with the more complex Islamic community, within which Arabs are a numerical minority. The Arab world, however, has its own human rights issues, centering around four areas: (1) the role of Arab countries in shaping and developing human rights norms; (2) the relationship of Arab countries to the ongoing global human rights movement; (3) the response of citizens in the Arab world to their countries' positions on human rights issues; and (4) the outlook the citizens share for the future of human rights in their respective countries.

First, on the matter of the role of Arab states in shaping human rights norms, references are often made to the 1948 behavior of **Saudi Arabia** as a way of creating a negative image of conduct supposedly typical of Arab countries. In that year, Saudi Arabia took one of the strongest stands against the **Universal Declaration of Human Rights** (UDHR). An even more negative image is created when the description of what took place in the vote to adopt the declaration includes the fact that Saudi Arabia joined with **apartheid South Africa** in abstaining when the vote was taken. What is rarely stated is that the Saudi government did not object to the declaration as a whole; it took strong exception to Article 18, which provides for religious liberty. In particular, it objected to the right to change one's religion—a position it continues to maintain and is reflected in its present criminal laws. Saudi Arabia's opposition to **lesbian and gay rights** is also used—especially in recent years—as an example to characterize its lack of commitment to human rights. Lebanon, however, also an Arab country, was among the leading states in the shaping of the declaration. Indeed, it may be said that few countries, except the **United States**, the **United Kingdom**, France, the former Soviet Union (and perhaps **China**) can match the role played by Lebanon. Countries such as **Iraq** and Egypt and were fairly strong supporters, also.

Second, the role of Arab countries in relation to the ongoing human rights movement, including the norms of that movement has been mixed. On the whole, Arab states, as a group, have been no less willing to ratify human rights treaties than other states. They have also been as selective in the process and pace of their ratifications as many other states have been. Tunisia, in North Africa, is an Arab country where the human rights movement has been gaining substantial momentum, as represented by some improvements in the principles of democratic entitlement, equality for women, and an enlightened and expanding effort to protect the rights of children, as provided by the Convention on the Rights of the Child. It has even been willing to allow some discussion on adapting the **Sharia**—without impairing its fundamental principles—to the norms of human rights. But there are Arab countries such as Algeria, **Kuwait, Saudi Arabia,** and Sudan that have trampled on the principles of democratic entitlement, given lip service to equality (women traditionally have had limited rights, such as the right to own property, but there is strong opposition to equality with men), and undermined most civil and political rights. Egypt and Lebanon have had governments that have vacillated in their support for human rights. That hesitation has been particularly evident in their efforts to move toward reforms of their laws, while at the same time giving support—along with other Arab states—to the Cairo Declaration on Human Rights in Islam (1990), which was adopted by the Organization of the Islamic Conference, an institution representing over fifty Muslim countries.

Article 1 of the Cairo Declaration deals with the right to life. It prohibits the taking of life, except for a "Sharia prescribed reason." But a Sharia prescribed reason, such as the death penalty by stoning for adultery, is a violation of the human rights norm against cruel, inhuman, and degrading treatment or punishment. Stoning, though it still exists, is no longer *widely* followed in Arab countries, but it illustrates the problem of the conservative-inspired Cairo Declaration.

Third, the issue of the response of Arab citizens to their governments' attitude toward human rights, is also mixed. Some have rejected human rights norms, which are seen to be in conflict with Islam. But others, such as those individual activists who formed, joined, and gave support to the Arab Organization for Human Rights (AOHR)—one of the few regional rather than country-specific, nongovernmental human rights groups—are among the strongest supporters of human rights anywhere in the world. Established in 1983, because its founders felt that Arab governments were depriving citizens of their freedom of thought and expression, their right to participate in government, and were, in a number of countries, subjecting citizens to murder, torture, and arbitrary detention, AOHR has set itself the task of documenting and publicizing those human rights abuses. Although pressured by governments, AOHR has succeeded in developing affiliated groups throughout the Arab region and gaining international standing outside the region, as exemplified in its recently obtained consultative status at the UN, after Arab states withdrew their objections. In individual countries, there are a number of human rights groups, such as the Association of Democratic Women in Tunisia, the Moroccan Association of Human Rights, and in Kuwait, the Committee for the Defense of Human Rights (the independence of the last group is uncertain).

Fourth, the future of the human rights movement in the Arab world is one that is likely to flower slowly, but it is one that governments of the region will find increasingly hard to curb. See also: Religion and Human Rights. *Further Reading:* H. Bielefeld, "Muslim Voices in the Human Rights Debate," *HRQ*, vol 17, no. 4 (1995); J. Crystal, "The Human Rights Movement in the Arab World," *HRQ*, vol. 16, no. 3 (1994); A. M. Mayer, *Islam and Human Rights: Tradition and Politics* (1991).

ARBITRARY ARREST AND DETENTION. One of the fundamental rights recognized by international human rights standards, according to Article 9 of the **Universal Declaration of Human Rights** (UDHR), is that of freedom from arbitrary arrest, detention, or exile. The scope of this right varies in regional human rights instruments, but at the global level, it is fully illuminated in Article 9 of the **International Covenant on Civil and Political Rights** (ICCPR):

1. Everyone has the right to liberty and security of person. No one shall be subjected to arbitrary arrest and detention. No one shall be deprived of his liberty

except on such grounds and in accordance with such procedures as are established by law.

2. Anyone who is arrested shall be informed, at the time of arrest, of the reasons for his arrest and shall be promptly informed of any charges against him.

3. Anyone arrested or detained on a criminal charge shall be brought promptly before a judge or other officer authorized by law to exercise judicial power and shall be entitled to trial within a reasonable time or to release.

4. Anyone who is deprived of his liberty by arrest or detention shall be entitled to take proceedings before a court, in order that that court may decide without delay on the lawfulness of his detention and order his release if the detention is not lawful.

5. Anyone who has been a victim of unlawful arrest or detention shall have an enforceable right to compensation.

See also: Derogation; Procedural Guarantees, Processes and Protections; Public Emergency. *Further Reading:* A. Cassese, *Inhuman States: Imprisonment, Detention and Torture in Europe Today* (1996); I. Omar, *Rights, Emergencies, and Judicial Review* (1996).

ARGENTINA. See MOTHERS OF THE PLAZA DE MAYO; NUNCA MAS.

ARMED CONFLICT. This term refers to the clash of armed forces between states, occupation of foreign territory by armed forces with or without armed resistance, as well as armed conflict taking place within a country. Conflicts that take place within the borders of countries are called noninternational armed conflicts, and those between countries are called international armed conflicts. The international community has shown concern about both types of armed conflicts and their bearing on the **human rights** of civilians, prisoners, and combatants, and it has taken steps, especially through the United Nations, to address those concerns.

At the 1968 International Conference on Human Rights, held in Teheran, Iran, attending countries noted "that widespread violence and brutality . . . including massacres, summary executions, tortures, inhuman treatment of prisoners, killing of civilians in armed conflict and the use of biological warfare, including napalm bombing, erode human rights." The conference, therefore, called upon the secretary-general of the UN to study steps that could be taken to improve the protection of human rights. In 1970, the United Nations **General Assembly** refined and affirmed eight basic principles for the protection of civilian populations during armed conflict. Principles 1, 2, 3, and 7, which capture the essence of that intended protection, are as follows:

1. Fundamental human rights, as accepted in international law and laid down in international instruments, continue to apply fully in situations of armed conflict.

2. In the conduct of military operations during armed conflicts, a distinction must be made at all times between persons actively taking part in hostilities and civilian populations.

3. In the conduct of military operations, every effort should be made to spare civilian populations from the ravages of war, and all necessary precautions should be taken to avoid injury, loss or damage to civilian populations. . . .

7. Civilian populations, or individual members thereof, should not be the object of reprisals, forcible transfers or other assaults on their integrity.

Further developments in this area of human rights include the 1974 UN **Declaration on the Protection of Women and Children in Emergency Armed Conflict** (Resolution XXIX), two 1977 international agreements (Protocol I and Protocol II of the 1949 Geneva Conventions), and a UN study, Impact of Armed Conflict on Children. Article 1 of the declaration states that "attacks and bombings on civilian populations . . . especially on women and children, who are the most vulnerable members of the population, shall be prohibited." Protocol I seeks to give further protection to victims of international armed conflicts, and Protocol II offers like protection to victims of noninternational armed conflicts. Finally, the secretary-general's appointed expert to study the impact of armed conflicts on children submitted a report to the 1996 UN General Assembly entitled *The Impact of Armed Conflict on Children*. That study details the multiple violations of the human rights of children that take place during armed conflicts and will likely influence further refinement of principles in this area of human rights. See also: Child, Rights of; Geneva Conventions; Proclamation of Teheran. *Further Reading:* G. Best, *Humanity in Warfare* (1980); I. Cohn and G. S. Goodwin-Gill, *Child Soldiers* (1994); J. Kuper, *International Law Concerning Child Civilians in Armed Conflict* (1997); UN Doc., *The Impact of Armed Conflict on Children*, A/51/306 and Add.1 (1996).

ARMENIA. See GENOCIDE; NAGORNO-KARABAKH.

ASIAN VALUES. This is an international term that is used to define a series of positions some Asian political and other leaders have taken in discourses with their Western counterparts on the nature of **human rights** and the emphasis that should be accorded to the norms of human rights. During those talks, differences surfaced—differences that have assumed international political and economic proportions and that are likely to have a profound impact on how the world evolves in the coming century. The talks and accompanying differences center around (1) the relationship between the individual and the community; (2) the link between rights and responsibilities; (3) the role of the state in social life; and (4) the ties between and among "social parts" within a given society, when the components of 1, 2, and 3 are in place.

On the issue of the relationship between the individual and the community, the West has shaped its societies on the view that individuals have claims or rights that are superior to those of the community and, except in circumstances where the individual's exercise of those rights results in or threatens imminent harm to the rights of other persons, that exercise should not be limited or otherwise regulated by the state. Many Asian countries, however, argue that individuals do not exist as independent, isolated units. They are in large measure the products of communities—families, villages, townships, schools, churches—on which they depend and through which they are nurtured and developed. These communities also have coexistent rights that may even at times supersede those of individuals.

The issue of the nature of the connection between rights and responsibilities bears an intimate relationship to the first issue. The West recognizes that for every right there is an *implicit* responsibility, but consistently expresses a preference for those responsibilities to remain implicit. Asian countries (and most of the non-West and perhaps even Central Europe) argue that responsibilities should be *explicit* and given an equivalent emphasis to those accorded to rights. Some countries, such as **Singapore**, Malaysia, and **China**, take a position that is consistent with the one taken by Latin American states in 1948, one that the United States then subscribed to: rights and responsibilities (or duties) are not only organically related, but fulfillment of duty is a *prerequisite* to the rights of all. Further, while rights exalt individual liberty, duties or responsibilities express the dignity of that liberty.

The role of the state in social life is implicated in the preceding two areas of discussion. For the West (especially the English-speaking West), the role of the state should be limited, since the sum of self-chosen individual goals should be that which defines society and social life. The extent of the state's involvement, in such a case, should ideally be merely to facilitate self-chosen aspirations and provide the institutional mechanisms through which redress may be had, when agreements in pursuit of those ends are breached. In contrast, Asian countries see communities and the *relationships* that define communities and individuals as having ends of their own. Additionally, the common good—societal good—does not emerge or result from the self-chosen interests of individuals; it must be consciously promoted by the state. In that conscious promotion, all the interests and relationships shaped by the interacting sectors that make up society (interests and relationships self-seeking individuals cannot fully see or embrace) can be properly followed. A greater focus on relationships and communities bears with it less emphasis on confrontation and litigation, and allows mediatory and conciliatory approaches to resolution of conflicts. It also bears with it a better balance of rights and responsibilities, say Asians.

In the human rights debate, the professed differences between Western values and Asian values express themselves in the tendency of the West, especially the **United States** and Great Britain, to place greater emphasis on the civil and political class of human rights. That tendency has been accompanied by a push to seek universalization of this emphasis. Asian (and a majority on non-Western) countries, however, tend to emphasize the economic, social, and cultural class of rights, or at least to suggest that they should have equal standing with their civil and political counterparts. Since both Asian and non-Asian countries, at least theoretically, accept the interdependence and universality of both classes of rights, the emphasis on either class by one side is viewed with suspicion and, sometimes, even hostility. See also: Bangkok Declaration; Civil and Political Rights; Declaration on the Right to Development; Economic, Social and Cultural Rights; Proclamation of Teheran; World Conference on Human Rights. *Further Reading:* D. A. Bell, "The East Asian Challenge to Human Rights," *HRQ*, vol. 18, no. 3 (1996); S. P. Huntington, "The Class of Civilizations," *For. Aff.*, vol. 72, no. 3 (1993); M. Mohammad, "East Asia Will Find Its Own Way," *IHT* (May 17, 1994); M. L. Davis, ed., *Human Rights and Chinese Values* (1995).

ASSEMBLY AND ASSOCIATION. The right of all people to the freedom of peaceful assembly and free association is found in a number of global and regional human rights instruments. The **International Bill of Human Rights** is particularly instructive on this specific right, as stated in each of its three components. The **Universal Declaration of Human Rights** (UDHR) states in Article 20 that

1. Everyone has the right to freedom of peaceful assembly and association.

2. No one may be compelled to belong to an association.

Article 23 (4) states that "Everyone has the right to form and to join trade unions for the protection of his interests."

The **International Covenant on Civil and Political Rights** (ICCPR) provides in Article 21 that

The right of peaceful assembly shall be recognized. No restrictions may be placed on the exercise of this right other than those imposed in conformity with the law and which are necessary in a democratic society in the interests of national security and public safety, public order . . . , the protection of public health or morals or the protection of the rights and freedoms of others. Article 22 (1). Everyone has the right to freedom of association with others, including the right to form and join trade unions for the protection of his interests.

Section 2 of Article 22 has the same exceptions as those found in Article 21 dealing with the freedom of peaceful assembly.

Article 8 of the **International Covenant on Economic, Social and Cultural Rights** elaborates the right to form and join trade unions, to establish national federations or confederations of such unions and to form or join international trade union organizations. See also: *Democratic Entitlement.*

ASSOCIATED COUNTRY WOMEN OF THE WORLD. Rural groups, especially women's groups, generally have not had a say in political affairs commensurate with their importance and numbers. In some cases, they have existed in isolation, away from the centers of power and unlinked to those with whom they share common interests. In 1933, the country women of the world, who had long suffered neglect at the hands of governments, formed the Associated Country Women of the World (ACWW) at a meeting in Stockholm, Sweden. At that time, the ACWW was only a step beyond its predecessor, the Liaison Committee of Rural Women's and Homemaker's Organizations, which had been founded in Vienna, Austria, in 1930, in seeking to pool the knowledge and efforts of women to effect a collective improvement in their condition. Since 1933, the ACWW has grown to become the largest international organization of rural women, extending to 172 countries and covering every region of the world. Today it is a respected **nongovernmental organization** (NGO) enjoying consultative status with the UN.

The aims of the organization are fivefold: (1) to raise the standard of living and education of women and their families worldwide, through community development projects and training programs; (2) to promote international goodwill, friendship, and understanding among women everywhere; (3) to work together for the relief of poverty and sickness, the protection and preservation of health, and the promotion of education; (4) to work for equal opportunities for women by eliminating **discrimination** because of gender, race, nationality, religion, or marital status; and (5) to act as a forum on international affairs for rural women, speaking for them with an informed voice in the councils of the world.

The ACWW pursues its aims independently, but also in coordination or partnership with international organizations like the **United Nations Educational, Scientific and Cultural Organization** (UNESCO). Such partnerships help satisfy **economic, social and cultural rights** in the areas of education, health, nutrition, income-generating strategems (especially in communities where women still do most of the agricultural work), leadership, and skills training. In some instances, the ACWW is involved in providing such basic services as clean water and basic sanitation. It is also involved in AIDS prevention projects. Among its publications is *The Country Woman*, a magazine published four times annually. *Further Information:* The Associated Country Women of the World, 6th Floor, Vincent House, Vincent Square, London, SW1P 2NB, England, Tel.: 011–44–171–834–8635.

ASYLUM. Asylum refers to the sanctuary or inviolable protection offered by a state to fugitives accused of political offenses or victims of persecution in other states. So long as recipients of asylum remain within the borders of the state granting asylum, the authority of the country from which the victims fled cannot legally reach them. The state granting asylum is also

required to observe the international prohibition of "non-refoulment"—
not to return summarily fugitives to the state from which they fled.

The right of asylum is recognized by the **Universal Declaration of Human
Rights** (UDHR) in Article 14.

1. Everyone has the right to seek and enjoy in other countries asylum from persecution.

2. This right may not be invoked in the case of prosecutions genuinely arising from
   non-political crimes or from acts contrary to the purposes and principles of the
   United Nations.

As Section 2 of the preceding article indicates, not everyone who seeks
asylum is entitled to it. The **Declaration on Territorial Asylum** speaks to a
class of persons who may not be given asylum. Article 1(2) of that declaration reads that

The right to seek and enjoy asylum may not be invoked by any person with respect
to whom there are serious reasons for considering that he has committed a crime
against peace, a war crime or a crime against humanity, as defined in the international instruments drawn up to make provisions in respect of such crimes.

See also: Convention Relating to the Status of Refugees; Crimes Against
Humanity; Crimes Against Peace; War Crimes. *Further Reading:* General Assembly, *Declaration on Territorial Asylum*, Resolution 2312 (XXII), December 14,
1967; A. W. Plaut, *Asylum: A Moral Dilemma* (1995).

ATLANTIC CHARTER. The Atlantic Charter is the name given to a joint
declaration issued on August 14, 1941, by **Franklin D. Roosevelt,** president
of the **United States,** and Winston Churchill, prime minister of the **United
Kingdom.** That charter, although technically not a human rights instrument, represents the first "common program of purposes and principles"
of the United Nations, and it served as a spiritual influence in shaping the
human rights agenda after 1945. Apart from the charter's call for the destruction of Nazi tyranny and the establishment of a permanent system of
general security for all nations, it incorporated in the third and fifth of its
eight principles the foundation for **civil and political rights** as well as **economic, social and cultural rights.** Principle 3 speaks of "respect for the right
of all peoples to choose the form of government under which they live"
and of "sovereign rights and self-government restored to those who have
been forcibly deprived of them." Principle 5 deals with the desire to "bring
about the fullest collaboration between all nations in the economic field
with the object of securing, for all, improved labor standards, and economic
advancement and social security." *Further Reading:* P. Drakidis, *The Atlantic
and United Nations Charters* (1995); T. A. Wilson, *The First Summit: Roosevelt
and Churchill at Placenta Bay* (1991); *Yearbook of the United Nations, 1946–1947*
(1947).

AUNG SAN SUU KYI. See BURMA.

AUSTRALIA. The Commonwealth of Australia is a federation, which has enjoyed a long history of parliamentary democracy. It has a population of approximately 18 million people, drawn from many countries (chiefly European), in addition to the Aboriginals who were present when European settlers first arrived in 1788. They now constitute about 2 percent of the population. English is the official language and Christianity is embraced by over 75 percent of the population. In general, the country ranks high among nations identified with a strong promotion and protection of **human rights**, and it has been particularly attentive to the rights of women, children, AIDS victims, and workers since the late 1980s. Two areas in which the country has consistent problems, however, are the rights of **indigenous peoples** (who have been discriminated against since the arrival of the Europeans) and immigrants.

Recognizing the persistence of the problem of **discrimination**, in 1975 Australia's parliament passed the Racial Discrimination Act, Section 10 of which provides for equality of treatment for all persons regardless of race, color, national, or ethnic origin. Despite the 1975 Act, Aboriginals continue to have inferior education, medical care, and employment opportunities. They are imprisoned sixteen times more often than non-Aboriginals, especially the young, among whom only 7 percent have post-secondary education; their average life expectancy is twenty years less than other members of the population; and the mortality rate of indigenous women is five times that of nonindigenous women.

In 1992, the country's Supreme Court overturned what was until then a legal precedent: that land belonged to no one before the Europeans arrived. With that ruling, along with 1993 Native Title Legislation, Aboriginals can claim title to land and improve their economic standing, providing they can prove maintained traditional title. But with the emergence of the One Nation Party—a recent political organization that has been gaining widespread popularity based on its anti-immigration and anti-indigenous persons stances—even the promise of the Court's ruling and the accompanying legislation may be frustrated.

First, by operation of the principle that Parliament cannot bind its successors, the 1993 legislation may become ineffective. Second, the more than 500 land claims by Aboriginals have incited anger among farmers, ranchers, and mining companies that hold over 40 percent of Australia's land under long-term leases and want the "easing of Indigenous land rights." Third, the fear that white Australians are culturally threatened by the inflow of migrants, especially from Asia, has invited anti-immigrant bashing. That fear has increased resentments against Aboriginals. See also Self-Determination. *Further Reading:* P. H. Bailey, *Human Rights: Australia in an*

International Context (1990); C. H. Furnsworth, "Anxious in Australia: Blaming It All on 'Them,' " *NYT* (May 11, 1997); M. Thornton, *The Liberal Promise* (1990).

AZERBAIJAN. See NAGORNO-KARABAKII.

B

BAHAI INTERNATIONAL COMMUNITY. An international **nongovernmental organization** (NGO), the Bahai community is a cross section of the **peoples** of the world, with over 5 million members in more than 187 countries. It represents one of the world's fastest growing religions (the Bahai), and is perhaps the most inclusive religious body, representing over 2,100 ethnic groups and encompassing all social, trade, and professional classes.

Founded in 1844 in Persia (present-day Iran) by Mizra Husayn-Ali, known as Baha'u'llah (1817–1892), the Bahai believes in the spiritual constitution of the individual and the fundamental oneness of humanity. Consistent with that belief, the Bahai International Community has participated in all the UN's activities concerned with human rights, and it has consultative status with the United Nations **Economic and Social Council** (ECOSOC) and the **United Nations Children's Fund** (UNICEF). It is also one of the international nongovernmental organizations that has been most committed to a universal auxiliary language, recognition of the essential oneness of the world's great religions, establishment of a democratic world federal system, elimination of all forms of discrimination, equality of the sexes, and elimination of poverty. Among its publications is the journal, *World Order. Further Reading:* Bahai International Community, *Turning Point For All Nations* (1995); *Gleanings from the Writings of Baha'u'llah* (1976). *Further Information:* Bahai International Community, 866 United Nations Plaza, Suite 120, New York, N.Y. 10017, Tel.: (212) 803–2500.

BALTIC STATES. See STALIN, JOSEPH V.

BANGKOK DECLARATION. From March 29 to April 2, 1993, most Asian states met in Bangkok, Thailand, in an effort to prepare collectively for the **World Conference on Human Rights**, which was scheduled to take place in Vienna, Austria, in June of that year. At the conclusion of the meeting, the countries adopted a declaration, which has come to be known as the Bangkok Declaration.

The declaration embraces a number of positions that the West, especially the **United States** and Britain, find more difficult to adopt, creating certain disagreements between most Asian states and the West. Those positions became important at the World Conference on Human Rights, which adopted some of them, including the principles of indivisibility, universality, and the inherent interrelationship between democracy and development.

The declaration stresses (1) "the universality, objectivity and non-selectivity of all human rights and the need to avoid double standards in the implementation of human rights"; (2) the right to development as "a universal and inalienable right and an integral part of fundamental human rights"; (3) the "need to develop the right of humankind regarding . . . a clean, safe and healthy environment"; and (4) that "poverty is one of the major obstacles to the full enjoyment of human rights." It also reiterates "the interdependence and indivisibility of economic, social, cultural, civil and political rights, and the inherent interrelationship between development, democracy, universal enjoyment of human rights, and social justice." Finally, among other things, it stresses the importance of protecting the rights of women and children, of creating international monitoring mechanisms to ensure realization of the right to development, and of strengthening the United Nations **Centre for Human Rights**, and calls for increased representation in the centre from developing countries.

The focus on selectivity, indivisibility, and development, while important in and of themselves, was also an attempt to confront the West, which is seen as focusing on **civil and political rights** to the neglect, by and large, of **economic, social and cultural rights** as well as the general right to development. And since the right to development, as well as the general class of economic, social and cultural rights require for their full implementation considerable government involvement in the economy, the emphasis in the Bangkok Declaration is one that essentially rejects the Western model of economic development—one that today emphasizes less and less government intervention in economic life. See also: Asian Values; Declaration on the Right to Development; Singapore. *Further Reading*: C. M. Cerra, "East Asian Approach to Human Rights," *BILJ*, vol. 2 no. 2 (1995); M. C. Davis, ed., *Human Rights and Chinese Values* (1995); Davis, ed., "Human Rights in Asia: China and the Bangkok Declaration," *BJIL*, vol. 2 no. 2 (1995).

BANGLADESH. The People's Republic of Bangladesh is located in south Asia on the Bay of Bengal, bordered by **India** and **Burma**. Its population of about 120 million people (98 percent Bangladeshi and 2 percent Bihari) is overwhelmingly Muslim (82 percent Islamic, 15 percent Hindu, and the rest other), and the people commonly speak Bengali (official), English, and Urdu.

The area that now forms Bangladesh was formerly part of Pakistan (and named East Pakistan), when British India was divided into India and Pakistan in 1947. For some twenty-five years, it remained East Pakistan, ruled by West Pakistan, from which it was separated by over 1,000 miles of Indian territory. But resentment at the discrimination visited on them by the non-Bengali, West Pakistan caused East Pakistan—led by a separatist party called the Awami League—to declare independence in 1971. A civil war followed, during which an estimated 1 million persons were killed, some deliberately massacred by the army of West Pakistan, and many thousands of women and girls were raped. Some 10 million Bangladeshi people sought protection in other countries, primarily in India.

While the world looked on at the killings, India intervened, principally to weaken its old foe, West Pakistan (now Pakistan), but also to stem the flow of refugees and offer some help to the victims of West Pakistan's brutality. That intervention, which began in December 1971, helped defeat Pakistan and assure the independence of East Pakistan, now renamed Bangladesh. Since independence, the country has struggled with deep poverty and natural disasters, especially cyclones and the almost annual monsoons that often devastate the country. It has begun to build a multiethnic and multireligious society (although the Bihari still face discrimination), and its constitution as well as its political policies exhibit considerable commitment to equality, including equality for women. The human and social destruction caused by the civil war, which led to the country's independence, has also forced many scholars and nations to modify their noninterventionist views in favor of intervention, when massive violations of human rights are taking place or are imminently threatened. Finally, the right of all individuals to financial credit (whether or not individuals have security in the form of land or other property for such credit) is a right that is espoused by scholars and human rights activists in Bangladesh, especially those who have come to accept that right as championed by Professor Muhammad Yunus, founder and managing director of the now world famous Grameen Bank.

The bank offers loans to the poor (over 90 percent to women), who have no means of security, on the basis of the belief that giving people a chance to better themselves socially is far more important than what is traditionally called security. The bank has established branches in over half of the country's 68,000 villages, extended loans amounting to nearly $2 billion, is transforming the lives of millions of peasants (especially women), and has a default rate 1.9 percent, which no conventional banker can boast. Of utmost importance for the future of Bangladesh will be the extent to which men and women, in this Muslim country where men dominate social and economic life, can come to accept the increasing economic independence of women. See also: Economic, Social and Cultural Rights; Interventionism; Rape; Self-Determination. *Further Reading:* K. Chaudhuri, *Genocide in Bangladesh* (1972); I. Hossain, "An Experiment in Sustainable Development: The Grameen Bank of Bangladesh," *JTWS*, vol. 15, no. 1 (1998); R. Payne, *Massacre* (1973); R. Sisson and L. E. Rose, *Secession: Pakistan, India, and the Creation of Bangladesh* (1990).

BANJUL CHARTER ON HUMAN AND PEOPLE'S RIGHTS. See AFRICAN CHARTER ON HUMAN AND PEOPLES' RIGHTS.

BASIC PRINCIPLES FOR THE PROTECTION OF CIVILIANS IN ARMED CONFLICT. See ARMED CONFLICT.

BASIC PRINCIPLES ON THE INDEPENDENCE OF THE JUDICIARY. See JUDICIARY.

BEIJING DECLARATION AND PLATFORM FOR ACTION. See WORLD CONFERENCES ON WOMEN.

BEIJING RULES. See UNITED NATIONS STANDARD MINIMUM RULES FOR THE ADMINISTRATION OF JUVENILE JUSTICE.

B'NAI B'RITH INTERNATIONAL. Also known as B'nai B'rith International Council, B'nai B'rith International (BBI) is a global Jewish service organization that was founded in 1843, in New York, to meet the needs of poor Jewish immigrants. Today, it is the world's largest Jewish organization, with over half a million people affiliated with its service activities in more than fifty-eight countries. And while its activities are centered around supporting or uniting persons of Jewish identity (relocating Ethiopian Jews, protecting a small beleaguered Jewish community in Syria, extending aid and/or forging links with Jewish communities in Latin America, India, and Eastern Europe), it has become one of the most passionate **nongovernmental organizations** in promoting **human rights** for all.

The organization is at the forefront in lending support to human rights instruments dealing with the rights of the child, eliminating racial discrimination and religious intolerance, preventing **genocide** and torture, and, lately, eliminating all forms of discrimination against women. Directed by a Board of Governors who are elected by its delegate conference, BBI is organized into chapters and smaller units. It has consultative status with many international organizations, including the UN, **Organization of American States** (OAS), and European Union (EU). Among its constituent organizations are the Anti-Defamation League of B'nai B'rith and the B'nai B'rith Youth Organization. The former functions as a watchdog organization, especially in combating anti-Semitism; the latter is an organization dedicated to the nurturing of Jewish children. See also: Child, Rights of; Racism. *Further Information:* B'nai B'rith International Council, 1640 Rhode Island Avenue N.W., Washington, D.C. 20036, Tel.: (202) 857–6600.

BONDED LABOR. Bonded labor or debt bondage is a term used to denote a human status or condition that arises when a person who is in debt pledges his or her personal services (or the services of a person or persons under his or her control) as security for that debt. Usually, the duration and nature of the pledged services are neither defined nor limited, and the services, when rendered, are not applied toward the liquidation of the debt. Alternatively, the person making the pledge is paid such low wages that he or she can merely survive, and therefore has no chance to pay off the debt. Such debtors remain indefinitely in debt, and in some instances their pledged obligations, on their deaths, are inherited by their children. In the case of children, the result is not only bonded labor, but another form of human exploitation—child labor.

Throughout the world today—in many countries of Africa, North and South America, Europe, and the Middle East, but especially in south Asia, including **India** and Pakistan—bonded labor is prevalent and found in occupations varying from prostitution and domestic service, to farm labor, mining, and carpet weaving. The practice of bonded labor constitutes involuntary servitude and is, therefore, a form of slavery. Increasingly, the international community has begun to direct its attention to the elimination of a practice that the Supreme Court of India calls an "affront to basic human dignity."

Bonded labor violates a considerable number of human rights instruments, including the **International Bill of Human Rights** and the Convention on the Rights of the Child (CRC). Article 4 of the **Universal Declaration of Human Rights** (UDHR) provides that "No one shall be held in slavery or servitude." Article 23 (1) also states that "Everyone has the right to . . . free choice of employment, to just and favourable conditions of work." Section 3 of Article 23 goes on to say that "Everyone who works has the right to just and favourable remuneration ensuring for himself and his family an existence worthy of human dignity." Article 8 of the **International Covenant on Civil and Political Rights** (ICCPR) provides that "No one shall be required to perform forced or compulsory labour."

In the case of children, the CRC offers very important protections. Article 54 of that convention, among other things, provides children with the right to protection from all exploitation; physical, mental, and sexual abuse; and the right to education, play, and protection from work that threatens their education, health, or development. See also: Child, Rights of; Child Labor; Convention for the Suppression of the Traffic in Persons and the Exploitation of the Prostitution of Others; Forced Labor; Slavery, the Slave Trade, and Slavery-like Practices. *Further Reading:* Anti-Slavery International, *Children in Bondage* (1991); Human Rights Watch, *The Small Hands of Slavery: Bonded Child Labor in India* (1996).

BOSNIA-HERZEGOVINA. The Republic of Bosnia and Herzegovina is populated by many ethnic and religious groups, the majority of which are Muslims, who constitute about 50 percent; Serbians, who make up about 30 percent; and Croats, who compose about 17 percent. The Serbs are predominantly Orthodox Christians and they use the Cyrillic alphabet (like the Russians, for example); the Croats are overwhelmingly Roman Catholic and use the Roman alphabet; and the Muslims are largely of Slavic origin, who embraced Islam when both Bosnia and Herzegovina were for many centuries subject to Turkish rule. All three groups speak the same language, Serbo-Croatian, are ethnically indistinguishable, and have, over the years, engaged in considerable intermarriage and other forms of social intermingling. Indeed, Sarajevo, the capital of Bosnia, had been regarded as one of the most cosmopolitan cities in the world.

After World War I, Bosnia-Herzegovina became part of the new kingdom of the Serbs, Croats, and Slovenes, later known as Yugoslavia. Yugoslavia (now called the former Yugoslavia, because it disintegrated in 1991), lasted from 1929–1991, and consisted of two autonomous provinces—Kosovo and Vojvodina—and the six republics of Bosnia-Herzegovina, Croatia, Macedonia, Montenegro, Slovenia, and **Serbia**. They coexisted, despite intermittent conflicts, because of relative economic prosperity, the central coordinating role of the Yugoslav Communist Party, led by Josip B. Tito, and the political containment of Serbia, which had always sought an unduly dominant role in the affairs of the country.

When the economic problems of the mid-1980s undermined the country's economy, the mass movement for democratic pluralism that had swept through the communist countries of Europe in the late 1980s forced the Yugoslav Communist Party to compete with other political parties, and Serbia took a more nationalist posture in the country. Slovenia and Croatia declared themselves independent in 1991; the following year, Bosnia-Herzegovina did likewise. But the Serbs in Bosnia-Herzegovina refused to secede from their fellow Serbs in Serbia, which then dominated the remaining portions of the former Yugoslavia. What followed was one of the bloodiest wars in human history, during which the Serbs of Bosnia-Herzegovina, supported by Serbia, sought to take control of more and more areas of Bosnia-Herzegovina; Croatia, turning against its former Muslim allies, sought to take and annex to Croatia non-Serb controlled areas; and the Muslims fought to preserve as much as possible of the areas belonging to the old Bosnia-Herzegovina. In addition, each side (especially the Serbs, but also the Croats) sought to make its community an ethnically homogeneous nation, by pursuing policies designed to exclude "others" (also called **ethnic cleansing**). Such policies included **expulsion**, mass **rape** (to humiliate or induce people to flee), **genocide**, massacre of civilians, especially when the Serbs defeated the Muslims in the city of Srebrenica, siege, bombardment, and wanton destruction of cities. Bosnia-Herzegovina, which prided itself in its intermingling of ethnic, religious, and other groups, and its general cosmopolitanism was ethnically, religiously, and socially lacerated. Numbers are uncertain, but it is estimated that tens of thousands were killed in the massacres.

The European Union (EU), the **United States**, and the UN, moved by the horror of what had taken place, intervened, and, especially with the help of the United States, a peace agreement was negotiated in 1995. That agreement created a loose federal state of Bosnia-Herzegovina, which is almost evenly divided among a Bosnia-Croat-Muslim federation and a Bosnia-Serb republic. It also provides for the protection of **human rights** and fundamental freedoms, as well as cooperation in the arrest, trial, and prosecution of those, such as the leader of the Bosnian Serbs, Radovan Karadzic, who are directly involved in sponsoring human rights violations. See also: Kosovo; Milosevic, Slobodan; War Crimes Tribunals. *Further Reading:* A. Bell-Fialkoff, *Ethnic Cleansing* (1996); L. J. Cohen, "Whose Bosnia? The Politics of Nation Building," *CH*, vol. 97, no. 617 (1998); L. Silber and A. Little, *Yugoslavia: Death of a Nation* (1996); A. Stiglmayer, ed., *Rape: The War Against Women in Bosnia-Herzegovina* (1994); UN Doco, *Report of the Special Rapperteur on the situation of human rights in the territory of the former Yugoslavia,* E/CN. 4/1998/ 63.

BRAZIL. The Federal Republic of Brazil is the largest country in South America, with a population of over 158 million people and a gross domestic product of more than $575 billion. The country is composed of twenty-six constitutional subdivisions called states and a federal district. Although its population has been influenced by several religions, the country is overwhelmingly (over 90 percent) Christian. Racially and ethnically, it is composed of indigenous Indians, immigrants from Japan and the countries of Europe, and Afro-Brazilians, who are principally descendants of slaves imported from Africa.

The Brazilian constitution admirably provides for **democratic entitlement** and other **human rights** of the civil and political kinds embodied in international human rights instruments. When one compares the textual provisions of the Brazilian constitution with the conduct of successive governments, however, one finds human rights violations in a number of areas, including the rights relating to respect for personal integrity, non-discrimination, **indigenous peoples**, children, and workers.

In the first area, a disturbing number of extrajudicial killings have occurred, especially in the industrial state of São Paulo, where military police have been responsible for instances of "mass murder." In other areas of the country, landless workers have been killed, again by military police.

Judges and lawyers who have sought to protect the rights of the landless have been threatened with violence, sometimes by **death squads** that are known to be in league with the police. The government's behavior with respect to the norms against **discrimination** and the rights of indigenous persons and children has been no better.

Women experience very high incidences (as many as 60 percent, according to some statistics) of physical abuse. And, although the Brazilian Supreme Court in 1991 struck down the now discredited concept of "defense of honor" as a justification for wife murder in cases of sexual infidelity, courts are still relatively unreceptive to the prosecution and conviction of men who attack their wives.

On average, women earn 54 percent of the salary earned by men, and some employers, in order to avoid compliance with the legal requirement of 120 days of maternity leave, either try to avoid hiring women of childbearing age or seek to obtain a sterilization certificate from women job applicants. The government rarely seeks to enforce the maternity leave law.

Brazil often presents itself as a "racial democracy," yet few blacks are found at the senior levels of government, in the armed forces, private businesses, or national cultural institutions, although they constitute approximately half the population. Black consciousness organizations, as well as churches, supply persuasive evidence of discrimination against blacks in employment, housing, and educational opportunities. These forms of discrimination are also present against indigenous persons who are often trapped into forced labor and confronted with inadequate medical care, progressive loss of their tribal lands, and assaults on their culture. Finally, according to a 1995 human rights report submitted by the U.S. State Department to Congress, Brazil has millions of children—many between the ages of ten and thirteen—who fail to get an education, must work to sustain themselves and do not have a place to live. See also: Child, Rights of; Civil and Political Rights; Convention on the Elimination of All Forms of Discrimination Against Women; Forced Labor; Indigenous Peoples; International Covenant as Civil and Political Rights. *Further Reading:* Amnesty International, *Brazil* (1988); Human Rights Watch, *Police Brutality in Urban Brazil* (1997); G. O'Connor, *Amazon Journal* (1996); R. Schneider, *Brazil: Culture and Politics in a New Industrial Powerhouse* (1996).

BRUTLAND COMMISSION. See ENVIRONMENT.

BUDDHISM. See RELIGION AND HUMAN RIGHTS.

BURMA. Burma or the Union of Myanmar, its current name, is located in southeast Asia, bordering **Bangladesh, China, India,** Laos, and Thailand. Its 44 million population, although predominantly Burmese (70 percent), is composed of a number of ethnic groups, including Shan (9 percent), Karen

(8 percent), Chinese (5 percent), and Indian (2 percent). Although over 80 percent of the population are Buddhist, Christianity, Islam, and Hinduism have important standing in Myanmar society.

Approximately six months before the country gained independence from Britain in 1948, its foremost nationalist and the person who was expected to become its first prime minister, U Aung San, was assassinated. Because of the suspicions and divisions caused by the assassination; security concerns because of its location; anxieties raised by the political challenge of the Shan and Karen (who had been fighting for political and cultural autonomy); as well as fears about economic domination by the Chinese and the Indians, successive authoritarian governments were able to use the banner of national unity to maintain control. That control was challenged in 1988, when widespread antigovernment protests forced the Burma Socialist Program Party, that had exercised a monopoly of power for some twenty-six years, to call for multiparty elections. During the protests, the government used torture, **rape**, and extrajudicial killings of an estimated 3,000 persons to reverse the popular uprising, but its conduct only undermined its legitimacy.

In March 1989, the United Nations **Commission on Human Rights** (CHR) adopted a stance entitled "Situation in Burma," which expressed concern about the government's violations of **human rights** and urged it to honor its undertaking to organize and hold fair multiparty democratic elections. Seeking to regain its claim to legitimacy and thinking that it could win an election in which it would encourage the participation of many political parties (some ninety parties ultimately participated), the government held elections in 1990. The result was a stunning victory for the main opposition party, the National League for Democracy (NLD) led by Aung San-Suu Kyi, then the 44-year-old daughter of U Aung San. The NLD won 392 of the 485 contested seats, but the governing military body, the State Law and Order Restoration Council (SLORC), voided the election and attacked the coalition of winning parties, many of whose leading members were intimidated, illegally detained, or placed under house arrest. It was not until 1992 that the regime began to relax its draconian rule, reopening universities, releasing some prisoners, and inviting many who had fled abroad to return. That relaxation has not stopped the regime's human rights violations, however, which have included limits on freedom of speech, religion, and association, torture, disappearances, and arbitrary arrests. Other violations include the right to organize and bargain collectively, the right against forced labor, and the minimum age for the employment of children.

In March 1995, the CHR adopted a resolution criticizing the authorities in Myanmar for their human rights abuses, and in December 1995, the United Nation **General Assembly** adopted a consensus resolution deploring the continued violations of human rights in that country. The European

Union (EU) and the **United States** have registered some protests, but the military regime has been winning some successes in avoiding moral and political isolation, as evidenced in the 1997 vote of the Association of Southeast Asian Nations to offer membership in that body to Burma. See also: Civil and Political Rights; Democratic Entitlement. *Further Reading:* B. Lintner, *Land of Jade: A Journey Though Insurgent Burma* (1990); G. M. Maung, *Burmese Political Values* (1983); E. T. Mirante, *Burmese Looking Glass: A Human Rights Adventure and a Jungle Revolution* (1993); Aung San Suu Kyi, *Freedom from Fear and Other Writings* (1991).

BUSINESS CORPORATIONS AND HUMAN RIGHTS. The human rights movement developed with a focus on the state as both the principal threat to and promoter-protector of **human rights**. Over the past decade, however, a vigorous debate has emerged concerning the connection between business activities of corporations and their respect for the promotion and protection of human rights.

At first, the debate was dominated by the stances of governments and business corporations, which held that international investment and trade would improve the chances for human rights protection and promotion. In particular, it was argued, corporations would promote **civil and political rights** such as the freedom of association and expression, equality and non-discrimination, as well as those **economic, social and cultural rights** that are realizable from improvements in the material conditions of human beings, including the right to food, clothing, and housing. This line of thinking has been very persuasive, because business corporations have not only become the center of economic activities but, in some cases, individual transnational business corporations (TNCs) enjoy economic power that exceeds that of many countries. Powerful TNCs are also effective in influencing the behavior of countries. Available evidence about corporate conduct suggests that, in many instances, corporations have been deeply involved in human rights violations.

These violations take many forms: support for repressive governments that deny people their **democratic entitlement;** opposition to the formation of unions (one of the rights to associate); and actual complicity with governments that deny or abridge economic, social, and cultural rights such as maternity protection, health-supporting labor conditions, fair wages, free choice of work, equal employment opportunity, and education.

In 1994, for example, a report of the United States Congress, "By the Sweat and Toil of Children," disclosed widespread complicity between governments and corporations in the exploitation of child labor. In 1996, the British Parliament passed a resolution condemning one of its TNCs, British Petroleum, for funding **death squads** in Columbia. In 1993, Germany, troubled by the exploitation of child labor in the carpet industry in east Asia, began to support consumer-based groups that had begun to organize against such exploitation. Sweatshop conditions in developing countries, in the **United States**—especially in garment factories in California and New York—as well as sex discrimination in Mexico's U.S.-owned export processing factories along the border, have begun to invite strong public resentment. National legislative bodies in **Canada**, Germany, Denmark, the **United Kingdom**, and the United States—spurred on by public concern— have also begun to debate what actions to take. But as of this writing, no effective governmental measure at the national or international level has been adopted. At the local level, however, political and civic leaders have been taking important actions.

In the 1980s, corporations that did business with the **apartheid** regime in **South Africa** were boycotted by units of local governments in the United States (and elsewhere) and by certain private groups. Because of the threat of consumer boycotts, a number of companies decided against doing business with **Burma** (Myanmar Republic); and the decision of cities such as Ann Arbor, Michigan, and San Francisco, California, to prohibit the purchase of goods and services from companies doing business in Burma has also had a salutary effect on business corporations. In April 1998, attorneys in California representing workers and consumers filed a civil suit against Nike, Inc., a maker of footwear, for allegedly misleading the public about the working conditions of hundreds of thousands of Vietnamese, Chinese, and Indonesian workers. These workers, the suit claims, are regularly subject to physical punishment and sexual abuse, and are often exposed to dangerous chemicals and forced labor, sometimes without pay.

Many of the corporations that have been accused of complicity in violating human rights deny the accusations but, in a considerable number of cases, however, the evidence supporting the charges is persuasive. One only has to review the Human Rights Watch's report on Royal Dutch/Shell's support for Nigerian dictators against the Ogoni people of their country, the previously mentioned British Petroleum's support for death squads in Columbia, and Zenith Corporation's mistreatment of pregnant workers in Mexico. See also: Child, Rights of; Child Labor. *Further Reading:* T. Regan, *Just Business: New Introductory Essays in Business Ethics* (1983); D. L. Spar, "The Spotlight and Bottom Line: How Multinationals Export Human Rights," *For. Aff.*, vol. 77, no. 2 (1998); R. P. Claude and B. H. Weston, eds., *Human Rights and the World Community: Issues and Action* (1992); R. J. Johnson, P. J. Taylor, and M. J. Watts, eds., *Geographies of Global Change* (1995).

C

CAIRO DECLARATION ON HUMAN RIGHTS IN ISLAM. See ARAB WORLD AND HUMAN RIGHTS.

CAMBODIA. Cambodia is a country located in southeast Asia and shares borders with the Gulf of Thailand, Laos, Thailand, and Vietnam. Its population, estimated by the UN (1996) to be about 9 million people, is ethnically composed of Khmers (90 percent) and Chinese (5 percent); the remaining percentages are made up of Burmese, Chams, and Vietnamese. The official language is Khmer, but French, Chinese, and Vietnamese are varyingly used. Buddhism is the dominant religion, but other religions, including Islam and Animism, are also observed.

After gaining independence from France and joining the UN in 1953, Cambodia's new government—a constitutional monarchy—was led by King Norodom Sihanouk until 1970, when it was overthrown by Lon Nol. Since 1970, the country has experienced little but social and political instability, including the 1997 coup d'état that overthrew the 1993 coalition government that a UN-sponsored election had put in office. Coupled with that instability have been some of the most egregious violations of human rights.

In 1964, the Khmer Rouge (Red or Communist Cambodians) began a peasant-led uprising against the king, but when he was overthrown in 1970 he joined forces with the Khmer Rouge, led by Saloth Sar (also known as Pol Pot) in a war of resistance against the increasingly repressive military regime of Lon Nol. In 1975, the Khmer Rouge succeeded in toppling the military regime and began what came to be called the "Cambodian genocide."

Committed to the racial, social, economic, ideological, and political purification of Cambodia, leaders of the Khmer Rouge, between 1975 and

1978, launched a revolution that had, in their words, "no precedent." All cities and towns were evacuated and a forced transfer of nearly half of the country's population to rural areas was effected; the liquidation of one to two million persons perceived as "class enemies" was carried out. Enemies included those who spoke foreign languages, had higher education, and were unwilling to accept the view that "various nationalities [did] not any longer exist in Kampuchea" (the briefly renamed Cambodia). Also included were those who opposed the abolition of money, markets, wages, private property, separation of children from their parents, or who were soiled by previous associations with the military regime. The Khmer Rouge also routinely used torture, starvation, and denial of medical care as political weapons.

Despite the **genocide** in the "killing fields of Cambodia," there was little international public pressure against Cambodia. In 1979, however, the Vietnamese invaded Cambodia—due in part to the ongoing genocide against ethnic Vietnamese. The invasion forced the Khmer Rouge to the areas along the borders of Thailand, where its leaders set up guerrilla bases and resisted the Vietnamese-installed puppet regime in Phnom Penh, the capital of Cambodia. Pressured by the international community, Vietnam withdrew its troops in 1989. In 1991, all Cambodian political factions, including the Khmer Rouge, signed a peace agreement providing for UN peacekeeping and democratic elections. Peace, however, is elusive, and political and social instability continues.

Today, the people of Cambodia—and this is not likely to change soon—are stripped of their **democratic entitlement**. They face limitations on religious freedom and **minorities** such as the Vietnamese are discriminated against. The government does not enforce the minimum age requirement for **child labor**. The Khmer Rouge has not been defeated. See also: Ethnic Cleansing. *Further Reading:* D. Chandler, *Brother Number One: A Political Biography of Pol Pot* (1992); H. Hannum, "International Law and Cambodian Genocide: The Sound of Silence," *HRQ*, vol 11, no. 1 (1989).

CANADA. Canada is the second largest country in the world in size. It has a population that is estimated by the UN (1996) to be about 28 million people, and it is racially, ethnically, and culturally diverse. English-speaking and French-speaking Canadians constitute the largest subnational groupings, but there are other nonlinguistic groups including Ukrainian; Italian; German; Dutch; east-, south-, and west-Asian; Caribbean; Polish; Jewish; and aboriginal peoples. (Aboriginals include Indians, Inuit or Eskimos, and Metis, who are people of mixed Indian and non-Indian descent.) The country is highly industrialized, boasts a market-based economy, and has one of the most admired **human rights** records in the world.

A good sense of Canada's human rights behavior can be arrived at by looking at its 1982 Charter of Rights and Freedoms, which provides a *national standard* to which all statutory legislation must conform. It also provides for equal benefits and nondiscrimination regardless of race, national or ethnic origin, color, religion, sex, age, or physical disability. "Sex," as used here, includes **lesbian and gay rights**, and in international forums, Canada has joined with Denmark, Norway, and the Netherlands in supporting the norm of nondiscrimination for lesbian and gay persons. Despite Canada's good record in protecting human rights, there are a few areas where problems have arisen and continue to exist: violence against women, treatment of Aboriginals, self-government for Quebec, anti-Semitism, and immigration policy.

Canadian law forbids violence, including spousal abuse, against women; yet, half of all Canadian women, after the age of sixteen, experienced at least one incident of violence by a male. According to a 1995 government report, over 200,000 women had been sexually abused by their husbands or common-law partner in the previous year. Because of discrimination against Aboriginals, they live in socioeconomic conditions plagued by drugs, alcoholism and drug addiction, poverty and family violence, unusually high crime rates, teenage suicide, and levels of unemployment as high as 80 percent. A Royal Commission, established in 1991, to examine Aboriginal concerns and make recommendations to the government, submitted its report in November 1996. One of its recommendations was that there should be "a new beginning in the relationship between Canada and its aboriginal nations," and as part of that new beginning, it proposed the infusion of some $27 billion over the next twenty years to improve housing, health care, job training, and education.

In the matter of self-government, Quebec—one of Canada's ten provinces and home of the overwhelming percentage of French-speaking Canadians—has been seeking that status for many years. The Canadian constitution protects linguistic and cultural minorities, and it now provides for a bilingual (English and French) country. Many Quebecers, however, feel dominated by the English-speaking majority and seek a separate society. In 1995, a Quebec sovereignty referendum was narrowly defeated (49.4 to 50.6 percent), and mutual recriminations between French-speaking and non-French-speaking Quebecers followed. To compound matters, the Cree (indigenous) Nation, whose land area represents a substantial portion of Quebec, not only opposes the idea of sovereignty for Quebec but takes the position that if the French-speaking community were to secede from Canada, it would secede from Quebec. Canada submitted the case of Quebec's call for a separate society to the Canadian Supreme Court. The Supreme Court ruled in August 1998 that while Quebec cannot by its own vote secede from Canada, if a clear majority of the people of that province wish to secede, Canada would be obligated to negotiate the terms of that secession.

In 1995, the B'nai B'rith League for Human Rights in Canada reported that Canada experienced its highest levels of anti-Semitism in thirteen years. On the issue of immigration, the government's policy has been discriminating in favor of would-be immigrants who are young, reasonably affluent, college-educated, and fluent in English or French. See also: Declaration on the Elimination of Violence Against Women; Indigenous Peoples; Racism; Self-Determination. *Further Reading:* G. Beaudoin and E. Mendes, eds., *The Canadian Charter of Rights and Freedoms* (1996); D. Schneiderman and K. Sutherland, eds., *Charting the Consequences: The Impact of Charter Rights on Canadian Law and Politics* (1997).

CAPITAL PUNISHMENT. Capital punishment, a subject of considerable international action, refers to punishment by death. It is currently one of the most vexing issues in the international **human rights** movement, with the controversy centered around the question of whether this form of punishment should be abolished.

Those who argue for its retention say it protects society in that it serves as a deterrent to potential criminal offenders and provides a sense of atonement, which, especially in cases of the most heinous crimes, might make society ungovernable. The argument continues that taking a criminal's life places a reasonable limit on the economic cost to society, which would otherwise have to offer indefinite support for his or her maintainance.

Arguments for those who seek its abolition are equally forceful. Abolition advocates contend that human life is sacred, and the state should, by its conduct, set an example of respect for the sanctity of human life, not repeat the crime by indulging in capital punishment, which degrades life as well. The death penalty is not a social deterrent, since crime statistics demonstrate that where there has been abolition, there have not been increases in crime. Capital punishment is administered unequally, especially against the poor who are the most powerless in society. Abolitionists also argue that capital punishment constitutes a form of cruelty and inhumanity that contradicts the moral and spiritual norms that define civilized conduct.

The above-mentioned arguments were some of those offered during the period when the **Universal Declaration of Human Rights** (UDHR) was being formulated. Then, Yugoslavia, Poland and the USSR proposed the universal repeal of capital punishment in peacetime; a majority of states voted against that proposal, however, giving advocates of the death penalty an apparent victory. When Article 3 of the UDHR recognized everyone's "right to life," therefore, that recognition did not bear with it support for abolition. However, since 1948—the date of the Universal of Human Rights Declaration—human rights advocates have been gaining support for the abolition of the death penalty. By 1966, when the **International Covenant on Civil and Political Rights** (ICCPR) was adopted by the UN, the momentum had clearly shifted. States—through Article 6 of the covenant— agreed that in countries where abolition had not yet come into force, the death penalty should apply only in cases of the most serious crimes; that no person under the age of eighteen or pregnant should be legally sentenced to death; and that nothing in the covenant should be interpreted to delay or prevent the abolition of capital punishment.

Article 6 of the ICCPR strengthened the argument that the death penalty is inconsistent with the right to life. And since 1976, when that covenant came into force, the number of countries that have abolished the death penalty has grown to become a majority, although a considerable number, including **China, Saudi Arabia,** Sudan and the United States continue the practice. Among the countries that have abolished capital punishment, fifty-eight (including **Australia,** Germany, and Venezuela) have abolished it for *all* crimes; fifteen (including **Canada, Mexico, South Africa** and **Israel)** have abolished it for all except the most serious crimes; and twenty-seven, which have not explicitly abolished it by law, have simply ceased employing the practice. Among the latter are Albania, Senegal, Sri Lanka, and Grenada. Article 1 of Protocol No. 6 of the European Convention for the Protection of Human Rights states that the death penalty shall be abolished. In 1989, the United Nations **General Assembly** adopted an additional protocol to the ICCPR—a protocol that has as its aim the abolition of the death penalty. See also: European Convention on Human Rights. *Further Reading:* R. Hood, *The Death Penalty* (1996); M. Kronenwetter, *Capital Punishment: A Reference Handbook* (1993); W. Schabas, *The Abolition of the Death Penalty in International Law* (1997).

CARTER, JIMMY (JAMES EARL, JR.) (1924–   ). Jimmy Carter was the thirty-ninth president of the United States from 1976 to 1980 and became associated with a number of foreign policy initiatives that were not very popular at the time of his tenure in office. One of those initiatives was that of making **human rights** the moral center of U.S. foreign policy.

Many who believe that foreign policy should be based on relationships of power disagreed with him. But, for the people in Argentina confronting a tyrannical military dictatorship, in **South Africa, apartheid,** or dissidents in **China** or Eastern Europe, the moral support that President Carter's initiative provided was welcomed. Since 1980, every president of the **United States** has adopted a human rights emphasis, even if he did not accept human rights in the same moral vein as President Carter did. Indeed, while other United States presidents have emphasized **civil and political rights,** Carter is the only U.S. president, apart from **Franklin D. Roosevelt,** to focus on **economic, social and cultural rights** as well. Since he left office, the former president devotes his time and energies to support people's right to housing, health care, education, and peace. Through Habitat for Humanity, he has himself helped to build some of that housing for the poor throughout the world and in the United States. He should be credited with having played an important role in the development of the of the inter-American human rights regime. See also: Roosevelt, Eleanor. *Further Reading:* A. G. Mower Jr., *Human Rights and American Foreign Policy: The Carter and Reagan Experiences* (1987); Mower, *The United States and Human Rights: The Eleanor Roosevelt and Jimmy Carter Eras* (1979).

CATHOLIC CHURCH. See HOLY SEE.

CENTRE FOR HUMAN RIGHTS. The Centre, located in Geneva, Switzerland, is part of the UN's office in that city and also a unit of the United Nations Secretariat. It functions in four major areas: (1) It provides management, administrative, and research services to UN organs that deal with **human rights** issues. These organs include the United Nations **Economic and Social Council (ECOSOC), General Assembly, Commission on Human Rights** (CHR) and **Human Rights Committee.** (2) It coordinates the work of the UN's specialized agencies concerned with questions of human rights, the **World Health Organization** (WHO), United Nations Educational, Scientific and Cultural Organization (UNESCO), and the **International Labor Organization** (ILO). (3) It cooperates with and lends support to regional intergovernmental organizations such as the **Organization of African Unity** (OAU), **Organization of American States** (OAS), and the **Council of Europe.** (4) It offers advisory services and technical assistance (the training of judges and police persons, for example) that help promote and protect human rights. Finally, the Centre serves as an important source of information to the public, especially to nongovernmental groups engaged in human rights concerns.

In July 1997, the UN secretary-general proposed the consolidation of the **Office of High Commissioner for Human Rights** and Centre for Human Rights into a single Office of High Commissioner. The proposed streamlined structure will focus on three areas: (1) information, analysis, and policy development; (2) support to human rights bodies and organs; and (3) actions for the promotion and protection of human rights. See also: Advisory Services in the Field of Human Rights. *Further Reading:* "Renewing the United Nations: A Programme for Reform," UN Doc./A51/950 (July 14, 1997).

CHARTER OF THE INTERNATIONAL MILITARY TRIBUNAL. See CRIMES AGAINST HUMANITY; CRIMES AGAINST PEACE.

CHARTER ON SEXUAL HARASSMENT IN THE WORKPLACE. See LESBIAN AND GAY RIGHTS.

"CHARTER 77." "Charter 77" refers to a free association of Czechoslovakian people of varied beliefs, preferences, and opinions who, in 1977, confronted their government and demanded that it live up to its assumed obligations under the **International Covenants on Human Rights** that it had signed in 1968 and ratified in 1975. The term also refers to a document, signed by some 1,000 Czechoslovakian citizens, containing the written confrontation and demand to the government. Many of those involved in the drafting and dissemination of the written "Charter of 77," including **Václav Havel,** were later imprisoned as the government tried to suppress the association. The charter, however, had too profound an effect to be covered up. First, it acquainted citizens with their rights (the ratification of the International Covenants was not known to the general public until 1977). Second, it incited the human rights movement in the country and heavily contributed to the 1989 "velvet revolution," which succeeded in overthrowing the communist regime and replacing it in 1990 with a democratically elected government, led by Havel.

From the day the government signed the covenants, the written charter claimed, "our citizens have the rights and the State the duty, to be guided by them." Far from being so guided, the charter charged that the government had engaged in systematic violations of the human rights contained in the covenants. Among those rights violated were the right to seek, receive, and impart information and ideas of all kinds, regardless of frontiers; the right to **thought, conscience and religion** (guaranteed by Articles 18 and 19 of the **International Covenant on Civil and Political Rights** [ICCPR]), and the right of individuals to form and join trade unions for the promotion and protection of their economic and social interests (Article 8 of the **International Covenant on Economic, Social and Cultural Rights**). The charter also pointed to the persistent violations of the **human rights** norms against arbitrary arrest, unlawful interference with privacy, family, home, and correspondence. *Further Reading:* J. Bradly, *Czechoslovakia's Velvet Revolution* (1992); O. Kreji, *Czechoslovak National Interest* (1996); U.S. Congress, *Human Rights and the Democratization of the Czech Republic* (1994).

CHECHNYA. Chechnya is a constituent republic of **Russia,** located in the southwest of that country. It borders Georgia and has a population of about 780,000 people, the overwhelming percentage of whom are Muslim. The republic, whose capital is Grozny, has significant deposits of natural gas, houses strategic rail lines from the Caspian Sea to the Black Sea, and is associated with important petroleum and chemical industries.

Chechens, who fought against Russian political control from the 1830s to the late 1850s, only acquiesced after they were defeated by **Russia** in 1859. Since that date, they have continued an uneasy relationship with Russia, including the period 1917 to 1991, during which Russia formed part of the USSR. In 1991, at about the time when the Soviet Union was at the last stages of dissolution and the Russian Federation was effecting its "new birth," Chechnya declared itself independent from the Federation and has been in a state of military and political confrontation with Russia ever since.

Following its declaration of independence, Russia sent troops to help support opposition groups that had differences with the new government in Grozny. When those efforts failed to temper the Chechen spirit of independence, the Russian government sent troops into Chechnya in 1994. The troops were initially repelled in their assault on Grozny, but by March 1995, the city was taken at the cost of its near destruction and heavy civilian casualities. For Russia, too, the number of dead soldiers was so high that its government became politically vulnerable. After a succession of failed cease-fires, Russian and Chechen leaders signed a peace agreement in May 1996. The agreement did not solve the issue of independence, however, and as early as August 1996, another cease-fire had to be negotiated. An important result was that Chechnya was offered (and it accepted) the prospect of early independence. In March 1998, however, in violation of the May 1996 agreement with Russia, Chechnya declared itself an Islamic republic (Russia is a predominantly Christian country) and began to institute Islamic legal code.

The Russia-Chechnya war of the 1990s involved a number of **human rights** violations. First, Chechnya's right to national **self-determination** was violated by Russia. Second, both parties to the conflict engaged in hostage-taking, and, in the case of Chechnya, even the right to the health of hospital patients was violated, when its rebels seized a southern Russian hospital, taking patients and members of the medical staff hostage. Third, the conflict also entailed indiscriminate killing of people, including large numbers of civilians, and the reckless destruction of property. Fourth, it involved the impairment of the physical and social environment, thus endangering elementary human rights such as those to food, clean water and air, education, and housing. See also: Geneva Conventions. *Further Reading:* D. Curran, F. Hill, and E. Kostritsyna, *The Search for Peace in Chechnya: Sourcebook, 1994–1996* (1997); K. Dawisha, "Russian Foreign Policy in the Near Abroad," *CH*, vol. 95 no. 607 (1996); V. Tolz, "The War in Chechnya," *CH*, vol. 95 no. 607 (1996).

CHILD, RIGHTS OF. Since 1924, when the League of Nations—the predecessor of the UN—adopted the Child Welfare Charter, international concern for the protection of children has been significant. Article 25 (2) of the **Universal Declaration of Human Rights** (UDHR), expressing that concern, reads as follows: "Motherhood and childhood are entitled to special care and assistance. All children, whether born in or out of wedlock, shall enjoy the same social protection."

In 1966, almost twenty years after the UDHR, the UN adopted two human rights covenants, which did not go much beyond what the UDHR had offered, although in the intervening years two important human rights instruments were adopted by the UN. The first was the 1959 **Declaration of the Rights of the Child** and the other was the 1965 **Declaration on the**

Promotion Among Youth of the Ideals of Peace, Mutual Respect and Understanding among peoples. These two instruments were never intended as legally binding on states; they were moral statements that sought to protect children against various forms of abuse and prepare them for a social and international life that was less exploitative in nature. It was not until 1989 when the UN adopted a comprehensive international treaty, the Convention on the Rights of the Child (CRC), that children received international recognition as persons with interests and rights independent of families, parents, and adults in general.

While other UN efforts, such as the creation of the **United Nations Children's Fund** (UNICEF), recognizes that children have special *needs*, the 1989 convention, in a revolutionary turn, says children have *rights* as well. These rights are civil and political as well as economic, social, and cultural—the very classes of rights adults have. As of early 1998, some 187 countries, not including the United States, have ratified the CRC.

Among the rights recognized by the CRC are the right to health care services; education; protection against discrimination on the basis of race, sex, religion, nationality, etc.; expression of one's views on important matters; protection against abuse, neglect, or injury; a name and nationality; protection against hazardous work and economic or other exploitation; rights against torture, cruel or inhuman or degrading treatment; and freedom of **thought, conscience and religion.** See also: Bonded Labor; Child Labor; Civil and Political Rights; Economic, Social and Cultural Rights; Slavery, the Slave Trade, and Slavery-like Practices; United Nations Standard Minimum Rules for the Administration of Juvenile Justice. *Further Reading:* M. Black, *Children First* (1996); C. P. Cohen, S. N. Hart, and S. M. Kosloske, "Monitoring the United Nations Convention on the Rights of the Child," *HRQ*, vol. 18 no. 2 (1996); Convention on the Rights of the Child, 28 *ILM* 1457 (1989); United Nations Children's Fund, *The State of the World's Children* (1997).

CHILD LABOR. Almost every country has laws that set limits on the employment of children. Several international treaties make it illegal for children to engage in work that is or is likely to be hazardous, impairs a child's health or physical, mental, or moral development, or that interferes with a child's education. In most countries, and from the content of **human rights** standards, the widely shared view is that the proper place for a child during adult working hours is the classroom, not the factory or the farm.

Notwithstanding that view, there is widespread use of child labor. The **International Labor Organization** (ILO) has estimated the total number of child laborers to be between 100–200 million, with over 90 percent in developing countries. The economic activities in which they engage are wide-ranging, including family-based agriculture, domestic and restaurant services, prostitution and small-scale manufacturing. Export-focused industries that typically employ children include the garment trade, carpet-making, mining, gem-polishing, leather tanning, shoe-making, and furniture-making.

The international community, as part of the human rights movement, has begun to exert some pressure to eliminate child labor. In Article 1(1) of the 1973 ILO Minimum Age Convention (no. C138), states undertake "to pursue a national policy designed to ensure the effective abolition of child labor and to raise progressively the minimum age for admission to employment." Paragraph 3 of the same article, in an effort to reinforce the child's right to education and define "minimum age," provides that the "minimum age . . . shall not be less than 15 years." There have been some reservation about the minimum age standard of fifteen, but with the advent of the 1989 Convention on the Rights of the Child (CRC), that standard has begun to receive increasing support. In January 1995, the labor ministers of Non-Aligned and Developing Countries met in New Delhi, India, and at the meeting issued an important statement, which has come to be called the Delhi Declaration, the essence of which is captured in the following portion of the statement: "We are aware and hold that the practice of exploitative child labour wherever it is practiced is a moral outrage and an affront to human dignity."

The last-quoted statement is important for several reasons. For one, it comes from leaders of countries in which child labor is most prevalent. The statement itself was formulated in Asia, the region of the world where child labor is over 50 percent, with the practice widespread in countries such as India, Indonesia, and Pakistan. The statement was accompanied by a promise to begin the process of eliminating child labor. The task will be formidable, because, as a U.S.-sponsored study on the subject shows that economic self-interest, public indifference, government corruption, and social prejudice, among other factors, conspire to preserve child labor.

In the case of economic self-interest, factory owners overwork, underpay, and otherwise take advantage of vulnerable children to increase profits. As children do not vote, political and media leaders often treat child labor as a nonissue, and some political leaders actually benefit materially from child labor. Finally, social prejudices that invite disregard for the poor and powerless contribute to public indifference. The human rights movement seeks to end that indifference. See also: Bonded Labor; Child, Rights of; Slavery, the Slave Trade, and Slavery-like Practices. *Further Reading:* C. Bellamy, *The State of the World's Children 1996* (1997); R. Sawyer, *Children Enslaved* (1988); U.S. Department of Labor, *By the Sweat and Toil of Children* (1994).

CHILE. Chile is a South American country, which shares its borders with the Pacific Ocean, Peru, Bolivia, and Argentina. It has a population of about 13.5 million people, 92 percent of whom are of mixed Spanish and Amerindian descent; the rest are Europeans and Indigenous Amerindians. The country gained its independence from Spain in 1818 and joined the

UN in 1945. Although Chile had been portrayed for years as a stable democracy, social and ideological differences divided the country with socialists and their leftist associates wanting to create a more egalitarian society and conservatives seeking to hold onto the privileges that caused great social inequalities. In 1970, Salvador Allende Gossens was elected president by a plurality of votes, with the support of socialists, communists, and other leftist groups. As Allende proceeded to introduce the social reforms he had promised, a military coup, led by General Augusto Pinochet Ugarte, overthrew him in 1973. By December 1974, Pinochet, supported by the United States, assumed the presidency, which he held until December 1989, when Chilean voters denied him his long sought opportunity of being "elected" to office, and instead elected Christian Democratic candidate Patricio Aylwin, to lead them back to civilian life.

During the years of Pinochet's military rule, there were grave violations of **human rights**. More than 100,000 Chileans were arbitrarily arrested and tortured, and thousands were killed or identified as "disappeared persons." The United Nations **Commission on Human Rights** (CHR), beginning in 1974, heard complaints of human rights violations and appointed a **working group**, which was later replaced by a special rapporteur, to examine the "situation in Chile." The commission, on receiving the special rapporteur's tenth report at its 1990 session, acknowledged some improvements in human rights in Chile. It also noted that the following were still pending: (1) judicial and administrative identification and punishment of the persons responsible for the crimes, disappearances, persecutions, and intimidations during military rule; (2) a return to the normal administration of justice, especially with regard to a reform of the system of military justice and a review of decisions made by military courts; and (3) a review of the rules by which persons charged with committing serious human rights violations are granted immunity.

With the above reforms pending, a new civilian government, and the so-called "Aylwin Doctrine" (named after the former president), which said courts should not close cases involving disappearances until bodies are found or credible evidence is provided to indicate that an individual is dead, many Chileans felt hopeful. But Pinochet had packed the Supreme Court with his judges and had remained, until early 1998, in control of the armed forces, and the dominant economic and social elites he had served were not anxious to facilitate the process of identifying and punishing those who had committed grave violations of human rights.

During early 1996, several cases of disappearances and extrajudicial executions were closed. The National Corporation of Reparation and Reconciliation, a general body created in 1991 to continue investigating human rights violations during the military regime, delivered its final report in August 1996, confirming 899 more "deaths by disappearances," thus bringing the total of such crimes to over three thousand. The much needed, far-reaching reforms of the Criminal Procedures Code, which were presented to the Chilean Congress in 1995—reforms necessary to protect human rights—are still under debate. To the credit of the Congress, a new privacy law, which bars obtaining and disseminating information secured by telephone intercepts or other surreptitious means, was passed in November 1995.

An effort is also being made to include over 1 million **indigenous peoples** in planning processes that concern them. Further, the government's former policy of assimilation for all indigenous persons has been replaced by a policy of bilingualism and cultural autonomy.

Abuse by police, including torture, continues in Chile. In November 1996, Special Rapporteur on Torture Nigel Radley concluded his report on Chile by noting that cases of torture were "sufficiently numerous and serious for authorities to continue giving attention to the problem." Since 1990, he has transmitted to the Chilean Government some 110 allegations of torture, but nothing has been done by the authorities there.

However, in October 1998, Pinochet (who was in the United Kingdom for medical treatment) was arrested by British police at the request of Spain. The warrant of arrest said he was wanted for questioning for "crimes of genocide and terrorism that include murder." This development will not only help Chile to deal with its own internal problem, but it will have worldwide implications for the future prosecution of alleged human rights violations under international law. See also: Declaration on the Protection of All Persons from Enforced Disappearance; Democratic Entitlement; Truth Commissions. *Further Reading:* J. Puryear, *Thinking Politics: Intellectuals and Democracy in Chile, 1973–1988* (1994); P. W. Drake and I. Jaksic, eds., *The Struggle for Democracy in Chile, 1982–1990* (1991).

CHINA. The People's Republic of China (PRC) has an estimated population of over 1.2 billion people. The Han Chinese constitute about 93 percent of the total, and some fifty-five designated minority groups including Zhuang and Tibetans compose the rest. Languages used in common include standard (official) Chinese, Mandarin, and Cantonese, along with a number of local dialects.

The PRC was established in 1949, after the Communist Party of China (CPC), led by **Mao Zedong** won a civil war against the Nationalist Party (the Koumintang), which had governed China since 1911. After its defeat, the Nationalist government, which had been recognized as the government of China, fled to the island of Taiwan, one of the provinces of China. There, it continued to claim that it was the legitimate government of China until the 1970s, when most of the remaining countries that had continued to recognize its legitimacy shifted recognition to the communist government in Beijing. In the meantime, the CPC had led a remarkable socioeconomic transformation of China.

In the process of that transformation, the CPC leader Mao Zedong, organized the Great Leap Forward (1958–1961), a campaign designed to bring about village industrialization and rural collectivization. He also launched the Great Proletarian Cultural Revolution (1966–1976), a movement led by groups of youths and especially students called the Red Guards, who campaigned against "old ideas, old culture, old habits, and old customs," as a way of purging the CPC of those who opposed the radical egalitarianism sought by Mao. Both campaigns involved mass brutality and grave violations of **human rights**—from the right to life, privacy, and free exercise of one's religion, to the right to a fair trial and freedom from arbitrary arrest and torture. Millions of persons were killed during these campaigns.

Since Mao's death in 1976, China has adopted a mixed economy and allowed a greater degree of personal freedom, although a 1989 pro-democracy protest in **Tienanmen Square** was met with strong government repression. That repression, apparently designed to prevent popular sentiments to dictate the nature and face of political democracy in China, has continued in the form of long-term imprisonment and arbitrary arrest of political activists. Even today, there has been no thorough accounting of all those killed or declared missing in connection with that repression. Current and future human rights issues involving China include the right to national **self-determination** and religious freedom, rights of children, women, and minorities, and the priority given to certain categories of human rights.

With regard to self-determination, both the people of Taiwan and Tibet may seek to exercise that right, but the CPC seeks the reclaimation of all territories formerly alienated from China especially during the "golden age of imperialism" (the eighteenth and nineteenth centuries) as well as the reunification of China as one of the tasks it must finish in order to complete its revolution. Tibet, however, has been seeking greater autonomy since 1959, and Taiwan, in July 1992, modified its constitution to remove its former "provincial status," thus making it constitutionally possible to proclaim national independence. In the area of religious freedom, China's constitution provides for the toleration of all religious beliefs, but government regulations actually restrict religious practices. For example, the CPC takes the position that party membership and religious beliefs are incompatible. The government assumed the authority to name the second-in-command to the **Dalai Lama** in the Buddhist community of Tibet, and although Catholic seminarians, Muslim clerics, and Buddhist clergy have been allowed to go abroad to further their studies, only those religious organizations that receive the state's stamp of approval can engage in public religious activities.

The rights of children, women, and **minorities** are also a concern. Women, for example, are subject to abuse, including abduction, to satisfy the demand for marriageable women, and although they textually have "equal rights with men in all spheres of life," they are the most likely to be fired in the restructuring of state enterprises. With children, the major problem is that a preference is accorded to the male child, particularly under the government's family planning policy, which restricts most urban couples to one child. This policy not only infringes on the right to found a family, but sometimes results—because of the cultural preference for boys—in the death of many infant girls. China has improved the life of minority groups in general, but some are discriminated against when they lack certain attributes—when they do not speak Mandarin, for example. Finally, China has given priority to a class of human rights that the West, especially the United States, has chosen to de-emphasize, a priority that has a bearing on matters of international economic relations and the development of the human rights movement.

The CPC has emphasized **economic, social and cultural rights**—the right to education, food, health care, and housing, for example. In this area of human rights it has done very well. It has not given, however, much emphasis to **civil and political rights**—the right to a free press, private property, and democratic entitlement. The West wants China to focus on civil and political rights in exchange for improved economic relations, and access to technology. China has been using its potentially vast market for Western goods to counter Western pressure, and its success or failure will be reflected in its dealings with Hong Kong which, in July 1997, was returned to China from Britain. Hong Kong's robust economy has been linked to "a capitalist focus on civil and political rights," and China has promised to integrate that economy by following a formula of "one country, two systems." The fate of Macao, the Portuguese colony that will be returned to China in 1999, will also be a test of that type of promised integration. Should China succeed, then Taiwan, which boasts a capitalist type of economic order and allows greater civil and political rights, may be less inclined to seek independence from China. Equally significant, China's success could demonstrate how to give equal emphasis to both classes of human rights—civil and political as well as economic, social, and cultural. China's failure, however, could mean a further deterioration in their focus on economic, social, and cultural rights. See also: Arbitrary Arrest and Detention; Asian Values. *Further Reading:* Cheng Li, *Rediscovering China: Dynamics and Dilemmas of Reform* (1997); M. C. Davis, ed., *Human Rights and Chinese Values* (1995); D. Soled, ed., *China: A Nation in Transition* (1995).

CHRISTIANITY. See RELIGION AND HUMAN RIGHTS.

CIRCUMCISION. See GENITAL MUTILATION.

CIVIL AND POLITICAL RIGHTS. The term refers to one of the classes of human rights that states are obligated to promote and protect. These rights, as defined and elaborated in the **International Covenant on Civil and Political Rights** (ICCPR) as well as in the **Universal Declaration of Human Rights** (UDHR), include:

- the right to life;
- the right not to be subjected to torture, or cruel, inhuman, or degrading treatment or punishment;
- the right not to be held in slavery or be subjected to forced or compulsory labor;
- the right to liberty and security of one's person;
- the right not to be subjected to arbitrary arrest and detention;
- the right to be brought promptly before a judge or other officer authorized by law if arrested and detained;
- the right to be informed, at the time of arrest, of the reason for that arrest;
- the right to compensation for unlawful arrest and detention;
- the right to challenge one's arrest and detention;
- the right to freedom of movement and to leave any country;
- the right to communicate with and have a lawyer;
- the right to freedom of religion and belief;
- the right to freedom of thought, conscience, and religion;
- the right to freedom of expression;
- the right to associate;
- the right to privacy; and
- the right to found a family.

See also: Economic, Social and Cultural Rights; Generations of Rights; International Bill of Human Rights. *Further Reading:* H. J. Steiner and P. Alston, *International Human Rights in Context* (1996); L. Henkin, ed., *The International Bill of Rights: The Covenant on Civil and Political Rights* (1981).

CLONING AND BIOMEDICINE. The term cloning denotes the process of human intervention, by embryo splitting or nuclear transfer technique, to create life-forms that are genetically identical. Cloning cells and tissues is, in general, viewed worldwide as socially and scientifically valuable and an ethically acceptable biomedical technique. Deliberately cloning human beings, however, is considered ethically unsupportable for three major reasons—all of which are said to compromise the fundamental concept of human rights. First, cloning bears with it the inevitable promotion of instrumentalism, which espouses the view that the use a product has for its producer determines its value. In human terms, the claim of human rights is that humans have ultimate value and cannot be measured by the extent to which they are useful to others. Second, human cloning destroys the protection against the predetermination of human genetic constitution by third parties. Such a predetermination removes the fortuitous equality humans have by virtue of the genetic process of their origins. Third, human cloning reduces the freedom that naturally occurring genetic recombination allows and robs people of their unique identities. The three reasons also share a common property: human cloning violates human dignity.

Many political and other leaders, including President Bill Clinton of the United States, have publicly opposed human cloning. Political leaders in Western Europe, however, have been the first to take action to outlaw it. They have done so through two human rights instruments: the Convention on Human Rights and Biomedicine (also known as the Convention for the Protection of Human Rights and Dignity with Regard to the Application of Biology and Medicine) and the Draft Additional Protocol to the Convention on Human Rights and Biomedicine on the Prohibition of Cloning Human Beings (also known as the Draft Additional Protocol to the Convention for the Protection of Human Rights and Dignity with Regard to the Application of Biology and Medicine on the Prohibition of Cloning Human Beings). The first was adopted by the Council of Europe on April 4, 1997, and the second on September 22, 1997. The convention's and the draft protocol's principal concerns are to prevent misuses in biology and medicine that could lead to acts endangering human dignity, and to ensure that progress in biology and medicine is used for the benefit of present and future generations. The following articles of the Convention on Human Rights and Biomedicine express those concerns:

Article 1   Purpose and object
Parties to the Convention shall protect the dignity and identity of all human beings and guarantee everyone, without discrimination, respect for their integrity and other rights and fundamental freedoms with regard to the application of biology and medicine.

Each Party shall take in its internal law the necessary measures to give effect to the provisions of this Convention.

Article 2   Primacy of the human being
The interests and welfare of human beings shall prevail over the sole interest of society and science.

Article 11   Non-discrimination
Any form of discrimination against a person on grounds of his or her genetic heritage is prohibited.

Article 12   Predictive genetic tests
Tests which are predictive of genetic diseases or which serve either to identify the subject as a carrier of a gene responsible for a disease or to detect a genetic predisposition or susceptibility to a disease may be performed only for health purposes or for scientific research linked to health purposes, and subject to appropriate genetic counselling.

Article 13   Intervention on the human genome
An intervention seeking to modify the human genome may only be undertaken

for preventive, diagnostic or therapeutic purposes and only if its aim is not to introduce any modification in the genome of any descendants.

Article 14   Non-selection of sex

The use of techniques of medically assisted procreation shall not be allowed for the purpose of choosing a future child's sex, except where a serious hereditary sex-related disease is to be avoided.

Article 21   Prohibition of financial gain

The human body and its parts shall not, as such, give rise to financial gain.

Article 22   Disposal of a removed part of the human body

When in the course of an intervention any part of a human body is removed, it may be stored and used for a purpose other than that for which it was removed, only if this is done in conformity with appropriate information and consent procedures.

The Draft Additional Protocol, seeking to protect the "dignity and identity of all human beings," and serving as an overall complement to the broader biomedical concerns of the convention, goes on to deal with cloning in more specific terms. It defines and outlaws human cloning and stipulates that there shall be no derogation of the limitations the convention imposes. The relevant articles state:

Article 1 Any intervention seeking to create a human being, whether living or dead, is prohibited.

For the purpose of this article, the term human being "genetically identical" to another human being means a human being sharing with another the same nuclear gene set.

Article 2 No derogation from the provisions of this Protocol shall be made under Article 26 paragraph 1 of the Convention.

Article 26 paragraph 1 of the Convention on Human Rights and Biomedicine provides that no restrictions shall be placed on the exercise of the rights and protective provisions that are contained within that convention, except those that are prescribed by law and are necessary in a democratic society in the interest of public safety, prevention of crime, protection of public health, or protection of the rights and freedoms of others.

On November 11, 1997, the 186 member states of the **United Nations Educational, Scientific and Cultural Organization** (UNESCO) adopted the Universal Declaration on the Human Genome and Human Rights, which seeks to ban human cloning. That instrument, because it is a declaration and not a treaty, does not by itself have the binding force of the European Convention on Human Rights and Biomedicine. It could, however, come to gain that status if states shape their behavior according to the spirit of its terms. Article 11 of the declaration provides that "Practices which are contrary to human dignity, such as reproductive cloning of human beings, shall not be permitted." See also: Declaration on the Use of Scientific and Technological Progress in the Interest of Peace and for the Benefit of Mankind. *Further Reading:* R. H. Blank and A. L. Bonnicksen, eds., *Emerging Issues in Biomedical Policy*, vol. 3 (1994); E. B. Brody, *Biomedical Technology and Human Rights* (1993); M. A. Rodwin, *Medicine, Money, and Morals* (1995); Convention on Human Rights and Biomedicine, *ILM*, vol. 36 no. 4 (1997); Draft Additional Protocol to the Convention on Human Rights and Biomedicine on the Prohibition of Cloning Human Beings, *ILM*, vol. 36 no. 6 (1997).

CODE OF CONDUCT FOR LAW ENFORCEMENT OFFICIALS. On December 17, 1979, the United Nations **General Assembly**, aware of the important role law enforcement officials play in the promotion and protection of **human rights** and aware, as well, of the abuses that often result from enforcement of the law, adopted a code of conduct for law enforcement officials. That code, which is really a body of principles with detailed commentaries, is not included here in full, but its first six principles, stated in the form of articles (without accompanying commentaries), are as follows:

Article 1. Law enforcement officials shall at all times fulfill the duty imposed upon them by law, by serving the community and by protecting all persons against illegal acts, consistent with the high degree of responsibility required by their profession.

Article 2. In the performance of their duty, law enforcement officials shall respect and protect human dignity and maintain and uphold the human rights of all persons.

Article 3. Law enforcement officials may use force only when strictly necessary and to the extent required for the performance of their duty.

Article 4. Matters of a confidential nature in the possession of law enforcement officials shall be kept confidential, unless the performance of duty or the ends of justice strictly require otherwise.

Article 5. No law enforcement official may inflict, instigate or tolerate any act of torture or cruel, inhuman or degrading treatment or punishment, nor may any law enforcement official invoke superior order or exceptional circumstances such as state of war or a threat of war, a threat to national security, internal political instability or any other public emergency as a justification of torture or other cruel, inhuman or degrading treatment or punishment.

Article 6. Law enforcement officials shall ensure the full protection of the health of persons in their custody and, in particular, shall take immediate action to secure medical attention whenever required.

See also: Arbitrary Arrest and Detention; Procedural Guarantees, Processes and Protections; Public Emergency; Superior Orders. *Further Reading:* General Assembly *Code of Conduct for Law Enforcement Officials*, Resolution 34/169 (December 17, 1979); United Nations, *Human Rights and Law Enforcement: A Manual on Human Rights Training for the Police* (1997).

COLLECTIVIZATION. This term refers to the act or process by which title and control of property are transferred from private to collective (often meaning state) ownership and control. Under communism, the act or process was often forcibly imposed, resulting in the death of many peasants who fought against it. In the case of the Soviet Union, for example, the government, led by **Joseph V. Stalin**, conducted a brutal campaign against rich peasants (*kulaks*), who had benefited from agricultural reforms that took place in **Russia** between 1906 and 1917. The same loss of life, torture, imprisonment, and starvation that many peasants experienced in the USSR (especially in Ukraine), were repeated in the collectivization process of a number of other communist countries, including **Cambodia** and **China**. See also: *Gulag Archipelago*. Further Reading: R. Conquest, *The Harvest of Sorrow: Soviet Collectivization and Terror-Famine* (1986); L. Viola, *The Best Sons of the Fatherland: Workers in the Vanguard of Soviet Collectivization* (1987).

COMMISSION ON HUMAN RIGHTS. Article 68 of the **United Nations Charter** authorizes the United Nations **Economic and Social Council** (ECO-SOC) to "set up commissions in the economic and social fields for the promotion of human rights." Consistent with that article, the ECOSOC established the United Nations Commission on Human Rights (CHR) in 1946. In accordance with its original mandate, the commission has been at the forefront of international action concerned with defining, promoting, and protecting **human rights**. For example, it proposed the initial drafts for the human rights instruments that together constitute the **International Bill of Human Rights**. It has also aided in drafting a number of other human rights instruments, including the **International Convention on the Elimination of All Forms of Racial Discrimination** and the **Convention Against Torture and Other Cruel, Inhuman or Degrading Treatment or Punishment**. The CHR has also developed a variety of means to help it carry out its task of promoting and protecting human rights, three of which are the use of qualified experts, working groups, and special procedures under the ECOSOC's Resolution 1503 (XLVIII) of 1970.

Experts, who are often designated special rapporteurs, special representatives, or special envoys, are persons chosen to take on fact-finding tasks on human rights issues such as torture, prostitution, or intolerance based on religion or belief. The commission also uses **working groups** to examine and report on human rights situations, such as involuntary disappearances, and to help draft conventions such as the 1989 Convention on the Rights of the Child (CRC). With regard to special procedures, the commission, under ECOSOC's Resolution 1503, may receive and examine, through its sub-commission, complaints that reveal a consistent pattern of human rights violations. The work of the commission in dealing with these complaints (including whatever report it makes to the ECOSOC) is confidential, unless the ECOSOC decides otherwise. The commission also works closely with other UN organs, countries, and **nongovernmental organizations** (NGOs) dealing with human rights.

In addition to the United Nations Commission on Human Rights, there are three other commissions on human rights: the European Commission on Human Rights, the Inter-American Commission on Human Rights, and the African Commission on Human and Peoples' Rights. See also: Human Rights Commissions. *Further Reading:* H. Tolley, *The U.N. Commission on Human Rights* (1987).

COMMISSION ON THE STATUS OF WOMEN. The United Nations Commission on the Status of Women (CSW) was created by the United Nations **Economic and Social Council** (ECOSOC) in 1946. Since the time of its creation, the CSW has served as the UN body primarily responsible for the advancement of women. Its work has included a wide variety of international actions to define, promote, and protect the human rights of women.

In defining and helping to elaborate standards of **human rights**, the commission has played the major role in preparing human rights treaties such as the 1953 **Convention on the Political Rights of Women** and the 1979 **Convention on the Elimination of All Forms of Discrimination Against Women** (CEDAW). In the area of promoting women's rights, the commission helped to prepare the United Nations Decade for Women (1976–1985), during which special emphasis was placed on studying and bringing the attention of the international community to the social plight of women throughout the world. It also helped prepare the United Nations–sponsored **world conferences on women**, which took place during the Decade for Women and culminated in the 1985 conference in Nairobi, Kenya, and the Nairobi Forward-Looking Strategies for the Advancement of Women. The strategies set ambitious but practicable agendas for governments to have in place by the year 2000, programs for achieving full equality for women. The commission was also instrumental in planning and organizing the Fourth World Conference on Women, which took place in Beijing in 1995.

At present, perhaps the most weighty task facing the commission is that of monitoring, reviewing, and appraising the implementation of the Nairobi Forward-Looking Strategies—a task assigned to it by the United Nations **General Assembly**, which endorsed those strategies—and of monitoring and reviewing the Programme of Action, which came out of the Beijing conference. Meeting the responsibilities of these assignments will no doubt go beyond the year 2000 and will require considerable coordination with many UN agencies, **nongovernmental organizations** (NGOs) and individual states.

On the matter of protecting human rights, in 1988 the commission established a Working Group on Communications. They have examined a number of complaints from countries, many of which deal with abuse and violence against women, as well as social and economic discrimination. Much of the information secured by the working group was helpful at the world conference in Beijing, and in future years should also prove helpful in the work of the **Committee on the Elimination of Discrimination Against Women,** which was created by CEDAW. *Further Reading:* Centre for Human Rights, *Discrimination Against Women: The Convention and the Committee* (1994).

COMMITTEE AGAINST TORTURE. Article 17 of the **Convention Against Torture and Other Cruel, Inhuman or Degrading Treatment or Punishment** requires that a Committee Against Torture (CAT) be created. That committee, the legal outlines of which were adopted by the United Nations **General Assembly** in 1984, came into force on June 26, 1987.

Under the terms of the convention, each state is responsible for taking appropriate legislative, administrative, judicial, and other measures to prevent acts of torture in areas under its jurisdiction. Each state is further required to make reports to CAT on the measures it has taken. In turn, CAT is vested with the authority to receive and consider those reports, make comments and observations about them, and include the comments and observations in its required annual report to the General Assembly. They are also forwarded to the state concerned.

Complaints to the committee may be made by states against other states, or by, or on behalf of, individuals against a state. In each case, before the complaint can be considered, the consent of the state against which the complaint is being made must have been previously obtained by CAT. *Further Reading:* Centre for Human Rights, *The Committee Against Torture* (1992); E. Peters, *Torture* (1996).

COMMITTEE OF MINISTERS OF THE COUNCIL OF EUROPE. The **Council of Europe,** created in 1949 to pursue European unity, is grounded in certain common ideals and principles shared by its members, among which are **human rights,** which have been elaborated in the **European Convention on Human Rights** and the **European Social Charter.** The European Convention, concerned primarily with **civil and political rights,** provides for a court of human rights and a **Commission on Human Rights.** The European Social Charter deals with **economic, social and cultural rights.**

The Committee of Ministers of the Council of Europe performs two very important functions within the framework of the convention: it executes the decisions of the **European Court of Human Rights** and, in instances when the European Commission on Human Rights forwards a case to it rather than the court, it is required to decide whether the convention has been violated. With respect to the European Social Charter, the committee receives biennial reports from states indicating their conduct under the terms of the charter. This essentially supervisory activity on the part of the committee is facilitated by its power to evaluate and comment on these reports as well as make recommendations to states. In addition, the committee, which is actually composed of the members of the Council of Europe, continuously reviews the two human rights instruments and refines their application. See also: Human Rights Commissions. *Further Reading:* Council of Europe, *The Council of Europe and Its Work Against Intolerance, Discrimination, and Racism* (1982); G. Gilbert, "The Council of Europe and Minority Rights," *HRQ,* vol. 18 no. 1 (1996).

COMMITTEE ON ECONOMIC, SOCIAL AND CULTURAL RIGHTS.
This committee was created in 1985 by the United Nations **Economic and Social Council** (ECOSOC), to help implement the terms of the **International Covenant on Economic, Social and Cultural Rights.**

Each state that accepts the obligations of the covenant agrees to take certain individual and collective steps in order to achieve the progressive realization of the rights recognized in the covenant. Additionally, states undertake to guarantee the promotion and protection of the rights in question without discrimination, and to ensure equal opportunities to men and women in the exercise and enjoyment of those rights. Countries are obligated to submit reports to the UN secretary-general on the steps they have taken and the progress they have made to comply with the terms of the covenant. ECOSOC, which receives the accounts, considers them and other reports, evaluates and summarizes them, and, where necessary, makes recommendations to individual countries. The Committee on Economic, Social and Cultural Rights plays a central role in reviewing, evaluating, and summarizing the reports and making recommendations. See also: *Economic, Social and Cultural Rights. Further Reading:* Centre for Human Rights, *Committee on Economic, Social and Cultural Rights* (1991); R. Beddard and D. M. Hill, eds., *Economic, Social and Cultural Rights: Progress and Achievement* (1992).

COMMITTEE ON NONGOVERNMENTAL ORGANIZATIONS.
Article 71 of the **United Nations Charter** authorizes the United Nations **Economic and Social Council** (ECOSOC) to "make suitable arrangements for consultation with **nongovernmental organizations** (NGOs) that are concerned with matters within its competence." Consistent with that authorization, ECOSOC established a Committee on Nongovernmental Organizations, including those organizations that are concerned with one of the most important areas of its focus: **human rights.**

The committee divides nongovernmental organizations into three category groupings: Category I consists of organizations that have basic interests in most of the council's activities; Category II includes groups that have concerns on fewer of the council's activities; they, however, have special capabilities that can be of help in the activities of the council; Category III is made up of groups that make periodic but important contributions to the work of the council. Amnesty International, for example, is a Category II organization, as are many others.

Organizations that are in one of these three groups are said to have consultative status, that is, they can send observers to all public meetings of the council. They may do the same with the council's subsidiary bodies, such as the **Commission on Human Rights**, its **Sub-Commission on the Prevention of Discrimination and Protection of Minorities**, and **Commission on the Status of Women**. At meetings, nongovernmental organizations can present their own views in verbal and written forms. The opportunity to participate in these meetings has helped give nongovernmental organizations considerable influence in the human rights activities of the United Nations. See also: Amnesty International; Anti-Slavery International; Physicians for Human Rights. *Further Reading:* M. H. Posner, "The Establishment of the Right of Non-Governmental Human Rights Groups to Operate," in *Human Rights: An Agenda for the Next Century*, ed. L. Henkia and J. L. Hargrove (1994).

COMMITTEE ON THE ELIMINATION OF DISCRIMINATION AGAINST WOMEN. Article 17 of the **Convention on the Elimination of All Forms of Discrimination Against Women** (CEDAW) requires that a Committee on the Elimination of Discrimination Against Women be established for "the purpose of considering the progress made in the implementation of the . . . Convention." The committee, made up of twenty-three experts, was established according to the terms of the convention, which was adopted in 1979.

In "considering the progress made," the committee is to bear in mind that states agree to pursue by "all appropriate means and without delay," a policy of eliminating discrimination against women. Through considerations of reports, which states are required to submit to the UN secretary-general, the committee gains a fair sense of what states are doing judicially, legislatively, and administratively to honor the terms of the convention. In addition, the committee, in conjunction with **nongovernmental organizations** (NGOs) and other intergovernmental groups both in and outside the United Nations **Economic and Social Council** (ECOSOC), can receive additional information. Finally, the committee, through Article 21 of the convention, has the authority to make suggestions and recommendations based on its review of reports and other information. In 1994, the committee began entertaining proposals for an Optional Protocol to the Convention. If a protocol is initiated, it would enable individuals and groups to submit written communications, including complaints, to the committee. See also: Commission on the Status of Women. *Further Reading:* A. C. Byrnes, "The 'Other' Human Rights Treaty Body: The Work of the Committee on the Elimination of Discrimination Against Women," *YJIL*, vol. 14 no. 1 (1989); Centre for Human Rights, *Discrimination Against Women: The Convention and the Committee* (1994).

COMMITTEE ON THE ELIMINATION OF RACIAL DISCRIMINATION. This committee was established as required by and in accordance with Articles 8 and 9 of the **International Convention on the Elimination of All Forms of Racial Discrimination**. The International Convention was adopted by the United Nations **General Assembly** in 1965, and states that are parties to the convention undertake to pursue a policy of eliminating racial discrimination in all forms and promoting understanding among races. The committee's responsibilities are to help ensure that elimination and promotion. It can discharge its responsibilities in three major ways: (1) consideration of *reports* by states; (2) consideration of *complaints* from states against other states; and (3) consideration and review of communications from individuals and nonstate groups, who allege racial discrimination on the part of states.

The first consideration also entails the duty of states to submit to the UN secretary-general, for consideration by the committee, reports of administrative, judicial, and legislative steps taken to achieve the terms of the convention. The committee has the authority to examine the reports, request additional information, and make suggestions and recommendations, based on its assessments, to the UN General Assembly. In the second case, a state that thinks another state is failing to fulfill its obligation to the convention may communicate that concern to the committee. In the third case, under Article 14 of the convention, the committee is empowered to receive and consider communications from individuals and nonstate groups that claim to be victims of racial discrimination. See also: Apartheid; Propaganda; Racism. *Further Reading:* Centre for Human Rights, *Committee on the Elimination of Racial Discrimination* (1991); International Convention on the Elimination of All Forms of Racial Discrimination, 666 *UNTS* 195.

COMMITTEE ON THE EXERCISE OF THE INALIENABLE RIGHTS OF THE PALESTINIAN PEOPLE. This committee was established in 1975 by the United Nations **General Assembly** for the purpose of recommending a program to the General Assembly that will enable Palestinians to accomplish three things: (1) the right to **self-determination** without outside interference; (2) the right to national independence and sovereignty; and (3), the right to return to their homes and property from which they have been displaced. See also: Intifadah; Israel; Palestine Liberation Organization.

COMPENSATION FOR VICTIMS OF HUMAN RIGHTS ABUSE. International law, through human rights instruments, now provides compensation for victims of gross violations of **human rights**. Article 8 of the **Universal Declaration of Human Rights** (UDHR) provides that "Everyone has the right to an effective remedy by the competent national tribunals for actions violating the fundamental rights granted him by the constitution or by law." The **International Covenant on Civil and Political Rights** (ICCPR) stipulates:

Article 14 (6). When a person has by final decision been convicted of a criminal offence and when subsequently his conviction has been reversed or he has been pardoned on the ground that a new or newly discovered fact shows conclusively that there has been a miscarriage of justice, the person who has suffered punishment as a result of such conviction shall be compensated according to law, unless it is proved that the non-disclosure of the unknown fact in time is wholly or partly attributable to him.

The **Convention Against Torture and Other Cruel, Inhuman or Degrading Treatment or Punishment** states in Article 14:

1. Each State Party shall ensure in its legal system that the victims of an act of torture obtains redress and has an enforceable right to fair and adequate compensation, including the means for as full rehabilitation as possible. In the event of the death of the victim as a result of an act of torture, his dependents shall be entitled to compensation.

2. Nothing in this article shall affect any right of the victim or other persons to compensation which may exist by law.

The 1985 UN **Declaration of Basic Principles of Justice for Victims of Crime and Abuse of Power** in Articles 8–17, provides for restitution, compensation, and other assistance to victims. *Further Reading:* General Assembly, *Declaration of Basic Principles of Justice for Victims of Crime and Abuse of Power,* Resolution 40/34 (November 29, 1985).

CONDITIONALITY. The term refers to a set of conditions that governments must meet when they seek to secure access to structural adjustment loans from the International Monetary Fund (IMF). The conditions, which vary slightly from state to state, generally include (1) elimination of price controls, (2) removal of food and housing subsides, (3) reductions in allocations to education, (4) general cuts in government spending, and (5) devaluation of the currency and/or tax increases. Women, children, and the poor are customarily and disproportionately affected and **economic, social and cultural rights** (the right to housing, food, health care, and education) are invariably undermined. At issue has been the extent to which the International Monetary Fund and other international lending agencies are committed to the promotion and protection of human rights. See also: Child, Rights of. *Further Reading:* B. Sadasivam, "The Impact of Structural Adjustment on Women: A Governance and Human Rights Agenda," *HRQ,* vol. 19 no. 3 (1997); S. I. Skogly, "Structural Adjustment and Development: Human Rights—An Agenda for Change," *HRQ,* vol. 11 no. 4 (1993).

CONVENTION AGAINST DISCRIMINATION IN EDUCATION. This convention, which was adopted by the General Conference of the **United Nations Educational, Scientific and Cultural Organization** (UNESCO) on December 14, 1960, has three general purposes: (1) to eliminate discrimination in education; (2) to promote equality in education; and (3) to have education contribute to the full development of each individual.

Taking its inspiration from the **Universal Declaration of Human Rights** (UDHR), the convention declares education to be a right and defines it as "all types and levels of education, and includ(ing) access to education, the standards and quality of education, and the conditions under which it is given." Under Article 1, the convention defines discrimination to include "any distinction, exclusion, limitation or preference which . . . based on race, colour, sex, language, religion, political and other opinion, national and social origin, economic condition or birth, has the purpose or effect of nullifying or impairing equality of treatment in education." Included in acts of discrimination are (1) limiting any person or group to an education of inferior standard, (2) depriving an individual or group of access to "education of any type or at any level," and (3) inflicting on them conditions that are incompatible with their dignity.

The convention requires states to: (1) provide free and compulsory primary education for all, (2) make secondary education accessible to all, and (3) ensure that higher education is equally available to everyone. Further, public educational institutions at the "same level" must have equivalent standards of education. See also: Apartheid; Discrimination; Education. *Further Reading:* UNTS, *Convention Against Discrimination in Education,* 429 UNTS 93.

CONVENTION AGAINST TORTURE AND OTHER CRUEL, INHUMAN OR DEGRADING TREATMENT OR PUNISHMENT. One of the most reprehensible areas of states' conduct has been that of torture or other forms of cruel and degrading treatment. On December 10, 1984, the United Nations **General Assembly** adopted a treaty aimed at outlawing the practice. That treaty entered into force on June 26, 1987.

The convention defines torture, commits states to take effective legislative, administrative, judicial, and other measures to prevent acts of torture "in any territory under [their] jurisdiction," and establishes, through Article 17, a **Committee Against Torture,** the function of which is to monitor the conduct of states under the terms of the convention. Article 1(1) of the convention, which defines torture, is as follows:

For purposes of this Convention, the term "torture" means any act by which severe pain or suffering, whether physical or mental, is intentionally inflicted on a person for such purposes as obtaining from him or a third person information or a confession, punishing him for an act he or a third person has committed or is suspected of having committed, or intimidating or coercing him or a third person, or for any reason based on discrimination of any kind, when such pain or suffering is inflicted by or at the instigation of or with the consent or acquiescence of a public official or other person acting in an official capacity. It does not include pain or suffering arising only from, inherent in or incidental to lawful sanctions.

See also: Compensation for Victims of Human Rights Abuse; Crimes Against Humanity. *Further Reading:* M. Basoglu, *Torture and Its Consequences* (1992); E. Peters, *Torture* (1996).

CONVENTION CONCERNING EQUAL OPPORTUNITIES AND EQUAL TREATMENT FOR MEN AND WOMEN WORKERS: WORKERS WITH FAMILY RESPONSIBILITIES. This convention was adopted on June 23, 1981, by the **International Labor Organization** (ILO), a specialized agency of the UN. It addresses one of the most important norms of **human rights,** that of equality, especially between men and women.

Since 1945, the UN has sought to bring about gender equality by adopting a number of human rights instruments, including the **Convention Concerning Equal Remuneration for Men and Women for Work of Equal Value.** Despite the adoption of such instruments, there has always been a subtle implication that "family responsibilities" are primarily women's concerns. Even the 1979 **Convention on the Elimination of All Forms of Discrimination Against Women** (CEDAW)—the single most important treaty dealing with women's rights—bears that implication. The 1981 convention, also known as the Workers with Family Responsibilities Convention (WFRC), deals with this important issue of human rights.

The WFRC takes the position that the care and upbringing of dependent children must be the shared responsibility of women and men as well as society as a whole. A comparable responsibility is shared by men and women workers "in relationship to other members of their immediate family who clearly need their care and support." The norm of equality becomes especially applicable, according to Article 1 of the convention, "where such responsibilities restrict their [men or women workers] possibilities for preparing for, entering and participating in or advancing in economic activity." Articles 4 and 5 of the convention require states to take *all measures* compatible with national conditions to (1) "enable workers with family responsibilities to exercise the right of free choice of employment"; (2) "take account of their needs in terms and conditions of employment and social security"; (3) "take account of the needs of workers with family responsibilities in community planning"; and (4) "develop and promote community services, public and private, such as child care and family services facilities." *Further Reading:* Convention (No. 156) Concerning Equal Opportunities and Equal Treatment for Men and Women Workers: Workers with Family Responsibilities 362 UNTS 32; K. D. Ewing, C. Gearty, and B. A. Hepple, eds., *Human Rights and Labour Law* (1994).

CONVENTION CONCERNING EQUAL REMUNERATION FOR MEN AND WOMEN WORKERS FOR WORK OF EQUAL VALUE. One area of social life that provokes one of the most debated questions is that relating to inequality in compensation that men and women receive for equivalent work or work of equal value. The UN, through one of its specialized agencies, the **International Labor Organization** (ILO), has taken steps to remove this inequality.

On June 29, 1957, the General Conference of the ILO adopted the Equal Remuneration Convention. Article 2 (1) of the convention requires that states "ensure the application to all workers of the principle of equal remuneration for men and women workers for work of equal value." Section 2 of the same article states that the principle of "equal remuneration" may "be applied by means of—(a) national laws or regulations; (b) legally established or recognized machinery for wage determination; (c) collective agreements between employers and workers; or (d) a combination of these various means."

The convention also defines "remuneration" and "equal remuneration" as follows:

Article 1. For purposes of this Convention—

a. the terms "remunerations" includes the ordinary, basic or minimum wage or salary and any additional emoluments whatever payable directly or indirectly, whether in cash or in kind, by the employer to the worker and arising out of the worker's employment.

b. the terms "equal remuneration for men and women workers for work of equal value" refers to rates of remuneration established without discrimination based on sex.

See also: Convention Concerning Equal Opportunities and Equal Treatment for Men and Women Workers: Workers with Family Responsibilities; Convention on the Elimination of All Forms of Discrimination Against Women; Economic, Social and Cultural Rights. *Further Reading:* UNTS, *Convention (No. 100) Concerning Equal Remuneration for Men and Women Workers for Work of Equal Value,* 165 UNTS 303.

CONVENTION CONCERNING MATERNITY PROTECTION. As early as 1919, the **International Labor Organization** (ILO), now a specialized agency of the UN, adopted a treaty dealing with women before and after childbirth. By the end of World War II, however, as the cross-pressures of family and job responsibilities increasingly demonstrated unfairness to women, states realized that the 1919 treaty needed to be updated, and on July 29, 1952, the ILO adopted the Convention concerning Maternity Protection.

The convention applies to "any female person, irrespective of age, nationality, race, or creed, whether married or unmarried," who is "employed in industrial and agricultural occupations, including . . . wage earners at home." A woman who produces "a medical certificate stating the presumed date of her confinement" is entitled to a period of maternity leave. That period, according to Article 3 (2) of the convention "shall be at least twelve weeks, and shall include a period of compulsory leave after confinement." Section 3 of the same article goes on to say that "the period of compulsory leave after confinement shall be prescribed by national laws or regulations, but shall in no case be less than six weeks; the remainder of the total period of maternity leave may be provided before the prescribed date of confinement," or it can follow the expiration of the compulsory leave period. While on leave, a woman is entitled to receive cash and medical benefits— benefits enough to ensure "full and healthy maintenance of herself and her child."

Medical benefits under the convention include prenatal, confinement, and postnatal care by qualified midwives or medical practitioners as well as hospitalization, where necessary. See also: Economic, Social and Cultural Rights; European Social Charter; Health. *Further Reading:* UNTS, *Convention (No. 103) Concerning Maternity Protection*, 214 UNTS 321.

CONVENTION FOR THE SUPPRESSION OF THE TRAFFIC IN PERSONS AND THE EXPLOITATION OF THE PROSTITUTION OF OTHERS. To many, prostitution is a violation of **human rights,** viewed as not only one of the uglier forms of exploitation and discrimination, but also as a degrading violation of human dignity. The spirit of every international human rights instrument supports this view, and this convention leaves no doubt about the human rights implications of prostitution.

Approved by the United Nations **General Assembly** on December 2, 1949, and entering into force on July 25, 1951, the preamble to the convention reads in part that "prostitution and the accompanying evil of traffic in persons for the purpose of prostitution are incompatible with the dignity and worth of the human person." States that accept the terms of the convention assume the obligation to punish any individual who "procures, entices, or leads away" another person for purpose of prostitution, or who exploits the prostitution of another person, even if that person consents. Further, states assume the duty to punish anyone who keeps, manages, or knowingly finances or takes part in financing a brothel, or rents a building or a part thereof "for the purpose of the prostitution of others." A person who *attempts* to commit any of the above-mentioned criminal acts or who engages in acts of preparation to commit any of the crimes is to be punished. In addition, the convention includes provisions for the extradition of wrongdoers, the exchange of victims of prostitution, temporary care, and repatriation.

Given the preceding examples of obligations states assume under the convention, it would be reasonable to think that prostitution is on the wane, however, this is not the case. Today, this form of human exploitation (especially of women and children) is an international scandal. Often, governments that maintain military bases abroad, countries that earn significant amounts of foreign exchange from tourism, and business persons seeking "periods of relaxation and fun" are part of the problem. Knowingly or unknowingly, they engage in what constitutes cooperation, if not complicity, with procurers and pimps, owners of houses of prostitution, massage parlors, saunas and *genelevs* (Turkish baths or public houses), in reducing many women and children to what amounts to slavery.

The old thinking, which sought to blame the victims on grounds of their supposed mental weaknesses or vicious inclinations, was exposed as without any foundation in a report authored by Jean Fernand-Laurent, Special Rapporteur. The report, commissioned by the secretary-general of the UN to "make a synthesis of the surveys and studies on the traffic of persons and the exploitation of the prostitution of others, was submitted to the UN **Economic and Social Council** (ECOSOC) in 1983. It speaks of the "poverty, emotional deprivation, trickery, and coercion" that procurers use to get women and girls into prostitution, the servitude the victims enter into once they have been procured, and the pressures, punishments, and rewards used to condition them psychologically. Only education, improvement in people's economic and social conditions, and uncompromising international cooperation in enforcing the terms of the convention will reverse the prostitution of others. See also: Child Labor; Slavery, the Slave Trader, and Slavery-like Practices; Traffic in Persons and Exploitation of the Prostitution of Others. *Further Reading:* Anti-Slavery International, *Forced Prostitution in Turkey* (1993); Kathleen Barry, *Female Sexual Slavery* (1975); United Nations Doc., *Report on Mr. Jean Laurent, Special Rapporteur on the suppression of the traffic in persons and the exploitation of the prostitution of others,* E/1983/7 (March 17, 1983).

CONVENTION ON CONSENT TO MARRIAGE, MINIMUM AGE FOR MARRIAGE AND REGISTRATION OF MARRIAGES.

A women's right to consent to marriage is an issue concerning the institution of marriage and the unequal role and standing of women in relation to that institution. Young women and girls of a "tender age," too young to consent, are often "given away" in marriage, or "spoken for." Many women are also victims of polygamy, especially where there are no provisions for the registration of marriages.

The convention, adopted by the United Nations **General Assembly** on December 10, 1962, and effective December 9, 1965, seeks to ensure, through the principles of consent and registration, a degree of equal rights for women and girls. Article 1 of the convention states that no "marriage shall be legally entered into without the full and free consent of both parties." That consent is to be expressed by "them in person after due publicity and in the presence of the authority" which, by law, is competent to solemnize marriages. Articles 2 and 3 deal with the issues of minimum age and registration and the obligations of states:

Article 2. States parties to the present Convention shall take legislative action to specify a minimum age for marriage. No marriage shall be legally entered into by any person under this age, except where a competent authority has granted a dispensation as to age, for serious reasons, in the interest of the intending spouses.

Article 3. All marriages shall be registered in an appropriate official register by the competent authority.

Although the convention does not specify a minimum age, a 1965 recommendation by the UN General Assembly urges fifteen years old as the minimum age. *Further Reading:* UNTS, *Convention on Consent to Marriage, Minimum Age for Marriage and Registration of Marriages,* 521 UNTS 231; General Assembly, *Recommendation on Consent to Marriage, Minimum Age for Marriage and Registration of Marriages,* Resolution 2018 (XX) (November 1, 1965).

CONVENTION ON HUMAN RIGHTS AND BIOMEDICINE. See CLONING AND BIOMEDICINE.

CONVENTION ON THE ELIMINATION OF ALL FORMS OF DISCRIMINATION AGAINST WOMEN. One of the most powerful and socially transforming national and international movements of modern times is the women's movement, which seeks equality for women and the development of a more just international society. The international spirit of that movement and the work of the United Nations **Commission on the Status of Women** (CSW), as well as the efforts of the United Nations **Economic and Social Council** (ECOSOC) in the area of women's rights, culminated in the adoption of this convention by the United Nations **General Assembly** on December 28, 1979, and its entering into force on September 3, 1981.

Under the terms of the Convention on the Elimination of All Forms of Discrimination Against Women (CEDAW), states are obligated to adopt laws, policies, and practices to improve the status of women in order to bring them to conditions of equality with men. Articles 1 and 2–16 give a reasonable sense of the convention's substantive terms. Article 1 states that

For the purposes of the present Convention, the term "discrimination against women" shall mean any distinction, exclusion or restriction made on the basis of sex which has the effect or purpose of impairing or nullifying the recognition, enjoyment or exercise by women, irrespective of their maritial status, on the basis of equality of men and women, of human rights and fundamental freedoms in the political, economic, social, civil or any other field.

Articles 2–16 elaborate the actions governments must take to eliminate discrimination and ensure equality. These actions include

• embodying the principle of equality in national constitutions or other appropriate legislation;

• establishing competent national tribunals and other public institutions to protect women;

- repealing discriminatory laws and adopting "temporary special measures" (affirmative action);
- ensuring equal access to education, health care, and employment;
- recognizing a wife's nationality independently of that of her husband's; and
- providing women the right to engage in financial and other socioeconomic transactions in their own names.

Articles 7 and 8 specifically recognize a woman's right to vote and participate in local, national, and international public life. Article 11 prohibits dismissal from employment on grounds of marriage or maternity and provides for maternity leave. Articles 15 and 16 deal with a range of social and economic rights, including the right to contract and administer property, and choose one's residence. The articles also include the entitlement to equal rights and responsibilities before, during, and at the dissolution of marriage.

Finally, the convention establishes a committee, the **Committee on the Elimination of Discrimination Against Women**, to monitor government compliance with the terms of the convention. See also: Affirmative Action; Discrimination; World Conferences on Women. *Further Reading:* R. Cook, *Human Rights of Women* (1994); K. Tomasenski, *Women and Human Rights* (1993).

CONVENTION ON THE NATIONALITY OF MARRIED WOMEN. The issue of the nationality of women has been of special concern since 1948, when the United Nation **Commission on the Status of Women** (CSW) informed the UN secretary-general of the many and varied forms of discrimination to which women were being subjected under existing nationality laws. In particular, women in many countries were forced by law to take the nationality of their husbands. Alien wives of such husbands lived under the constant threat of "lost nationality" if they were divorced by their husbands. After further study of the issue, CSW, at its third session in 1949, recommended that a convention on the nationality of married women be promptly prepared. The proposed convention would assure equality with men in the area of nationality.

The proposal was endorsed by the United Nations **Economic and Social Council** (ECOSOC), which later approved a draft of the Convention on the Nationality of Married Women and forwarded it to the United Nations **General Assembly**. It was adopted by the General Assembly on January 29, 1957.

Affirming the right of everyone, as recognized in Article 15 of the **Universal Declaration of Human Rights** (UDHR), "to a nationality" as well as the right not to be "arbitrarily deprived of [that] nationality or be "denied the right to change [one's] nationality," the first two articles of the Convention on the Nationality of Women provide the following:

Article 1. Each Contracting State agrees that neither the celebration nor the dissolution of a marriage between one of its nationals and an alien, nor change of nationality by the husband during marriage, shall automatically affect the nationality of the wife.

Article 2. Each Contracting State agrees that neither the voluntary acquisition of the nationality of another State nor the renunciation of its nationality by one of its nationals shall prevent the retention of its nationality by the wife of such national.

Article 3 of the convention confers on alien wives, at their request, the right to acquire the nationality of their husbands. The convention, which entered into force on August 11, 1958, unfortunately does not address another important area of discrimination: the right of wives to transfer their nationality to alien husbands, as husbands can freely do in many countries, for their alien wives. In countries such as the United States and Canada, the issue has been addressed. *Further Reading:* UNTS, *Convention on the Nationality of Married Women*, 309 UNTS 65; P. Weis, *Nationality and Statelessness in International Law* (1979).

CONVENTION ON THE NON-APPLICABILITY OF THE STATUTORY LIMITATIONS TO WAR CRIMES AND CRIMES AGAINST HUMANITY.

After World War II, states committed themselves to identify, prosecute, and punish perpetrators of war crimes and crimes against humanity. Studies by the UN Security Council, however, revealed that statutory limitations in a number of countries would prevent the trial or punishment of such perpetrators after certain specified dates.

This convention, adopted by the United Nations **General Assembly** on November 28, 1968, stipulates in Article 1 that under international law, no statutory limitation shall exist for the prosecution and conviction of those people who are known to be responsible for war crimes and crimes against humanity. Article 2 identifies those who may be held liable for the crimes: representatives of state authorities or private individuals who participate, or who directly or indirectly incite others to the commission of those crimes, or who conspire to commit them, irrespective of the degree of completion. Representatives of state authorities who tolerate the commission of such crimes are also liable. Articles 3 and 4 deal with the undertaking by states to adopt the necessary legislative and other measures to make extradition possible, and make certain that statutory limitations do not apply to crimes against humanity and war crimes. See also: Crimes Against Humanity; War Crimes. *Further Reading:* UNTS, *Convention on the Non-Applicability of the Statutory Limitations to War Crimes and Crimes Against Humanity*, 754 UNTS 73; C. M. Bassiouni, *Crimes Against Humanity in International Law* (1992).

CONVENTION ON THE POLITICAL RIGHTS OF WOMEN.

Although this UN convention's provisions are now incorporated into the most important treaty dealing with women's rights, the **Convention on the Elimination of All Forms of Discrimination Against Women** (CEDAW), it is an important convention because it represents four developments for women: (1) it was the first global instrument under which states assumed the obligation to ensure political equality for women; (2) it continued the political momentum of the work of the UN **Commission on the Status of Women** (CSW), which played a central role in the drafting of the convention; (3) it affirmed the self-evident truth that there can be no political democracy when over half the population does not have the right to vote; and (4) it vindicated and gave support to the efforts of Inter-American countries which, in 1948, adopted a regional instrument on women's political rights, the Inter-American Convention on the Granting of Political Rights to Women.

This 1952 UN Convention on the Political Rights of Women entered into force on July 7, 1954. Its most important terms are contained in the first three articles:

Article 1. Women shall be entitled to vote in all elections on equal terms with men, without discrimination.

Article 2. Women shall be eligible for election to all publicly elected bodies, established by law, on equal terms with men, without discrimination.

Article 3. Women shall be entitled to hold public office and to exercise all public functions, established by law, on equal terms with men, without discrimination.

Some states, such as **Kuwait** and **Saudi Arabia,** do not recognize the right of women to vote. See also: Inter-American Commission of Women. *Further Reading:* UNTS, *Convention on the Political Rights of Women,* 193 UNTS 135.

CONVENTION ON THE PREVENTION AND PUNISHMENT OF THE CRIME OF GENOCIDE. One of the most odious moral outrages humans have to confront is **genocide.** At its second session in 1946, the United Nations **General Assembly** affirmed that genocide is a crime under international law and that persons who engage in it, under whatever circumstances, are punishable. To provide some of the needed international legal machinery for such punishment, the United Nations **Economic and Social Council** (ECOSOC) supervised the drafting of an international convention on genocide and forwarded it to the General Assembly where it was adopted on December 9, 1948. Under the convention, states undertake to adopt the necessary legislation to accomplish its provisions. Those provisions include providing effective penalties for those convicted of the crime of genocide and allowing extradition of persons, under their jurisdiction, who may be charged with genocide.

Articles 1–4 stipulate that states must confirm the crime, define the crime, indicate the acts that are punishable, and identify the classes of persons who may be punished.

Article 1. The Contracting Parties confirm that genocide, whether committed in time of peace or in time of war, is a crime under international law which they undertake to prevent and punish.

Article 2. In the present Convention, genocide means any of the following acts committed with the intent to destroy, in whole or in part, a national, ethnical, racial or religious group, as such:

   a. Killing members of the group;

   b. Causing serious bodily or mental harm to members of the group;

   c. Deliberately inflicting on the group conditions of life calculated to bring about its physical destruction in whole or in part;

   d. Imposing measures intended to prevent births within the group;

   e. Forcibly transferring children of the group to another group.

Article 3. The following acts shall be punishable:

   a. Genocide;

   b. Conspiracy to commit genocide;

   c. Direct and public incitement to commit genocide;

   d. Attempt to commit genocide;

   e. Complicity to commit genocide.

Article 4. Persons committing genocide or any other act enumerated in article 3 shall be punished, whether they are constitutionally responsible rulers, public officials or private individuals.

The Convention entered into force on January 12, 1951. See also: Cambodia; Crimes Against Humanity; East Timor; Ethnic Cleansing; Rwanda. *Further Reading:* UNTS, *Convention on the Prevention and Punishment of the Crime of Genocide*, 78 UNTS 277; C. B. Strozer and M. Flynn, eds., *Genocide, War, and Human Survival* (1996); C. M. Bassiouni, *Crimes Against Humanity in International Law* (1992).

CONVENTION ON THE REDUCTION OF STATELESSNESS. Statelessness refers to the condition of an individual who is not recognized by any state as one of its nationals. Historically, statelessness has arisen from dislocations caused by wars, revolutions, and political persecutions, conflicts of nationality laws, or uncertainty about the place of one's birth or about one's parents. In the case of women, for example, marriage to foreigners has always been risky, since, in many cases, they must take the nationality of their husbands. But if they were divorced by their husbands, they would often lose their new nationality. Since statelessness means that individuals have no legal claim to the protection of any specific country, such individuals have always been in danger of having their human rights violated. The Convention on the Reduction of Statelessness represents the UN's efforts to reduce, if not eliminate, the condition of statelessness.

   First, the convention specifies the circumstances (marriage, divorce, adoption, expatriation, and naturalization) under which individuals should not lose their nationality, if in so doing, they run the risk of becoming stateless. Second, it identifies situations under which individuals may lose their nationality: voluntary renunciation of one's nationality; swearing allegiance to another state; obtaining nationality by fraud; and engaging in the act of treason. Under Article 9, the Convention prohibits states from depriving "any person or group of persons of their nationality on racial, ethnic, religious or political grounds." It further provides, under Article 2, that foundlings—infants six months old or less—found in the territory of a state, in the absence of proof to the contrary, should be "considered to have been born within that territory of parents possessing the nationality of that state." Finally, the convention provides for the establishment of a body, within the UN system, to which persons seeking assistance under the convention may apply. The Office of the **United Nations High Commissioner for Refugees** provides such assistance.

The convention was adopted on August 30, 1961, by a Conference of Plenipotentiaries; it entered into force on December 13, 1975. See also: Aliens; Convention Relating to the Status of Stateless Persons; Declaration on the Human Rights of Individuals Who Are Not Nationals of the Country in Which They Live. *Further Reading:* A. Ghoshal and T. M. Crowley, "Refugees and Immigrants: A Human Rights Dilemma," *HRQ*, vol. 5 no. 3 (1983); R. K. Goldman and S. M. Martin, "International Legal Standards Relating to the Rights of Aliens and Refugees and United States Immigration Law," *HRQ*, vol. 5 no. 3 (1983); P. Weis, *Nationality and Statelessness in International Law* (1979).

CONVENTION ON THE RIGHTS OF THE CHILD. See CHILD, RIGHTS OF.

CONVENTION RELATING TO THE STATUS OF REFUGEES. Unlike a stateless person who has no nationality, a refugee is a person who has been expelled or deported, or who fled from his or her place of nationality or residence. The vast uprooting of people caused by Nazi invasions, the regime's attempt to exterminate all Jews, and its ruthless enslavement of the people in territories it occupied, resulted in a major refugee problem after World War II. Additionally, the extension (sometimes through coercion) of communist regimes to China and Eastern Europe after 1945 increased the number of refugees with whom states had to cope. Relief and rehabilitation efforts during and immediately after the war proved relatively ineffectual, especially in face of the fact that refugees had no political rights.

The UN's efforts to deal with the issue resulted in the 1951 Convention Relating to the Status of Refugees. Article 1 of that convention defines a refugee as a person

[who] owing to [a] well-founded fear of being persecuted for reasons of race, religion, nationality, membership of a particular social group or political opinion, is

outside the country of his nationality and is unable or, owing to such fear, is unwilling to avail himself of the protection of that country.

Because the "well-founded fear of being persecuted" had to have arisen from events linked to World War II or associated with "events occurring in Europe before January 1, 1951," the application of the convention was initially confined to a narrow time span and geographical area. The UN corrected that problem on December 16, 1966, when the **General Assembly** adopted the Convention Relating to the Status of Refugees: Protocol. The protocol removed the time limits of the 1951 convention and extended to the globe at large the area covered by its terms. Today, on account of authoritarian regimes, religious persecution, civil wars, and **genocide**, there are over 20 million refugees worldwide.

Substantively, the **human rights** protections afforded by the convention are governed by two principles: the first is that of nonreturn (or nonrefoulment, as it is termed in French). This principle means that a country cannot return refugees who have entered its territory, by whatever means, to their state if they have a well-founded fear of persecution. The only exception is if refugees constitute a threat to the national security of the host state. The second principle provides that refugees who have entered a country, even if illegally, may not be punished or subjected to discriminatory treatment. Human rights protection for refugees include the right of association, access to courts, gainful employment, public education, property, social security, and freedom of religion. See also: Asylum; Convention Relating to the Status of Stateless Persons; Ethnic Cleansing. *Further Reading:* A. Ager, *Refugees* (1998); L. A. Camino and R. M. Krufeld, *Reconstructing Lives, Recapturing Meaning: Refugee Identity, Gender, and Culture Change* (1994); Centre for Human Rights, *Human Rights and Refugees* (1993); Tom Farer, "How the Inter-American System Copes with Involuntary Migration," *HRQ*, vol. 17 no. 1 (1995).

CONVENTION RELATING TO THE STATUS OF REFUGEES: PROTOCOL. See Convention Relating to the Status of Refugees.

CONVENTION RELATING TO THE STATUS OF STATELESS PERSONS. This convention, unlike the **Convention on the Reduction of Statelessness,** deals with the status and the **human rights** of those who remain or become stateless. The day-to-day problems of stateless people can assume almost unimaginable complexities, which have the effect of undermining their human rights. Concerns about travel documents, identity papers, work permits, language competence—matters about which citizens and legal aliens are spared—are often issues of survival for stateless individuals.

On September 28, 1954, a Conference of Plenipotentiaries convened by the United Nations **Economic and Social Council** (ECOSOC) adopted the convention, with the aim of not only guaranteeing the survival of stateless persons, but of ensuring the protection of their human rights as well. Article 1 of the convention defines a stateless person as an individual "who is not considered as a national by any State under the operation of its law." Article 2 obligates countries that ratify the convention to apply its terms to "stateless persons without discrimination as to race, religion or country of origin." Under article 4, states undertake to accord to "stateless persons within their territories treatment at least a favorable as that accorded to their nationals with respect to freedom of religion, including "the religious education of their children."

Other rights to which stateless persons are entitled, at least on terms as favorable as those allowed legal aliens, include the right

- of access to courts,
- of association,
- to hold property,
- to public education,
- to social security,
- to public relief, and
- to administrative assistance in obtaining identity papers, travel documents, and the transfer of assets.

The convention entered into force on June 6, 1960. See also: Aliens; Asylum; Convention Relating to the Status of Refugees; Visas. *Further Reading:* P. Weis, *Nationality and Statelessness in International Law* (1979).

COPENHAGEN DECLARATION AND PROGRAMME OF ACTION. See POVERTY.

COSTA RICA. See UNIVERSITY FOR PEACE.

COUNCIL OF EUROPE. The Council of Europe is a regional intergovernmental organization located in Strasbourg, France, that was established in 1949, with Belgium, Denmark, France, Great Britain, Ireland, Italy, Luxembourg, the Netherlands, Norway, and Sweden as founding members. Over the years, membership has increased to include states such as Austria, Germany, Greece, Malta, Switzerland, and **Turkey.** As the countries of Eastern Europe such as Poland and the Czech Republic have moved away from communism, they have applied for membership in the council. Among the purposes for which the council was established are those that pursue the political unity of its members and protect and promote human rights and fundamental freedoms.

The council's organizational structure consists of two bodies, the first, a Consultative Assembly, which functions as the deliberative body composed of all members of the Council, and the second, a Committee of Ministers, which is composed of the foreign ministers of member states or their alternates. The Committee of Ministers has the sole power to make decisions; it makes recommendations to member governments and approves treaties and other international agreements. When such agreements are ratified by member states, they assume the status of international legislation for members. Among the treaties recommended and approved is the **European Convention on Human Rights**. In 1997, it recommended to member states for adoption the ground-breaking Convention on Human Rights and Biomedicine. That convention allows individuals to appeal beyond their national courts to the **European Court of Human Rights** and the European Commission on Human Rights. Such appeals sometimes reach the Committee of Ministers when they are not resolved or resolvable by either the Court or the Commission.

Since 1981, the council has awarded the Council of Europe Human Rights Prize for outstanding work in the protection and promotion of human rights. Its publications include the *Yearbook of the European Convention on Human Rights*. See also: Cloning and Biomedicine; Committee of Ministers of the Council of Europe; Human Rights Commissions.

CRIMES AGAINST HUMANITY. At the end of World War II, the governments of the Allied forces entered into an agreement for the prosecution and punishment of the major war criminals of the European Axis powers. That agreement also included the Charter of the International Military Tribunal (also known as the Nuremberg Tribunal) under which the trials were conducted. On December 11, 1946, the United Nations **General Assembly** affirmed the principles of the charter, which are now part of human rights law. One of the categories of crimes prosecuted under the charter was that of crimes against humanity. These crimes include: "murder, extermination, enslavement, deportation, and other inhumane acts committed against any civilian population, before or during [a] war . . . whether or not in violation of the domestic law of the country where perpetrated."

Today, crimes against humanity include at least three other crimes: torture and **genocide**, which fit the category of "other inhumane acts," and **apartheid**. See also: Convention Against Torture and Other Cruel, Inhuman or Degrading Treatment or Punishment; International Criminal Court. *Further Reading:* T. Meron, *Human Rights and Humanitarian Norms as Customary International Law* (1989); D. Warner, *Human Rights and Humanitarian Law* (1997).

CRIMES AGAINST PEACE. These are one of the three categories of crimes enunciated in the Charter of the International Military Tribunal, which was created in 1945 to try and punish the criminals of the European Axis powers. It is the most detailed of the three categories because it entails not only the sovereign right of the state to make war but to plan the unlawful use of force. Indeed, it has served as the basis, in part, for a later claim to a human right to peace. Crimes against peace include: "planning, preparation, initiation or waging of a war of aggression, or a war in violation of international treaties, agreements or assurances, or participation in a common plan or conspiracy for the accomplishment of any of the foregoing." See also: Crimes Against Humanity; Declaration on the Right of Peoples to Peace; War Crimes; War Crimes Tribunals. *Further Reading:* UNTS, *Agreement for the Prosecution and Punishment of the Major War Criminals of the European Axis Powers and the Charter of the International Military Tribunal*, 82 UNTS 279.

CROATIA. See BOSNIA-HERZEGOVINA; ETHNIC CLEANSING.

CUBA. The Republic of Cuba is the largest of the West Indian Islands and has a population that is estimated by the UN (1996) to be about 11 million people. It gained its independence from Spain in 1899 and became a member of the UN in 1945. In 1956, a rebellion led by Fidel Castro began, and by 1959 the guerrillas succeeded in overthrowing the dictatorship of Fulgencio Batista and establishing a socialist society, with Castro as its leader. He has since led Cuba, with the aim of establishing a lasting, communist society. Cuba's **human rights** record has been mixed.

In the area of **economic, social and cultural rights**, it has one of the better records in the world. Its constitution provides for the right to education, adequate means of subsistence, medical care, jobs, and culture and recreation. Children are guaranteed the right to "schooling, food, and clothing." These constitutional provisions have been largely met, and the right to housing has been supported by the government. **Civil and political rights**, however, have not been as well protected. In fact, Cuba has violated many of these rights, including the right to associate, to change one's government, to leave and return to one's country, to pursue one's religious convictions, and to freedom of the press.

In the case of freedom of association, for example, Cuba does not allow workers to form unions; neither does it allow citizens to form political parties that might compete with the Communist Party. The recently created Cuban Council (Concilio Cubano), a coalition of over 130 nongovernmental organizations, has had a number of its members arrested or detained. Article 13 of the **Universal Declaration of Human Rights** (UDHR) recognizes the right of all people "to leave any country, including his own," but Cuba's criminal code continues to criminalize "illegal exit."

In the area of religion, Cuba amended its constitution in 1992 to prohibit religious discrimination, and the government has been less restrictive since then in its conduct toward religion, especially Roman Catholicism. Groups such as the Seventh Day Adventists and Jehovah's Witnesses, however, continue to be persecuted as enemies of the revolution. In January 1998, Pope John Paul II visited Cuba, and although he praised the country for pursuing social justice, he was critical of its limits on civil and political rights. The Pope was also critical of other countries, such as the United States, which have sought to use economic sanctions to make social and economic life difficult for the Cuban people. See also: Democratic Entitlement. *Further Reading:* L. A. Perez Jr., *Cuba: Between Reform and Revolution* (1995); L. M. Smith and A. Padula, *Sex and Revolution: Women in Socialist Cuba* (1996).

CULTURAL LIFE. The right of every individual to participate in cultural life is one that is recognized by a number of international human rights instruments, in particular, the **Universal Declaration of Human Rights (UDHR)** and the **International Covenant on Economic, Social and Cultural Rights.**
The Universal Declaration of Human Rights states in Article 27 that

1. Everyone has the right freely to participate in the cultural life of the community, to enjoy the arts and to share in scientific advancement and its benefits.

2. Everyone has the right to the protection of the moral and material interests resulting from any scientific, literary or artistic production of which he is the author.

The International Covenant on Economic, Social and Cultural Rights, going even further, stipulates in Article is that

1. The States Parties to the present Covenant recognize the right of everyone:

   a. To take part in cultural life;

   b. To enjoy the benefits of scientific progress and its applications;

   c. To benefit from the protection of the moral and material interests resulting from any scientific, literary or artistic production of which he is the author.

2. The steps taken by the States Parties to the present Covenant to achieve the full realization of this right shall include those necessary for the conservation, the development and the diffusion of science and culture.

Further Reading: C. Lury, *Cultural Rights* (1993); I. Szabo, *Cultural Rights* (1974).

CZECHOSLOVAKIA. See CHARTER 77.

D

DALAI LAMA. Dalai Lama is the title given to the one who enjoys the highest spiritual rank in Lamaism, a Tibetan form of Buddhism introduced into Tibet in the seventh century A.D. The person who has this title is generally not only the religious leader of Tibet, but its political leader, as well. The current Dalai Lama (the fourteenth Dalai Lama), Tenzin Gyatso (1935–), fled in 1959 from Tibet to **India**, where he has remained, following a failed Tibetan revolt against Chinese rule. Since the time of his exile, the Dalai Lama has devoted his efforts toward the international promotion of **self-determination** for Tibet, nonviolence, and international peace on a global scale. In orthodox Buddhist tradition, he maintains that the transformation of social and political life sufficient to nurture the full enjoyment of **human rights** must come primarily through the self-cultivation of love, compassion, and nonviolence.

In the view of some, the focus on nonviolence has hampered the Dalai Lama's efforts to gain self-determination for his people. He has insisted, especially since 1988, that Tibet be given political autonomy, with a Western-type model of democracy, but **China**, while willing to concede some autonomy, is uneasy about the Western model of democracy. He also insists that the political goal of self-determination be won in a nonviolent way, placing him in conflict with some of his supporters in Tibet. In 1989 he was awarded the Nobel Peace Prize. *Further Reading:* M. Goldstein, "The Dalai Lama's Dilemma," *For. Aff.*, vol. 77 no. 1 (1998); C. Levenson, *The Dalai Lama: A Biography* (1988).

DALITS. See INDIA.

DAYTON ACCORDS. See SERBIA.

DEATH PENALTY. See CAPITAL PUNISHMENT.

DEATH SQUADS. A term given to paramilitary units that are most often associated with or directly part of the security forces of a country. These units are used to eliminate a regime's perceived opponents, often in ways with which a regime is unwilling to be publicly associated. The term became part of the popular national and international political vocabulary during the 1970s and early 1980s military terror in Argentina and, to an extent, **Chile.** It then became a descriptive term for what took place in South Africa, El Salvador, Guatemala, and elsewhere in Central America in the 1980s, and today it is generally applied to the phenomenon, wherever it takes place in the world, including **Algeria.** Torture, **arbitrary arrest and detention**, disappearances, denial of a fair and public trial are but a few of the human rights violations associated with death squads. See also: Haiti; *Nunca Mas. Further Reading:* S. Anderson, *Inside the League* (1986); J. Pauw, *The Heart of the Whore: The Story of Apartheid Death Squads* (1991).

DEBT BONDAGE. See BONDED LABOR.

DECALOGUE. See HELSINKI ACCORDS.

DECLARATION CONCERNING ESSENTIALS OF PEACE. This declaration resulted from an intense debate in the United Nations **General Assembly** over two peace proposals, one submitted by the **United Kingdom** and the **United States,** and the other by the USSR. The latter's proposal, which was criticized as an attempt to supplant the United Nations **Security Council,** sought to have the five permanent members of the council conclude among themselves a treaty for strengthening peace. The United Kingdom–United States proposal, although it was criticized as "inadequate," was adopted by a vote of 53 to 5. There are thirteen points in the proposal, but only the first six are cited below from General Assembly Resolution 290 (4) of December 1, 1949:

The General Assembly

1. Declares that the Charter of the United Nations, the most solemn pact of peace in history, lays down basic principles necessary for an enduring peace; that disregard of these principles is primarily responsible for the continuance of international tension; and that it is urgently necessary for all Members to act in accordance with these principles in the spirit of co-operation on which the United Nations was founded;

Calls upon every nation

2. To refrain from threatening or using force contrary to the Charter;

3. To refrain from any threats or acts, direct or indirect, aimed at impairing the

freedom, independence or integrity of any State, or at fomenting civil strife and subverting the will of the people in any State;

4. To carry out in good faith its international agreements;

5. To afford all United Nations bodies full co-operation and free access in the performance of the tasks assigned to them under the Charter;

6. To promote, in recognition of the paramount importance of preserving the dignity and worth of the human person, full freedom for the peaceful expression of political opposition, full opportunity for the exercise of religious freedom and full respect for all the fundamental rights expressed in the Universal Declaration of Human Rights.

See also: Crimes Against Peace; Declaration on the Right of Peoples to Peace. *Further Reading:* Institute of Peace, *Bibliography on Peace, Security, and International Conflict Management* (1993); I. R. Irwin, *Building a Peace System* (1989); E. L. Long, *Peace Thinking in a Warring World* (1993).

DECLARATION FOR THE PROTECTION OF WAR VICTIMS. This declaration was adopted on September 1, 1993, at the International Conference for the Protection of War Victims, held from August 30 to September 1, 1993, in Geneva, Switzerland.

The declaration does three things:

1. It condemns:

a. war, violence, hatred, and the grave and systematic violations of fundamental rights of persons;

b. violations of humanitarian law; and

c. acts of violence against civilians, which constitute a breach of international humanitarian law.

2. It assigns responsibilities:

a. to states to disseminate international humanitarian law to their respective general populations, public administrators, and military personnel;

b. to adopt and enforce implementing legislation;

c. to recognize the competence of international fact-finding commissions;

d. to prosecute war crimes;

e. to support international humanitarian organizations; and

f. to ensure the protection of cultural property, places of worship, and the environment.

3. It obligates states to undertake and demand, in cooperation with the UN and in accordance with the **United Nations Charter**, cooperation with peace-keeping forces.

See also: Crimes Against Peace; Declaration Concerning the Essentials of Peace; Declaration on the Right of Peoples to Peace. *Further Reading:* General Assembly, *Declaration for the Protection of War Victims*, UN Doc. A/48/742, Annex (December 8, 1993); *ILM*, vol. 33 no. 1 (1994); E. L. Long, *Peace Thinking in a Warring World* (1993).

DECLARATION OF A GLOBAL ETHIC. This declaration is the product of two years of consultation among 200 scholars and theologians representing the world's community of faith. It was discussed on September 2–4, 1993, by an assembly of religious and spiritual leaders who were meeting as part of the 1993 Parliament of the World's Religions, in Chicago, Illinois. The parliament adopted the declaration as an initial effort, "a point of beginning for a world sorely in need of ethical consensus." Among the elements of the Declaration of a Global Ethic are:

1. No global order without a new global ethic.
   - a better global order cannot be created or enforced by laws, prescriptions, and conventions alone;
   - the realization of peace, justice and the protection of the earth depends on the insight and readiness of men and women to act justly;
   - action in favor of rights and freedoms presume a consciousness of responsibility and duty, and therefore both the minds and hearts of women and men must be addressed;
2. Every human being must be treated humanely.

   This means that every human being without distinction . . . possesses an inalienable and untouchable dignity, and everyone, the individual as well as the state, is therefore obliged to honor this dignity and protect it. Humans must always be the subjects of rights, must be ends, never mere means, never objects of commercialization and industrialization economics, politics and media, in research institutes and industrial corporations. No one stands "above good and evil"—no human being, no social class, no influential interest group, no cartel, no police apparatus, no army, no state.

3. Irrevocable directives
   - commitment to a culture of non-violence and respect for life.
   - commitment to a culture of solidarity and a just economic order.
   - commitment to a culture of tolerance and a life of truthfulness.
   - commitment to a culture of equal rights and partnership between men and women.

See also: Asian Values; Duties; Religion and Human Rights. *Further Reading:* Council for a Parliament of the World's Religions, *Towards a Global Ethic* (1993).

DECLARATION OF THE BASIC PRINCIPLES OF JUSTICE FOR VICTIMS OF CRIME AND ABUSE OF POWER. This declaration came about because the UN became increasingly aware that millions of people, who are victims of crime and abuse of power throughout the world, are not adequately acknowledged or protected, morally or legally. The declaration is designed to give recognition to these persons, define them as victims, and aid national governments and international organizations in assisting them. Adopted on November 25, 1985, by the United Nations **General Assembly**, the text of the declaration is divided into two parts: Part A deals with victims of crime and Part B with victims of abuse of power.

In Part A, victims are defined as people who, individually or collectively, have suffered harm—including physical, mental, or emotional injury—economic loss, or substantial impairment of their fundamental rights. Harm can result from either acts or omissions that are in violation of the criminal laws of countries, whether or not the perpetrator is identified, apprehended, prosecuted or convicted, and regardless of the relationship between the perpetrator and the victim. Victims also include immediate family members or dependents and persons who have suffered harm in intervening to assist others—witnesses, lawyers, or physicians, for example. The declaration provides for access to justice, compensation, and restitution to the victims, as well as protection of their privacy and medical, psychological, and social assistance.

In Part B, victims are defined in the same manner as in Part A, with one major exception: victimization results not so much from violations of a country's criminal law, "but of internationally recognized norms relating to human rights." The remedies Part B provides for or encourages are the same as those found in Part A. See also: Compensation for Victims of Human Rights Abuse. *Further Reading:* General Assembly, *Compensation for Victims of Human Rights Violations* General Assembly Resolution 40/34 (November 29, 1985).

DECLARATION OF THE RIGHTS OF THE CHILD. Because the 1989 Convention on the Rights of the Child (CRC) incorporated, augmented, and refined the norms of this declaration, it is not discussed in detail here. It is noteworthy, however, that this declaration represents an important milestone in the evolution of children's rights.

Immediately after World War II, the prevailing view was that the interests of children and their parents were essentially one and the same. In the Declaration of the Rights of the Child, however, the UN admitted for the first time that the interests and needs of children might be different from those of their parents or other adult members of families. Hence, this instrument. It was adopted by the United Nations **General Assembly** on November 20, 1959. See also: Child, Rights of. *Further Reading:* M. A. Jensen and S. G. Coffin, eds., *Visions of Entitlements: The Care and Education of America's Children* (1993); United Nations Children Fund, *The State of the World's Children* (1997).

DECLARATION ON PERMANENT SOVEREIGNTY OVER NATURAL RESOURCES. The human rights movement has been principally concerned with the rights of individuals, as distinct from the rights of groups. One of the few groups that has been recognized as having rights in the human rights campaign is one called **peoples**, often equated with a nation or any group of persons with a long heritage of distinctive cultural identity. Peoples, such as the Navajos or other American Indian groups and the Saami of Scandinavia, are said to have the right to **self-determination**, and the right to permanent sovereignty over their natural resources is seen as inseparable from the right to self-determination. Concerned in large measure about the potentially adverse relationship between peoples' rights to their natural resources and the growing power of transnational economic interests, on December 14, 1962, the United Nations **General Assembly** adopted the Declaration on Permanent Sovereignty Over Natural Resources. Principles 1–3 of the text, which contain its most important norms, read as follows:

1. The right of peoples and nations to permanent sovereignty over their natural wealth and resources must be exercised in the interest of their national development and of the well-being of the people of the State concerned.

2. The exploration, development and disposition of such resources, as well as the import of foreign capital required for those purposes, should be in conformity with the rules and conditions which the peoples and nations freely consider to be necessary or desirable with regard to the authorization, restriction or prohibition of such activities.

3. In cases where authorization is granted, the capital imported and the earnings on that capital shall be governed by the terms thereof, the national legislation in force, and by international law. The profits derived must be shared in the proportions freely agreed upon, in each case, between investors and recipient State, due care being taken to ensure that there is no impairment, for any reason, of that State's sovereignty over its natural wealth and resources.

Principles 4–8 provide that violation of the right of peoples to their natural resources is contrary to the spirit of the **United Nations Charter**. They also require that if nationalization of resources takes place it should be on grounds of public utility, security, or national interest, and that adequate compensation should be given to the owners of the nationalized property. See also: *Indigenous Peoples*. *Further Reading:* General Assembly, *Permanent Sovereignty Over Natural Resources*, General Assembly Resolution 1803 (XVII) (December 14, 1962).

DECLARATION ON RACE AND RACIAL PREJUDICE. See RACISM.

DECLARATION ON SOCIAL AND LEGAL PRINCIPLES RELATING TO THE PROTECTION AND WELFARE OF CHILDREN, WITH SPECIAL REFERENCE TO FOSTER PLACEMENT AND ADOPTION NATIONALLY AND INTERNATIONALLY. The adoption of this declaration by the United Nations **General Assembly** on December 3, 1986, was prompted by the concern that many children throughout the world did not have the benefit of growing up under the responsible care of their parents, and that foster placement and national and international adoption could offer the moral and material security those children need. The General Assembly was also concerned that the large numbers of children who are routinely abandoned or orphaned due to violence, armed conflict, natural disasters, or economic and social problems, create conditions in which the best interests of the children are not adequately considered. To ensure that the interests of the children remain paramount in foster placement and adoption, this declaration was adopted.

Articles 1–9 deal with general family and child welfare, and assert that since the child's welfare is dependent on family welfare, states should give priority to good family welfare. They also provide that foster placement and adoption should take place only when care by the "child's own parents is unavailable or inappropriate," and that placing the child "outside the care of the child's own parents, the best interest of the child, especially his or her need for affection and the right to security and continuing care," should be the paramount consideration. The relevant articles then go on to state that persons responsible for foster placement and adoption should have professional and other training; that the child should *at all times* have a name, a nationality, and a legal representative; and that the need of a foster or adopted child to know "about his or her background should be recognized, unless contrary to the child's best interest."

Articles 10–12 deal with foster placement, and they provide that such placements shall be regulated by law, and that foster family care, "though temporary in nature," may continue, if necessary, until adulthood, but should not preclude either prior return to the child's own parents or adoption." Articles 13–24 deal with national and international adoption; requirements for counseling the parents of the to-be-adopted child, the child, and the prospective adoptive parents; the right of the child to be recognized "in law as a member of the adoptive family"; and with the obligation of governments to establish "policy, legislation and effective supervision for the protection of children involved in intercountry adoption." See also: Child, Rights of. *Further Reading:* General Assembly, *Declaration on Social and Legal Principles Relating to the Protection and the Welfare of Children, with Special Reference to Foster Placement and Adoption Nationally and Internationally,* General Assembly Resolution 41/85 (December 3, 1986).

DECLARATION ON TERRITORIAL ASYLUM. Article 13(2) of the **Universal Declaration of Human Rights** (UDHR), proclaims the right of everyone "to leave any country, including his own, and return to his country." Article 14(1) of the UDHR states that "Everyone has the right to seek and to enjoy in other countries asylum from persecution," although section 2 of the article says that "This right may not be invoked in case of prose-cution genuinely arising from non-political crimes or from acts contrary to the purposes and principles of the United Nations."

To ensure that states comply with the right to territorial asylum and assist them in achieving compliance, the United Nation **General Assembly**, on December 17, 1967, adopted this declaration. Article 1 of the declara-tion provides that **asylum** granted by one state to persons entitled to invoke Article 14 of the UDHR—including persons struggling against colonial-ism—shall be respected by all other states. It also requires that if there are serious grounds for considering that individuals have committed **war crimes, crimes against peace**, or **crimes against humanity**, the right to asy-lum may not be invoked. Article 2 (2) states that where a country finds it difficult to grant or continue to grant asylum, other countries—individu-ally, jointly, or with the UN—should consider appropriate measures to lighten the burden on such a country. Article 3 (1) provides that no person who is eligible for asylum "shall be subjected to measures such as rejection at the frontier." And if he [or she] has already entered the territory in which asylum is being sought, such a person may not be expelled or forced "to return to any State where he [or she] may be subjected to persecution." Exceptions to the provisions of Article 3 are allowed only for "overriding reasons of national security or in order to safeguard the population, as in the case of a mass influx of persons." In the case of the exceptions, the state involved should consider ways, including provisional asylum, of fa-cilitating the process by which asylum-seekers may go to other states. See also: Convention Relating to the Status of Refugees. *Further Reading:* M. R. Garcia-Mora, *International Law and Asylum as a Human Right* (1956); G. W. Plaut, *Asylum: A Moral Dilemma* (1995).

DECLARATION ON THE ELIMINATION OF ALL FORMS OF IN-TOLERANCE AND OF DISCRIMINATION BASED ON RELIGION OR BELIEF. The United Nations **General Assembly** felt there was a need to reinforce the **International Bill of Human Rights,** which proclaims the prin-ciples of nondiscrimination and equality before the law and the right to freedom of thought, conscience, religion or belief. Likewise, the importance of affirming the view that religion or belief, for individuals who profess either, is a fundamental feature of their conception of life; and the convic-tion that protecting persons from discrimination or intolerance on the basis of religion or belief can contribute to friendly relations between countries.

This declaration provides for the right of all people to freedom of thought, conscience, religion, and belief as well as the right to manifest personal choice in any of these areas, either individually or in community with others, and in public or private. Freedom to manifest one's religion or belief may be subject only to such limitations "as are prescribed by law and are necessary for public safety, order, health or morals or the funda-mental rights and freedoms of others."

Article 2 of the declaration defines discrimination and identifies the parties who may not engage in it.

1. No one shall be subject to discrimination by any State, institution, group of persons, or person on grounds of religion or other belief.

2. For the purposes of the present Declaration, the expression "intolerance and discrimination based on religion or belief" means any distinction, exclusion, restriction, or preference based on religion or belief and having as its purpose or its effect nullification or impairment of the recognition, enjoyment or exercise of human rights and fundamental freedoms on an equal basis.

The remainder of the declaration deals with the obligation of states to take effective measures—including enacting or rescinding legislation—to prevent and eliminate discrimination on grounds of religion or belief, the right of children to have access to education "in the matter of religion or belief in accordance with the wishes" of parents or legal guardians, and the right to a number of specific freedoms under Article 6, subject only to the limitations mentioned above.

[T]he right to freedom of conscience, religion or belief shall include, *inter alia* [among other things], the following freedoms:

a. To worship or assemble in connection with a religion or belief, and to estab lish and maintain places for these purposes;

b. To establish and maintain appropriate charitable or humanitarian institutions;

c. To make, acquire and use to an adequate extent the necessary articles and materials related to the rites and customs of a religion or belief;

d. To write, issue and disseminate relevant publications in these areas;

e. To teach a religion or belief in places suitable for these purposes;

f. To solicit and receive voluntary financial and other contributions from individuals and institutions;

g. To train, appoint, and elect or designate by succession appropriate leaders called for by the requirements and standards of any religion or belief;

h. To observe days of rest and to celebrate holidays and ceremonies in accordance with the precepts of one's religion or belief;

i. To establish and maintain communications with individuals and communities in matters of religion and belief at the national and international levels.

The declaration was adopted by the UN General Assembly on November 25, 1981. See also: China; Declaration of a Global Ethic; Discrimination; Fundamentalism; Religion and Human Rights; Sharia; Thought, Conscience and Religion. *Further Reading:* Commission on Human Rights, *Implementation of the Declaration on the Elimination of All Forms of Intolerance and Discrimination Based on Religion or Belief*, UN Doc. E/CN.4/1994/79 (January 20, 1994); John C. Green et al., eds., *Religion and the Culture Wars* (1996).

DECLARATION ON THE ELIMINATION OF VIOLENCE AGAINST WOMEN. Violence against women is a moral disgrace that every modern society has to face. At the World Conference to Review and Appraise the Achievements of the United Nations Decade for Women, held in Nairobi, Kenya, July 15–26, 1985, violence against women was one of the major issues of concern. And while the United Nations **General Assembly** endorsed the Forward-Looking Strategies for the Advancement of Women that emanated from that conference—strategies that include plans to eliminate violence against women—states, as a whole, did little to eliminate violence. With a push from the **Commission on the Status of Women** (CSW) on February 23, 1994, the General Assembly adopted the Declaration on the Elimination of Violence Against Women.

The declaration affirms that "violence against women constitutes a violation of the rights and fundamental freedoms of women and impairs their enjoyment of those rights and freedoms." It recognizes that "violence against women is a manifestation of the historically unequal power relationship between men and women" that leads to domination and **discrimination** against women by men, and that this very domination prevents the advancement of women. It also acknowledges that some groups of women, such as minority, indigenous, refugee, migrant, destitute, disabled, the elderly, as well as women in rural and remote communities, in detention or other institutions, in situations of armed conflict, and female children are "especially vulnerable to violence." Further, the declaration takes the position that violence against women "is an obstacle to the achievement of equality, development, and peace."

Under the declaration, states undertake to condemn violence against women; to not invoke any custom, tradition, or religious considerations to avoid their obligation to eliminate it; and to pursue, "by all appropriate means and without delay," a policy of eliminating violence against women. Those means include the development of penal, civil, labor, and other administrative sanctions in domestic legislation to punish and redress the wrongs caused to women who are subjected to violence; and budgetary allocations to support activities—research, collection of data, compilation of statistics, for instance—designed to eliminate violence against women. Articles 1 and 2, which define violence, read as follows:

Article 1. For purposes of this Declaration, the term "violence against women" means any act of gender-based violence that results in, or is likely to result in physical, sexual or psychological harm or suffering to women, including threats of such acts, coercion or arbitrary deprivation of liberty occurring in public or in private life.

Article 2. Violence against women shall be understood to encompass, but not limited to, the following:

  a. Physical, sexual and psychological violence occurring in the family, including battering, sexual abuse of female children in the household, dowry-related violence, marital rape, female genital mutilation and other traditional practices harmful to women, non-spousal violence and violence related exploitation;

b. Physical, sexual and psychological violence occurring within the general community, including rape, sexual abuse, sexual harassments and intimidation at work, in educational institutions and elsewhere, trafficking in women and forced prostitution;

c. Physical, sexual and psychological violence perpetrated or condoned by the state, whatever it occurs.

See also: Bonded Labor; Forced Labor; Sexual Harassment; Slavery, the Slave Trade, and Slavery-like Practices. *Further Reading:* General Assembly, *Declaration on the Elimination of Violence Against Women*, Resolution A/44/104 (February 23, 1994); text of the declaration may also be found in *ILM*, vol. 33 no. 4 (1994).

DECLARATION ON THE GRANTING OF INDEPENDENCE TO COLONIAL COUNTRIES AND PEOPLES.

When the United Nations was created in 1945, there were just over fifty members; today membership has grown to 185 countries. One reason for the increase in membership is the formation of newly independent countries, now free from colonial rule and politically independent. This declaration has supported the aspirations of people seeking to end colonialism and clamoring for political independence.

The declaration was proposed by the leader of the Soviet Union, Nikita Khrushchev, and was adopted by the **General Assembly** on December 14, 1960. It "Solemnly proclaims the necessity of bringing to a speedy and unconditional end colonialism in all its forms and manifestations;

And to this end

Declares that:

1. The subjection of peoples to alien subjugation, domination and exploitation constitutes a denial of fundamental human rights, is contrary to the Charter of the United Nations and is an impediment to the promotion of world peace and cooperation.

2. All peoples have the right to self-determination; by virtue of that right they freely determine their political status and freely pursue their economic, social and cultural development.

3. Inadequacy of political, economic, social or educational preparedness should never serve as a pretext for delaying independence.

4. All armed action or repressive measures of all kinds directed against dependent peoples shall cease in order to enable them to exercise peacefully and freely their right to complete independence, and the integrity of their national territory shall be respected.

The remaining portions of the declaration deal with the obligation of all states to act in accordance with the **United Nations Charter**, the **Universal**

Declaration of Human Rights (UDHR), and the provisions of this declaration, and specifically to respect the territorial integrity of states. See also: Self-Determination. *Further Reading:* General Assembly, *Declaration on the Granting of Independence to Colonial Countries and Peoples*, Resolution 1514 (XV) (December 1960); O. Mendelsohn and U. Baxi, eds., *The Rights of Subordinated Peoples* (1994).

DECLARATION ON THE HUMAN RIGHTS OF INDIVIDUALS WHO ARE NOT NATIONALS OF THE COUNTRY IN WHICH THEY LIVE. This declaration is in large measure a reaffirmation of the provisions contained in the **International Bill of Human Rights** respecting persons who are not nationals of the country in which they live. The bill proclaims that all human beings are born free and have equal rights, without distinction as to race, color, or *nationality*. It also states that everyone has the right to recognition *everywhere* as a person before the law and is entitled, without distinction as to nationality, to the equal protection of the law. States that are parties to the **International Covenants** that are part of the International Bill of Human Rights undertake to guarantee the rights contained within the bill.

Consistent with the International Bill of Human Rights, this declaration seeks to ensure that the **human rights** of individuals who are not nationals of the country in which they live are fully protected, in accordance with some detailed provisions. For example, they have the right to leave the country in which they live, to freedom of expression, and to peaceful assembly, subject to restrictions deemed necessary to protect national security, public safety, and public health and morals. It was adopted by United Nations **General Assembly** Resolution 40/144, December 13, 1985. See also: Aliens. *Further Reading:* F. G. Dawson, *International Tribunals and the Rights of Aliens* (1971); R. B. Lilich, *The Human Rights of Aliens in Contemporary International Law* (1984).

DECLARATION ON THE PROMOTION AMONG YOUTH OF THE IDEALS OF PEACE, MUTUAL RESPECT AND UNDERSTANDING BETWEEN PEOPLES. Respect for human beings and their rights, regardless of sex, nationality, race, or social origin, is not easily achieved among peoples and nations. It must be taught and carefully cultivated. The United Nations **General Assembly** believes that through teaching and cultivation respect emerges, especially when teaching begins with children.

On January 7, 1965, the General Assembly, convinced that the type of education children receive is crucial in the promotion and protection of **human rights**, adopted the Declaration on the Promotion Among Youth of the Ideals of Peace, Mutual Respect and Understanding Between Peoples. The declaration contains six principles; cited below are Principles I–III and VI. The fourth and fifth principles deal with encouraging exchanges, travel, and tourism among young people as well as the development of national and international associations of youths.

Principle I. Young people should be brought up in the spirit of peace, justice, freedom, mutual respect and understanding in order to promote equal rights for all human beings and all nations, economic and social progress, disarmament and the maintenance of international peace and security.

Principle II. All means of education . . . intended for the young should foster among them the ideals of peace, humanity, liberty and international solidarity . . . and [should] acquaint them with the role entrusted to the United Nations as a means of preserving and maintaining peace and promoting international understanding and co-operation.

Principle III. Young people should be brought up in the knowledge of the dignity and equality of all men, without distinction as to race, colour, ethnic origins or beliefs, and in respect for fundamental human rights and for the right of peoples to self-determination.

Principle VI. Young people must become conscious of their responsibilities in the world they will be called upon to manage and should be inspired with confidence in the future of the happiness of [hu]mankind.

See also: Child, Rights of. *Further Reading:* R. I. Irwin, *Building a Peace System* (1989); W. E. Langley, "Children, a Global Ethic, and Zones of Peace," *Peace Review*, vol. 9 no. 2 (1997).

DECLARATION ON THE PROTECTION OF ALL PERSONS FROM BEING SUBJECT TO TORTURE AND OTHER CRUEL, INHUMAN OR DEGRADING TREATMENT OR PUNISHMENT. As is the case of certain other human rights mechanisms cited in this volume, this 1975 declaration has been supplanted by another instrument, the 1987 **Convention Against Torture and Other Cruel, Inhuman or Degrading Treatment or Punishment**. The declaration, adopted by the **General Assembly** on December 9, 1975, is nevertheless important, because it represents the first time that the global community attempted and pushed for comprehensive legislative action against torture and other cruel, inhuman, or degrading treatment or punishment. *Further Reading:* Amnesty International, *Human Rights in Chile: The Role of the Medical Profession* (1986); Physicians for Human Rights, *Torture in Turkey & Its Unwilling Accomplices* (1996); United Nations Commission on Human Rights, United Nations Doc., *Question of the Human Rights of All Persons Subjected to any Form of Detention or Imprisonment, Torture and Other Cruel, Inhuman or Degrading Treatment or Punishment* E/CN.4/1987/ 13.

DECLARATION ON THE PROTECTION OF ALL PERSONS FROM ENFORCED DISAPPEARANCE. In many countries throughout the world, there have been enforced disappearances of people, that is, people have been arrested, detained, abducted, or otherwise deprived of their freedom by governments, organized groups, or private individuals acting on behalf of such governments. Most alarming, the fate and whereabouts of the victims are not disclosed; many are never found. To protect people from such a fate, on February 12, 1993, the United Nations **General Assembly** adopted this declaration. Articles 1, 2, 3, and 7, which include most of the essential protections under the declaration, are included below.

Article 1 (1). Any act of enforced disappearance is an offense to human dignity. It is condemned as a denial of the purposes of the Charter of the United Nations and as a grave and flagrant violation of human rights and fundamental freedoms . . .

(2). Any act of enforced disappearance . . . constitutes a violation of . . . the right to recognition as a person before the law, the right to liberty and security of person and the right not to be subject to torture and other cruel, inhuman or degrading treatment of punishment. It also violates or constitutes a grave threat to the right to life.

Article 2 (1). No state shall practice, permit or tolerate enforced disappearances.

Article 3. Each State shall take effective legislative, administrative, judicial or other measures to prevent and terminate acts of enforced disappearances in any territory under its jurisdiction.

Article 7. No circumstances whatsoever, whether a threat of war, a state of war, internal political instability or any other emergency, may be invoked to justify enforced disappearances.

Other articles provide that no state may expel, return, or extradite a person to another state where there are grounds to believe such a person would be in danger of enforced disappearance. Article 10 requires that *any person* "deprived of liberty must be held in an officially recognized place of detention . . . and be brought before a judicial authority promptly after detention." It also requires the keeping of records of detention. See also: Death Squads; Nunca Mas. *Further Reading:* Amnesty International, *Disappearances: A Workbook* (1981); *Declaration on the Protection of All Persons from Enforced Disappearances, ILM,* vol. 32 no. 3 (1993).

DECLARATION ON THE PROTECTION OF WOMEN AND CHILDREN IN EMERGENCY ARMED CONFLICT.

Women and children are among the most vulnerable in circumstances of **armed conflict.** On December 14, 1974, the United Nations **General Assembly** adopted this six-paragraph declaration to offer them protection during armed conflict.

The first paragraph states that attacks on the civilian population, "inflicting incalculable suffering, especially on women and children, who are the most vulnerable in the population, shall be prohibited." Paragraphs 2 and 3 indicate that the use of chemical and biological weapons, which inflict heavy losses on defenseless women and children in the course of military operations, is condemned, and that armed conflicts do not suspend the need to protect human rights.

(Paragraph) 4. All efforts shall be made by States involved in armed conflicts . . . to spare women and children from the ravages of war.

(Paragraph) 5. All forms of repression and cruel and inhuman treatment of women and children including imprisonment, torture, shooting, mass arrests . . . destruction of dwellings and forcible eviction, committed by belligerents in the course of military operations or in occupied territories shall be considered criminal.

(Paragraph) 6. Women and children belonging to the civilian population and finding themselves in circumstances of emergency and armed conflict in the struggle for peace, self-determination, national liberation and independence, who live in occupied territories, shall not be denied shelter, food, medical aid or other inalienable rights . . . [in accordance with the International Bill of Human Rights].

See also: Child, Rights of. *Further Reading:* General Assembly, *Declaration on the Protection of Women and Children in Emergency and Armed Conflict,* Resolution 3318 (XXIX) (December 14, 1974); United Nations Children's Fund, *State of the World's Children, 1997* (1997).

DECLARATION ON THE RIGHT OF PEOPLES TO PEACE.

DECLARATION ON THE RIGHT OF PEOPLES TO PEACE. This declaration, adopted by the United Nations **General Assembly** on November 12, 1984, was inspired largely by the emerging international understanding that the enjoyment of the right to peace is a precondition for the proper implementation and full enjoyment of fundamental **human rights**. The four paragraphs (without the preamble) of the declaration read as follows:

The General Assembly,

1. *Solemnly proclaims* that the maintenance of a peaceful life for peoples is the sacred duty of each State;

2. *Solemnly declares* that the preservation of the right of the peoples to peace and the promotion of its implementation constitute a fundamental obligation of each State;

3. *Emphasizes* that ensuring the exercise of the right of peoples to peace demands that the policies of States be directed towards the elimination of the threat of war, particularly nuclear war, the renunciation of the use of force in international relations and the settlement of international disputes by peaceful means on the basis of the Charter of the United Nations;

4. *Appeals* to all States and international organizations to do their utmost to assist in implementing the right of peoples to peace through the adoption of appropriate measures at both the national and international level.

See also: Crimes Against Peace; Declaration Concerning Essentials of Peace. *Further Reading:* General Assembly, *Declaration on the Right of Peoples to Peace,* Resolution 39/11 (November 12, 1984); R. I. Irwin, *Building a Peace System* (1989).

DECLARATION ON THE RIGHTS OF DISABLED PERSONS.

DECLARATION ON THE RIGHTS OF DISABLED PERSONS. Generally, disabled persons have been among the most discriminated against groups in the world. The United Nations **General Assembly**, on December 9, 1975, adopted this declaration to help protect the **human rights** of the disabled, regardless on their "race, colour, sex, language, religion, political or other opinions, national or social origin, state of wealth, birth or any other situation applying either to the disabled person himself or herself or to his or his family." Paragraphs 1 and 3–11 which contain the essence of this thirteen-paragraph declaration are as follows:

1. The term "disabled person" means any person unable to ensure by himself or herself, wholly or partly, the necessities of a normal individual and/or social life, as a result of deficiency, either congenital or not, in his or her physical or mental capabilities.

3. Disabled persons have the inherent right to respect for their dignity. Disabled persons, whatever the origin, nature and seriousness of their handicaps and disabilities, have the same fundamental rights [plus the special ones in this Declaration] as their fellow-citizens of the same age, which implies first and foremost the right to enjoy a decent life, as normal and full as possible.

4. Disabled persons have the same civil and political rights as other human beings; paragraph 7 of the Declaration on the Rights of Mentally Retarded Persons applies to any possible limitation or suppression of those rights for mentally disabled persons.

5. Disabled persons are entitled to the measures designed to enable them to become as self-reliant as possible.

6. Disabled persons have the right to medical, psychological and functional treatment, including prosthetic and orthotic appliances, to medical and social rehabilitation, aid, counselling, placement services and other services which will enable them to develop their capabilities and skills to the maximum and will hasten the process of their social integration or reintegration.

7. Disabled persons have the right to economic and social security and to a decent level of living. They have the right, according to their capabilities, to secure and retain employment or to engage in a useful, productive and remunerative occupation and to join trade unions.

8. Disabled persons are entitled to have special needs taken into consideration at all stages of economic and social planning.

9. Disabled persons have the right to live with their families or with foster parents and to participate in all social, creative or recreational activities. . . . If the stay of a disabled person in a specialized establishment is indispensable, the environment and living conditions therein shall be as close as possible to those of the normal life of a person of his or her age.

10. Disabled persons shall be protected against all exploitation, all regulations and all treatment of a discriminatory, abusive or degrading nature.

11. Disabled persons shall be able to avail themselves of qualified legal aid when such aid proves indispensable for the protection of their persons and property. If judicial proceedings are instituted against them, the legal procedure applied shall take their physical or mental condition fully into account.

See also: Declaration on the Rights of Mentally Retarded Persons. *Further Reading:* T. Degener and Y. Koster-Deese, eds., *Human Rights and Disabled Persons* (1995); L. Despouy, *Human Rights and Disabled Persons* (1993).

DECLARATION ON THE RIGHTS OF MENTALLY RETARDED PERSONS. The principal objectives of this declaration are to ensure the promotion and protection of the **human rights** of mentally retarded persons, including the development of "their abilities in various fields of activities" and the promotion of "their integration as far as possible in normal life." The declaration, adopted by the United Nations **General Assembly** on December 20, 1971, reads as follows:

The General Assembly . . . *Proclaims* this Declaration . . . and calls for national and international action to ensure that it will be used as a common basis and frame of reference for the protection of these rights:

1. The mentally retarded person has, to the maximum degree of feasibility, the same right as other human beings.

2. The mentally retarded person has a right to proper medical care and physical therapy and to such education, training, rehabilitation and guidance as will enable him to develop his ability and maximum potential.

3. The mentally retarded person has the right to economic security and to a decent standard of living. He has a right to perform productive work or to engage in other meaningful occupation to the fullest possible extent of his capabilities.

4. Whenever possible, the mentally retarded person should live with his own family or with foster parents and participate in different forms of community life. The family with which he lives should receive assistance. If care in an institution becomes necessary, it should be provided in surroundings and other circumstances as close as possible to those of normal life.

5. The mentally retarded person has a right to a qualified guardian when this is required to protect his personal well-being and interests.

6. The mentally retarded person has a right to protection from exploitation, abuse and degrading treatment. If prosecuted for any offense, he shall have a right to due process of law with full recognition being given to his degree of mental responsibility.

7. Whenever mentally retarded persons are unable, because of the severity of their handicap, to exercise all their rights in a meaningful way or it should become necessary to restrict or deny some or all of these rights, the procedure used for that restriction or denial of rights must contain proper legal safeguards against every form of abuse. This procedure must be based on an evaluation of the social capability of the mentally retarded person by qualified experts and must be subject to periodic review and to the right of appeal to higher authorities.

See also: Declaration on the Rights of Disabled Persons. *Further Reading:* General Assembly, *Declaration on the Rights of Mentally Retarded Persons,* Resolution 2856 (XXVI) (December 20, 1971); L. Despouy, *Human Rights and Disabled Persons* (1993).

DECLARATION ON THE RIGHTS OF PERSONS BELONGING TO NATIONAL OR ETHNIC, RELIGIOUS AND LINGUISTIC MINORITIES. Article 27 of the **International Covenant on Civil and Political Rights** (ICCPR) stipulates that "In those States in which ethnic, religious or linguistic minorities exist, persons belonging to such minorities shall not be denied the right, in community with the other members of their group, to enjoy their own culture, to profess and practise their own religion, or to use their own language." Despite these clearly stated rights, ethnic and other **minorities** have had these rights violated in many countries. The United Nations **General Assembly**, in order to ensure more "effective implementation of the international human rights" that minorities possess, adopted this declaration on February 3, 1993.

Article 1 indicates what states must do; Article 2 spells out the rights of the minorities in question; and Article 3 (3) says how the rights may be enjoyed. The other articles, not included below, refine the specific actions countries must take to implement the rights recognized in the declaration.

Article 1 (1). States shall protect the existence and the national or ethnic, cultural, religious and linguistic identity of minorities within their respective territories and shall encourage conditions for the promotion of that identity.

(2). States shall adopt appropriate legislative and other measures to achieve those ends.

Article 2 (1). Persons belonging to national or ethnic, religious and linguistic minorities . . . have the right to enjoy their own culture, to profess and practice their own religion, and to use their own language, in private or in public, freely and without interference or any form of discrimination.

(2). Persons belonging to minorities have the right to participate effectively in cultural, religious, social, economic and public life.

(3). Persons belonging to minorities have the right to participate directly in decisions on the national and, where appropriate, regional level concerning the minority to which they belong or the region in which they live, in a manner not incompatible with national legislation.

(4). Persons belonging to minorities have the right to establish and maintain, without any discrimination, free and peaceful contacts with other members of their group and with persons belonging to other minorities, as well as contacts across frontiers with citizens of other states to whom they are related by national or ethnic, religious or linguistic ties.

Article 3 (1). Persons belonging to minorities may exercise their rights, including those set forth in the present Declaration, individually as well as in community with other members of their group, without any discrimination.

See also: Ethnic Cleansing; Genocide; Racism. *Further Reading:* Declaration on the Rights of Persons Belonging to National or Ethnic, Religious or Linguistic Minorities, *ILM*, vol. 32 no. 3 (1993); Y. N. Kay, *Popular Guide to Minority Rights* (1995); O. Mendelsohn and U. Baxi, eds., *The Rights of Subordinated Peo-*

ples (1994); N. S. Rodley, "Conceptual Problems in the Protection of Minorities," *HRQ*, vol. 17 no. 1 (1995).

DECLARATION ON THE RIGHT TO DEVELOPMENT. The right to development is one that was earlier associated with groups, not individuals, and was thus somewhat controversial. It is, however, also an individual right, as implied in the **International Bill of Human Rights** and explicitly indicated in this declaration. Today, the right to development is taken for granted, and, like the right to peace, is seen as central to the full realization of all **human rights**. The declaration, adopted by the United Nations **General Assembly** on December 4, 1986, defines development in Article 1; identifies the subject, as well as the object, of development in Article 2; and spells out the relationship among the rights and freedoms recognized by the UN and the global community in article 6 (2). In Article 8 (1), it indicates some additional responsibilities of states.

Article 1 (1). The right to development is an inalienable human right by virtue of which every human person and all peoples are entitled to participate in, contribute to, and enjoy economic, social, cultural and political development, in which all human rights and fundamental freedoms can be fully realized.

(2). The human right to development also implies the full realization of the rights of peoples to self-determination, which includes, subject to the relevant provisions of both International Covenants on Human Rights, the exercise of their inalienable right to full sovereignty over all their natural wealth and resources.

Article 2 (1). The human person is the central subject of development and should be the active participant and beneficiary of the right to development.

(2). All human beings have a responsibility for development, individually and collectively, taking into account the need for full respect for their human rights and fundamental freedoms as well as their duties to the community, which alone can ensure the free and complete fulfillment of the human being, and they should therefore promote and protect an appropriate political, social and economic order for development.

(3). States have the right and the duty to formulate appropriate national development policies that aim at the constant improvement of the well-being of the entire population and of all individuals, on the basis of their active, free and meaningful participation in development and in the fair distribution of the benefits resulting therefrom.

Article 3 (1). States have the primary responsibility for the creation of national and international conditions favourable to the realization of the right to development.

Article 6 (2). All human rights and fundamental freedoms are indivisible and interdependent; equal attention and urgent consideration should be given to the implementation, promotion and protection of civil, political, economic, social and cultural rights.

Article 8 (1). States should undertake at the national level, all necessary measures for the realization of the right to development and shall ensure, *inter alia* [among other things], equality of opportunity for all in their access to basic resources, education, health services, food, housing, employment and the fair distribution of income. Effective measures should be taken to ensure that women have an active role in the development process.

See also: International Covenants on Human Rights, Self-Determination, World Conferences on Women. *Further Reading:* General Assembly, *Declaration on the Right to Development*, Resolution 41/128 (December 4, 1986); J. O'Manique, "Human Rights and Development," *HRQ*, vol. 14 no. 1 (1992); S. I. Skogly, "Structural Adjustment and Development: Human Rights—An Agenda for Peace," *HRQ*, vol. 15 no. 4 (1993).

DECLARATION ON THE USE OF SCIENTIFIC AND TECHNOLOGICAL PROGRESS IN THE INTEREST OF PEACE AND FOR THE BENEFIT OF MANKIND. Since the late 1960s, the UN has been concerned about the general impact of scientific and technological progress on **human rights**. While that progress had been among the most important factors in the evolution of human societies, evolution has often threatened or impaired human rights and fundamental freedoms, especially one's right to know, health, equality, privacy, and a nurturing natural environment. To help ensure that scientific and technical advances do not threaten human rights, on November 10, 1975, the United Nations **General Assembly** adopted this declaration.

Paragraph 2 of the declaration asserts that all states promise to "take appropriate measures to prevent the use of scientific and technological development . . . to limit or interfere with the enjoyment of the human rights and fundamental freedoms of the individual enshrined" in the **International Bill of Human Rights** and other human rights instruments. Paragraph 3 deals with the commitment of states to take measures "to ensure that scientific and technological achievements satisfy the material and spiritual needs for all sectors of the population," and Paragraph 4 deals with the prohibition against the use, by states, of scientific and technological achievements to wage aggressive wars, violate the sovereignty of other states, pursue a policy of racial discrimination, or interfere in the internal affairs of other countries. Paragraphs 6 and 7, which deal most fully with human rights read as follows:

6. All States shall take measures to extend the benefits of science and technology to all strata of the population and to protect them, both socially and materially, from possible harmful effects of the misuse of scientific and technological developments, including their misuse to infringe upon the rights of the individual or the group, particularly with regard to respect for privacy and the protection of the human personality and its physical and intellectual integrity.

7. All States shall take the necessary measures, including legislative measures, to ensure that the utilization of scientific and technological achievements promotes

the fullest realization of human rights and fundamental freedoms without any discrimination whatsoever on grounds of race, sex, language or religious beliefs.

See also: Cloning and Biomedicine. *Further Reading:* L. Kass, *Toward A More Natural Science: Biology and Human Affairs* (1985); J. F. Metzel, "Information Technology and Human Rights," *HRQ*, vol. 18 no. 4 (1996).

DEFENSE FOR CHILDREN INTERNATIONAL. As the UN became increasingly concerned about the welfare of children throughout the world, it designated 1979 as the Year of the Child. At that time, however, there was no international **nongovernmental organization** (NGO) with the specific aim of advancing and protecting the rights of the child. Defense for Children International (DCI) was founded by private parties in Geneva, Switzerland, in the midst of the Year of the Child to help promote children's rights.

DCI is nongovernmental, nonconfessional, and nonpolitical in character. It enjoys consultative status with the United Nations **Economic and Social Council** (ECOSOC), the **Council of Europe**, and the **United Nations Children's Fund** (UNICEF). The organization has grown to include forty affiliated national sections and has individual members in sixty countries. DCI, which played an important role in helping draft the Convention on the Rights of the Child (CRC), has the following goals: (1) to increase awareness and create solidarity on children's rights issues worldwide; (2) to encourage, monitor, and evaluate the implementation of children's rights, especially the Convention on the Rights of the Child; and (3) to foster national, regional, and global cooperation to improve the mechanism for protecting children's rights.

DCI has an impressive publication program, including its internationally respected *Children's Rights Monitor.* See also: Child, Rights of; Nongovernmental Organizations. *Further Information:* Defense for Children International, PO Box 88, CH-1211 Geneva 20, Switzerland. Tel. 011–41–22–734–05–58.

DELHI DECLARATION. See CHILD LABOR.

DEMOCRATIC ENTITLEMENT. This term refers to a cluster of political rights which together entitle each citizen of every state to live in a democratic society. That cluster of rights is authorized by Articles 2, 21, 22, and 23 of the **International Covenant on Civil and Political Rights** (ICCPR) and Articles 20 and 21 of the **Universal Declaration of Human Rights** (UDHR), and is linked to five principles: (1) nondiscrimination, (2) participation in public life, (3) popular elections, (4) association, and (5) the moral foundation of political authority.

The principle of nondiscrimination states that every citizen has the right to participate in the governance of her or his country, without restriction as to race, color, sex, language, political or other opinion, national or social origin, property, birth or other status. It also states that restrictions on any other grounds must be reasonable. For example, a state may make reasonable restrictions on a citizen's rights based on age (minors), mental illness, criminal conduct, and residency. According to the principle of participation in public life, every citizen has the right to take part in the conduct of public affairs, either directly or through freely chosen representatives.

If the right to participate in the conduct of public affairs is to be effectively realized—participation including the right to freely choose one's representatives—it must be coupled with a process by which that participation can be reliably assured. The principle of popular elections means that citizens have the right to vote and be elected through *genuine periodic elections*. Voting by secret ballot guarantees the free expression of the will of the voters to choose from among two or more candidates for office. Democratic entitlement, therefore, includes the right to associate freely, the right to freedom of speech (both for the candidates whose political programs must be freely communicated and prospective voters, who wish to communicate with the candidates and other would-be voters), and the right to form and join political parties and other groups.

The right to vote, associate, participate in the conduct of public affairs, and be free from discrimination in the exercise of those rights is based on the principle of the moral and political sovereignty of citizens. The right of a state to govern is not original, but is derived from the consent of the governed, to whom all governments remains politically and morally accountable. Article 21 (3) of the **Universal Declaration of Human Rights** (UDHR) states the essence of the principle: "The will of the people shall be the basis of the authority of government."

Democratic entitlement is a basic tenet of **human rights**. In an effort to promote it around the globe, the UN has begun to supervise elections in some countries. The 1989 UN-supervised elections in Namibia and Nicaragua, and the 1990 and 1996 elections in **Haiti** are recent examples of international supervision. This international supervision systematically undermines the traditional claims of countries to the "right of nonintervention" in their internal affairs, and in the future, international recognition of governments most likely will be determined by the extent to which those governments have complied with or are themselves the result of the full expression of the principles of democratic entitlement. Last, the concept of democratic entitlement reinforces the human right to individual and collective **self-determination**. See also: *Civil and Political Rights. Further Reading:* G. H. Fox, "The Right to Political Participation in International Law," *TYJIL*, vol. 17 no. 2 (1992); T. M. Franck, "The Emerging Right to Democratic Governnance," *AJIL*, vol. 86 no. 1 (1992); L. H. Miller, *Global Order: Values and Power in International Politics* (1990).

DEPORTATION. See ETHNIC CLEANSING.

DEROGATION. Under the **International Bill of Human Rights**, if the life of a nation were threatened, it is permissible for the period of that threat to derogate from (to give inferior protection to) certain **human rights**. Article 4 (1) of the **International Covenant on Civil and Political Rights** (ICCPR) speaks of the scope of permissible derogation; (2) specifies which rights are nonderogable; and (3) stipulates that states that avail themselves of the authority to engage in derogation should "immediately inform," through the UN secretary-general, the other states which are parties to the covenant.

Article 4 (1). In time of public emergency which threatens the life of the nation and the existence of which is officially proclaimed, States Parties to the present Covenant may take measures derogating from their obligations under the present Covenant to the extent strictly required by the exigencies of the situation, provided that such measures are not inconsistent with their other obligations under international law and do not involve discrimination solely on the ground of race, colour, sex, language, religion or social origin.

No derogation of certain rights, is allowed, even in emergencies. Those rights are found in Article 6, the right to life; Article 7, the prohibition against torture and cruel, inhuman and degrading treatment or punishment; Article 8, the prohibition against slavery, slave trade, servitude, and imprisonment for nonfulfillment of contractual obligations; Article 15, the prohibition against retroactive application of criminal laws; Article 16, the right to be recognized as a person before the law; and Article 18, the right to freedom of thought, conscience and religion. See also: Convention Against Torture and Other Cruel, Inhuman or Degrading Treatment or Punishment; Declaration on the Protection of All Persons from Enforced Disappearance; Public Emergency. *Further Reading:* T. Buergenthal, "To Respect and Ensure; State Obligations and Permissible Derogation" in *The International Bill of Rights: The Covenant on Civil and Political Rights*, L. Henkin, ed. (1981); "Symposium: Limitation and Derogation in the International Covenant on Civil and Political Rights," *HRQ*, vol. 7 no. 1 (1985).

DETENTION. Detention is an international term that describes the practice of governments, administrative authorities, or other groups, working in complicity with those authorities, of detaining individuals without legal charges or trial by an independent judicial authority. Explanations given for detentions include mental illness, prevention or suppression of alleged disturbances of public order, and protection of the civilian population during warfare. Many detentions, however, result in the torture, death, or disappearance of the persons detained.

Concern about the issue of detention, especially as it violates **human rights** and fundamental freedoms (freedom of movement, right to life, right to security of person, for example), led the United Nations to conduct a number of studies in the area and to prepare guidelines for law enforcement officials. Some of these studies contributed to the 1993 adoption by the United Nations **General Assembly** of the **Declaration on the Protection of All Persons from Enforced Disappearance**. Article 10 of that declaration spells out provisions to protect the rights of those detained:

Article 10 (1). Any person deprived of liberty shall be held in an officially recognized place of detention and, in conformity with national law, by brought before a judicial authority promptly after detention.

(2). Accurate information on the detention of such persons and their place or places of detention, including transfers, shall be made promptly available to their family members, their counsel or to any other persons having a legitimate interest in the information unless a wish to the contrary has been manifested by the person concerned.

(3). An official up-to-date register of all persons deprived of their liberty shall be maintained in every place of detention. Additionally, each State shall take steps to maintain similar centralized registers.

The information contained in these registers shall be made available to the persons mentioned in the preceding paragraph, to any judicial or other competent and independent national authority and to any other competent authority entitled under the law of the State concerned or any international legal instrument to which the State concerned is a party, seeking to trace the whereabouts of a detained person.

See also: Code of Conduct for Law Enforcement Officials; Judiciary. *Further Reading:* United Nations, *Human Rights and Law Enforcement: A Manual on Human Rights Training for the Police* (1997); United Nations, *Human Rights and Pretrial Detention* (1994).

DEVELOPMENT. See DECLARATION ON THE RIGHT TO DEVELOPMENT.

DISABLED PERSONS. See DECLARATION ON THE RIGHTS OF DISABLED PERSONS.

DISAPPEARANCE OF PERSONS. See DECLARATION ON THE PROTECTION OF ALL PERSONS FROM ENFORCED DISAPPEARANCE.

DISCRIMINATION. The norm against discrimination is one of the basic standards of **human rights**. It is to be found in every human rights instrument, and is the exclusive focus of some, such as the **Convention on the Elimination of All Forms of Discrimination Against Women** (CEDAW) and the **International Convention on the Elimination of All Forms of Racial Discrimination**. Every human being is entitled to the rights recognized by the human rights instruments without distinction of any kind such as race, color, sex, language, religion, political or other opinion, national or social origin, property, birth or other status. *Further Reading:* J. Hucker, "Antidiscrimination Laws in Canada," *HRQ*, vol. 19 no. 3 (1997); V. Van Dyke, *Human Rights, Ethnicity, and Discrimination* (1985).

DOMESTIC VIOLENCE. Certain forms of violence have been seen historically as punishable wrongs against society as well as against individual victims. Domestic violence against women, however, even when it entails **rape** and murder, until recently, has been treated as a private matter to be dealt with by "family government." Family government has been traditionally controlled by men, generally the authors of domestic violence. Indeed, in countries like Brazil, a husband can still preserve his "honor" by murdering his unfaithful wife. Domestic violence in many industrially advanced countries, including the **United States**, has assumed epidemic proportions.

With the support of the women's movement, especially through the **Commission on the Status of Women** (CSW) and the first three of the four **World Conferences on Women**, the United Nations **General Assembly** became fully aware of domestic violence. In 1994, it adopted the **Declaration on the Elimination of Violence Against Women**. This declaration, which recognizes that violence against women is a violation of their fundamental **human rights**, deals with violence in general, but also focuses on the domestic sphere, as spelled out in Article 2 (a). The declaration forbids such violence, and makes states that condone or permit it accountable under international law.

Article 1. [T]he term "violence against women" means any act of gender-based violence that results in, or is likely to result in, physical, sexual or psychological harm or suffering to women, including threats of such acts, coercion or arbitrary deprivation of liberty, whether occurring in public or private life.

Article 2. Violence against women shall be understood to encompass, but not limited to, the following: a. Physical, sexual and psychological violence occurring in the family, including battering, sexual abuse of female children in the household, dowry-related violence, marital rape, female genital mutilation and other traditional practices harmful to women, non-spousal violence and violence related to exploitation.

See also: Slavery, the Slave Trade, and Slavery-like Practices. *Further Reading*: D. Q. Thomas and M. F. Beasley, "Domestic Violence as a Human Rights Issue," *HRQ*, vol. 15 no. 1 (1993); United Nations, *Violence Against Women in the Family* (1989); L. E. Walker, *The Battered Woman* (1979).

DRAFT ADDITIONAL PROTOCOL TO THE CONVENTION ON HUMAN RIGHTS AND BIOMEDICINE ON THE PROHIBITION OF CLONING HUMAN BEINGS. See CLONING AND BIOMEDICINE.

DRUGS AND HUMAN RIGHTS. The issue of drugs and human rights is complex. First, it entails the extent to which governments are involved in using drugs to undermine the right to life and to social opportunities of unfavored or less-favored groups, including minorities—in and outside their borders—by making drugs available to members of such groups. The **United States**, for example, was accused in 1995 and 1996 by members of its black community, of channeling drugs to their neighborhoods. Similar charges have been made against the **United Kingdom** by some members of the Irish Catholic community in **Northern Ireland**. Second, the issue involves antidrug policies of governments that sometimes discriminate against members of less-favored social groups or other disadvantaged communities. Since the norms of **human rights** require equality of treatment and nondiscrimination, targeting members of certain communities—(gays, blacks, political dissidents, religious, linguistic, cultural or other groups—is a clear violation of human rights. The frequency of arrests and prosecutions, as well as the severity of punishment inflicted on members of such communities—when compared to members of the more socially favored communities—testifies to such discrimination throughout the world. Other abuses of human rights in relationship to drugs are well known.

In Bolivia, for example, antinarcotic policies against poor coca growers (cocaine comes from coca leaves) often entail death-producing human rights violations by security forces, and even in the most civil-rights conscious countries such as the United States and the United Kingdom, the right to privacy is often violated. Further, few governments have policies in place to deal effectively with law-enforcement personnel who, in the pursuit of antidrug policies, abuse the human rights of individuals. Finally, the fairness of the trials of persons accused of using prohibited drugs is often nonexistent. See also: Equality; Fair Trial; Privacy. *Further Reading:* C. Castillo and D. Harmon, *Powderburns: Cocaine, Contras and the Drug War* (1994); D. McClintick, *Swordfish: A True Story of Ambition, Savagery and Betrayal* (1993); D. W. Rasmussen and B. L. Benson, *The Economic Anatomy of a Drug War* (1994).

DUTIES. In dealing with **human rights**, very few people ever speak of duties or responsibilities. At the international level, except for the **American Declaration of the Rights and Duties of Man** and the **African Charter on Human and Peoples' Rights**, there is not a single human rights instrument that emphasizes—as distinct from mentioning them in passing—duties or responsibilities. States are understood to have obligations or responsibilities to enforce human rights, but what of the duties or responsibilities of individuals?

The West, which for years dominated the human rights debate, took the position that rights *imply* duties or responsibilities, that focusing on duties could undermine rights, and that, in any event, Article 29 of the **Universal Declaration of Human Rights** (UDHR) deals with duties. That article reads as follows:

Article 29 (1). Everyone has duties to the community in which alone the free and full development of his personality is possible.

(2). In the exercise of his rights and freedoms, everyone shall be subject only to such limitations as are determined by law solely for the purpose of securing due recognition and respect for the rights and freedoms of others and of meeting the just requirements of morality, public order and the general welfare in a democratic society.

(3). These rights and freedoms may in no case be exercised contrary to the purposes and principles of the United Nations.

References to Article 29 did not always help, and many countries, especially those outside the West, contend that an emphasis on rights alone reflects a Western cultural bias, a focus on individualism, and a neglect of the community and society. It also overlooks the traditions of societies in which rights are more intimately tied to responsibilities. With goodwill, a group of twenty-four former chiefs of state or government, including **Brazil, Canada**, France, Germany, Korea, Japan, Singapore, and the **United States**, has developed a draft version of the Universal Declaration of Human Responsibilities. It was submitted to the United Nations **General Assembly** on the fiftieth anniversary of the Universal Declaration of Human Rights, December 10, 1998, for adoption. See also: Asian Values. *Further Reading:* Parliament of the World's Religions, *The Declaration of a Global Ethnic* (1993); W. Pfaff, "Beyond Universal Rights," *BG* (January 12, 1998); M. C. Davis, ed., *Human Rights and Chinese Values* (1995).

E _____

EARTH CHARTER. See ENVIRONMENT.

EAST TIMOR. Timor is an island located south of the Philippines, east of Indonesia, and northwest of **Australia**. From the early 1600s, the Portuguese and the Dutch fought to gain control of the island, but they later concluded agreements to divide it, with the Dutch owning the western half and the Portuguese the eastern half. When the former Dutch East Indies won its independence and became the Republic of Indonesia in 1950, West Timor was incorporated into it. East Timor remained a Portuguese colony until 1974, when a democratic revolution took place in Portugal. As a result, East Timor joined other Portuguese colonies that sought to exercise the right to **self-determination**. Indonesia, which had always coveted East Timor, intervened military in the country in 1975, and has retained an overwhelming military force there since.

Indonesia claimed that its intervention prevented wholesale disorder, but evidence suggests the contrary. In 1975, East Timor had a population of about 700,000. In the last twenty three years, over 200,000 people have died as a result of Indonesia's occupation—the equivalent of some 74 million Americans dying. The deaths have been associated with widespread repression, forced relocations, extrajudicial killings, arbitrary detention, disappearances, torture, and attempts to obliterate the cultural identity of the East Timorese people. As part of the last course of conduct, Indonesia has been encouraging the migration of large numbers of Indonesians to East Timor. As of this writing, conditions have not materially improved except that with the fall of Radan Suharto, leader of Indonesia since 1967, in the popular uprising of July–August 1998, there appears to be a greater willingness on the part of Indonesia to talk about autonomy for east Timor.

In November 1996, two East Timorese nationalists and forceful opponents of Indonesia's occupation, Bishop Carlos Ximenes Belo and Jose Ramos-Horta, were awarded the Nobel Peace Prize. It was initially believed that this prestigious award would bring pressure to bear on the Indonesian government to show more respect for the **human rights** of East Timorese, but this has not been the case. In March 1996, the European Parliament adopted a resolution calling for Indonesia to release political prisoners and asking member states to halt all military assistance to the country. The United States signaled its displeasure over Indonesia's violations of human rights, but has done little more. In the spring of 1997, the United Nations **Commission on Human Rights** (CHR), while welcoming Indonesia's statement of commitment to a continuing dialogue toward "a just, comprehensive and internationally acceptable solution to the question of East Timor," expressed deep concern about (1) reports of continued extrajudicial killings, disappearances, torture, and arbitrary detentions; (2) nonfulfillment of a commitment to invite working groups of the commission to East Timor in 1997 and (3) "the policy of systematic migration of persons to East Timor."

The economic problems faced by Indonesia, especially in face of a worsening of those problems during the spring and summer of 1998, make the situation in East Timor all the more uncertain. See also: Declaration on the Protection of All Persons from Enforced Disappearance; Ethnic Cleansing. *Further Reading:* C. Budiardjo, *Surviving Indonesia's Gulag* (1996); M. Jardine, *East Timor: Genocide in Paradise* (1995); P. Carey and G. C. Bentley, eds., *East Timor at the Crossroads* (1995). United Nations Doc., *Report of the Secretary General on the Situation of Human Rights in East Timor*, E/CN.4/1998/59.

ECONOMIC AND SOCIAL COUNCIL. The Economic and Social Council (ECOSOC) is one of the six principal organs of the United Nations, created by Article 7 of the **United Nations Charter**. It has many functions, among which are those specified in Article 62 of the UN Charter:

1. to initiate studies and reports with respect to international economic, social, cultural, educational, health and related matters and to make recommendations on such matters to the General Assembly, to members of the UN, and to UN specialized agencies;

2. to make "recommendations for purposes of promoting respect for, and observance of, human rights and fundamental freedoms for all"; and

3. to "prepare draft conventions for submission to the General Assembly with respect to matter falling within its competence."

The ECOSOC is also authorized under Article 55 of the UN Charter not simply to make *recommendations* for the purposes of promoting **human rights,** but to act directly to promote "universal respect for, and observance of" those rights for all without distinction as to race, sex, language, or religion. States pledge themselves in Article 56 of the charter "to take joint and separate action in co-operation" with the UN to achieve the objectives indicated in Article 55.

To help achieve its human rights goals, the ECOSOC is divided into a number of subsidiary bodies, including (1) functional commissions, (2) sub-commissions, (3) standing committees, and (4) **working groups**. In the first of these bodies, there are for example, the **Commission on Human Rights** (CHR) and the **Commission on the Status of Women** (CSW). In the second, an example is the **Sub-Commission on the Prevention of Discrimination and Protection of Minorities.** With regard to the third, there is the **Committee on Economic, Social and Cultural Rights**; and in the fourth subsidiary body, there are working groups on slavery, **indigenous peoples,** and disappearances. The ECOSOC also works closely with human rights bodies such as the **Committee Against Torture** (CAT), the Committee on the Rights of the Child, and the **Committee on the Elimination of Discrimination Against Women**. Finally, the ECOSOC works in coordination with the United Nations **General Assembly,** the **Center for Human Rights,** and the **Office of High Commissioner for Human Rights.** See also: Nongovernmental Organizations. *Further Reading:* P. Alston, *The United Nations and Human Rights* (1995); J.T.P. Humphrey, *Human Rights and the United Nations* (1984).

ECONOMIC, SOCIAL AND CULTURAL RIGHTS. The West, especially the United States and the **United Kingdom,** generally thinks of **human rights** in civil and political terms. There is another class of human rights, however, which are equally important and are organically linked to their civil and political relatives: economic, social and cultural rights. Articles 22–28 of the **Universal Declaration of Human Rights** (UDHR) specify some of these rights and the **International Covenant on Economic, Social and Cultural Rights** elaborates them. The **European Social Charter** and the Additional Protocol to the **American Convention on Human Rights** in the Area of Economic, Social and Cultural Rights, as well as many of the human rights instruments adopted by the **International Labor Organization** (ILO) and the **United Nations Educational, Scientific and Cultural Organization** (UNESCO) also deal with those rights. For purposes of this volume, the emphasis is on the **Universal Declaration of Human Rights** (UDHR) and the **International Covenants on Human Rights.**

The rights to which every person regardless of sex, race, color, religion, national or social origin, are entitled include:

- social security;
- work;
- free choice of employment;
- just and favorable conditions of work and protection against unemployment;
- just and favorable remuneration;

- equal pay for equal work;
- form and join trade unions for the protection of one's interests;
- strike;
- rest and leisure, including reasonable limitation on working hours;
- standard of living adequate for the health and well-being of one's family, including food, clothing, housing, medical care, and necessary social services;
- security in the event of unemployment, sickness, disability, widowhood, old age, or other lack of livelihood in circumstances beyond one's control;
- education;
- highest standard of physical and mental health;
- participate freely in the cultural life of the community;
- enjoy the arts and share in the scientific advancement and its benefits; and
- social and international order in which all the rights and freedoms indicated can be fully realized.

In the micro social order, **motherhood and childhood** are entitled to special protection, and all children, whether born in or out of wedlock, have the right to the same social protection.

Many non-Western countries, especially Asian ones, tend to focus on the economic, social, and cultural rights. Socialist countries, also, have tended either to give equal weight to both categories of rights or assign more emphasis to the economic, social, and cultural. The women's movement has been pressing for the coequal standing of both categories of rights, a standing that the UN has always supported and those who launched the human rights movement also intended. See also: Civil and Political Rights; Bangkok Declaration; Declaration on the Right to Development; World Conferences on Human Rights. *Further Reading:* R. Beddard and D. M. Hill, eds., *Economic, Social and Cultural Rights: Progress and Achievement* (1992); A. Side, C. Krause, and A. Rosas, eds., *Economic, Social and Cultural Rights: A Textbook* (1995).

EDUCATION. The right to education is one that both the **Universal Declaration of Human Rights** (UDHR) and the **International Covenant on Economic, Social and Cultural Rights** recognizes. These two human rights instruments not only specify the right to education, but the purposes that right should serve. Article 26 of the UDHR reads:

Article 26 (1). Everyone has the right to education. Education shall be free, at least in the elementary and fundamental stages. Elementary education shall be compulsory. Technical and professional education shall be made generally available and higher education shall be equally accessible to all on the basis of merit.

(2). Education shall be directed to the full development of the human personality and to the strengthening of respect for human rights and fundamental freedoms. It shall promote understanding, tolerance and friendship among all nations, racial or religious groups, and shall further the activities of the United Nations for the maintenance of peace.

(3). Parents have a prior right to choose the kind of education that shall be given to their children.

The International Covenant on Economic, Social and Cultural Rights, in Article 13 (1), covers the right to education in much the same manner as the UDHR does. There are a few areas of difference, however, which are significant enough to mention. Section 1 of Article 13 adds another purpose that education should serve: it should "enable all persons to participate effectively in a free society." Section 2 (c) of Article 13 not only speaks of making higher education accessible to all on the basis of capacity or merit, but that steps should be taken to implement the "progressive introduction of free education" at this level also. Section 2 (d) provides that fundamental education shall be "encouraged or intensified as far as possible for those persons who have not received or completed the whole period of their primary education." See also: Convention Against Discrimination in Education. *Further Reading:* UNTS, *Convention Against Discrimination in Education,* 429 *UNTS* 93; W. G. Langley, "Children, Moral Development, and Global Transformation," *World Order,* vol. 28 no. 3 (1978); N. B. Tarrow, ed., *Human Rights and Education* (1987); UNESCO, *World Education Report 1995* (1997).

EMPLOYMENT. The right to employment is one of the **economic, social and cultural rights** recognized by the **International Bill of Human Rights.** Article 23 of the **Universal Declaration of Human Rights** (UDHR) provides that

1. Everyone has a right to work, to free choice of employment, to just and favourable conditions of work and to protection against unemployment.

2. Everyone, without any discrimination, has the right to equal pay for equal work.

3. Everyone who works has the right to just and favourable remuneration ensuring for himself and his family an existence worthy of human dignity, and supplemented, if necessary, by other means of social protection.

4. Everyone has the right to form and to join trade unions for the protection of his interests.

The **International Covenant on Economic, Social and Cultural Rights** in Article 7 affirms the rights indicated above in the Universal Declaration of Human Rights. In addition, however, Article 7 (c) also includes the right to "Equal opportunity for everyone to be promoted in his employment to an appropriate higher level, subject to no considerations other than those of seniority and competence." In addition to "equal pay for equal work," Article 7 (a) (i) of the covenant speaks to "Fair wages and equal remuneration for work of equal value without distinction of any kind, in particular women being guaranteed conditions of work not inferior to those enjoyed by men, with equal pay for equal work." Article 6 of the covenant also provides some affirmative duties that states must discharge, in relationship to employment:

1. The States Parties to the present Covenant recognize the right to work, which includes the right of everyone to the opportunity to gain his living by work which he freely chooses or accepts, and will take appropriate steps to safeguard this right.

2. The steps to be taken by a State Party to the present Covenant to achieve the full realization of this right shall include technical and vocational guidance and training programmes, policies and techniques to achieve steady economic, social and cultural development and full and productive employment under conditions safeguarding fundamental political and economic freedoms to the individual.

See also: Convention Concerning Equal Opportunities and Equal Treatment for Men and Women Workers: Workers with Family Responsibilities. *Further Reading:* N. Valticos and G. W. von Potobsky, *International Labour Law* (1995); K. D. Ewing, C. A. Gearty, and B. A. Hepple, eds., *Human Rights and Labour Law* (1994).

ENVIRONMENT. One of the most important generation of rights is the fourth (or third, some advocates would argue) to an environment that is not only life-sustaining but also makes possible the full enjoyment of all the other rights recognized in the human rights instruments. Notwithstanding its importance, it has had difficulties gaining the merited support of states. Article 28 of the **Universal Declaration of Human Rights** (UDHR) refers to the right individuals have to a social and international order in which the rights and freedoms recognized can be fully realized, but there is no reference to the environment. Almost twenty-five years after the 1948 proclamation of the UDHR, however, a strong and growing worldwide environmental movement had developed, and people became aware that without a biophysical order, there could be no social and international order. So in 1972, spurred on by the environmental movement, a United Nations Conference on the Human Environment met in Stockholm, Sweden, from June 5–15.

The purpose of the meeting was to consider the need for the adoption of a common outlook and common principles to "inspire and guide the peoples of the world in the preservation and enhancement of the human environment." After due consideration, the conference of 112 nations unanimously adopted the Stockholm Declaration of the United Nations Conference on the Human Environment on June 16, 1972. The declaration's twenty-six principles, which were endorsed by the United Nations **General Assembly,** constitute an important body of common views and agreed on standards by which the conduct of states toward the environment may be judged. Included in the common outlook is the view that human beings, through rapid acceleration in science and technology, have transformed the natural environment, and that both components of the human environment, "the natural and the man-made, are essential to (one's) well-being and to the enjoyment of basic human rights—even the right to life itself." The first two principles of the declaration reinforce and elaborate this view.

Principle 1. Man has a fundamental right to freedom, equality and adequate conditions of life, in an environment of a quality that permits a life of dignity and well-being, and he bears a solemn responsibility to protect and improve the environment for present and future generations.

Principle 2. The natural resources of the earth, including air, water, land, flora and fauna and especially representative samples of natural ecosystems, must be safeguarded for the benefit of present and future generations through careful planning or management, as appropriate.

Despite the virtues of the Stockholm Declaration, it became the object of considerable criticism, because (1) it did not go beyond the *human* environment; (2) it did not sufficiently link the life and welfare of human beings to other life forms; and (3) it failed to vest individuals with sufficient rights to ensure the protection of the ecological system. On October 24, 1982, the UN General Assembly, responding to some of these criticisms, adopted a **World Charter for Nature**, which proclaims that "Every form of life is unique, warranting respect regardless of its worth to man, and [that] to accord other organisms such recognition, man must be guided by a moral code of action." It also acknowledges that civilization is rooted in nature. The response of states to the World Charter of Nature has been ambiguous.

On the one hand, they have supported, through the UN, the creation in 1983 of the World Commission on Environment and Development (WCED), also called the Brutland Commission, and the 1992 United Nations Conference on Environment and Development (UNCED), called the Earth Summit, held in Rio de Janeiro, Brazil. On the other hand, states have not acted in accordance with the concern that appears to support those UN efforts.

The World Commission's report, *Our Common Future*, was published in 1987. It made some important recommendations, including the necessity of integrating economic, development, and environmental concerns; of reorienting technology so that it can better manage risk; and of adopting a universal declaration on environmental protection and sustainable development. The report also stated a number of general principles, the first of which is that "All human beings have the fundamental right to an environment adequate for their health and well-being." The second principle speaks to the issue of intergenerational equity: "States shall conserve the use of the environment and natural resources for the benefit of present and future generations."

The convening of UNCED was largely influenced by *Our Common Future*, but the conference, because of the reluctance of states, did not create the hoped for "new norms . . . needed to maintain livelihood and life on our shared planet," as the Brutland Commission had recommended. Even the Rio Declaration that came out of that conference—a declaration through which states committed themselves to adopt measures protective of the environment—has been largely disregarded. Since 1992, the rights of individuals and peoples to food, safe water, health, and social security continue to be threatened and violated by acid rain, global warming, ozone depletion, deserts consuming agricultural lands, and the accelerating extinction of plant and animal species. But there are signs that the basis for future action in the area of **human rights** and the environment may be improving. At the interstate level, a 1994 Draft Declaration of Principles on Human Rights and the Environment (Draft Declaration), sponsored by the UN **Sub-Commission on Prevention of Discrimination and Protection of Minorities**, provides a framework from which a global treaty can be fashioned. And while a 1997 international agreement, called the Kyoto Protocol on Climate Change, does not make human rights its principal focus, that agreement, by seeking to freeze the amount of emissions of greenhouse gases from the world's thirty-eight developed countries to current levels, sets in motion a process for the evolution of a broad international legal framework to reduce carbon emissions, and offers a psychological boost to the human rights–environment movement, which has been increasing its pressure on governments. A number of **nongovernmental organizations**, such as the World Conservation Union (WCU), the Earth Council, and **Soka Gakkai International**, have been "organizing and planning at the grassroots" to gain support for a proposed International Covenant on Environment and Development (prepared largely by WCU), and a proposed Earth Charter (sponsored by the Earth Council), which has as its aim a statement of a moral standard for interstate, intercommunity, and individual conduct. It is questionable, of course, whether states will support the efforts of these private groups.

The first principle of the proposed Earth Charter reads: "Respect Earth and all Life. Earth, each life form, and all living beings possess intrinsic value and warrant respect independently of their utilitarian value to humanity."

The proposed International Covenant, the articles of which considerably complement those of the Draft Declaration, states the following in its fourth article: "Peace, development, environmental protection and respect for human rights and fundamental freedoms are interdependent."

Principle I of the Draft Declaration of Principles on Human Rights and the Environment provides that "Human rights, an ecologically sound environment, sustainable development and peace are interdependent and indivisible."

At the international regional level, both the **African Charter on Human and Peoples' Rights** and the **American Convention on Human Rights** (through its protocol on **economic, social and cultural rights**) explicitly provide for the right to an environment that is life-sustaining. *Further Reading:* M. Anderson, *Human Rights Approaches to Environmental Protection* (1996); Boston Research Center for the Twenty-First Century, *Buddhist Perspectives on the Earth Charter* (1997); N.A.F. Popovic, "In Pursuit of Environmental Human Rights: Commentary on the Draft of the Declaration of Principles on Human Rights and the Environment," *CHRLR*, vol. 27 no. 3 (1996); United Nations Environment Programme, *Global Environment Outlook* (1997); World Commission on Environment and Development, *Our Common Future* (1989).

EQUALITY. The norm of equality, so much a part of moral teaching and reasoning throughout the world, is a central principle of the **International Bill of Human Rights.** In its first instrument, the **Universal Declaration of Human Rights** (UDHR), the norm of equality is proclaimed as follows:

Article 1. All human beings are born free and equal in dignity and rights. They are endowed with reason and conscience and should act towards one another in the spirit of brotherhood.

Article 2. Everyone is entitled to the rights and freedoms set forth in this Declaration, without distinction of any kind, such as race, colour, sex, language, religion, political or other opinion, national or social origin, property, birth or other status.

Article 7. All are equal before the law and are entitled without any discrimination to equal protection of the law. All are entitled to equal protection against any discrimination in violation of this Declaration and against any incitement to such discrimination.

In the second instrument, the **International Covenant on Economic, Social and Cultural Rights,** though modified in its phrasing, asserts the same principle of equality in

Article 2 (2). The State Parties to the present Covenant undertake to guarantee that the rights enunciated in the present Covenant will be exercised without discrimination of any kind as to race, colour, sex, language, religion, political or other opinion, national or social origin, property, birth or other status.

Article 3. The States Parties to the present Covenant undertake to ensure the equal right of men and women to the enjoyment of all economic, social and cultural rights set forth in the present Covenant.

The third instrument in the International Bill of Human Rights, the **International Covenant on Civil and Political Rights** (ICCPR), enunciates the norm of equality in

Article 2 (1). Each State Party to the present Covenant undertakes to respect and to ensure to all individuals within its territory and subject to its jurisdiction the rights recognized in the present Covenant, without distinction of any kind, such as race, colour, sex, language, religion, political or other opinion, national or social origin, property, birth or other status.

Article 3. The States Parties to the present Covenant undertake to ensure the equal right of men and women to the enjoyment of all civil and political rights set forth in the present Covenant.

Other articles in the International Covenant on Civil and Political Rights, as well as other regional and global human rights instruments, also speak to the norm of equality, and while they may not do so explicitly, all human rights instruments implicitly support that norm. See also: Convention Against Discrimination in Education; Convention on the Elimination of All Forms of Discrimination Against Women; Discrimination; International Convention on the Elimination of all Forms of Racial Discrimination. *Further Reading:* S. L. Martin and K. E. Mahoney, *Equality and Judicial Neutrality* (1987); W. A. McKean, *Equality and Discrimination under International Law* (1983); M. Minoan, *Making All the Difference: Inclusion, Exclusion, and American Law* (1990).

ETHNIC CLEANSING. This is a term that gained currency during the Third Balkan War (1991–1995), the First and Second taking place in 1912 and 1913. It is now generally used to denote the practice, long a part of human history, of planned forcible **expulsion** of certain members of a civilian population, generally citizens, who are distinguished by one or more characteristics such as ethnicity, race, class, religion, language, or sexual orientation. Tactics used to execute such expulsions include the use of terror, mass rape, summary executions, forced disappearances, torture and **genocide.**

In the break up of the former Yugoslavia, for example, Serbs who sought control of territories in which Croats and Bosnia-Herzegovinians (including Muslims) lived, used terror and many of the other tactics mentioned above to expel or "cleanse" non-Serbs—those with different ethnic, racial, or religious characteristics than the Serbs. Croats and Bosnians, in many instances, reciprocated. During World War II, Nazi Germany used ethnic cleansing to justify the attempted Final Solution against Jews and Gypsies (or Roma people). In **Cambodia** and **Rwanda**, the world has witnessed recent examples of this practice.

Ethnic cleansing violates almost every norm of human rights, including the right to equality, non-discrimination; nationality; life; security of person against torture, inhuman or other degrading treatment or punishment; freedom of movement and residence; and against arbitrary arrest and detention. Article 3 (1) of Protocol IV of the **European Convention on Human Rights,** for example, provides that no one "shall be expelled, by means either of an individual or collective measure, from the territory of a State of which he [or she] is a national." Article 4 of Protocol IV also states that "collective expulsion of aliens is prohibited." See also: Bosnia-Herzegovina; Convention Against Torture and Other Cruel, Inhuman or Degrading

Treatment or Punishment; East Timor; Milosevic, Slobodan; Rape; Serbia. *Further Reading:* A. Bell-Fialkoff, *Ethnic Cleansing* (1996); A. N. Dragnich, *Yugoslavia's Disintegration and the Struggle for Truth* (1996); G. Prunier, *The Rwanda Crisis: History of Genocide* (1995).

EUROPEAN COMMISSION ON HUMAN RIGHTS. See HUMAN RIGHTS COMMISSION (REGIONAL).

EUROPEAN CONVENTION ON HUMAN RIGHTS. Officially entitled the Convention for the Protection of Human Rights and Fundamental Freedoms, this regional treaty is the first collective effort of its kind, on the part of states, to comply with their assumed **human rights** obligations under the **United Nation Charter**. It is also the first to provide collective enforcement for the human rights proclaimed in the **Universal Declaration of Human Rights** (UDHR). The convention, which was prepared under the jurisdiction of the **Council of Europe**, does four things: (1) it states and defines the rights and freedoms that are the concerns of its members; (2) it stipulates the permissible limitations which may be placed upon those rights and freedoms; (3) it creates institutions to implement the rights and freedoms defined; and (4) in providing the first three, it elaborates a model that has been and is being emulated outside the European region.

The two principal institutions created by the convention are the **European Commission** and the **European Court of Human Rights**. The two work in coordination with the **Committee of Ministers of the Council of Europe** to protect the rights recognized.

The convention, which has been supplemented by a number of protocols, provides a comprehensive body of rights and freedoms, including the right to life, liberty, and security; respect for privacy and family life, home and correspondence; freedom of thought, conscience and religion; freedom of expression; freedom of peaceful assembly and freedom of association; and freedom to marry and found a family. The convention also recognizes that individuals have the right not to be held in slavery or servitude; be subject to torture, inhuman or other degrading treatment; and be deprived of liberty, except by way of lawful arrest or detention, among other defined procedures.

While the preceding body of rights deals primarily with **civil and political rights**, readers should note that the **European Social Charter** deals with certain **economic, social and cultural rights**. It should also be noted that Protocol I, which was added to the convention in 1952, provides for the right to education and peaceful enjoyment of one's property. Protocol IV forbids deprivation of liberty on the grounds of one's inability to fulfill one's contractual obligations. The convention was concluded in Rome, Italy, on November 4, 1950, and entered into force on September 3, 1953. See also: Human Rights Commission. *Further Reading:* UNTS, *Convention for* *the Protection of Human Rights and Fundamental Freedoms*, 213 UNTS 221. B. Dickson, *European Rights and the European Convention* (1996); D. Kinley, *The European Convention of Human Rights* (1993).

EUROPEAN COURT OF HUMAN RIGHTS. This court is the judicial organ of the **European Convention on Human Rights.** It was created in accordance with Article 19 of the convention and it is empowered to judge cases relating to **human rights** complaints. Complaints may be brought before it by a signatory state whose national is a victim of human rights violation, a signatory against which a complaint has been lodged; a signatory that has referred a case to the **European Commission on Human Rights;** or by the European Commission itself. The court also has the authority to give advisory opinions when they are requested by the **Committee of Ministers of the Council of Europe.**

Not all complaints of alleged human rights violations reach the court. Indeed, complaints are deemed admissible before it only after the European Commission has examined them and been unable to arrive at a "friendly settlement." Judgments of the court are final, and they are executed by the Committee of Ministers of the Council of Europe. Without doubt, this court has been the most successful international judicial institution in the field of human rights. See also: Human Rights Commission; Inter-American Court of Human Rights. *Further Reading:* A. Clapham, *Human Rights and the European Community* (1991); A. Cassesse, A. Clapham, and J. Weiler, eds., *Human Rights and the European Community: Method of Protection* (1991).

EUROPEAN SOCIAL CHARTER. This charter, signed in 1961, over a decade after the largely **civil and political rights** were recognized in the **European Convention of Human Rights,** represents Europe's commitment to **economic, social and cultural rights.** The rights to which everyone is entitled without **discrimination** on grounds of race, color, sex, religion, political opinion, national or social origin, are too many to enumerate here. Included in Part I of the charter are

- the right to earn one's living in an occupation freely entered into;
- to just conditions of work;
- to safe and healthy working conditions;
- to fair remuneration sufficient for a decent standard of living for one and one's family;
- to freedom of association in national and international organizations for the protection of one's economic and social interests;
- to collective bargaining;
- to social and medical assistance;
- to social security;

- to social welfare services;
- to appropriate facilities for vocational training; and
- (for the young) the right to special protection against physical and moral hazards.

The right of employed women to protection, as elaborated in Part II, Article 8, is very instructive.

With a view to ensuring the effective exercise of the right of employed women to protection, the Contracting Parties undertake:

1. to provide either by paid leave, by adequate social security benefits or by benefits from public funds for women to take leave before and after childbirth up to a total of 12 weeks;

2. to consider it unlawful for an employer to give a woman notice of dismissal during her absence on maternity leave or to give her notice of dismissal at such a time that the notice will expire during her absence;

3. to provide that mothers who are nursing their infants shall be entitled to sufficient time off for this purpose.

The charter was signed on October 18, 1961, and entered into force on February 26, 1965. See also: Convention Concerning Maternity Protection; International Convention Economic, Social and Cultural Rights. *Further Reading:* F. Fabricius, *Human Rights and European Politics: The Legal-Political Status of Workers* (1992); A.C.M. Jaspers and L. Betton, eds., *25 Years, European Social Charter* (1988).

EXPULSION. Expulsion is the official act of removing from the territory of a state **aliens** who have been previously legally admitted or settled there. Reasons often given for expulsion include alleged threats to the security of the state engaging in the expulsion or the social or moral undesirability of the aliens.

Every state enjoys the authority to admit and refuse admission to aliens. Each state also has the authority to expel them. Because there had been few international legal principles defining what constitutes just or unjust causes for expulsion, the only traditional limit on the abuse of that authority by a state had been the fear of equivalent reciprocal action toward its citizens living in other countries. The human rights movement has provided some principles and procedures to remove the weakness in this often abused area of interstate conduct. Those principles are found in Article 13 of the **International Covenant on Civil and Political Rights** (ICCPR):

Article 13. An alien lawfully in the territory of a State Party to the present Covenant may be expelled therefrom only in pursuance of a decision reached in accordance with the law and shall, except where compelling reasons of national security otherwise require, be allowed to submit the reasons against his expulsion and to have his case reviewed by, and be represented for the purpose before, the competent authority or a person or persons especially designated by the competent authority.

Article 4 of Protocol IV of the **European Convention on Human Rights** provides that "Collective expulsion of aliens is prohibited." Article 12 (5) of the **African Charter on Human and Peoples' Rights** provides that "mass expulsion of non-nationals shall be prohibited," and goes on to define mass expulsion as that "which is aimed at national, racial, ethnic, or religious groups." See also: Declaration on the Rights of Individuals Who Are Not Nationals of the Country in Which They Live; Ethnic Cleansing. *Further Reading:* C. H. Goldman, *Human Rights and the Migratory Labour System* (1985); P. Weis, *Nationality and Statelessness in International Law* (1979).

F

FACT-FINDING. In order to advance and protect **human rights**, it is not enough that there are norms and that people and institutions become aware of those norms and are committed to them. There are additional needs, one of which is uncovering the facts that can help demonstrate the compliance or noncompliance of states with what the norms of human rights require. Uncovering those facts or fact-finding, however, is demanding, especially due to the nature of human rights law and the behavior of states.

The portion of international law that is concerned with human rights not only regulates the behavior of states toward each other; it regulates their behavior toward nonstate groups and individuals, including their own citizens. In many instances of human rights complaints, it is usually an aggrieved national who brings the complaint of human rights abuse against the government. Proof of violation or noncompliance, however, requires refined procedures as well as a keen appreciation of the multiple means involved in gaining access to the reliable information necessary for proof. States are not eager to help in fact-finding and gathering information that is potentially damaging to them. In fact, in many cases, governments engage in cover-ups. **Nongovernmental organizations** (NGOs) such as **Amnesty International, Defense for Children International,** or **Physicians for Human Rights** help in fact-finding.

In the 1980s, the United Nations **Commission on Human Rights** oversaw the creation of a series of human rights procedures and mechanisms intended to improve the UN's ability to analyze global trends in the field of human rights. The procedures and mechanisms are also intended to help the UN recommend appropriate policy actions to government, and, perhaps most important, to respond to complaints brought to the UN on behalf of individuals who have been victims of human rights abuse.

The procedures (sometimes called "specialized procedures") include the appointment of a country-specific rapporteur, representative, or expert group, usually for a year, although the commission can renew the mandate by resolution. These experts study and assess a country's human rights situation, taking into account its human rights laws, policies, and individual cases of human rights abuse. The result of the study and assessment is then presented to the United Nations **Commission on Human Rights** (CHR) and sometimes the United Nations **General Assembly**. There is also the appointment of "thematic" rapporteurs or **working groups** to consider particular forms of human rights abuse such as the sale of children, disappearances, or torture and **discrimination** against **indigenous peoples**. This class of experts is appointed for three years, and they consider the specific conditions that contribute to abuse around the world. Because of the global scope of their enquiry, governments are more apt to cooperate with thematic rapporteurs than with country-specific rapporteurs.

There are many problems with these fact-finding efforts. Many of the findings, while shared with other UN bodies, are not made public because of opposition from the countries in question. Governments, which fear adverse reports, are not always willing to allow experts into their borders; and representation in these expert bodies, in terms of cultural, ethnic, and gender diversity, is not always adequate. See also: Economic and Social Council; Truth Commissions. *Further Reading:* S. Cohen, "Government Responses to Human Rights Reports," *HRQ*, vol. 18 no. 3 (1996); M. O'Flaherty, "The Reporting Obligation under Article 40 of the International Covenant on Civil and Political Rights," *HRQ*, vol. 16 no. 3 (1994); R. G. Ramcharan, *International Law and Fact-Finding in the Field of Human Rights* (1982); R. B. Lillich, ed., *Fact-Finding Before International Tribunals* (1992).

FAIR TRIAL. The right to a fair trial, in the case of a criminal charge, is one that is recognized by regional and global human rights instruments. At the global level, Articles 10 and 11 of the **Universal Declaration of Human Rights** (UDHR) and Article 14 of the **International Covenant on Civil and Political Rights** (ICCPR) deal with that right. Because Article 14 of the International Covenant incorporates the principles in the Universal Declaration, this entry will concentrate on its seven major provisions for a fair trial.

First, a fair trial entails the element of equality, that is, the persons charged must be given a full and equal opportunity in the proceedings before the tribunal. Second, the proceedings should be public and before a competent, independent, and impartial tribunal established by law (exceptions to public proceedings are allowed in circumstances such as national security and the interest of juveniles). Third, alleged wrongdoers are presumed to be innocent until proven guilty. Fourth, persons should have certain "minimum guarantees," including, according to Article 14 (3):

a. To be informed promptly and in detail in a language which he understands of the nature and cause of the charge against him;

b. To have adequate time and facilities for the preparation of his defence and to communicate with counsel of his own choosing;

c. To be tried without undue delay;

d. To be tried in his presence, and to defend himself in person or through legal assistance of his own choosing; . . .

e. To examine, or have examined, the witnesses against him and to obtain the attendance and examination of witnesses on his behalf under the same conditions as witness against him;

f. To have the free assistance of an interpreter if he cannot understand or speak the language used in court;

g. Not to be compelled to testify against himself or to confess guilt.

If convicted, states the fifth provision, one has the right to appeal that conviction. Sixth, if after a person is convicted that conviction is reversed or overturned on grounds that a new or newly discovered fact shows that there has been a miscarriage of justice, the person who has suffered punishment as a result of the conviction shall be compensated. Seventh, each person has the right not to be tried twice for the same crime. Regional human rights instruments, especially those of the Inter-Americas and Western Europe, recognize comparable, if not as extensive, procedural rights in the norm of fair trials. *Further Reading:* D. J. Bodenhamer, *Fair Trial* (1992); C. Crane and M. Mackarel, eds., *Human Rights and the Administration of Justice* (1997).

FAMILY. The overwhelming body of human rights instruments focuses on individuals, as distinct from groups. One of the few groups, however, where those instruments have placed emphasis is on that of the family, which, according to the **International Bill of Human Rights,** is "the natural and fundamental group unit of society." As such, according to Article 16 of the **Universal Declaration of Human Rights** (UDHR) and Article 23 (1) of the **International Covenant on Civil and Political Rights** (ICCPR) "it is entitled to protection by society and the State." Article 10 (1) of the **International Covenant on Economic, Social and Cultural Rights** goes further. It provides that the "widest possible protection and assistance should be accorded to the family . . . particularly for its establishment and while it is responsible for the care and education of dependent children."

Article 16 of the **European Social Charter** gives a fuller view of the family's rights. It states that "With a view of ensuring the necessary conditions for full development of the family, . . . the Contracting Parties undertake to promote the economic, legal and social protection of family life by such means as social and family benefits, fiscal arrangements, provisions for family housing, benefits for newly married, and other appropriate means." Article 18 (2) of the Banjul Charter provides that the state "shall have the duty to assist the family which is the custodian of morals and traditional values recognized by the community." The **American Convention on Human Rights** imposes the same duty on states.

Because of the claimed importance of the family, the International Bill of Human Rights recognizes "special protection" for **motherhood and childhood.** Another area of rights relating to the family is the right to found one. Article 16 (1) of the Universal Declaration provides that "Men and women of full age, without any limitation due to race, nationality or religion, have the right to marry and to found a family." Women and men are entitled to "equal rights as to marriage, during marriage and at its dissolution."

The drafters of the earlier human rights instruments thought in terms of the "traditional family unit" but they did not define what that meant. Today, as illustrated in the 1991 **International Convention on the Protection of the Rights of All Migrant Workers and Members of Their Families** and in the efforts of gay and lesbian couples to found families, that definition is broadening. Article 4 of the convention states that

members of the family refers to persons married to migrant workers or having with them a relationship that, according to applicable law, produces effects equivalent to marriage, as well as their dependent children and other dependent persons recognized as members of the family.

Gay and lesbian couples are arguing, in jurisdictions that have refused to recognize their right to found a family, that their relationships are producing effects—effects of care and commitment—that are equivalent to marriage. *Further Reading:* C. Kagitcibasi, *Family and Human Development Across Cultures* (1996); G. Van Buren, "The International Protection of Family Members' Rights as the 21st Century Approaches," *HRQ*, vol. 17 no. 4 (1995).

FINAL SOLUTION. See GENOCIDE.

FINLAND. See SAAMI.

FIRST GENERATION RIGHTS. See GENERATIONS OF RIGHTS.

FIRST TRANCHE. The word *tranche* is French and means slice. Tranches are slices of credit to which member states of the International Monetary Fund (IMF) may have access. First tranche refers to the first slice of a country's allocation or quota of credit (usually determined mainly by that country's contribution to the IMF), and any member country of the IMF can have access to that tranche without condition. If a country needs to have credit beyond the first tranche, however, it progressively subjects itself to conditions imposed by the IMF. These conditions—structural adjustments—generally include modifications in the exchange rates of national currencies and drastic reductions in government spending. Reduction in government spending usually means elimination, partly or wholly, of support for education, food, rent, and health care, and, thus, the undermining of **economic, social and cultural** rights. In general, women, children, and the poor are most vulnerable. See also: Conditionality. *Further Reading:* P. Dasgupta, *An Enquiry into Well-Being and Destitution* (1993); A. G. Smith, *Human Rights and Choice in Poverty* (1997).

FOOD. Although many in the world go hungry or are undernourished, the right of every person to food is proclaimed in the **Universal Declaration of Human Rights** (UDHR) and recognized in the **International Covenant on Economic, Social and Cultural Rights.** Article 25 (1) of the UDHR provides that "Everyone has the right to a standard of living adequate for health . . . including food." And the International Covenant states in:

Article 11(1). The States Parties to the present Covenant recognize the right of everyone to an adequate standard of living . . . including . . . food . . .

(2). The States Parties to the present Covenant, recognizing the fundamental right of everyone to be free from hunger, shall take, individually and through international co-operation, the measures, including specific programmes, which are needed.

   a. To improve methods of production, conservation and distribution of food by making full use of technical and scientific knowledge, by disseminating knowledge of the principles of nutrition and by developing or reforming agrarian systems . . .

   b. Taking into account the problems of both food-importing and food-exporting countries, to ensure an equitable distribution of world food supplies in relation to need.

As part of taking international measures to implement the right to food, a 1974 World Food Conference, convened under United Nations **General Assembly** Resolution 3180, adopted the **Universal Declaration on the Eradication of Hunger and Malnutrition.** Paragraph 1 of that declaration states that "Every man, woman and child has the inalienable right to be free from hunger and malnutrition in order to develop fully and maintain their physical and mental faculties." See also: Universal Declaration on the Eradication of Hunger and Malnutrition. *Further Reading:* Institute on Hunger and Development, *Bread for the World* (1990); A. G. Smith, *Human Rights and Choice in Poverty* (1997).

FORCED LABOR. Compulsory or forced labor is regarded as a practice that is similar to slavery. On June 28, 1930, the General Conference of the **International Labor Organization** (ILO), concerned that forced and compulsory labor had become widespread in former colonial areas, adopted Convention (No. 29) Concerning Forced and Compulsory Labor. The convention defined "forced and compulsory labor" as "all work or service which is exacted from any person under the menace of any penalty or for which the said person has not offered himself [or herself] voluntarily."

States agreed to a complete suppression of compulsory labor, after exempting from its meaning military service, work during emergencies such as famine, epidemic diseases, and the work of legally supervised convicted persons.

After the creation of the UN in 1945, forced labor continued. And from an **Economic and Social Council**-ILO jointly sponsored study of the phenomenon, the world learned that compulsory labor was alive and well, and spreading. That study, completed in 1953, noted that compulsory labor was taking place not only in dependent territories, but in independent countries; it also noted that there were two principal forms of compulsory labor: (1) that used as a means of political coercion—something that took place in Nazi Germany, for example, against the Jews and others, in the former Soviet Union, and, recently, in **Cambodia**; and (2), that used as a system of forced labor for economic purposes—for example, the Five-Year Economic Plans in early Stalinist Soviet **Russia**, the Great Leap Forward in **China**, and the forced prostitution of women and children.

To deal with the problem, on June 25, 1957, the ILO adopted Convention (No. 105) Concerning the Abolition of Forced Labor. Under this convention, which entered into force January 17, 1959, states undertake, in accordance with Article 1, to suppress and not make use of any form of compulsory labor:

a. As a means of political coercion or education or as punishment for holding or expressing political views or views ideologically opposed to the established political, social or economic system;

b. As a method of mobilizing and using labour for purposes of economic development;

c. As a means of labour discipline;

d. As punishment for having participated in strikes;

e. As a means of racial, social, national or religious discrimination.

See also: Bonded Labor; Gulag Archipelago; Slavery, the Slave Trade, and Slavery-like Practices. *Further Reading:* E. Bacon, *The Gulag at War* (1994); D. Dallin, *Forced Labor in Soviet Russia* (1947).

FRAMEWORK CONVENTION FOR THE PROTECTION OF NATIONAL MINORITIES. The social and economic changes that have taken place in Europe since 1991, when the former Soviet Union collapsed and communism lost it influence in the region, have sponsored a reawakening of issues concerned with minority rights. Some of the issues are at the root of many international problems that affect Europe and, indeed, the world. The **Council of Europe** recognizes that "the upheavals of European history have shown that protection of national minorities is essential to stability, democratic security and peace in the continent." It has acknowledged as well that a pluralist and genuinely democratic society should not only respect the ethnic, cultural, linguistic, and religious identity of each person belonging to a national minority, but also "create appropriate conditions enabling them to express, preserve and develop this identity."

With the above acknowledgment and recognition, as well as the assumed obligation of its members under international human rights instruments to protect minorities, the Council of Europe, on February 1, 1995, concluded a Framework Convention for the Protection of National Minorities. Article 1 of the convention, linking what Europe seeks to do with broader ongoing international developments, states that "The protection of national minorities and the rights and freedoms belonging to those minorities forms an integral part of the international protection of human rights, and as such, falls within the scope of international co-operation." Article 3 (1) spells out the rights of individuals in relationship to any given national minority: "Every person belonging to a national minority shall have the right freely to choose to be treated or not to be treated as such and no disadvantage shall result from this choice or from the exercise of the rights which are connected to that choice." States undertake in Article 5 (1) "to promote the conditions necessary for persons belonging to national minorities to maintain and develop their culture, and to preserve the essential elements of their identity," namely, their religion, language, traditions, and general cultural heritage. And while countries can pursue their general policies of integration, those policies "shall refrain from . . . practices aimed at assimilation of persons belonging to national minorities against their will."

The Framework Convention, like the **International Covenant on Civil and Political Rights** (ICCPR) does not define minority, it simply refers to certain categories of people—religious, linguistic, and ethnic, for example. Rights under the Framework Convention do not fall under the implementation of the **European Court of Human Rights** or the European Commission of Human Rights. The **Committee of Ministers of the Council of Europe** will monitor its implementation. *Further Reading:* G. Gilbert, "The Council of Europe and Minority Rights," *HRQ*, vol. 18 no. 1 (1996); Text of the Framework Convention, *ILM*, vol. 34 no. 2 (1995).

FREEDOM OF INFORMATION. See NEW WORLD INFORMATION AND COMMUNICATIONS ORDER.

FREEDOM OF THOUGHT, CONSCIENCE AND RELIGION. See THOUGHT, CONSCIENCE AND RELIGION.

FRIENDS WORLD COMMITTEE FOR CONSULTATION. This is a worldwide Quaker body that is recognized by the UN as an international **nongovernmental organization** (NGO) and has been granted consultative status with the United Nations **Economic and Social Council** (ECOSOC).

The committee (FWCC), which was established in 1937, has as its aim transcending differences of language, culture, and nationality and learning how to rejoice in the richness and variety of those differences.

Ever since the early days, when two of its leaders (William Penn in 1693 and John Belles in 1710) published proposals for international peacekeeping organizations, Quakers have supported initiatives like the UN for the maintenance of international peace. Today, FWCC is intimately involved in a wide range of UN-related activities, including **human rights**. Its work in human rights is guided by its religious doctrine that states that there is a spiritual property called Light that dwells in every human being—a light that endows each human life with a sacred dimension, "so that it must not be debased or exploited or destroyed for any reason or under any circumstances." FWCC's work supports the rights of refugees, victims of war, children, indigenous peoples (especially in Australia and New Zealand), disabled, women, and economically deprived people. Its work on children serving as soldiers, particularly in African countries, has been particularly enlightening to the world. Because of its stance on certain issues—criticism of governments for their reluctance to embrace disarmament; Israel, for alleged violations of Palestinian rights; and the United States for its actions in Vietnam—it has been subject to some criticism, also. *Further Reading:* R. Brett, M. McCallin, and R. O'Shea, *Children: The Invisible Soldiers* (1995); J. D. Wood, *The Background to Quaker Work at the United Nations* (1993). *Further Information:* Friends World Committee for Consultation, 4 Byng Place, London, WC1E 7JH, U.K., Tel.: 011–44–171–388–0497.

FUNDAMENTALISM. Fundamentalism is a term used to denote an outlook and attitude opposed to secularism. Secularism, on the one hand, is a social and political outlook that has for centuries worked to free social and public policy from what it sees as the restrictions of religion or religion-informed ideologies, and rejects the religious as inappropriate to the definition and application of public affairs. For secularists, the modernization process brings with it a faith in the human capacity of **self-determination**. The process sponsors great social, economic, aesthetic, moral, scientific, and technological diversity, which only a pluralistic belief system and political arrangement can accommodate.

Fundamentalism, on the other hand, takes the position that human beings are dependent on an authority outside themselves—an authority that is locatable in a set of principles derived from holy texts such as the Bible, the Torah, and the Koran. These texts are to be interpreted literally and, sometimes, exclusively of other points of view. Christian fundamentalists have gained considerable influence in the United States where they have been influencing areas of foreign policy, including **China**, which they see as limiting religious freedom and women's reproductive rights. In **Israel**, Jewish fundamentalists have, on occasions, exercised veto power over issues of self-determination for the Palestinians and on matters of marriage and Jewish identity. In many Islamic countries such as Iran, Pakistan, and Sudan, fundamentalists have sought to exclude all expressions of cultural pluralism. In **India**, Hindu fundamentalists now threaten the fifty-year old interreligious compromise that has provided the country with significant democratic stability.

The insistence on the part of fundamentalists that holy texts should have literal interpretation and be the basis for public policy, tends to limit freedoms—freedom of speech, information, founding a family, association, religion, belief, and conscience. See also: Declaration on the Elimination of All Forms of Intolerance and of Discrimination Based on Religion or Belief; Religion and Human Rights; Thought, Conscience and Religion. *Further Reading:* A. A. An-Naim, *Human Rights and Religious Values* (1995); A.J.M. Milne, *Human Rights and Human Diversity* (1986).

G

GANDHI, MOHANDAS K. ARAMCHAND, (1869–1948). Gandhi was the most important figure in helping **India** win political independence from Britain in 1947. In the process of leading a mass movement against the British (and earlier a confrontation with **apartheid** in **South Africa**), he was able to elaborate a philosophy of life that touches on almost all the fundamental areas of **human rights**: a review of swaraj, ahimsa, tolerance, equality, development, and the environment should help illustrate this claim.

The concept of swaraj deals with the principle of **self-determination**—the right of India to enjoy independence from Britain. But it also entails the acquisition of the capacity by people at large to resist, regulate, and control authority. To Gandhi, a precondition for swaraj was the education of all individuals—an education incorporating the life experience of the individual. Linked to the idea of swaraj—the right to self-determination and the capacity to resist authority—is the concept of ahimsa, defined as nonviolence or noninjury.

While nationalists generally accept violence as a necessary means to win political independence and preserve independence through war, Gandhi took the position that violence damages not only the physical and spiritual constitutions of its victims but also its practitioners, it reinforces aggression, impairs the moral dignity of all, and teaches hatred. To gain independence, individuals must learn to love and resist those that one loves, but without violence. Gandhi saw intolerance as a form of violence—something that cuts off the true development of people's moral and intellectual personalities and impairs the relationship that people seek to develop with the natural and the supernatural order. He was therefore against all forms of intolerance.

With respect to equality, Gandhi took the position that human dignity cannot be preserved in a system of inequality, and neither can the true independence of a nation be formed in a system of inequality. He challenged India to eliminate the caste system and particularly untouchability (the lowest caste system that is associated with poverty, illiteracy and powerlessness), as its primary social objective. To demonstrate his commitment to equality, he lived among the untouchables.

In the areas of development and the **environment**, Gandhi anticipated many contemporary discussions. He opined that economic growth is not the same as development. Development refers to the transformation of society and people toward an ethical commitment to social justice, income distribution, and the spiritual unfolding of the individual and collective personality. The natural environment, which is necessary for the development of the cultural environment, must be carefully tended and cultivated, as he sought to do in the ashrams (conventional retreats) where he liked to live. And in the true sense of human rights, Gandhi thought that all nations should work to *rediscover* the unity of the human family. In doing so, leaders and followers should seek to pursue the elimination of the seven social sins: politics without principles; commerce without morality; wealth without work; education without character; science without humanity; pleasure without conscience; and worship without sacrifice. See also: Religion and Human Rights. *Further Reading:* K. Kriplani, ed., *All Men Are Brothers: Life and Thoughts of Mahatma Gandhi as Told in His Own Words* (1958); N. Radhakrishnan, ed., *Gandhian Perspective of Nation-Building for World Peace* (1992).

GAY RIGHTS. See LESBIAN AND GAY RIGHTS.

GENERAL ASSEMBLY. This institution is one of the six principal organs of the United Nations. Its major functions and powers include (1) discussing any issue that is within the scope of the United Nations **Charter;** (2) considering general principles of cooperation for the maintenance of international peace and security and making recommendations based on those principles; and (3) calling to the attention of the United Nations **Security Council** any situation that is likely to endanger international peace and security. In addition to its discuss-and-recommend functions, which have emerged as an important political instrument within the UN, the General Assembly has a supervisory role in overseeing and coordinating many activities of the United Nations: it is responsible for the finances of the UN; it elects (either on its own or in conjunction with the Security Council) members of other UN organs; it approves amendments to the charter; and it admits (on the recommendation of the Security Council) states to membership and expulsion from the United Nations.

From the standpoint of this volume, the powers given to the General Assembly by Article 13 (b) of the United Nations Charter are most relevant:

it authorizes the General Assembly to make recommendations for the purpose of "promoting international co-operation in the economic, social, cultural, educational and health field, and assisting in the realization of human rights and fundamental freedoms without distinction as to race, sex, language or religion." This authority, when combined with other areas, including its work as a virtual "world parliament," enables the General Assembly to study, consider, adopt, and recommend to member states human rights instruments or actions relating to those instruments. It has been on the basis of the General Assembly's recommendations that we have most of the human rights instruments, such as those which make up the International Bill of Human Rights, we have examined in this volume. See also: Economic and Social Council; International Bill of Human Rights; The International Court of Justice. *Further Reading:* P. Alston, *The United Nations and Human Rights: A Critical Appraisal* (1992); M. J. Peterson, *The General Assembly* (1986).

GENERATIONS OF RIGHTS. Since the 1980s, in an effort to assign categories to the body of rights that have evolved since 1948, scholars developed the concept of three generations of interdependent rights. First generation rights are called civil and political—those that, in general, focus on freedom "from" various types of feared or threatened abuses, including arbitrary detention, torture, slavery, **expulsion**, and **genocide**. There are also rights "to"—to a fair trial, to freedom of **thought, conscience and religion**, and to recognition as a person before the law.

Second generation rights are economic, social, and cultural. These are overwhelmingly rights "to" and deal with the right to education, to work, to equal pay for equal work, to an adequate standard of living, to health care, to participate in the cultural life of the community, and to enjoy the fruits of technological and scientific progress.

Third generation rights are frequently called "solidarity rights," because they require for fulfillment the consistent cooperation of many groups at local, national, and international levels. They include the right to development, to human security (not security of states), to peace, to **self-determination**, and, to an extent, the rights of women. The right of **indigenous peoples** and the right of a life-sustaining and nurturing **environment** are sometimes called fourth generation rights, although many would include them in the third category. See also: Civil and Political Rights; Economic, Social and Cultural Rights. *Further Reading:* H. Hannum, *Autonomy, Sovereignty and Self-Determination* (1990); P. Alston, *The United Nations and Human Rights: A Critical Appraisal* (1992).

GENEVA CONVENTIONS. These are four treaties that represent agreements, updates, and codifications of international humanitarian law for the protection of war victims, including prisoners of war and civilians. Civilians include political prisoners, women, children, and other noncombat personnel. Sometimes called the Red Cross Conventions, they were drafted under the aegis of the **International Committee of the Red Cross** and approved by some forty-eight countries at a diplomatic conference held in Geneva, Switzerland, on August 12, 1949. For the purpose of this volume, Conventions III and IV are of primary concern; they were revised and supplemented by two protocols in 1977–1978, but they share a basic body of protections for war victims, as presented in Article 3, the content of which is common to both conventions:

In case of armed conflict . . . each Party to the conflict shall be bound to apply as a minimum, the following provisions:

1. Persons taking no active part in hostilities, including members of the armed forces who have laid down their arms . . . shall in all circumstances be treated humanely . . .

To this end the following acts are and shall remain prohibited at any time and in any place whatever with respect to the above-mentioned persons:

a. violence to life and person, in particular murder of all kinds, mutilation, cruel treatment and torture;

b. taking hostage;

c. outrages upon personal dignity, in particular humiliating and degrading treatment;

d. the passing of sentences and carrying out of executions without previous judgment pronounced by a regularly constituted court, affording all judicial guarantees which are recognized as indispensable by civilized peoples.

2. The wounded and sick shall be collected and cared for.

An impartial humanitarian body, such as the International Committee of the Red Cross, may offer its services to the Parties to the conflict.

One of the more divisive issues in international relations is centered on the fact that **human rights** must not be suspended during times of war. Those who think the interstate system cannot be without war and that war is, by definition, inhumane, often frown on the limitations placed on states by humanitarian and human rights laws. *Further Reading:* G. Best, *Humanity in Warfare* (1980); D. Forsythe, "Human Rights and the International Committee of the Red Cross," *HRQ*, vol. 12 no. 2 (1990); J. F. Hutchinson, *Champions of Charity: War and the Rise of the Red Cross* (1996).

GENITAL MUTILATION. Genital mutilation, sometimes called female circumcision, is a practice that entails cutting away part of a woman's external genitalia, which is composed of the clitoris, the inner folds (*labia minora*), and the outer folds (*labia majora*). The practice, which until the 1930s took place in some areas of the **United States**, is today found in over forty countries, primarily in North and West Africa, west and central Asia, some areas of Southeast Asia, as well as Peru, Brazil, eastern Mexico, and among the **indigenous peoples of Australia.** In all of the societies in which the practice takes place, it is not so much that governments have promoted or engaged in the practice, it is because of the force of custom (and some leaders of government may actually accept the custom), that governments have failed to arrest and eliminate the practice.

Controversy surrounds the practice, because of the pain involved, the physical and health risks (many of the excisions take place under conditions where antibiotics and anesthetics are either not widely used or unavailable), the psychological trauma, and the deaths that result. Equally important, although there are cultural factors associated with female genital mutilation—initiation into adulthood and the preservation of virginity, for example—there is a common, underlying social logic: the control of women and their reproductive faculties. A final area of controversy centers around the claim that the practice is a violation of **human rights,** which are universal in character.

Those who claim that the norms of human rights are essentially Western in concept and content, and without proper appreciation of other cultures, view the attempt to subject genital mutilation to human rights principles as efforts to engage in a form of cultural imperialism. To date, the controversy is moving in the direction of favoring an increasingly strong opposition to the practice throughout the world, Article 2 of the 1994 UN **Declaration on the Elimination of Violence Against Women** specifically prohibits "female genital mutilation and other practices harmful to women." Egyptian courts in 1995 upheld a decision declaring the practice illegal. And in June 1996, the U.S. Board of Immigration Appeals ruled that Fauziya Kasinga, a nineteen-year-old citizen of Togo, was eligible for political **asylum** in the United States on grounds that she would be forced to undergo genital mutilation were she to return to Togo.

Female genital mutilation violates a number of human rights norms. Among them are the right to life; to liberty and security of person; to physical integrity; to health; and not to be subject to cruel, inhuman, and degrading treatment. *Further Reading:* A. T. Slack, "Female Circumcision: A Critical Appraisal," *HRQ*, vol. 10 no. 4 (1988); A. Thiam, *Black Sisters Speak Out* (1986).

GENOCIDE. Regarded as the ultimate crime and the gravest possible violation of **human rights,** genocide occupies a prominent place in human history, including twentieth-century history. In 1915, for example, the Ottoman Turks conducted the systematic extermination of over an estimated 1 million Armenians. During World War II, through **forced labor,** sterilization, starvation, gassings and mass murder in concentration camps, some six million Jews, along with an uncertain numbers of homosexuals, Roma people (Gypsies), and others were killed by Nazi Germany. In the case of the Jews, the effort was designed to effect the Final Solution (from the standpoint of the Nazis) to their undesirable and undeserved presence in Europe. It was the reaction of the global community to the killing of the Jews that prompted the United Nations to adopt the **Convention on the Prevention and Punishment of the Crime of Genocide** in 1948.

Since 1945, there have been repeated examples of genocide: the killing of Cambodians during the Pol Pot regime; the Indonesian slaughter of the people of East Timor; and most recently, the occurrences in **Rwanda** and the former Yugoslavia. See also: Cambodia; Ethnic Cleansing. *Further Reading:* A. Bell, *Ethnic Cleansing* (1996); G. J. Andreopoulos, ed., *Genocide: Conceptual and Historical Dimensions* (1994).

GLOBAL CIVIL SOCIETY. See NONGOVERNMENTAL ORGANIZATIONS.

GLOBAL ETHIC. See DECLARATION OF A GLOBAL ETHIC.

GORBACHEV, MIKHAIL S., (1931–   ). Mikhail Gorbachev was born and grew up in the USSR, which dissolved in 1991, replaced by the Russian Federation. From 1985 to 1991, he served as leader of the Soviet Union and during that time was engaged in a number of policy decisions that not only transformed the structure of world politics but improved **human rights** prospects for many people throughout the world.

First, he renounced the Brezhnev Doctrine—Leonid I. Brezhnev (1906–1982), a leader of the Soviet Union—that claimed the right to intervene in the internal affairs of other socialist countries under the guise of preserving socialism or the socialist commonwealth. In renouncing the Brezhna Doctrine, Gorbachev gave strong support to the principle of **self-determination.** The peoples of Eastern Europe, the Baltic states (Estonia, Latvia, and Lithuania), as well as many other nations within the Soviet empire such as Ukraine, Armenia, Georgia, and Azerbaijan owe their present independence to his policy of change, as does the reunified Germany.

Second, Gorbachev's policy of *glasnost* (political openess) at home destroyed the political monopoly that the Communist Party enjoyed. The **civil and political rights** that the party denied for more than seventy years have begun to take root in **Russia.**

Third, while his policies of arms control and disarmament caused a considerable relaxation of tension throughout the world and allowed for greater freedom in the areas formerly controlled by the Soviet Union, old ethnic, religious, and other rivalries reemerged in some of those areas (Nagorno-Karabakh and Ckechnya, for example) with calls for **ethnic cleansing** surprising the global community. There are two other major areas of human rights on which Gorbachev's policies have had an impact: protection of **economic, social and cultural rights** in Russia and the implementation of certain civil and political rights.

In the first area, he was unable to put into operation his restructuring of the former Soviet Union's economy (*perestroika*), in part because he was unwilling to move to capitalism in the sense that the West wanted, and because of opposition at home to any fundamental change in the state-controlled economy. This failure allowed those who succeeded to disregard, by and large, the economic, social, and cultural rights about which the former Soviet Union was so proud. Today, with unregulated capitalism in Russia, education, health care, housing, and old age benefits have all been undermined, if not totally discarded, and the voices for those rights in the international arena have been less vigorous. In the West, very little attention has been focused on economic, social, and cultural rights for Russian citizens.

Finally, Gorbachev supported the creation within the UN of a strong, unbiased authority to impose sanctions on those who violate human rights; he also supported the creation of the **Human Dimension (Mechanism)**, which is an institution that helps promote human rights among the members of the **Organization for Security and Co-operation in Europe (OSCE)**. He was awarded the Nobel Peace Prize in 1990. See also: Russia. *Further Reading*: D. Doder, *Gorbachev: Heretic in the Kremlin* (1990); M. Lewin, *The Gorbachev Phenomenon* (1991).

GREAT PROLETARIAN CULTURAL REVOLUTION. See CHINA.

GUATEMALA. See TRUTH COMMISSIONS.

GULAG ARCHIPELAGO. This is the title of a novel that was published by the Soviet (now Russian) writer, Alexandr I. Solzhenitsyn (1918–   ). The term GULAG is an acronym in Russian for "The Main Camp Administration" or, as is translated by some, "The Main Administration of Corrective Labour Camps." The term "archipelago" normally refers to an expanse of water with many scattered islands, and the Gulag in this case was characterized by an institutional expanse with widely scattered islands of labor camps. Archipelago refers to an archipelago of the mind—a mind scattered and conditioned by the actual prison camps and slave labor within the Soviet Union.

Beginning some time in the early 1930s during the leadership of **Joseph V. Stalin**, who controlled the Soviet Union from 1924 to his death in 1953, labor camps were organized. They were established because of the view that keeping prisoners in them was "economically" sounder than detaining them in prison. It was also argued that labor camps would facilitate and expedite industrial construction in the Urals, Siberia, and the Far East, where it was difficult to attract free labor. Solzenhitsyn was one of the millions of political prisoners who were sent to GULAG (an estimated 35–40 million people were sent, a majority of whom are believed to have died from beatings, overwork, and even starvation).

These forced-labor camps, where political prisoners, peasants who opposed collectivization in agriculture, dissidents, and others were sent, were largely emptied after Stalin's death, but criminals were still used as forced laborers until the dissolution of the Soviet Union. The current leader of Russia, Boris Yeltsin (1931–   ) is said to have abolished **forced labor**. It is this forced labor about which Solzenhitsyn wrote in *The Gulag Archipelago*; it is also this forced labor which, in part, marks the Soviet Union as having been in such grave violations of **human rights**. See also: Slavery, the Slave Trade, and Slavery-like Practices. *Further Reading:* E. Bacon, *The Gulag at War* (1994); R. Conquest, *The Great Terror: A Reassessment* (1990); A. Solzhenitsyn, *The Gulag Archipelago* (1974).

H

HAITI. Haiti is a country that is located in the western third of the island of Hispaniola, in the West Indies. Its eastern border is with the Dominican Republic, which occupies the rest of the island. The country has a population of about 7 million people, 90 percent of whom are of African descent. The other 10 percent is almost equally divided between Europeans and people of mixed descent (those who trace their ancestry from both European and African). Haiti is overwhelmingly Christian, with Roman Catholicism dominant. The country is one of the poorest in the world, and is the poorest in the Western Hemisphere, with urban poverty existing at a 65 percent level and rural at 80 percent.

Haiti won its independence from France in 1804, and until 1957 underwent a succession of authoritarian regimes. Each failed to address the country's social problems, which have been rooted in the selfish control of society by a small number of persons of mixed descent and their internal and external supporters. In 1957, François Duvalier (1907–1971) took control of the government and quickly established one of the most brutal dictatorships, supported by a paramilitary group called the Tonton Macoutes, which in turn controlled a number of **death squads**. Duvalier used death squads and the Tonton Macoutes to tyrannize the population and take vengeance on some of the social elites. At his death, he was succeeded by his son, Jean-Claude Duvalier (1951–), who ruled until 1986, when he was deposed following two years of popular unrest.

Elections in 1988 were negated by successive military coups. In 1990, Jean Bertrand Aristide (1953–), a Catholic priest who was strongly committed to the poor was elected president. He, too, was overthrown by the military after only seven months in office. This latest military coup so outraged the international community that it, under the sponsorship of the UN, imposed economic sanctions and a blockade against Haiti. In September 1994, a U.S.-led military force, under UN authority, entered Haiti. The force helped restore Aristide to power and prepare for new elections. The U.S.-led force was replaced in March 1996, by a UN mission, which has remained there. In February 1996, a new president, René Préval, was elected with over 88 percent of the vote.

Although torture, disappearances, summary executions—among some of the worst human rights abuses that were taking place in Haiti—have largely ceased, the country is still socially divided. The issue of poverty will have to be dealt with, if political stability is to mature and last. The right to education, health care, housing for the poor, and the right to organize and develop strong political parties must now be promoted. See also: Death Squads; Human Rights. *Further Reading:* Amnesty International, *Haiti* (1985); A. Dupuy, *Haiti in the New World Order* (1997); D. McFayen et al., eds., *Haiti: Dangerous Crossroads* (1995).

HAMAS. See INTIFADAH.

HAVEL, VÁCLAV (1946–   ). Former president of Czechoslovakia (1989–1992) and president of the Czech Republic since 1993, Václav Havel is also a dramatist and an important human rights activist. He was imprisoned twice by the former communist regime of Czechoslovakia, and was one of the principal authors of the human rights manifesto, **Charter 77**, which served as a major embarrassment to the communists in power, and became an important mobilizing force in toppling of the regime in 1989.

Havel's other contributions to the human rights movement are many. Among them is his support for the principle of national **self-determination,** his championing of **civil and political rights** in general, and his fierce defense of the right to freedom of **thought, conscience and religion.** On the matter of national self-determination—the right of people to freely determine their political status and pursue their economic, social, and cultural development—he has been consistent. To give concrete expression to this right, he fought for Czechoslovakia's independence from the former Soviet Union; and, despite some misgivings, also presided over the 1992 *peaceful* dissolution of Czechoslovakia and the creation of two states, the Czech Republic and Slovakia.

Havel believes that it is not enough, as the world has attempted to do since 1945, to create new international political organizations or insist that the basis of a new world order must be respect for **human rights.** Doing both, he contends in his writings and speeches, helps express the "single interconnected [world] civilization" that has been emerging. If building such organizations and a new world order is to be meaningful and successful, however, there must be another objective: the foundation must be grounded in a cultural environment that respects "the miracle of Being, the miracle of the universe and the miracle of our own existence"—an existence that is intimately bound up with and connected to the very evolution of the universe.

The right to freedom of thought, conscience, and religion is required not only to create and discover the connection and to understand the mystery of Being, but is critical to the pursuit of truth and the reclamation and preservation of the truthfulness of our diminished integrity. See also: Declaration of a Global Ethic. *Further Reading:* P. Berman, "The Philosopher King," *New York Times Magazine* (May 11, 1997); V. Havel, *Living the Truth* (1986).

HEALTH. The right to health is one of the most important human rights. Not many countries have acted to implement this right, however, and in some states it is controversial. Article 25 (1) of the **Universal Declaration of Human Rights** (UDHR) provides that "Everyone has the right to a standard of living adequate for . . . health and well-being." Article 12 of the **International Covenant on Economic, Social and Cultural Rights**, elaborates this right:

Article 12 (1). The States Parties to the present Covenant recognize the right of everyone to the enjoyment of the highest attainable standard of physical and mental health.

(2). The steps to be taken by the States . . . to achieve the full realization of this right shall include those necessary for:

a. The provision for the reduction of the stillbirth-rate and of infant mortality and for the healthy development of the child;

b. The improvement of all aspects of environmental and industrial hygiene;

c. The prevention, treatment and control of epidemic, endemic, occupational and other diseases;

d. The creation of conditions which would assure to all medical service and medical attention in the event of sickness.

Other human rights instruments, such as the **Convention on the Elimination of All Forms of Discrimination Against Women** (CEDAW) (Article 12), the Banjul Charter on Human and Peoples' Rights (Article 16), and the Convention on the Rights of the Child (CRC) (Article 24) also provide for the right to health. Emphasis on the protection of the **environment** from hazardous waste, chemical additives, and land mines as well as safe water supplies, proper inspection of food, and the impact of science and technology are linked to one's right to health. See also: African Charter on Human and People's Rights; Child, Rights of; Declaration on the Use of Scientific and Technological Progress in the Interest of Peace and for the Benefit of Mankind. *Further Reading:* L. O. Gostin, *Human Rights and Public Health in the AIDS Pandemic* (1997); B. S. Levy and V. W. Sidel, *War and Public Health* (1996); E. I. Pavolon, *Human Rights and Health Care Law* (1980); A. E. Yamin, "Defining Questions: Situating Issues of Power in the Formation of a Right to Health Under International Law," *HRQ*, vol. 18 no. 2 (1996).

HELSINKI ACCORDS. This is the name given to a diplomatic agreement that was signed in Helsinki, Finland, at the conclusion of the Conference on Security and Co-operation in Europe (CSCE), which lasted from 1973 to 1975. The agreement, sometimes called the Helsinki Final Act, had as its purpose the creation of stability and peace in Europe between the then East–West Cold War blocs. On January 1, 1995, CSCE was transformed from a series of conferences to a permanent institutional arrangement called the **Organization for Security and Co-operation in Europe** (OSCE).

The **human rights** component of the Helsinki Accords is made up of ten Guiding Principles, often called the Decalogue. Principle VII of the Decalogue is entitled "Respect for Human Rights and Fundamental Freedoms, Including Freedom of Thought, Conscience, and Religion or Belief." A section of the accords, "Human Contact," calls for meetings on the basis of **family** ties and travel for personal and professional reasons. These provided-for contacts were seen as "an important element in the strengthening of friendly relations and trust among peoples." The human rights concept and provisions converged to form what is now called the "human dimension" focus of OSCE. On January 15, 1989, the **Human Dimension (Mechanism)** was created to supervise the human dimension (human rights) focus of OSCE.

When the Helsinki Accords were initially agreed to by some thirty-five participating countries, including **Canada** and the **United States**, little hope was held out for affirmative results in the human rights field. Many in the West, including the United States and the **United Kingdom**, felt that the Eastern bloc had "won" the bargaining, and pointed to the fact that the accords had ratified the existing borders of Europe, some of which (those parts of the USSR that covered Estonia, Latvia, and Lithuania, for example) were illegal. Leaders of the former Soviet Union thought they had won also, since the agreement provided for the inviolability of frontiers and noninterference in the internal affairs of states. Although the focus has been primarily on civil and political rights, it is the human rights area that has become most important.

Among the beneficial results of the accords are increased Jewish emigration, freer movement of people in and out of Eastern Europe, granting of amnesty and release of political prisoners, and emergence of human rights groups within the former Soviet bloc. These groups are now monitoring implementation of the human rights component of the accords. Finally, it is largely due to the work of the OSCE—a product of the accords—that the international tribunal for the former Yugoslavia was created. See also: Human Rights International Helsinki Federation; War Crimes Tribunals. *Further Reading:* R. Brett, "Human Rights and the OSCE," *HRQ*, vol. 18 no. 3 (1996); Organization for Security and Co-operation in Europe: Budapest Summit Declaration on Genuine Partnership in a New Era, *ILM*, vol. 33 no. 3 (1995); A. Rotfeld, ed., *From Helsinki to Helsinki and Beyond* (1996).

HELSINKI WATCH. See INTERNATIONAL HELSINKI FEDERATION.

HIGH COMMISSIONER. See OFFICE OF HIGH COMMISSIONER FOR HUMAN RIGHTS.

HINDUISM. See RELIGION AND HUMAN RIGHTS.

HOLY SEE. The term refers to the Vatican city-state, located in central Rome with an area of about 108 acres. The area defining this state is also the site of the central administration of the Catholic Church, the largest Christian denomination numbering about 1 billion people. The Vatican city-state and the administrators of the Catholic Church have a population of about 1,000 people and are headed by the Pope, who exercises both spiritual and secular authority over Vatican City. The Holy See has elected not to be a member of the UN, although it has observer status, because it seeks to maintain its independence from the partisan compromises it sometimes finds so prevalent in the UN. Through the Papal secretary of state, however, Vatican City maintains extensive diplomatic relations with over 100 countries. It has been notably involved in a number of areas of human rights, especially since the papacy of the former Polish cardinal, Karol Wojtyla (1920–) who became John Paul II in 1978.

In **Poland,** for example, the Holy See supported Solidarity, a Polish trade union movement that sought **self-determination** for Poland against the Soviet Union and **civil and political rights** against the Communist Party of Poland. It also supports the people of **East Timor** against Indonesia and the Palestinians against **Israel.** In 1993, it was one of the few voices raised in accusing the Sudanese government of committing genocide against Christians in Sudan; it has used Papal visits (in Nicaragua and **Chile** in 1983 and 1987, for example) to win relaxation of curbs on civil and political rights. A similar visit to Cuba in January 1998, was preceded by improved religious freedom in that country. While celebrating new respect for civil and political rights, which it contributed to bringing about in Eastern Europe and the former Soviet Union, the Holy See is troubled by the decline of **economic, social and cultural rights** in those areas; it is also reluctant to criticize **Cuba,** as some do in the West, especially in the **United States,** because it sees Cuba as attending to the economic, social, and cultural categories of human rights. The Vatican, however, seems inconsistent in not supporting many of the initiatives of liberation theologians, who seek a socioeconomic transformation of society, especially in Latin America, to improve the condition of the poor.

One of the areas in which the Holy See's actions are most controversial is its position taken at the September 1994 Conference on Population and Development, held in Cairo, Egypt. There, a position backed by the United States sought to recognize women as having the right to contraception and safe, legal, and accessible abortions. The right was seen as part of the norm of equality—political and marital. The Holy See, however, took the position that the Church stands opposed to the "imposition of limits on family size and the promotion of methods of limiting births which separate the unitive and procreative dimensions of marital intercourse, which is contrary to the moral law." To support that opposition, the Vatican used its immense moral clout to forge a coalition with Latin American countries, Islamic states, such as Iran and Saudi Arabia, and a number of others to win the day in an explicit statement that "in no case should abortion be promoted as a method of family planning." See also: Liberation Theology. *Further Reading:* John Paul II, "Address of Pope John Paul II," in *Taking Sides: Clashing Views on Controversial Issues in World Politics*, ed. John Rouke (1995); John Paul II, *The Holy See at the Service of Peace* (1988).

HOMOSEXUALITY. See LESBIAN AND GAY RIGHTS.

HOUSING. Among the rights recognized by the **Universal Declaration of Human Rights** (UDHR) is the right of all people to housing. Article 25 of the declaration includes it as part of an overall right to a decent standard of living adequate for health that includes "food, clothing, housing and medical care." Article 11 of the **International Covenant on Economic, Social and Cultural Rights** also provides for this right. Few governments, except those that publicly consider themselves socialist in political orientation, assert this right in public.

Homelessness is, of course, a problem throughout the world, and it is present in societies that are materially affluent. Much of the problem has to do with complex sets of issues such as the right to own land, security of tenure, building codes, credit facilities, education, poverty, and even government neglect. All these problems have to be addressed if the right to housing is to be realized. See also: Declaration on the Right to Development; Standard of Living. *Further Reading:* D. Cowan, *Homelessness* (1997); P. Hunt, *Reclaiming Social Rights* (1996).

HUMAN DIMENSION (MECHANISM). One of the weaknesses of the **Helsinki Accords** is that it failed to provide any means by which the human dimension (human rights) features of the agreement could be monitored and implemented. In 1989, however, at one of the meetings of the former Conference on Security and Co-operation in Europe (CSCE) (now the Organization for Security and Co-operation in Europe, OSCE), an implementation process was created.

Known as the Human Rights Dimension Mechanism (or the Vienna Mechanism), the process provides a defined means by which issues of human rights and fundamental freedoms could be raised and addressed. There are four steps in the process: (1) exchanging information and/or response to claims on questions of human rights; (2) holding bilateral meetings, on request, between participating (accused and accusing states, for example) to examine both *situations* and specific *cases* relating to human rights issues. The objective, at this stage, is to resolve, if possible, whatever problems there may be; (3) allowing states to bring situations and cases, including those in the preceding two stages, to the attention of *other* participating countries, and if the issues are not resolved, they may be raised and action taken at step 4; (4) a future meeting of the OSCE.

A review of the four steps discloses that the procedures for implementation of the human rights standards, as defined in the human dimension focus of the Helsinki process, have no impartial third-party institution. States, both complaining and respondent, are left to deal with matters in the traditional modes or processes of diplomacy. In such a process, a state's need to preserve "good" inter-state relations may supersede its concerns about human rights abuse. This weakness is understood by members of the OSCE, but they have been able to address it only partially, through what has come to be called the Moscow Mechanism, a supplement to the Vienna Mechanism.

Adopted in 1991, the Moscow Human Dimension Mechanism adds the procedure of an on-site investigation by independent experts to the implementation process. With this additional procedure, a participating country can invite a mission of experts into its borders, or it can be requested by another country that has employed stage one or two to invite such a mission. If the country to which the request is directed does not act, or if the requesting state is persuaded that the issue remains unresolved, a mission of experts can be sent for an on-site investigation, without first receiving the consent of the state to be visited. *Further Reading:* R. Brett, "Human Rights and the OSCE," *HRQ,* vol. 18 no. 3 (1996); text of the Vienna Human Dimension Mechanism, *ILM,* vol. 28 no. 2 (1989).

HUMAN RIGHTS. Human Rights is an international term that refers to certain moral and legal entitlements, which all human beings are said to have. These rights differ from others that individuals have been recognized to have throughout human history. For example, people have rights by virtue of membership in a state—citizenship; others have rights because of their membership in social classes, religious communities, labor unions, political parties, blood lineage, and racial, gender, or linguistic groups. In the case of human rights, the only membership the individual needs is that of the human family. By virtue of membership in the human family, one is said to have rights that are *inherent,* that is to say, rights that are an inseparable part of what it is to be truly human.

The rights to which every human being is entitled include **civil and political** rights such as the right to life, liberty, security of person, equality before the law, and privacy, **thought, conscience and religion,** and nationality, and freedom of movement and residence. They also include **economic, social and cultural rights**, including the right to food, housing, health care, employment, education, and participation in the cultural life of the community.

The history of human rights is long and goes as far back in human history as the reign of Amenhotep IV of Egypt (1380–1362 B.C.E.), and its expression is found in every culture. The modern emphasis on human rights and its growth into a powerful contemporary movement is largely due to revolutionary doctrines that sponsored political and moral changes in the West, especially during the eighteenth, nineteenth, and twentieth centuries. The American (1776) and French (1789) revolutions were particularly influential; so, too, was the Russian Revolution (1917), which gave much impetus to **economic, social and cultural rights**, unlike the American and French, which gave greater emphasis to **civil and political rights**. Also influential in the human rights movement was the wholesale violation of human rights during World War II, culminating in **genocide** against the Jews. After the war, those political leaders who participated in organizing the post–World War II international order sought to establish international standards that would give recognition to rights that were formerly linked only in varying rudimentary degrees in national laws and constitutions. They did more: they made the promotion and protection of human rights and fundamental freedoms one of the purposes as well as one of the founding principles of the United Nations. Today, the idea that protection of human rights knows no international boundaries and that the international community has an obligation to ensure that governments guarantee and protect human rights has gained widespread acceptance and has excited the imagination of people everywhere about their possibilities.

International activities in the field of human rights promotion and protection have been mainly carried on, since 1945, within the United Nations, primarily through the **Economic and Social Council** (ECOSOC) and the **General Assembly**. Activities include (1) setting and enunciating common standards such as those contained in the **Universal Declaration of Human Rights** (UDHR); (2) adopting multilateral treaties that refine those standards and offer enforceable guarantees of the norms of human rights; (3) developing means by which information and assistance can be provided to states' and nonstate entities; and (4) nurturing mechanisms to help enforce those norms. On a regional level, the **European** and **American Conventions on Human Rights**, the **African Charter on Human and Peoples' Rights**, and the **Helsinki Accords** play important roles—especially in the case of the European Convention—in advancing the cause of human rights.

HUMAN RIGHTS AND PEACE. See DECLARATION ON THE RIGHT OF PEOPLES TO PEACE.

HUMAN RIGHTS AND YOUTH. Part of the emphasis of the UN's human rights program has been specifically directed at young people for three major reasons. First, according to the 1965 Declaration on the Promotion among Youth of the Ideals of Peace, Mutual Respect and Understanding between Peoples, they "have had to suffer" and "have had the greatest number of victims" in the "conflagrations which have affected [hu]mankind." Second, the conflagrations and dominant modes by which they have been fought have been due overwhelmingly to a lack of respect for human rights and fundamental freedoms. Third, a better future for humankind can only be assured by respect for those rights and freedoms, and a culture of respect can come about only through the young. See also: Child, Rights of; Declaration on the Promotion Among Youth of the Ideals of Peace, Mutual Respect and Understanding Among Nations.

HUMAN RIGHTS COMMISSIONS (REGIONAL). In addition to the United Nations **Commission on Human Rights** (CHR), there are three other international human rights commissions. Each is regional in scope: the African Commission on Human and Peoples' Rights, the European Commission on Human Rights, and the Inter-American Commission on Human Rights. All are charged with the responsibility of monitoring and helping to implement the human rights standards provided by their respective regional human rights instruments.

The African Commission on Human and Peoples' Rights, the youngest of the regional commissions, was created in 1981 by the **African Charter on Human and Peoples' Rights**. It has the responsibility to "ensure the protection" of **human rights**, through cooperation with African and other international institutions with similar concerns; to formulate principles and rules aimed at solving problems relating to human rights; and to undertake studies and research, organize seminars, symposia, and conferences, as well as offering views and recommendations to governments. In addition, the African Commission has the responsibility to interpret *all* provisions of the African Charter at the request of member states, the **Organization of African Unity** (OAU), and to "perform any other tasks entrusted to it by the Assembly," the supreme organ of the OAU.

Complaints to the commission may be brought by states that are parties to the charter or by other entities such as individuals and **nongovernmental organizations** (NGOs). In the case of states, if a state has grounds that another signatory to the African Charter has violated the charter's terms, it may, by written communication, bring the alleged breach to the attention of the claimed violator, with copies to the secretary-general of the OAU and the African Commission. If, within three months of the communicated violation, no satisfactory resolution is reached between the complaining and the complained-about state, then either may refer the issue to the commission. Alternatively, a state may elect to submit a charge directly to the commission, providing that local remedies have been exhausted or are likely to cause undue delay. Communications from other entities can be considered, if a simple majority of the commission is in favor of so doing.

Unlike the other regional commissions, the African Commission does not have the help of a court of human rights, because African states have argued that a court system would be too adversarial. They claim to prefer mediation and conciliation to the area of human rights. So the commission must decide cases and depend on the OAU's Assembly to support its decisions.

The European Commission, a creation of the **Council of Europe**, was established in 1955, in accordance with Article 19 of the **European Convention on Human Rights**. Its responsibility, along with the **European Court of Human Rights**, is to "ensure the observance" of the commitments undertaken by states that are parties to the European Convention.

The process by which the European Commission discharges its responsibility is as follows: any state that is a party to the European Convention may refer alleged breaches of the convention to the European Commission. In addition, under Article 25 of the convention, the commission may receive petitions from individuals, groups of individuals, and **nongovernmental organizations** "claiming to be the victim of violation . . . of one of the rights set forth in the Convention." Unlike complaints brought by one state against another, the petitions of individuals or groups of individuals can be received by the commission only if the state against which the alleged breach is being made agrees that the commission may receive such petitions. If the commission finds that a petition is admissible—that is, if it is not abusive of the right to petition, is well founded, and has exhausted local remedies—it has the authority to conduct hearings and investigations and to try, as in all cases before it, to find a friendly settlement.

If a friendly settlement cannot be arrived at, the commission prepares a detailed report that it gives to the concerned parties and the **Committee of Ministers of the Council of Europe**. The commission may also refer the problem to the European Court of Human Rights. In cases in which the commission has neither reached a settlement, forwarded a report to the Committee of Ministers, nor referred the problem to the European Court of Human Rights, the Council of Europe is left with the obligation to determine whether a breach of obligation under the convention has taken place, and, if so, what penalty is to be assessed. The most severe penalty in such cases is expulsion from the Council of Europe.

The Inter-American Commission is an organ of the **Organization of American States** (OAS). It was established in 1959, and in 1965 it was given powers to examine complaints from individuals under the **American Declaration of the Rights and Duties of Man** (ADRDM). Today, it functions primarily under the **American Convention on Human Rights**, which entered into force in 1978. Under that convention, the Inter-American Commission's principal purpose is to "promote respect for and defense of human rights." In pursuit of that purpose, it has responsibility to "exercise . . . the following functions and powers":

1. to develop an awareness of human rights among the people of the Americas;
2. to make recommendations to the governments of member states on progressive measures that may further observance of those rights;
3. to prepare studies and reports it deems advisable;
4. to request member states to supply it with information on measures they have adopted in matters of human rights;
5. to respond to enquires from member states and provide them, where possible, with advisory services;
6. to take action on petitions and other communications under the terms of the convention; and
7. to submit annual reports to the OAS.

With respect to point "6," the commission is authorized, under Article 45, to receive and examine communications from any signatory state alleging that another signatory state has committed a violation under the convention. The receipt of such a communication, however, is conditioned on the acceptance by both states of the commission's competence to receive it. Petitions from individuals or groups of individuals, or nongovernmental organizations legally recognized in any one or more member states, however, can be received by the commission without the consent of states. Such petitions of course, must describe alleged violations of the convention by a signatory state.

If the commission finds the communications or petitions admissable, it can then begin its investigation (including gathering information from the alleged wrongdoer) to determine whether grounds exist for the communications or petitions. If such grounds exist, it seeks to determine that fact and find a friendly settlement. If a settlement is reached, the commission prepares a report that it forwards to the states and the secretary-general of the OAS; if no such settlement is arrived at, the commission also prepares a report, that is transmitted confidentially to the state concerned. If the issue is not settled within three months, or if neither the states concerned nor the commission have taken the matter to the **Inter-American Court of Human Rights**—a course of action each has the right to take—the commission may further act as follows: it may, by an absolute majority of its members, set out the conclusions and opinions and make recommendations, along with a stipulated time for the state to take measures to remedy the problem brought before it. If those measures are not taken, it may publish its report by the vote of an absolute majority of its members. *Further Reading:* T. Farer, "The Rise of the Inter-American Human Rights Regime," *HRQ,* vol. 19 no. 3 (1997); D. Kinley, *The European Convention on Human Rights* (1993); C. E. Welch, "The African Commission on Human and Peoples' Rights," *HRQ*, vol. 14 no. 1 (1992).

HUMAN RIGHTS COMMITTEE. This committee was established as provided by Article 28 of the **International Covenant on Civil and Political Rights** (ICCPR). Under Article 3, each signatory state undertakes "to ensure the equal rights of men and women to the enjoyment of all the civil and political rights" recognized in the covenant. The Human Rights Committee's responsibility is to monitor Article 3 and ensure that it is honored by signatory states.

To discharge its responsibility, the committee is required to engage in three fundamental areas: (1) to consider reports of signatory states indicating the legislative and other measures they have adopted or plan to adopt to fulfill their pledges concerning human rights; (2) to examine and consider complaints of signatory states against other signatory states; and (3) to consider communications from individuals who are victims of human rights abuse.

The powers of the committee to pursue its defined functions are severely limited, however. Many states, claiming sovereign status, will not allow the committee to disclose its findings on any complaint, without their consent. Rules of confidentiality not only prevent embarrassing disclosures of states' conduct, but very often allows abusers of **human rights** to exhibit the appearance of compliant members of the international community. Even the competence of the committee to receive and consider complaints must be consented to by states. And in cases of individual communications, which are permitted against countries that sign the Optional Protocol to the Covenant, the committee merely engages in "confidential" exchanges with the states against which the communication is directed. It has no power to resolve the problem, it can only "forward its views" to the alleged wrongdoer. See also: Human Rights Commissions. *Further Reading:* S. Cohen, "Government Response to Human Rights Reports," *HRQ*, vol. 18 no. 3 (1996); Human Rights Committee, *Selected Decisions Under the Optional Protocol* (1989); M. O'Flaherty, *Human Rights and the UN: Practice Before Treaty Bodies* (1996); United Nations, *Manual on Human Rights Reporting* (1991).

HUMAN RIGHTS DAY. December 10, 1948, is the day on which the first part of the **International Bill of Human Rights, the Universal Declaration of Human Rights** (UDHR), was adopted by the United Nations **General Assembly.** On December 4, 1950, the General Assembly invited states to adopt December 10 of each year as Human Rights Day—a day of observance, celebration, and collective recommitment of the global community to the concept of **human rights** and specific criteria embraced by the Universal Declaration of Human Rights. Since 1950, therefore, December 10 is celebrated as Human Rights Day.

Programs of celebration throughout the world include meditation on the touchstones of the declaration, teach-ins at universities, colleges, high schools and similar institutions, special proclamations by state and local governments, and sharing experiences among groups that have had their lives changed by the declaration.

HUMAN RIGHTS WATCH. This is a **nongovernmental organization** (NGO) that was founded in 1978 as Helsinki Watch (now Human Rights Watch/Helsinki). It was established in response to urgent calls for help from embattled local groups in Moscow, Prague, and Warsaw that had been organized to monitor the compliance of governments in the Soviet Union and Eastern Europe with the human rights pledges of the **Helsinki Accords.** Today, Human Rights Watch (HRW) monitors and promotes the observance of **human rights** in Africa, the Americas, Asia, the Middle East, and among the signatories to the Helsinki Accords. It has come to be recognized internationally as one of the most effective nongovernmental organizations in the field of human rights. A sample of its activities includes complaints against **forced labor**, torture, and arbitrary arrest in **Burma;** efforts to protect evidence of **genocide** in **Rwanda;** actions to help refugees from the former Yugoslavia return to their homes; and exposure of racial discrimination in the criminal justice system in the **United States.** Its publications include the influential *Human Rights Watch and World Report.* See also: International Helsinki Federation. *Further Information:* Human Rights Watch, 485 Fifth Avenue, New York, N.Y. 10017–1604. Tel.: 212–972–8400.

HUNGER AND MALNUTRITION. See UNIVERSAL DECLARATION ON THE ERADICATION OF HUNGER AND MALNUTRITION.

I ────────────────────────────────

INDIA. The Republic of India is a country located in south Asia, sharing borders with Bhutan, **China**, and Nepal to the north, Pakistan to the west, **Bangladesh** and **Burma** to the east, and the Indian Ocean to the south. It has a population of about 970 million people and is home perhaps to the most socially and culturally complex society in the world, with seventeen official languages (and 1,500 dialects), some 2,000 ethnic groups, and five major religions—Buddhism, Christianity, Hinduism, Islam, and Zoroastrianism. Jainism, Judaism, Sikhism, and other religious faiths are also significantly represented. In addition, the country is divided socially into castes—hereditary social classes within Hinduism, whose members are rigidly restricted in social and occupational aspirations. Politically, India has faced violent secessionist movements, the most acute of which have been in the northwest, in **Kashmir**. With its predominantly Muslim population, Kashmir is clamoring for independence and has the support of Pakistan, a Muslim country.

India gained its independence in 1947 from Britain. From 1947 to 1996, it has been led almost continuously by the Congress Party of India. In 1996, the Congress Party was defeated by a coalition of other parties, including one dominated by Hindu fundamentalists that want to see India more fully Hindu in its social, cultural, and political life. Throughout its more than fifty years of independence, however, India has remained a strong democracy, protecting **civil and political rights** such as freedom of the press, religion, and thought; association; fair trail; and leaving and returning to one's country. It has also achieved some victories in the areas of discrimination and inequality. In the area of inequality, it is significant that **Mohandas Karamchand Gandhi's** ideal of a caste-free society and full social inclusion for over 150 million Dalits or "untouchables"—the lowest social caste—has recently received a boost: an untouchable, K. R. Narayanan, became president of India in July 1997. Women and other discriminated against groups have also been helped by affirmative action programs, and India's record of receiving and protecting refugees has been excellent.

India has many problems, however. Extrajudicial killings, especially in **Kashmir,** take place throughout the country, and domestic violence against women as well as unequal pay—despite its Equal Remuneration Act—is widespread. Further, "deep poverty," though decreasing as a percentage of the population, still affects over 300 million people; child labor and forced prostitution continues with little abatement; and some political violence and arbitrary detentions have been reported. The government of India has been attempting to deal with these problem areas: in 1995, for example, it worked out an agreement with the **International Committee of the Red Cross** for prison visits in Kashmir and to ensure the right of communication for detainees, especially communication with their families. See also: Bonded Labor; Child Labor. *Further Reading:* C. Jeffrelot, *The Hindu Nationalist Movement in India, 1925–1993* (1996); P. Sarbadhikari, *Reconstituting India* (1996).

INDIGENOUS PEOPLES. The expression is an international term that has come to designate persons who had been variously named aboriginals, Indians, tribal people, natives, **minorities,** earth people, first people, and even the Fourth World. While the term has found a considerable degree of contemporary acceptance, there is still controversy about the groups to which it is properly applicable, the international status such groups should enjoy, the rights accorded to that status, and the parties that should be involved in resolving controversy and protecting rights, if any, that are recognized.

There is no agreement about how many persons or groups are properly identifiable as indigenous peoples, but there are an estimated 4,500 groups in the international system, with a population ranging from 250 to 300 million people. These groups vary from the Crees of Quebec, **Canada,** the Sioux in the United States (as well as other North American Indian tribes), and the **Saami** (the Lapps) in Scandinavian countries, to the Inuit of Greenland, the Mayan of Guatemala, and the Maori of New Zealand.

In an effort to help deal more precisely with the matter of identity, the international community, though the **International Labor Organization** (ILO) and its 1989 Convention (No. 169) Concerning Indigenous and Tribal Peoples in Independent countries, offered a definition. They stated that indigenous peoples are "peoples in independent countries who are regarded as indigenous on account of their descent from the populations that inhabited the country, or a geographical region to which the country belongs, at the time of conquest or colonialization or the establishment of the present state boundaries and who . . . retain some or all of their social, cultural, and political institutions." That definition was rejected by indigenous peoples on a number of grounds: (1) it dealt with persons in independent countries, only; (2) it employed the word tribal, which many indigenous people dislike because of its implication of cultural backwardness; (3) it exhibited a bias in favor of assimilating indigenous persons into the dominant culture of existing states; (4) there was little participation of the generally recognized representatives of indigenous groups in drafting the convention; and (5) while the expression "peoples" (as distinct from merely population) was used in the convention, the rights attached to the concept, especially the right to **self-determination**, were not emphasized.

The issue of the right to **self-determination** is very important, since it carries with it the right to sovereign political independence, and since that right also implies the potential political and territorial divisions of existing states, they have been reluctant to concede it. As the international community comes to know more about indigenous peoples—especially since the 1982 establishment of the UN Working Group on Indigenous Populations and the 1993 UN International Year of the World's Indigenous People—some of the ignorance and stereotypes about native persons has been removed. No longer are such persons or groups seen as primitive, ignorant, and incapable of governing themselves, but as groups with values that are important for today's world—the devotion to future generations, an ethical respect for nature, and a commitment to community.

On August 26, 1994, the UN **Sub-Commission on Prevention of Discrimination and Protection of Minorities** adopted a UN Draft Declaration on the Rights of Indigenous Peoples, and on March 3, 1995, the United Nations **Commission on Human Rights** (CHR) voted to establish a **working group** to elaborate that draft. While still a preliminary document, the draft recognizes a number of rights for indigenous peoples.

Part I emphasizes their right to all **human rights** and fundamental freedoms, including the equal right of all peoples to self-determination. Part II deals with the right to exist as a distinct people and be free from **genocide** and other acts of violence, including the removal of children from their communities. Part III focuses on the right to cultural and spiritual integrity, and recognizes the right to maintain and revitalize traditional culture and transmit the heritage of that culture to future generations. Part IV emphasizes the right to education, information, and the right to work, while Part V deals with the right to political participation and to control the nature and pace of their development. Part VI deals with the inalienable right to own and control their lands and the resources of those lands as well as their intellectual and cultural properties. Parts VII–X deal with the right to self-government. Organizations of indigenous peoples have been participating in the elaboration of the draft. *Further Reading:* S. J. Anaya, *Indigenous Peoples in International Law* (1996); J. J. Corntassel and T. H. Primeau, "Indigenous 'Sovereignty' and International Laws," *HRQ*, vol. 17 no. 2 (1995).

INDIVIDUAL PETITION. See HUMAN RIGHTS COMMISSIONS.

INDONESIA. See EAST TIMOR.

INFORMATION. The right to know and to communicate is one of the fundamental **human rights**. It is implicit in the right to free expression, to participate in the political and cultural life of the community, and to freedom of opinion, among others. Furthermore, it is critical to the choices individuals make about work, housing, health, food, education, the environment, political leaders, policies of government, and the right to life itself.

On October 18, 1978, the United Nations **General Assembly** passed Resolution 33/115B proclaiming the need to create a fairer and more effective international information and communication order. By means of another resolution (33/115B) on the same date, the General Assembly also required the **United Nations Educational, Scientific and Cultural Organization** (UNESCO) to prepare and submit to it a report on the establishment of such an order. UNESCO, in turn, at its 1980 General Conference in Belgrade, Yugoslavia, elaborated a number of considerations on which a just and effective information and communication order could be based. After mentioning the usual principles such as freedom of the press, and freedom of journalists and professionals in the field of communications media, it focused on individuals and groups. The agreement from that conference was that such an order required respect for the right of all peoples to participate in international exchanges of information, on the basis of equality and mutual benefit, and respect for the "right of public, ethnic, and social groups and of individuals to have access to information sources and to participate actively in the communication process."

Point 7.2 of the Programme of Action of the 1994 International Conference on Population and Development in Cairo, Egypt, states that implicit in the right to health and a satisfying and freely ordered reproductive life is the "right of men and women to be informed and to have access to safe, effective, affordable methods of family planning of their choice." See also: Opinion and Expression; New World Communication and Information Order. *Further Reading:* UNESCO, *Many Voices One World* (1980); S. Coliver, ed., *The Right to Know: Human Rights and Access to Reproductive Health Information* (1995).

INKATHA. See SOUTH AFRICA.

INTER-AMERICAN CHARTER OF SOCIAL GUARANTEES. Almost twenty years before the UN adopted the **International Covenant on Economic, Social and Cultural Rights**, and almost as long before Western Europe adopted the **European Social Charter**, the American states, on May 2, 1948, adopted a Charter of Social Guarantees. The aim of the charter, according to its first article, is "to proclaim the fundamental principles that must protect workers of all kinds, and . . . [to] set forth the minimum rights they must enjoy in the American States." Articles 2–5 deal with some of these principles.

Article 2. The following principles are considered to be fundamental in all social legislations in American countries:

a. Labour is a social function; it enjoys the special protection of the States and must not be considered a commodity.

b. Every worker must have the opportunity for a decent existence and the right to fair working conditions.

c. Intellectual, as well as technical and manual labour, must enjoy the guarantees established by labour laws . . .

d. There should be equal compensation for equal work, regardless of the sex, race, creed or nationality of the worker . . .

e. The rights established in favour of workers may not be renounced . . .

Article 3. Every worker has the right to engage in his occupation and to devote himself to whatever activity suits him. He is likewise free to change employment.

Article 4. Every worker has the right to receive vocational and technical training in order to perfect his skills and knowledge . . .

Article 5. Workers have the right to share in the equitable distribution of the national well-being, by obtaining necessary food, clothing, and housing at reasonable prices.

The rest of the charter elaborates issues of wages, child labor, rest and vacation, domestic and rural workers, social security, labor courts, the right to strike, and public employees. See also: Economic, Social and Cultural Rights. *Further Reading:* F. Fabricius, *Human Rights and European Politics: The Legal and Political Status of Workers in the European Community* (1992); K. D. Ewing, C. A. Gearty, and B. A. Hepple, eds., *Human Rights and Labour Law* (1994).

INTER-AMERICAN COMMISSION OF WOMEN. This commission, now an autonomous specialized agency of the **Organization of American States** (OAS), was created in 1928 by the Sixth International Conference of American States. Over the years, it has done important work on women's rights issues, including preparing the drafts for the Inter-American Convention on the Granting of Civil Rights to Women (1948) and the Inter-American Convention on the Granting of Political Rights to Women (1948). These two conventions entered into force in 1949. The first convention provides that "The American States agree to grant to women the same civil rights that men enjoy," and the second states that "the right to vote and be elected to national office shall not be denied or abridged by reason of sex."

The experience gained through the preparatory work done for the above-mentioned conventions as well as other human rights instruments, was effectively used in the push for and the drafting of the 1952 UN **Convention on the Political Rights of Women,** the 1979 **Convention on the Elimination of All Forms of Discrimination Against Women** (CEDAW), and the 1994 **Inter-American Convention on the Prevention, Punishment and Eradication of Violence Against Women.** Among the aims of the commission are the mobilization, training, and organizing of women in the Americas for continuing effective participation in development programs and the formulation of strategies to shape new concepts about the role of women and men in society. See also: Commission on the Status of Women; World Conferences on Women.

INTER-AMERICAN COMMISSION ON HUMAN RIGHTS. See HUMAN RIGHTS COMMISSIONS.

INTER-AMERICAN CONVENTION ON THE FORCED DISAPPEARANCE OF PERSONS. As is the case in the general global community, the countries of the Americas are concerned about forced disappearances. Because the phenomenon has been most prevalent in Central America and South America, the states of the region have been prompted to go beyond the efforts of the global community in devising ways to deal with it. Hence, while the UN has adopted a *declaration* (Declaration on the Protection of All Persons from Enforced Disappearance), on the phenomenon—an instrument which, by itself, is not legally binding, the states of the Americas have adopted a legally binding instrument, a *convention*. That convention, the Inter-American Convention on the Forced Disappearance of Persons, was adopted at Belém, Brazil, on June 9, 1994. Articles 1 and 2 spell out the undertakings of states and the definition of the crime of forced disappearance.

Article 1. The States to this Convention undertake:

a. Not to practice, permit, or tolerate the forced disappearance of persons, even in a state of emergency or suspension of individual guarantees;

b. To punish within their jurisdictions those persons who commit or attempt to commit the crime of forced disappearance of persons and their accomplices and accessories;

c. To cooperate with one another in helping to prevent, punish and eliminate the forced disappearance of persons;

d. To take legislative, administrative, judicial and other measures necessary to comply with the commitments undertaken in this Convention.

Article 2. For the purpose of this Convention, forced disappearance is considered to be the act of depriving a person or persons of his or their freedom, in whatever way, perpetrated by agents of the state or by persons or groups of persons acting with the authorization, support, or acquiescence of the state, followed by an absence of information or a refusal to acknowledge, that deprivation of freedom or to give information on the whereabouts of that person, thereby impeding his or her recourse to the applicable legal remedies and procedural guarantees.

Article 4 deals with issues of jurisdiction and makes the crime of forced disappearance an offense not only within the state in whose borders it takes place but in *every* state ratifying the convention. Article 5 deals with extradition and exempts the crime of forced disappearance from "political crimes," which are not extradictable. And, as in the UN declaration, the convention requires states to establish and maintain official up-to-date registries of their detainees and allow the detainees access to relatives, attorneys, and other persons having a "legitimate interest in their cases." See also: Declaration on the Protection of All Persons from Enforced Disappearance. *Further Reading:* From the text of the Declaration on the Protection of All Persons from Enforced Disappearance, *ILM*, vol. 33 no. 6 (1994); R. Brody and F. Gonzalez, "Nunca Mas: An Analysis of International Instruments on Disappearances," *HRQ*, vol. 19 no. 2 (1997); *Report of the Working Group on Enforced or Involuntary Disappearances*, UN Doc. E/CN.4/1996/38 (1996).

INTER-AMERICAN CONVENTION ON THE GRANTING OF CIVIL RIGHTS TO WOMEN. See INTER-AMERICAN COMMISSION OF WOMEN.

INTER-AMERICAN CONVENTION ON THE GRANTING OF POLITICAL RIGHTS TO WOMEN. See INTER-AMERICAN COMMISSION OF WOMEN.

INTER-AMERICAN CONVENTION ON THE PREVENTION, PUNISHMENT AND ERADICATION OF VIOLENCE AGAINST WOMEN.
Known as the Convention of Belém Do Pará, after the city in Brazil were it was adopted on June 9, 1994, this convention is largely the product of the influence of the women's rights movement and the growing international concern about widespread violence against women. It also reflects important work done in this area by the **Inter-American Commission of Women.**

Affirming, as does the UN **Declaration on the Elimination of Violence Against Women,** that violence against women constitutes a violation of their **human rights,** the convention takes the position that the elimination of violence against women is "essential to their individual and social development and their full and equal participation in all walks of life." Articles 1 and 2 define and identify expressions of violence as follows:

Article 1. For the purposes of this Convention, violence against women shall be understood as any act or conduct, based on gender, which causes death or physical, sexual or psychological harm or suffering to women, whether in the public or the private sphere.

Article 2. Violence against women shall be understood to include physical, sexual and psychological violence:

a. that occurs within a family or domestic unit or within any other interpersonal relationship, whether or not the perpetrator shares or has shared the same residence with the woman, including among others, rape, battery and sexual abuse;

b. that occurs in the community and is perpetrated by any person, including among others, rape, sexual abuse, torture, trafficking in persons, forced prostitution, kidnapping and sexual harassment in the workplace, as well as in educational institutions, health facilities or any other place; and

c. that is perpetrated or condoned by the state or its agents regardless of where it occurs.

Articles 3–6 deal with the right of women to their physical and mental integrity and their right to be protected against violence. Articles 7–9 focus on the duties of states, including the duty to pursue "by all appropriate means and without delay" policies to prevent, punish, and eradicate violence against women. For example, education of all those involved in the administration of justice, amending or repealing of existing laws, and provisions for penalties for violence against women. Articles 10–12 deal with enforcement through the Inter-American Commission on Human Rights and the **Inter-American Court of Human Rights**. Articles 13–25 contain general provisions.

One major weakness of the convention is that, unlike the UN declaration, it does not explicitly mention **genital mutilation**. Latin America is one of the regions of the world where this form of violence against women occurs, so it is to be hoped that the definition in this convention will be construed to include that form of violence. See also: Forced Labor; Human Rights Commissions; Slavery, the Slave Trader, and Slavery-like Practices. *Further Reading:* For text of the Inter-American Convention on the Prevention, Punishment and Eradication of Violence Against Women see *ILM*, vol. 33 no. 6 (1994); J. S. Davidson, *The Inter-American Legal Rights System* (1997).

INTER-AMERICAN COURT OF HUMAN RIGHTS. Article 33 of the **American Convention on Human Rights** provides for the creation of two forums to enforce the norms and principles of that convention. They are the Inter-American Commission on Human Rights and the Inter-American Court of Human Rights. The two principal functions of the court are (1) to deal with cases involving alleged violations of **human rights** that it has been asked to adjudicate by either a signatory state to the convention or the Inter-American Commission (individual petitions are presented to the court by the Inter-American Commission), and (2) to offer advisory opinions.

The court gains jurisdiction in a case against a state when that state, either through a declaration or by a special agreement, recognizes the court's competence. If the court has jurisdiction in a case and finds that a signatory state has violated a right or freedom protected by the convention, it has the authority to "rule that the injured party be ensured the enjoyment of his [her] right or freedom that was violated." It can also rule, if appropriate, that specific measures be taken to remedy the consequences that have resulted from breaches of such a right or freedom and that "fair compensation be paid to the injured party" (Article 63.1). In circumstances of "extreme gravity and urgency," when it is "necessary to avoid irreparable damage to persons," the court may adopt provisional measures, including the granting of temporary injunctions.

With regard to advisory opinions, under Article 64 of the convention, the court has the authority to offer advice (respecting the interpretation of the convention and other human rights instruments among American states), to states, bodies, and specialized agencies of the **Organization of American States** (OAS), including the General Assembly of the OAS, the InterAmerican Commission on Human Rights, and the **Inter-American Commission of Women**. The decisions of the court are final and not subject to appeal. It is located in San Jose, Costa Rica. See also: European Court of Human Rights; Human Rights Commissions. *Further Reading:* J. S. Davidson, *The Inter-American Legal Rights System* (1997); T. Farer, "The Rise of the Inter-American Human Rights Regime," *HRQ*, vol. 19 no. 3 (1997).

INTER-AMERICAN DECLARATION ON RACIAL INTEGRATION IN THE AMERICAS. While the UN and other international entities were dealing in the 1960s with matters of racial *discrimination*, the American states at the 1965 Second Special Inter-American Conference, held in Rio de Janeiro, Brazil, adopted a policy on racial *integration*. Views on this course of action vary, but some claim that the emphasis on integration is an attempt to mask, especially in Latin America, the scope of discrimination that traditionally has taken place in the Americas. The idea of "complete integration of all elements of their citizenry" appears to imply cultural assimilation contrary to the rights of racial minorities, who would prefer not to be assimilated. And, especially in the case of indigenous peoples, some of whom are a numerical majority in a country like Guatemala, they have an internationally recognized right to cultural autonomy.

The declaration, adopted on November 30, 1965, reads as follows:

The Second Special Inter-American Conference Declares:

1. That racial discrimination is deeply contrary to the sense of justice of the peoples of the Americas.

2. That it reiterates that the democratic concept of the state, a basic principle on which the conduct of nations and of the hemisphere is based, must guarantee to all individuals, without regard to race, decent living conditions, access to

culture and employment, and opportunities for the pursuit of their legitimate activities.

3. That it reaffirms the goal of all governments to develop a policy tending toward complete integration of all elements of their citizenry, without distinction of any nature based on racial origin.

See also: Discrimination; International Convention on the Elimination of All Forms of Racial Discrimination; Minorities. *Further Reading:* M. Banton, *International Action Against Racial Discrimination* (1996); A. Sarat, *Race, Law and Culture* (1997).

INTERNATIONAL BILL OF HUMAN RIGHTS. The International Bill of Human Rights is a collective term that is used internationally to denote four international human rights instruments. Together, they form the core of the universally recognized rights that human beings enjoy: the **Universal Declaration of Human Rights** (UDHR), the **International Covenant on Economic, Social and Cultural Rights**, the **International Covenant on Civil and Political Rights** (ICCPR), and the Optional Protocol to the International Covenant on Civil and Political Rights. The last instrument, often implied in the ICCPR, is not often specifically cited, and therefore, in some cases, references are made to three rather than four instruments. See also: International Covenants on Human Rights. *Further Reading:* P. Sieghart, *The Lawful Rights of Mankind* (1985); L. Henkin, ed., *The International Bill of Rights: The Convenant on Civil and Political Rights* (1981).

INTERNATIONAL CAMPAIGN TO BAN LAND MINES. See LAND MINES.

INTERNATIONAL CATHOLIC CHILD BUREAU. An international **nongovernmental organization** (NGO) that was founded in 1948 to nurture the holistic growth of children, the International Catholic Child Bureau (ICCB) gives paramount attention to the most deprived, and disabled child victims of the street, drugs, war, and sex trade. The ICBB played an important role in helping shape the 1989 Convention on the Rights of the Child (CRC), and has associative status with the United Nations **Economic and Social Council** (ECOSOC), the **United Nations Children's Fund** (UNICEF), and the **United Nations Educational, Scientific and Cultural Organization** (UNESCO).

Its publications include *Surviving Violence: A Recovery Program for Children and Families* (1995), *Street Children: Problems or Persons?* (1995) and its newsletter, *ICCB News*. See also: Child, Rights of. *Further Information:* International Catholic Child Bureau: 63 rue de Laussanne, CH-1202, Geneva, Switzerland, Tel.: 011–41–22–731–3248.

INTERNATIONAL COMMITTEE OF THE RED CROSS. An international **nongovernmental organization** (NGO) with more than 250 million individual members and over 150 affiliated national groups, the International Committee of the Red Cross (ICRC) has consultative status with the United Nations **Economic and Social Council** (ECOSOC) and is perhaps the most internationally influential group of its kind.

The organization, which had its birth in 1863, came out of the Red Cross Movement that began with the initiative of a Swiss citizen, Henri Dunant, who had organized relief efforts for the wounded in the battle of Solferino in 1859—one of the important battles in the war of Italian unification). Since its founding, the ICRC has devoted itself to three major goals: (1) encouraging the formation of national Red Cross Societies; (2) insuring that victims (whether civilians or soldiers), in times of national and international armed conflicts, receive protection and humanitarian assistance; and (3) influencing the content, application, and development of international humanitarian law.

Today the Red Cross Movement falls into three groups: the ICRC; the National Red Cross societies; and the League of Red Cross Societies, which is a federation of all national societies. A national society becomes affiliated only after it has been recognized by the ICRC, but thereafter operates independently within its national borders. National societies work outside their borders when they participate in relief activities organized by the League of Red Cross Societies. The ICRC, which is composed exclusively of Swiss citizens, always operates internationally and maintains an international reputation for strict impartiality in matters of politics, ideology, religion, or cultural orientation. Their reputation for impartiality has enabled the ICRC, for over a century and a half, to intervene in national and international armed conflicts, intervention made all the more remarkable because of the jealously with which states guard their sovereignty.

In recent years, the ICRC has become involved with political prisoners and forced disappearances. One of its subsidiary organs, the Central Tracing Agency, performs an important service in establishing the whereabouts of persons missing as a result of war or disappearances. It received the Nobel Peace Prize for humanitarian service in 1917, 1944, and 1963. See also: Geneva Conventions. *Further Reading:* D. P. Forsythe, *Humanitarian Politics: The International Committee of the Red Cross* (1977); J. F. Hutchinson, *Champions of Charity: War and the Rise of the Red Cross* (1996); *Further Information:* International Committee of the Red Cross: 17 Avenue de la Paix, CH-1202, Geneva, Switzerland, Tel.: 011–41–22–34–6001.

INTERNATIONAL CONFERENCE ON HUMAN RIGHTS. See PROCLAMATION OF TEHERAN.

INTERNATIONAL CONVENTION ON THE ELIMINATION OF ALL FORMS OF RACIAL DISCRIMINATION. This convention, which was adopted by the United Nations **General Assembly** on December 21, 1965, was inspired by many factors, among them (1) a conviction that doctrines of superiority based on racial differentiation is scientifically false, morally condemnable, and socially unjust; (2) that such doctrines had played a major role in the genocidal actions against Jews and others during World War II; (3) that the existence of racial barriers is repugnant to the ideals of human society, as expressed in human rights instruments; and (4) that manifestations of racial discrimination are still evident in many areas of the world, threatening international peace and security.

The convention, which entered into force in 1969, defines racial discrimination, specifies actions states should take to eliminate it, and provides a mechanism to monitor its terms. In the matter of definition Article 1(1) provides that

In this Convention, the term "racial discrimination" shall mean any distinction, exclusion, restriction or preference based on race, colour, descent, or national or ethnic origin which has the purpose or effect of nullifying or impairing the recognition, enjoyment or exercise, on an equal footing, of human rights and fundamental freedoms in the political, economic, social, cultural or any other field of public life.

Restrictions or preferences made by states between citizens and noncitizens are not affected by the above definition. Neither are special measures taken by states for the *sole* purpose of enabling individuals or groups to have equal enjoyment or exercise of their **human rights**. States specifically undertake to condemn racial discrimination and adopt legislative and other measures to eliminate it. And, in an area that has become particularly controversial in the United States, because it is said to violate that country's Constitution, Article 4 of the convention requires states to declare that "all dissemination of ideas based on racial superiority and hatred" are an "offense punishable by law." Article 4 also requires states to "declare illegal and prohibit" organizations that promote and incite racial discrimination.

The convention, under Article 8, creates a **Committee on the Elimination of Racial Discrimination** to monitor its terms. See also: Propaganda; Racism. *Further Reading:* M. Banton, *International Action Against Racial Discrimination* (1996); A. Sarat, *Race, Law and Culture* (1997); B. Hepple and E. M. Szyszczak, eds., *Discrimination: The Limits of the Law* (1992).

INTERNATIONAL CONVENTION ON THE PROTECTION OF THE RIGHTS OF ALL MIGRANT WORKERS AND MEMBERS OF THEIR FAMILIES. The adoption of this convention by the United Nation **General Assembly** on February 25, 1991, was influenced by several considerations, among which were (1) the importance and extent of the migration phenomenon in the international community; (2) the vulnerability of migrant workers and their families to exploitation and other abuses; (3), the emerging clandestine movement in the trafficking of migrant workers and the insufficient protection of their rights; and (4) the need to harmonize international standards by which such workers are treated.

Part I of the convention, covering Articles 1–6, deals with the definition of migrant workers. According to Article 1, they are persons and their families who are or have been "engaged in a remunerative activity in a state" of which they are not nationals. Article 2 then elaborates the scope of the definition by identifying categories of workers that fall within its embrace: frontier workers, seasonal workers, seafarers, workers on offshore installations, itinerant workers and project-tied workers, among others. Article 3 focuses on excluding from the definition of migrant workers, persons such as those sent abroad to work on behalf of national governments and international organizations. Article 4 defines "members of their families" as those "persons married to migrant workers or having with them a relationship that, according to applicable law, produces effects equivalent to marriage, as well as children and other dependent persons." Articles 5 and 6 deal with issues of documentation, such as that determining migrant workers' country of origin and country of destination.

Part II of the convention prohibits states from discriminating against migrant workers; Part III, which covers Articles 8–35, elaborates their **civil and political rights** and their **economic, social and cultural rights**. These rights include the right to life; freedom of movement; privacy; property; liberty and security of person; **thought, conscience and religion;** organize and bargain collectively; not subject to torture, cruel, or inhuman treatment or punishment; and the right against collective expulsion. Migrant workers also have the right to be treated on a par with citizens in their right to social security, access to courts, and health care. Finally, they have a right to travel documents, access to consular and diplomatic authorities, education, and cultural identity. Parts IV, V, and VI, which cover articles 36–78, deal with the right of migrant workers to education, vocational training, housing, social services, humane and equitable treatment, and the establishment of a Committee on the Protection of the Rights of Migrant Workers and Members of Their Families to monitor the rights provided by the convention. *Further Reading:* International Convention on the Protection of the Right of All Migrant Workers and Members of Their Families, *ILM*, vol. 30 no. 6 (1991); S. S. Juss, *Immigration, Nationality, and Citizenship* (1994); R. Miles and D. Thranhardt, eds., *Migration and European Integration: The Dynamics of Inclusion and Exclusion* (1995).

INTERNATIONAL CONVENTION ON THE SUPPRESSION AND PUNISHMENT OF THE CRIME OF APARTHEID. Troubled by the racial discrimination that resides at the root of **apartheid**, concerned by the many similarities between some of the practices under apartheid and the crime of **genocide,** and alarmed by what appeared in the late 1960s and early 1970s as an emerging expansion of apartheid from **South Africa** into Namibia and Zimbabwe, the United Nations **General Assembly** adopted this convention on November 30, 1973. The convention, which entered into force on July 18, 1976, declares in Article I that apartheid is a **crime against humanity**; it also makes criminal "those organizations, institutions and individuals committing the crime of Apartheid."

Article II defines and applies the crime of apartheid to "the following inhuman acts committed for the purpose of establishing and maintaining domination by one racial group of persons over any other racial group of persons and systematically oppressing them:

a. Denial to a member or members of a racial group or groups of the right to life and liberty of person:

  i. By murder of members of a racial group or groups;

  ii. By infliction upon members of a racial group or groups of serious bodily injury or mental harm . . . or subjecting them to torture or cruel, inhuman or degrading treatment or punishment;

  iii. By arbitrary arrest and illegal imprisonment of members of the racial group or groups;

b. Deliberate imposition on a racial group or groups of living conditions calculated to cause its or their physical destruction in whole or in part;

c. Any legislative measures and other measures calculated to prevent a racial group or groups from participation in the political, social, economic and cultural life of the country . . . ;

d. Any measure, including legislative measures, designed to divide the population along racial lines by the creation of separate reserves and ghettos for the members of a racial group or groups, the prohibition of mixed marriages among members of various racial groups . . . ;

e. Exploitation of the labour of the members of a racial group or groups, in particular by submitting them to forced labour;

f. Persecution of organizations and persons, by depriving them of fundamental rights and freedoms, because they oppose *apartheid*.

In Article IV, states undertake to adopt legislative and other measures necessary to suppress as well as prevent any encouragement of the crime of apartheid. They also undertake to adopt legislative, judicial, and administrative measures to prosecute, bring to trial and punish persons responsible for or accused of the acts defined in Article II. See also: *Discrimination*; Mandela, Nelson; Racism; South Africa. *Further Reading*: International Convention on the Suppression and Punishment of the Crime of Apartheid, *ILM*, vol. 13 no. 8 (1974); M. Benton, *International Action Against Racial Discrimination* (1996).

INTERNATIONAL COURT OF JUSTICE. This is the name given to the supreme judicial body of the United Nations and one of that world organization's six principal organs. It is located in The Hague, Holland, and has competence or legal authority to hear any case brought to it by states parties to a dispute that have accepted its jurisdiction. The International Court of Justice (ICJ) may also render advisory opinions on any legal matter referred to it by states, other principal organs of the UN, and by most of the UN's specialized agencies. To reach a decision, the court applies treaties, international customs, general principles of law, judicial decisions, and the teachings of qualified writers in the field of international law. The court may also make decisions *ex aequo et bono*—according to what is just and fair, rather than the international law. The ICJ, also called the World Court, has fifteen judges, and decisions are made by a majority vote, which cannot be appealed.

Because only states or international organizations whose members are states can bring cases before the ICJ, it has not been very involved in matters of **human rights**. States, which are the principal violators of human rights, are not likely to accuse themselves, and are reluctant to accuse others, if that accusation entails actual legal action before a court. Proposals have been made, therefore, to reform the ICJ, so that it gains jurisdiction to adjudicate problems brought by nonstate groups and individuals. See also: Adjudication; International Criminal Court; War Crimes Tribunals. *Further Reading:* S. Rosenne, *The World Court and How It Works* (1994); L. F. Domrosch, ed., *International Court of Justice at the Crossroads* (1987).

INTERNATIONAL COVENANT ON CIVIL AND POLITICAL RIGHTS. This covenant is one of the four instruments that form the **International Bill of Human Rights**. It is paired with the fourth of these instruments, the Optional Protocol to the International Covenant on Civil and Political Rights.

The International Covenant on Civil and Political Rights (ICCPR), which was adopted by the United Nations **General Assembly** on December 16, 1966, and entered into force on March 23, 1976, defines the **civil and political rights** to which all persons are entitled. It also specifies the permissible limitations that, under certain conditions, may be placed on the enjoyment of those rights. For example, scattered throughout the covenant are provisions (Articles 12, 14, 22) that the exercise of the rights recognized are subject to restrictions provided by law to protect the rights of others, national security, public order, and public health. Further, it provides for the establishment of a **Human Rights Committee**, which is authorized to monitor the compliance of signatories to the covenant and receive complaints from signatory states against others. The Optional Protocol authorizes the committee to deal with complaints from individuals who are victims of human rights abuse. *Further Reading:* M. O'Flaherty, *Human Rights and the UN: Practice Before Treaty Bodies* (1996); L. Henkin, ed., *The International Bill of Rights: The Covenant on Civil and Political Rights* (1981).

INTERNATIONAL COVENANT ON ECONOMIC, SOCIAL AND CULTURAL RIGHTS. This covenant is the second of the four human rights instruments that compose the **International Bill of Human Rights.** It was adopted by the United Nations **General Assembly** on December 16, 1966, and entered into force on January 3, 1976.

Among the factors that prompted its creation and adoption was the international recognition, as stated in its preamble that the "ideals of human beings enjoying freedom from fear and want can only be achieved if conditions are created whereby everyone may enjoy his [her] economic, social and cultural rights, as well as . . . civil and political rights." The covenant defines the **economic, social and cultural rights** that individuals have, the conditions under which the enjoyment of those rights may be limited, and, along with its sister covenant, the **International covenant on Civil and Political Rights** (ICCPR), provides for the right of peoples to self-determination. In the matter of limitation, article 8 of this Covenant states that the exercise of the rights reorganized may be limited by law in the interest of public order, national security, or for the protection of the rights and freedoms of others. In 1985, the United Nations **Economic and Social Council** (ECOSOC) established the **Committee on Economic, Social and Cultural Rights** to help monitor the terms of the International Covenant on Economic, Social and Cultural Rights. *See also:* International Covenants on Human Rights. *Further Reading:* P. Alston, "Out of the Abyss: The Challenge Confronting the New UN Committee on Economic, Social and Cultural Rights," *HRQ*, vol. 9 no. 3 (1987); A. R. Chapman, "A 'Violations Approach' for Monitoring the International Covenant on Economic, Social and Cultural Rights," *HRQ*, vol. 18 no. 1 (1996).

INTERNATIONAL COVENANTS ON HUMAN RIGHTS. This is an international term that refers to two international human rights instruments, the **International Covenant on Economic, Social and Cultural Rights,** and the **International Covenant on Civil and Political Rights** (ICCPR). The latter associated with an Optional Protocol to the Covenant on Civil and Political Rights. Both were adopted by the United Nations **General Assembly** on December 16, 1966, after years of international negotiations. In a sense, it represents a failure on the part of those who wanted both **civil and political rights** and **economic, social and cultural rights** included in a single document: the separation of the two categories of rights often results in some states giving greater emphasis to one or the other category of rights.

The use of the term covenant instead of convention to entitle the treaties indicates the sacred character of the international pledges that are contained within the two covenants. The two covenants give legally binding effect to the Universal Declaration of Human Rights, and with that Declaration house the core of human rights. See also: International Bill of Human Rights.

INTERNATIONAL CRIMINAL COURT. On December 17, 1996, the United Nations **General Assembly**, by consensus, adopted Resolution 51/ 207 on the establishment of an International Criminal Court (ICC). The decision to adopt the resolution represents the culmination of determined efforts, since 1945, to find an international mechanism to hold individuals accountable for violations of international humanitarian and, to an extent, human rights laws. It also represents some current challenges and a promising future.

In 1948 the UN adopted the **Convention on the Prevention and Punishment of Genocide**, which makes it an international crime to commit defined criminal acts with the intent to destroy a national, ethnic, racial, or religious group. There was no criminal court, however, before which the convention could be adjudicated, therefore, in the 1950s, the **International Law Commission** (ILC), a UN agency, was authorized to codify (systematize and classify) the Nuremberg principles and prepare a draft statute to create an international criminal court. Because of the Cold War, however, that preparation was brought to a standstill. In 1989, the country of Trinidad and Tobago reintroduced the idea of a permanent court before the General Assembly, and this time, with the waning of the Cold War and the outbreak of violence in the former Yugoslavia, the idea drew more attention. The General Assembly, therefore, requested the ILC to prepare a draft statute for a permanent criminal court.

In 1993 and 1994, respectively, the **Security Council** of the United Nations established ad hoc **War Crimes Tribunals** for the former Yugoslavia and **Rwanda**, following allegations of **genocide** in each country. In 1994 year, the ILC completed and submitted to the General Assembly a draft statute on a proposed International Criminal Court (ICC) and recommended calling a conference of plenipotentiaries to draw up a treaty to enact the statute. On the basis of that recommendation, in November 1995, the General Assembly created a preparatory committee to meet and finalize the draft text so that it could be presented to an international conference for acceptance in 1998.

In July 1998, the statute and constitution of the Court was approved, and the ICC will have jurisdiction to try: (1) crimes of genocide; (2) crimes against humanity; (3) war crimes; and (4) crimes of aggression. Crimes against humanity is the broadest category, which includes murder, extermination, enslavement, torture, rape, forced prostitution, forced disappearance of persons, and apartheid.

In the area of present challenge, a number of member states of the UN, including the United States, have reservations about the creation of such a court, although their numbers have been substantially reduced. Other issues likely to continue include questions about the ICC's broad jurisdiction and the relationship of that jurisdiction to the UN Security Council. The future holds some promise.

Unlike the ad hoc tribunals for Rwanda and the former Yugoslavia, the ICC will be permanent. Also, unlike those tribunals, the ICC will not be geographically bound—it will be able to deal with cases from anywhere in the world. Unlike the **Nuremberg War Crimes Trials**, the ICC will be free of the taint of a victors' court. And finally, unlike the **International Court of Justice** (ICJ), where only states or intergovernmental organizations can bring complaints, the ICC will deal with nonstate groups. See also: Adjudication; Geneva Conventions. *Further Reading:* Rome Statute of the International Criminal Court, *ILM*, vol. 37 no. 5 (1998).

INTERNATIONAL HELSINKI FEDERATION. This institution is an international **nongovernmental organization** that monitors compliance with the human rights provisions of the **Helsinki Accords** and its follow-up documents such as the Vienna Human Dimension Mechanism. Based in Vienna, Austria, the International Helsinki Federation (IHF) represents thirty Helsinki monitoring groups in Europe (**Russia, Poland,** Solvenia, Greece, Sweden, and the **United Kingdom,** for example) and North America (**Canada** and the **United States**). It also has direct links with individuals and groups supporting **human rights** in countries, such as Chechnya, where Helsinki committees do not exist.

The organization had it beginnings as Helsinki watch in 1976, when the Moscow Helsinki Group was formed by Yelena Bonner and Anatoly Shchransky and others who sought to have their country uphold the human rights principles of the Helsinki Accords. Similar groups were created later in other countries such as Poland, Czechoslovakia, and the United States. In 1982, the Moscow group was forced to disband, although it reestablished itself in 1989. In 1982, the IHF was founded to provide a structure through which the independent Helsinki committees could support each other. In 1989, it was awarded the Human Rights Prize of the **Council of Europe.** *Further Information:* International Helsinki Federation of Human Rights Rummelhardtgasse Z/18, 1090 Vienna, Austria, Tel.: 011–43–1–402–7387.

INTERNATIONAL LABOR ORGANIZATION. This intergovernmental organization was founded in 1919 to promote social justice for all. It has sought to achieve this goal through a number of worldwide means, including: (1) full employment and the progressive improvement in standards of living; (2) improvement in working conditions; (3) advocacy of equality in education and vocational training; (4) recognition and support for collective bargaining; and (5) support for social security and health care. Since 1945, it has collaborated with the UN in all these areas, giving special support to **economic, social and cultural rights.** Support, in many cases, has taken the form of international conventions that its member states (most members of the UN are members of the ILO) have ratified. In addition, the ILO generally provides recommendations to its members to help them develop policies to put the conventions it sponsors into effect.

Among the conventions in the human rights area that the ILO has drafted, sponsored, and has had accepted by the international community are: Convention (No. 156) Concerning Equal Opportunities and Equal Treatment for Men and Women Workers (1981); Convention (No. 100) Concerning Equal Remuneration for Men and Women Workers for Work of Equal Value (1953); Convention (No. 103) Concerning Maternity Protection (1952); and Convention (No. 98) Concerning the Application of the Principles of the Right to Organize and Bargain Collectively (1949).

The ILO conventions are monitored by its Committee of Experts on the Application of Conventions and Recommendations. See also Employment, International Covenant on Economic, Social and Cultural Rights. *Further Reading*: The Constitution of the International Labour Organization, 15 UNTS 140 and 466 UNTS 323; W. Galenson, *The International Labor Organization* (1981); D. Strang and P. M. Chang, "The International Labor Organization and the Welfare State," *IO*, vol. 47 no. 2 (1993).

INTERNATIONAL LAW COMMISSION. This institution, an agency of the United Nations, was created in 1947, by the **General Assembly** to help it carry out its responsibilities according to Article 13 of the **United Nations Charter**, those responsibilities include working to "initiate studies and make recommendations . . . [promotive of] the progressive development of international law and its codification." The term "progressive development of international law" refers to the preparation of draft conventions in subject areas that either have not been previously regulated by international law, or, though previously regulated, have been insufficiently developed through customary practice of states. In contrast, "codification of international law" means the refined analysis, formulation, and systematic classification of international law in areas where there extensive state practice and doctrine already exists.

The International Law Commission (ILC) has prepared and presented a variety of reports to the General Assembly; it also has presented numerous draft conventions with the recommendation that the General Assembly convene international conferences to consider them. If the recommendations are followed and the conferences adopt the drafts, they become law-making treaties that are binding on the states that ratify them.

In the area of **human rights**, the ILC has been responsible for drafting several instruments, including the **Convention on the Nationality of Married Women** and the **Convention Relating to the Status of Stateless Persons**. More recently, it has been involved in the drafting of the statute for the **International Criminal Court** (ICC). *Further Reading*: B. G. Ramcharan, *The International Law Commission: Its Approach to Codification* (1977); I. M. Sinclair, *The International Law Commission* (1987).

INTERNATIONAL TRIBUNALS. See WAR CRIMES TRIBUNALS.

INTER-PARLIAMENTARY UNION. See AMNESTY INTERNA-TIONAL.

INTERVENTIONISM. One of the more jealously protected norms of international life is that of nonintervention. That is, states, as sovereign entities, generally claim the right to exclusive authority over what takes place within their borders. Since all states claim and seek to exercise that right, the right of nonintervention has come to be viewed as a basic attribute of the principle of sovereign equality of states. Should one state or a group of states interfere in the internal affairs of another state, therefore, that interference would be seen as a violation of **sovereignty** and sovereign equality. Interference, and the body of doctrines and ideas associated with it, including those justifying intervention in some circumstances, is called interventionism.

The advent of the human rights movement brought with it a moral, philosophical, and legal change in the way international relations are conducted. Each state, under human rights norms, is now obligated to protect the rights of all humans—not just their own citizens—everywhere. And if the protection of **human rights** is an obligation, then interference in the internal affairs of the country guilty of violating human rights is a duty. Most states, however, holding to the old practices *before* the development of the human rights movement, are reluctant to allow intervention. Some, like **China**, reject it, and others—primarily in the industrially less developed countries—fear that human rights could be used as an excuse to undermine the right to **self-determination**, export "Western values" and even "structure cultural imperialism." See also: Democratic Entitlement; Relativism and Universalism; South Africa. *Further Reading:* D. P. Forsythe and K. K. Pease, "Human Rights, Humanitarian Intervention, and World Politics," *HRQ*, vol. 15 no. 2 (1993); F. R. Teson, *Humanitarian Intervention: An Enquiry Into Law and Morality* (1988); L. F. Damrosch, ed., *Enforcing Restraint: Collective Intervention in Internal Conflicts* (1993).

INTIFADAH. The term, which means "shaking" or "shivering," may have first come into use among the Arabs during the 1920s and 1930s to characterize their uneasy confrontation in fighting against Jewish settlements in Palestine. Today, it refers to the 1988 uprising that began among young Palestinians in the occupied territories in Gaza and the West Bank against Israel's control of those territories. The uprising, which was initially spontaneous and essentially defined by stone throwing and jeers, was quickly organized by a number of radical Palestinians, including Hamas, perhaps the most radical of existing Palestinian groups, which often use terrorism and the threat of terrorism against Israeli civilians, often bombing, maiming, and murdering them. Hamas, which now has strong grassroots links among the Palestinian poor whom it has helped to feed, clothe, and house for a number of years, had come to view the **Palestine Liberation Organization** (PLO)—the internationally recognized representative of the Palestinians—as being "out of touch" with those it claimed to represent and too cautious and conservative. The organization they fashioned for the stone-throwers entailed the substitution of guns, knives, and explosives for stones and jeers to confront the Israelis. Many Israelis, as well as some moderate Palestinians, question whether Hamas want to see peace between Israel and the Palestinians.

Israel retaliated with deliberate armed violence against Hamas and its suspected enclaves, in the process killing hundreds of Palestinians, including children, and seriously wounding thousands of others. As the Intifadah crossed into Israel itself, there were further killings on both sides, with leaders of the Intifadah killing other Palestinians whom they suspected of collaborating with Israel. The **human rights** violations on both sides were many, including violations of the right to life, security of person, and the prohibition against torture, arbitrary arrest, and detention. But the uprising did have a major effect: it served to convince a considerable number of Israelis that exchanging "land for peace"—returning portions of the occupied territories—and supporting Palestinian **self-determination**, in return for secure borders, should be explored. *Further Reading:* R. Khalidi, *Palestinian Identity* (1997); I. Gershoni and J. P. Jankowski, eds., *Rethinking Nationalism in the Arab Middle East* (1997).

IRAQ. Iraq is an Arab state that gained its independence from Britain in 1932. Located in western Asia, the country shares borders with Iran, **Kuwait,** Jordan, **Saudi Arabia**, Syria, and **Turkey**, and has a estimated population of about 19.8 million people. The population, which is ethnically and linguistically diverse, is composed of Arabs, Kurds, Yazidis, Turkomans, and Armenians. The country is composed of Shi'a and Sunni Muslims, Christians, and Jews, although most of the Jews have migrated.

The government of Iraq, which took the form of a republic in 1958, has been somewhat unstable, principally due to the number of military coups it has undergone since the late 1950s. Instability has also come from other sources as well, including the establishment of a single party, the Arab Ba'ath Socialist Party, which has dominated the country's life since 1963. The party does not represent most Iraqis. Its leader since 1979, President Saddam Hussein, is himself dependent on the support of a small but dedicated number of related families from his home area of Tikrit and the largely affluent Sunni minority within a society of relatively poor Shi'a majority. Further, the country is faced with a demand for **self-determination** by the Kurds, a linguistic minority who make up about 20 percent of the population. In 1980, Hussein led an invasion of Shi'a-dominated Iran, in a dispute over the control of a waterway between them.

The consequences of the Iran-Iraq War (1980–1988) included an intensification of the efforts on the part of the Kurds to win their independence, the increased militarization of Iraqi society, as well as the depletion of its financial resources and the wholesale violation of **human rights**. Large numbers of persons disappeared, many of them Shi'ites who were arrested during the war; some Shi'ites were also expelled to Iran. With respect to the Kurds, many were killed extrajudicially with the objective of silencing dissent and suppressing political opposition. Matters got worse as Iraq invaded Kuwait in 1990, claiming that the country was part of Iraq. The UN quickly imposed an embargo and demanded Iraqi withdrawal. In 1991, a U.S.-led, UN-sanctioned war (Persian Gulf War,) resulted in Iraq's defeat, its explusion from Kuwait, and the restoration of Kuwait's government.

The disappearances continue in Iraq; thousands are held in incommunicado **detention**; physical and psychological torture is prevalent, with torture techniques varying from branding and burning with hot irons to the administration of electric shocks to the genitals. Cruel, inhuman, and degrading treatment and punishment is routinely engaged in, with the amputation of ears and hands for crimes varying from theft to military desertion.

Because of the continuing UN sanctions, in order to have Iraqi compliance with inspections of its territory for weapons of mass destruction, child mortality rates have quadrupled since 1990. And according to a 1995 joint UN Food and Agricultural Organization-World Food Program assessment, some 4 million Iraqis, mostly children or nursing women, were at serious risk of malnutrition. Both Iraq and the international community bear the burden here, since starvation cannot be morally or legally used as a weapon of warfare. See also: Civil and Political Rights; Convention against Torture and Other Cruel, Inhuman or Degrading Treatment or Punishment; Kurdistan; United States. *Further Reading:* O. Bengio, *Saddam's Word* (1997); S. al-Khalil, *The Republic of Fear* (1989); P. S. Marr, *The Modern History of Iraq* (1985).

ISLAM. See RELIGION AND HUMAN RIGHTS.

ISRAEL. Israel is located in western Asia and shares its borders with Egypt, Jordan, Lebanon, Syria and the Mediterranean Sea. The country earned its independence in 1948, is a parliamentary democracy, and boasts an advanced economy that affords its citizens a materially high standard of living. It has a population of about 5.2 million people, composed of Jews (over 80 percent), Muslims (about 18 percent), Christians (2.5 percent), and Druze (about 1.4 percent). Official languages include Hebrew and Arabic, and English is also widely spoken. Many national languages, such as German, Russian, or Persian, of the largely immigrant population are also used.

Since 1948, the country has been in a state of war with its Arab neighbors, with the exception of Egypt and Jordan, with which it signed peace treaties in 1979 and 1994, respectively. As a result of the 1967 War, Israel occupied the West Bank of the Jordan River the Gaza Strip, the eastern sector of Jerusalem (areas at the time populated almost exclusively by Palestinians and claimed by them) and the Golan Heights, which belong to Syria. The Palestinians and Syria seek the return of the occupied territories; Israel insists that the land will only be returned in exchange for a genuine peace and territorial adjustments to ensure its security. With the Palestinians using violence to make good their aim, Israel has responded in kind.

In 1995, a historic breakthrough in the process of Israeli–Palestinian reconciliation began, with a signed agreement between them—the Oslo Accords—providing for the redeployment of Israeli Defense Forces from certain Palestinian areas and the transfer of a variety of civil powers to a Palestinian Authority, headed by the **Palestine Liberation Organization** (PLO). In addition, the Oslo Accords call for the release of Palestinian prisoners and future negotiations to determine the status of Jerusalem and the political status of the Palestinians. Some Israelis and Palestinians oppose the agreement, and, on both sides, there are those who seek to sabotage the accords through a variety of tactics, including terrorism.

In Israel, **civil and political rights** are generally respected and promoted, as are many **economic, social and cultural rights**, which are often overlooked by some countries in the West. The prohibition against **discrimination**, however, is not always honored. First, women routinely receive lower wages for comparable work than their male counterparts, and domestic violence, including "honor killings" by male Israeli relatives for alleged misconduct, has been reported by local **human rights** groups. Second, the government does not provide Israeli Arabs with the same quality of education, housing, employment, and social services, according to the United States 1995 Department of State Country Reports on Human Rights. On the other hand, the country has one of the strongest commitments to the rights of children.

With respect to the occupied territories, chiefly the West Bank and Gaza, Israel released some 1,000 Palestinian prisoners in 1995–1996, but its security forces still have under detention large numbers of Palestinians. According to **Amnesty International** (AI) and **Human Rights Watch** (HRW), Israel's security forces have been guilty of torture and cruel and inhuman treatment of Palestinian detainees. Specifically, it contends that the forces subject Palestinian detainees to abuses of body positioning, beatings, hooding (covering of the head to blindfold a person), and sleep-deprivation. Israel denies the charges of torture, but admits that it does use some force during certain interrogations. Under a 1979 law, Palestinians may be kept in detention for up to a year without charge. Likewise, Israel has no consensus on whether the Palestinians claim to **self-determination** (in this case, the right to form a state) should be supported. However, Israel signed an

October 1998 agreement with the Palestinians transfering to their control an additional 13 percent of the West Bank while the Palestinians promised to renounce their Charter provision that calls for the destruction of the state of Israel. See also: Intifadah; Zionism. *Further Reading:* Amnesty International, *Israel and the Occupied Territories: Amnesty International's Response to the Comments of the Israeli Ministry of Justice on Amnesty International Reports, 1990 and 1991* (1991); M. Dumper, *The Politics of Jerusalem Since 1967* (1992); A. Elon, *A Blood-Dimmed Tide: Dispatches from the Middle East* (1997).

J

JOURNALISTS. The promotion, protection, and exercise of **human rights** cannot effectively take place unless the right of the individual and the public to know or to be fully informed is also protected. The press and other means of mass communication are critical to the flow of information enabling people to be informed. And since journalists and other mass media make possible much of the flow of information, including information about violations of **human rights**, it follows that journalists, too, should be protected under human rights declarations.

Freedom of the press and freedom of information are tied to the freedom of the professionals who deal with the flow of information. Journalists, given the impact that what they disseminate can have on people's lives and rights, have a duty to help create and support an international order within which recognized human rights and freedoms can be fully realized. See also: Information; Opinion and Expression. *Further Reading:* General Assembly, *Convention on the International Rights of Correction*, Resolution 630 (VII) (December 16, 1952), A. Parlow, "Beyond the 'Official Story': What Journalists Need to Know," in *Human Rights Education for the Twenty-First Century*, G. J. Andreopoulos and R. P. Claude, eds. (1997).

JUDAISM. See RELIGION AND HUMAN RIGHTS.

JUDICIARY. In the field of **human rights**, few institutions are as important as the judiciary, that branch of government in which the judicial power of a country is vested. It generally consists of judges, a body of laws that includes a constitution, and a system of courts. Because the promotion and protection of human rights are so deeply implicated in the often shifting political, social, religious, and larger cultural contexts of states, however, the mere existence of a judiciary does not guarantee the protection and promotion of human rights. What is absolutely necessary for the effective protection of those rights is an *independent, competent* (having legal authority) and *impartial* judiciary.

Articles 7, 8, and 10 of the **Universal Declaration of Human Rights** (UDHR) provide for **equality** before the law and the right to a fair hearing by competent, independent, and impartial tribunals. Article 2 (2) of the **International Covenant on Economic, Social and Cultural Rights** guarantees the exercise of the rights it recognizes without **discrimination**; and the **International Covenant on Civil and Political Rights** (ICCPR) not only provides for an equivalent guarantee, but ensures trial without delay. The United Nations **General Assembly**, by Resolutions 40/32 of November 29, 1985, and 40/146 of December 13, 1985, adopted a very important human rights instrument, the Basic Principles on the Independence of the Judiciary.

Not all twenty principles included in the instrument are included here, but the following principles capture its essence:

1. The independence of the judiciary shall be guaranteed by the State and enshrined in the Constitution or the law of the country . . .

2. The judiciary shall decide matters before them impartially, on the basis of facts and in accordance with the law, without any restrictions, improper influences, inducements, pressures, threats or inferences, direct or indirect, from any quarter or for any reason.

3. The judiciary shall have jurisdiction over all issues of a judicial nature and shall have exclusive authority to decide whether an issue submitted for its decision is within its competence as defined by law.

11. The term of office of judges, their independence, security, adequate remuneration, condition of service, pensions and the age of retirement shall be adequately secured by law.

12. Judges, whether appointed or elected, shall be guaranteed tenure and a mandatory retirement age or the expiry of their term of office, where such exists.

14. The assignment of cases to judges within the court to which they belong is an internal matter of judicial administration.

15. The judiciary shall be bound by professional secrecy with regard to their deliberations and to confidential information acquired in the course of their duties other than in public proceedings, and shall not be compelled to testify on such matters.

Other principles of the document deal with discipline, suspension, and removal as well as the personal immunity of judges from civil suits for monetary damages, on account of acts or omissions in the exercise of their judicial functions. See also: Adjudication; Fair Trial; Procedural Guarantees, Processes and Protections. *Further Reading:* D. M. Beatty, ed., *Human Rights and Judicial Review* (1994); C. Gane and M. Mackarel, eds., *Human Rights and the Administration of Justice* (1997).

K

KASHMIR. Kashmir is a disputed territory in the extreme north of the Indian subcontinent. The area, which is over 85,000 square miles, has a population of nearly 10 million people, the majority of whom are Muslim, and shares borders with Pakistan in the west, **Afghanistan** to the north, **China** to the northeast, and **India** to its south and southwest. Kashmir has been a center of dispute between India and Pakistan as well as an area of human rights abuse since 1947.

In 1947, British India was subdivided into India and Pakistan. Areas that were predominantly Hindu became India and those that were primarily Muslim formed Pakistan. The scheme of division did not include what were then called "princely states"—domains ruled by hereditary princes that included Kashmir. Both India and Pakistan sought to have the ruler of Kashmir, a Hindu, join their respective countries, but he initially avoided joining either one. Pakistani Muslims, however, invaded Kashmir in an attempt to unite it with their country, and maharaja Hari Singh appealed to India for military help, which it quickly gave, and was rewarded with a 1947 agreement to make Kashmir a part of India.

The agreement incited a war between India and Pakistan, both of which filed complaints with the United Nations. The UN brokered a cease-fire in January 1949, and later that year they agreed to *temporary* borders of the areas under their respective control. UN resolutions were later passed calling for the withdrawal of troops and holding a plebiscite (election) to determine the political status of the area. To date, no such plebiscite has been held.

The cease-fire lines (temporary boundaries) left Pakistan with the northwestern third of Kashmir—a region the Pakistani call Azad (free) Kashmir. The rest, under India's control (except for a portion seized by China in 1962 during its border war with India), was annexed to India in 1957 and has been administered since then by India as Jammu and Kashmir. The annexation was protested by both Pakistan and the UN, and since 1957, the so-called Free Kashmir Movement, made up of Muslims in Pakistan and Kashmir, has contested India's control of any portion of Kashmir. Military conflicts between India and Pakistan in 1965 and again in 1971 resulted in considerable fighting in Kashmir, but cease-fire agreements were worked out in each case. Since the late 1980s, however, Muslims in the Indian part of Kashmir have staged protests against Indian rule and with significant support from Pakistani who feverishly seek the unification of Pakistan and Kashmir. Some of the Muslims in the India-controlled portion of Kashmir seek independence; others want union with Pakistan.

India has increased its troop presence in Kashmir and has used repressive measures, including extrajudicial killings and illegal detentions, to contain the protests. It has indicated its willingness to go to war, if necessary, to retain its portion of Kashmir. Since Pakistan is no less committed to dislodging Kashmir from India's control, war between the two countries is an ever-present threat. Their recent activities in the detonation of nuclear weapons make that threat even more dangerous. See also: Bangladesh; Self-Determination. *Further Reading:* S. Gupta, *Kashmir: A Story in India-Pakistan Relations* (1966); Jagmohan, *My Frozen Turbulence in Kashmir* (1991); V. Schonfield, *Kashmir: In the Crossfire* (1996).

KENT STATE TRAGEDY. This expression takes its name from Kent State University, located in Kent, Ohio, in the United States, where four students were killed during a student protest of U.S. actions in the Vietnam War. The war, which began in the 1940s between Vietnam and Japan, continued as a conflict between Vietnam and France, and became part of a bitter struggle between the **United States** and Vietnam after the French were defeated at Dien Bien Phu in 1954. In 1954, the country was divided into North and South Vietnam, with the United States supporting South Vietnam against the communist North. The war continued at varying levels of intensity until 1975, when a peace treaty earlier agreed to and the goal of North Vietnam to unify all of Vietnam had been realized.

During the war, the North Vietnamese used guerrilla tactics, terror, and assassination to pursue its objectives. The United States, with its South Vietnamese ally, used guerrilla tactics and assassination, too, but it also tried to defeat the North Vietnamese by conventional means, through search-and-destroy missions and massive bombing strikes against the North's cities and general infrastructure (roads, bridges, and airports, for example). The brutality and the human and material damage, caused by both sides, were immense. As the war dragged on, people in the United States not only became increasingly morally disgusted with the killing, but began to harbor suspicions about the truthfulness of their government's explanations of its policies and conduct. In particular, they began to question whether the right of the Vietnamese to **self-determination** was being compromised under the guise of fighting communism. Outside the United States, people in many countries—including some allies—also began to protest the war, opposition to which increased broadly, especially after 1968.

Nowhere was the opposition in the United States more intense than on college and university campuses, where antiwar rallies assumed threatening political dimensions. Although opposition was nationwide, the event that had the most profound political impact on the nation and aroused the greatest feelings of concern about the war was the killing of four students at Kent State University; it was as if all the moral and psychological anxieties about the war became concentrated on this event.

On May 4, 1970, National Guardsmen, who had been called to Kent State to disperse a planned and ongoing antiwar rally, opened fire on the students. This was done without warning, resulting in the deaths of four students and the wounding of ten others. The immediate cause of the shooting was never determined, responsibility never acknowledged, and blame never assigned. But when the shock and numbness of the event wore off, it aroused enough moral and political passion to spur political leaders, especially President Nixon and his advisors, to take further steps to end the war, although the United States did not withdraw from that war until 1973, following the Paris Peace Accords of that year.

The shooting violated the students' **human rights** to freedom of expression and assembly, to impart and receive information, and, in a broader sense, to **democratic entitlement** (something the United States claimed to be fighting for in Vietnam). Of course, their right to life, security of person, and the dignity associated with the expression of their moral convictions, were all violated. See also: Civil and Political Rights; My Lai Massacre. *Further Reading:* J. Kelner, *The Kent State Coverup* (1980); U.S. Presidents' Commission on Campus Unrest, *The Kent State Tragedy* (1988).

KHMER ROUGE. See CAMBODIA.

KING, RODNEY G. Rodney King, a black American, was arrested on March 3, 1991, by Los Angeles, California, police for a speeding violation. The police, who claimed to have been exercising great caution in making his arrest, ordered him to get out of his car and lie face down on the pavement. There, according to eyewitness accounts, he was severely beaten by white policemen.

At first, the allegations of "needless cruelty" were denied by the police, and King was depicted as an aggressive and dangerous male. A two-minute videotape by an onlooker of what had taken place, however, exposed to a shocked **United States** and the world the substantial falsity of the police claims and also showed that while King was lying on the ground, cowering with his hands over his face, he was beaten, pounded on his head with a baton, and repeatedly kicked. In the hospital, he was treated for fifteen facial fractures and a broken leg. The police also delayed helping King obtain needed medical help, and some police officers made light of their abusive activities.

With respect to the delay, the police officer assigned to take King to the hospital told a "war story" in the squad room, while the wounded King waited in a patrol car for transportation to the hospital. Transcripts of computer messages between the police officers involved in the beating indicated that the officers were joking about their abusive activities. "Oops," one of the messages said after the beating, "I haven't beaten anyone this bad in a long time," according to released transcripts of computer messages between squad cars of officers.

In 1992, a largely white jury, with no blacks, acquitted all four policemen who were charged with wrongdoing. That acquittal, plus the racial tensions that had increased during the trial, the appearance of bias in the judicial proceedings, and intemperate statements by some public officials, caused the eruption of riots, and people's rage found antisocial expression in the burning of buildings, the beating of people, and the killing of some fifty-four persons.

The manner in which the beatings, the riots, and the general mayhem was treated and reported also incited tensions, as pictorial and other representations emphasized what whites were doing to blacks and blacks to whites. Very little attempt was made by the media to point out, for example, that not all of the two-minute tape had been seen by the public, or that for every black who was beating whites there were other blacks trying to protect them.

The federal government, troubled by the rising racial tensions—by then extending beyond Los Angeles—tried the four officers on federal civil rights violations, and two were found guilty in 1993. They were, however, given relatively light jail sentences. In 1994, King won a $3.8 million award in a civil-action lawsuit against the city of Los Angeles.

While the account presents violations of King's civil rights, there are broader issues implicated under international human rights standards. First, the police committed a number of violations under the **Code of Conduct for Law Enforcement Officials**. The code requires officers to protect the dignity of each person in their custody; to "ensure full protection of the health" of persons under their control; and to "take immediate action to secure medical attention whenever required." Second, they violated the prohibition against cruel and degrading treatment; and, in particular, they abused their power, as police officers. The media, in its uneven reporting, and local political leaders, in their intemperate statements, also contributed to an atmosphere that incited discriminatory actions.

Those people who were killed and had their properties destroyed were also victims of **human rights** abuse and racial **discrimination**. And to the extent that the imbalance of the presentation by the news media, excessive statements by political leaders, and the appearance of bias on the part of judges materially contributed to an incitement to riot, those standards of human rights that place particular responsibilities on the media and political leaders were also violated.

Finally, other human rights violations that may have contributed to the riots and mayhem were not always reported or otherwise touched on in the King case. The resentments, which in part sponsored the riots, were, in part, born out of a "pattern of police beating of the underclass" in Los Angeles, without anyone seeming to care. They were also born out of the social squalor in which many of the poor lived, going without food and education, for instance. This is the type of social neglect and abandonment that the implementation of **economic, social and cultural** rights might have prevented. See also: Civil and Political Rights; Louima, Abner. *Further Reading:* Lou Cannon, *Official Negligence: How Rodney King and the Riots Changed Los Angeles and the LAPD* (1997); David Nyhan, " 'Official Negligence': The Last Word on LA Riots," *BG* (January 25, 1968); United Nations, *Human Rights and Law Enforcement: A Manual on Human Rights Training for the Police* (1997).

KOSOVO. Kosovo is a province in southern **Serbia**. It borders Montenegro to the west, Albania to the southwest, and Macedonia to the south. The province, scene of the medieval Serbian empire's defeat by the Ottoman Turks in 1389, and the site of Serbia's most revered religious shrines, is also home to 2 million people, 90 percent of whom are ethnic Albanians. Because of its Albanian majority—a majority that was an ethnic minority in Serbia as a whole, Kosovo was made an autonomous region in the former Yugoslavia in 1974. That status allowed Kosovars to fly their own flag; recognized the Albanian language; promoted Albanian culture; and nurtured Albanian-language educational institutions.

In 1981, a year after the death of Marshal Tito (Josip Broz, 1892–1980), the late president of the former Yugoslavia and the person who presided over the creation and development of autonomous status for Kosovo, riots in support of linking Kosovo to Albania (a "Greater Albanian state") took place in Kosovo. The riots reignited fears among Serbs about the loyalty of Kosovo. As the federation of the former Yugoslavia was threatened with dissolution in the late 1980s, nationalist political leaders in Serbia played on those fears as they sought to create a "Greater Serbia." In 1989, the autonomous status of Kosovo was revoked by the increasingly repressive government of the former Yugoslavia, then dominated by Serbia. Kosovar Albanians resisted the revocation by creating a Kosovar Albanian shadow government led by Ibrahim Rugova, which has largely functioned outside the political arrangements through which Serbia has sought to govern Kosovo.

The resistance to Serbian control, though tension-filled, was mostly peaceful until 1996, when some members of the Kosovo Liberation Army (KLA), the armed wing of the Albanian Kosovar nationalist movement, began killing members of the Serbian security forces. The Serbian government responded with excessive and indiscriminate use of force, in many cases against innocent persons. This Serbian response, accompanied by the increased popularity of the Movement for the Unification of All Albanians (over 20 percent of adjacent Macedonia's 2 million people are also Albanians), as well as pressure from some Albanian Kosovars to declare full independence, raised the prospect of interethnic violence and an even wider Balkan and European war, given the ties of countries such as **Turkey, Russia,** and Greece, among others, to the region. And when, in January 1998, the KLA declared that it had launched an armed struggle to effect the unification of Kosovo and Albania, and Serbian leaders responded by promising, at all costs, to preserve Kosovo as part of Serbia, that prospect became a grimmer reality.

The **United States** and its major allies have indicated to Serbia that they will not tolerate any repetition in Kosovo of the widespread violations of human rights, including **ethnic cleansing**, which took place in **Bosnia-Herzegovina** in the early 1990s. Serbia has been threatened with a military attack by the United States and its major allies. The allies have also indicated that they are not prepared to support independence for Kosovo. A Contact Group—Britain, France, Germany, Italy, Russia, and the United States—has begun efforts to find a compromise between Serbia and the Albanian Kosovars nationalist movement. Any success on the part of this group, however, will likely have to coexist with the continued demand for **self-determination** by the Albanian Kosovars, as well as considerable external support, including arms and money, from sympathetic communities throughout the world. *Further Reading:* D. Hautin-Guiraut, "It's Time to Recognize Kosovo's Independence," *MGW* (April 25, 1988); O. Kesic, "Serbian Roulette," *CH*, vol. 97 no. 617 (1998); D. Perry, "Destiny on Hold: Macedonia and the Dangers of Ethnic Discord," *CH*, vol. 97 no. 617 (1998); R. Stavenhagen, *Ethnic Conflicts and the Nation-State* (1996).

KURDISTAN. This name, which means land of the Kurds, describes an area in west Asia. It is populated by Kurdish-speaking people and forms part of eastern **Turkey**, northeastern Syria, northern **Iraq**, and northwestern Iran, western Azerbaijan, and southwestern Armenia. The area has been the subject of international disputes between Turkey and Iran since the seventeenth century. After World War I, the major powers agreed to the idea of Kurdistan's independence under the terms of the Treaty of Sevres (1920). The treaty was never implemented, however, and many Kurds, who today constitute over 22 million people redoubled their efforts in the struggle for independence. After World War II, the struggle intensified, and in

1947 Iranian Kurdistan was proclaimed the Kurdish Republic. The republic was short-lived, however, as Iranian forces defeated the insurrectionists. Similar rebellions in Iraq and Turkey were also crushed.

Since 1947, the fight for national **self-determination** has gone through several phases. Kurdish nationalist guerrilla leaders have been in military confrontations with Iraq from 1961 to 1979, and again in the 1980s, during which both periods an estimated 200,000 Kurds were killed by Iraq. Since Iraq was defeated in the 1991 Gulf War, the Kurds have again challenged Iraq militarily. With respect to Turkey, it has faced rebellion from the Kurds almost continuously since 1945, with the period 1978–1979 and 1984 to the present being the most challenging years. In 1993, Turkey met with Syria and Iran to forge a common front against Kurdish independence, but agreement among those countries has not reduced the passion for Kurdish national independence.

Iran, Iraq, Syria, and Turkey are all been guilty of violating the norm of national self-determination. In addition, countries such as Turkey and Iraq are guilty of torture and cruel and inhuman treatment of the Kurds. Western Europe has refused to consider Turkey for the European Union (EU) because of its human rights record, especially with respect to the Kurds. The countries of Western Europe are also concerned that Turkey's policies toward the Kurds are causing unacceptable numbers of Kurds to flee to their societies from Turkey. See also: Asylum. *Further Reading:* H. J. Barkey and G. H. Fuller, *Turkey's Kurdish Question* (1997); R. Hutchings and J. Rugman, *Ataturk's Children: Turkey and the Kurds* (1996); L. M. Meho, *The Kurds and Kurdistan: A Selected and Annotated Bibliography* (1997).

KUWAIT. This country, located on the Arabian Peninsula at the head of the Persian Gulf, was founded in 1759 as a province of the Ottoman Empire. From 1899 to 1961, when Kuwait gained independence, it existed as a British protectorate. Its independence was protested by **Iraq,** which contended that the area constituting Kuwait should properly be part of Iraq. Iraq's claim seemed to have been settled when it recognized Kuwait in 1963, but that claim was reasserted in 1990, when President Saddam Hussein of Iraq invaded Kuwait, claiming it as Iraq's Province 19. The international community did not agree with Hussein and a UN-sponsored, U.S.-led coalition evicted Iraq from Kuwait during the Gulf War.

Kuwait has a population of about 2 million citizens and perhaps as many or more workers, including Palestinians, from many countries throughout the world. During the war involving Iraq, many Palestinians, including some in Kuwait, supported Iraq because of its support for the Palestinians' fight against Israel. The Kuwaiti government, which had fled during Iraq's invasion, expelled a considerable number of Palestinians upon its return to Kuwait. It also executed others extrajudicially. Indeed, Kuwait, which has been the beneficiary of international support for the right to **self-determination,** has been violating a number of other **human rights**.

It has continued to refuse women the right to vote, and it has rendered over 100,000 longtime inhabitants, known as "Bedoons," stateless. These inhabitants, many of whom know no other country, have been declared illegal residents, and because of that attributed status, they are restricted in their movements, barred from employment, and denied education for their children. They live under constant threat of arbitrary arrest. Kuwait has also been preventing some of the stateless persons, "Iraqi and Palestinians," from leaving for "their" countries. Finally, domestic servants, many of whom are from south and southeast Asian countries, are often forced to work forty-eight hours per week, treated as criminals if they escape from their employers, and deported if they seek to organize themselves.

The country's constitution prohibits **discrimination** based on race, national origin, or language, among other categories, but women and non-Kuwaitis face widespread discrimination. And while the right of association is constitutionally protected, political parties are banned. See also: Civil and Political Rights; Convention on the Elimination of All Forms of Discrimination Against Women. *Further Reading:* D. H. Finnie, *Shifting Lines in the Sand: Kuwait's Elusive Frontier with Iraq* (1992); Human Rights Watch, *The Bedoons of Kuwait* (1995).

KYOTO PROTOCOL ON CLIMATE CHANGE. See ENVIRONMENT.

L

LAND MINES. One of the most commonly used weapons in warfare, land mines are encased explosives designed to destroy enemy personnel. They are particularly effective against enemy soldiers because of their invisible presence. Placed beneath the surface of the ground, they detonate when weight is unknowingly placed on them. Land mines are often placed in buildings, as well as under roads, or in fields or ditches, and are also dangerous to civilians, because they can maim and kill decades after they are planted and war has ceased. Today, there are an estimated 110 million land mines in over sixty countries throughout the world, and the United Nations has estimated that some 25,000 persons, mostly civilians, including women, children, and farmers, are killed or dismembered annually by land mines. The social and economic costs are considerable, especially in damage done, preventing reconstruction efforts, delaying agricultural development, and undermining trade and transportation systems. And when loss of life coupled with lost economic and social opportunities and the price of reconstruction are added to what it will take to rid the world of land mines, the sum is astounding.

From the standpoint of **human rights**, the elimination of land mines is very important, because their use violates some of the most basic human rights norms, for example, the right to life, liberty and security of person, freedom of movement and residence, individual and collective development, and the right not to be arbitrarily deprived of one's property. In the case of children, it entails the right to be protected against all forms of cruelty and the right to opportunities for play and recreation.

It is within the above contexts of the dangers land mines represent that human rights advocates joined the recent International Campaign to Ban Land Mines, a coalition of over 1,000 organizations in more than sixty countries. That coalition, begun by Robert Muller, a United States Vietnam veteran who lost his legs during the Vietnam war, and coordinated by Jody Williams, also an American, succeeded in winning the approval of nearly 100 governments of a draft treaty to ban land mines. That treaty was signed in Ottawa, Canada, in December 1997. Jody Williams received the 1997 Nobel Peace Prize for her work on the campaign. *Further Reading:* K. M. Cahill, *Clearing the Fields: Solutions to Global Land Mines* (1995); B. Boutros-Ghali, "The Land Mine Crisis," *For Aff.*, vol. 73 no. 5 (1994).

LATVIA. See STALIN, JOSEPH V.

LAWS OF WAR. See GENEVA CONVENTIONS.

LESBIAN AND GAY RIGHTS. Among the individuals and groups that are most widely disciminated against are women and men (and the groups with which they are associated) who are homosexual. So deeply imbedded is this **discrimination,** that in spite of broad, contemporary nondiscrimination measures on behalf of other groups, attempts at removing even the most basic features of discriminatory practices toward lesbians and gays are met with hostile, and sometimes violent, opposition.

As homosexuals have become more open in asserting their identities, they have gained wider political support and even made possible the existence of organizations such as the International Lesbian and Gay Association (ILGA), which was founded in 1978. ILGA now has more than 300 member organizations throughout the world, including some of the most conservative states. It has been able to advance the interests of lesbians and gays in international forums, including the United Nations **Economic and Social Council** (ECOSOC), with which it has consultative status.

In more substantive terms, homosexual groups, as well as their supporters, have pointed to international human rights instruments as entitling them to protection. Using the **Universal Declaration of Human Rights** (UDHR) as one example, the following provisions are noted:

Article 1. All human beings are born free and equal in dignity and rights. . . .

Article 2. Everyone is entitled to all the rights and freedoms set forth in this Declaration, without distinction of any kind, such as race, colour, sex . . . birth or other status.

Article 3. Everyone has the right to life, liberty and security of person.

Article 5. No one shall be subjected to torture or to cruel, inhuman or degrading treatment or punishment.

Article 12. No one shall be subjected to arbitrary interference with his privacy, family, home or correspondence, nor to attacks upon his honour and reputation. Everyone has the right to the protection of the law against such interference or attacks.

Article 13 (1). Everyone has a right to freedom of movement and residence within the borders of each State.

(2). Everyone has the right to leave any country, including his own, and return to his country.

Article 14 (1). Everyone has the right to seek and to enjoy in other countries asylum from persecution.

Lesbians and gays point to the fact that they have never been treated with equal dignity, especially in view of the fact that the very assertion of their identity is frowned on; that the ban of discrimination on the basis of sex applies to them; that security of their persons is socially undermined by the discrimination against them; and that the social and cultural contempt exhibited toward them—often with the sanction and support of the state through its laws—is a form of inhuman and degrading treatment. They also contend that even when they seek to escape from the discrimination of local communities in order to form associations with others of the same sex in the anonymity of large cities or foreign countries, they have to reinvent themselves. And in the process of seeking such escape, their right of movement and residence within their country and, their right to leave a given country—even in face of overt persecution—are often compromised by discriminatory immigration laws that will not allow them to enter and/or stay within other countries. Finally, their right to privacy is not respected.

In recent years, political agitation from gay and lesbian groups and their supporters have resulted in some **human rights** gains, especially in Western Europe, and in other selected countries. The 1981 *Dungeon v. United Kingdom* case has proved to be of central importance. Jeffrey Dungeon, an activist with the **Northern Ireland** Gay Rights Association, challenged a **United Kingdom** law that criminalized adult homosexual activity in Northern Ireland. The **European Court of Human Rights** ruled that the criminal prohibition against adult homosexuality violated the right to privacy and is, therefore, a violation of the **European Convention on Human Rights**. Since the ruling of the European Court has Europe-wide impact, lesbians and gays gained a major victory. Parallel developments have taken place through other European institutions such as the European Parliament. In 1994, the parliament, which three years earlier had included protection for homosexuals under its adopted Charter on Sexual Harassment in the Workplace, passed a resolution that should have even greater impact. That resolution

5. Calls on the Member States to abolish all legal provisions which criminalize and discriminate against sexual activities between persons of the same sex;

6. Calls for the same age of consent to apply to homosexual and heterosexual activities alike;

7. Calls for an end to the unequal treatment of persons with homosexual orientation under the legal and administrative provisions of the social security system and where social benefits, adoption law, laws of inheritance, and housing and criminal law and all related legal provisions are concerned;

10. Calls on the Member States, together with the national lesbian and homosexual organizations, to take measures and initiate campaigns to combat all forms of social discrimination against homosexuals;

11. Recommends that Member States take steps to ensure that homosexual women's and men's social and cultural organizations have access to national funds on the same basis as other social and cultural organizations.

The repeal of criminal prohibition against homosexual activity, which is a legislative action that customarily precedes nondiscrimination policies, has been the usual course of legislative conduct found most prevalently in areas of the world outside Europe. With the exception of **Chile**, Nicaragua, and a few others, Latin America has decriminalized homosexual activities, so have states in the Balkans. Estonia, Latvia, Lithuania, Cyprus, Moldova, Ukraine, Hungary, **Russia**, and Kazakhstan have also decriminalized such activities. In some countries, including the **United States**, gay and lesbian marriages have received the support of some religious communities, and although the U.S. Congress, through its Defense of Marriage Act, permits "states within the U.S." to refuse recognition to such marriages, court decisions in Hawaii and Vermont could undermine that act. Many members of Congress are determined, however, to limit the rights of gay people.

On the global level, the United Nations **Sub-Commission on the Prevention of Discrimination and Protection of Minorities** is reviewing this area of human rights and nongovernmental organizations (NGOs) such as Human Rights Watch (HRW) are beginning to give support to the human rights of lesbians and gays. Human Rights Watch has adopted a policy opposing state tolerated "violence, detention, prosecution and discrimination on the basis of sexual orientation." In 1991, it requested the American Psychiatric Association to review cases of alleged psychiatric treatment of young people to change their sexual orientation. Although in 1973 homosexuality was removed from the official list of mental disorders, there have been reports that the diagnostic category of "Gender Identity Disorder" has been employed to institutionalize children who exhibit what are "perceived as gay and lesbian traits." See also: European Court of Human Rights; United Kingdom. *Further Reading:* B. Cant, *Invented Identities: Lesbians and Gays Talk About Migration* (1996); E. Heinze, *Sexual Orientation: A Human Right* (1995); D. Saunders, "Getting Lesbian and Gay Issues on the International Human Rights Agenda," *HRQ*, vol. 19 no. 1 (1996); R. Wintemute, *Sexual Orientation and Human Rights: The United States Constitution, the European Convention, and the Canadian Charter* (1996).

LIBERATION THEOLOGY. The term refers to a social and theological movement within Christianity (especially the Catholic Church) in Latin

America, the Caribbean, and the **Philippines**, and, to some extent, in Eastern Europe. The movement may be described as one that is (1) suspicious of the hierarchical structures of the established or official Christian church (which has never accepted the movement); (2) rejecting of church-state alliances, which have often reinforced "existing power relationships," many of which are coercive and violate human rights; and (3) questioning of the "neutral" stances that religious leaders often take in face of oppression and powerlessness. In an affirmative vein, liberation theology concerns itself with an interpretation of the Christian faith as one of suffering, struggle, and hope for the poor. It also elaborates a theory of action to sustain that struggle and hope.

In the approach of liberation theology, its advocates believe that theory and action must be linked, so theory begins with building blocks of concrete circumstances from people's lives—poverty and powerlessness, for example—that are used to demonstrate that those conditions were part of the core around which Christ's ministry was centered. Contrast is then shown between Christ's ministry and the position of the established church. In addition, emphasis is placed on the *causes* of poverty and powerlessness, to show that they are both *socially created* and that God expects Christians to act (not simply to believe) to relieve poverty and powerlessness.

If Christ's ministry was to bring relief to the poor and the powerless, then it is the duty of the Church to do the same. In taking the latter position, liberation theology has been at the center of support for the right to development, to **economic, social and cultural rights** and even the right to radically alter the social system in order to have those rights fully implemented. See also: Holy See. *Further Reading:* P. Berryman, *Liberation Theology* (1987); M. Pena, *Liberation Theologies* (1995).

LIBERTY. See LIBERTY AND SECURITY OF PERSON.

LIBERTY AND SECURITY OF PERSON. The right of everyone to liberty, which is an independent right in itself, is one that is also linked to the right to security of person. This linkage is born of long experience, which has shown that one's physical security (and even one's life at times) is an inseparable part of the deprivation of liberty. Article 3 of the **Universal Declaration of Human Rights** (UDHR) recognizing this inseparability, reads as follows: "Everyone has a right to life, liberty and security of person." And Articles 9 and 10 of the **International Covenant on Civil and Political Rights** (ICCPR), also recognizes the link between liberty and security of person, as they elaborate protections dealt with in the entry on **detention**. Article 9 (1) of the International Covenant on Civil and Political Rights provides that "Everyone has the right to liberty and security of person. No one shall be subjected to arbitrary arrest or detention. No one shall be deprived of his liberty except on such grounds and in accordance with such procedures as are established by law."

The right to liberty and security of person is found in all regional human rights instruments that are the basis of the respective regions' standards. The European and American conventions on human rights as well as the International Covenant on Civil and Political Rights (Article 11) also seek to protect liberty by prohibiting imprisonment solely on the grounds of the inability to fulfill a contractual obligation. See also: American Convention on Human Rights, Derogation, European Convention on Human Rights. *Further Reading:* D. A. Carter, *The Deadly Sin of Terrorism* (1994); B. Barret-Kriegel, *The State and the Rule of Law* (1995).

LOUIMA, ABNER. On August 9, 1997, Abner Louima, a black Haitian immigrant who had lived in New York for six years, was charged with assault and arrested by white policemen, who then took him to the 70th Police Precinct station in New York City. The arrest followed a brawl outside the Club Rendez-Vous, where Louima was allegedly mistaken for someone who had punched a police officer as the officer was trying to break up the melee. While at the police station, Louima was physically attacked by police officers, who dragged him into the bathroom, beat him, and rammed a stick (believed to be the handle of a toilet plunger) into his rectum. The stick was then, reportedly, shoved into his mouth. Louima also alleged that in the midst of the abuse by officers, he was repeatedly called "nigger"—a disparaging racial slur.

Although a police officer at the station played an important role in the disclosure of the alleged wrongdoing, public anger—especially in minority communities—was strong, and demonstrations calling for a public investigation into police conduct took place. The mayor of New York City, Rudolph Giuliani, who was slow in responding to the problem, was forced by public pressure to appoint a commission to investigate the police's conduct, especially when it was disclosed that a 1996 study by **Amnesty International** (AI) indicated that there was a persistent, widespread "pattern of brutality," especially against minorities, by that city's police.

The police officers at fault were indicted on assault, harassment, and other charges. But the incident, one of the most brutal in the history of police conduct, encompasses a broader range of human rights abuses, including the abuse of the protection against torture, inhuman, and degrading treatment, and, if the allegations about race are correct, discrimination based on race. They also include violations of the right to **liberty and security of person**, and presumption of innocence. See also: Discrimination. *Further Reading:* Associated Press, "7,000 Protest Police, Giuliani Marchers Vent Ire Over Abuse Case,"*BG* (August 30, 1997); Associated Press, "2 NYC Officers Get New Charge in Haitian's Beating Alleged in Sex Brutality Case," *BG* (September 9, 1997); P. Chevigny, *Edge of the Knife: Police Violence in the Americas* (1995); W. A. Geller and H. Toch, eds., *Police Violence: Understanding and Controlling Abuse of Force* (1996).

M _____

MANDELA, NELSON (1918–). Nelson Mandela is a South African nationalist who played a pivotal role during the 1950s in organizing and defining the political program of the African National Congress (ANC), then a South African multiracial organization that was created to promote peaceful and democratic reforms of **South Africa**. The ANC later led a violent struggle against the government from 1960 to 1990 and is today the political party that leads South Africa. Mandela was imprisoned from 1962 to 1990 because of his opposition to **apartheid**, and by the time he was released from prison, he had become not only the world's most famous prisoner but was viewed as a person of immense moral stature and political courage.

Immediately after his release from prison, Mandela assumed the leadership of ANC and became the undisputed spokesperson for those who sought a democratic and multiracial South Africa. He used his position to negotiate the end of apartheid which, by 1993, was legally abolished. In 1994, he became South Africa's first democratically elected president.

Nelson Mandela's contribution to the promotion of **human rights** are many. First, his entire public life has been devoted to and involved in supporting the right to **self-determination** and the prohibition of racial **discrimination**. Second, he led the way in creating a constitution for South Africa that is second to none in the world in incorporating of the norms of human rights. Those rights not only include **civil and political rights** and **economic, social and cultural rights**, but third generation rights such as "the right [of individuals] to an environment which is not detrimental to his or her health and well-being." In addition, rather than bend to the political winds seeking revenge against apartheid leaders who had killed, tortured, and otherwise abused nonwhite South Africans, or members of the ANC who had also abused the rights of South Africans, Mandela also initiated the creation of the Truth and Reconciliation Commission, which has sought to establish the truth about crimes, often committed in secret, as a step toward granting amnesty to wrongdoers who help establish the truth and effect interethnic and interracial reconciliation. See also: Environment; Generations of Rights; Truth Commissions. *Further Reading:* T. J. Juckels, *Opposition in South Africa* (1995); N. Mandela, *Long Walk to Freedom* (1994).

MAO ZEDONG (1893–1976). Mao Zedong was the leader of a revolution that succeeded in establishing communism in **China** in 1949. From that date, he led the People's Republic of China (PRC) until his death. As a young man, Mao steadily became more leftist in his political ideas, and by 1920 he had become a committed Marxist. In 1921, he was one of the founders of the Communist Party of China, whose leadership he assumed in 1935. He then skillfully led the party to power, after fighting a civil war against the Nationalist Party (the Kuomintang), which had led China since 1911–1912.

Mao originally accepted the orthodox Marxist position that the ideal society should be one that is socially grounded in industrial workers. Since China had an overwhelmingly peasant population, he had to modify that position, as he sought and won support for the communist party from the peasantry. In his fight against the Nationalists, Mao's base of support was always in the countryside. He retained this support until his death in 1976, because in addition to the general modernization of Chinese society and its transformation from an essentially capitalist economy to a socialist one, he championed social and economic rights for the Chinese people. In particular, the right to education, health care, food, and housing was emphasized. But there were major human rights violations in other areas, especially in **civil and political rights,** during the time he led China.

Mao's regime did not tolerate dissent, and when he appeared to change the policy of intolerance in the late 1950s through the Hundred Flowers Campaign—a campaign that sought to encourage the free exchange of thoughts and ideas—it turned out to have been largely a trap to identify people who disagreed with his regime's policies. Many were imprisoned or killed.

Further, Mao introduced radical land reforms, including the collectivization of agriculture, and forced peasants to work in "people's collectives." Collectivization produced considerable social dislocation and later, famine. The effects of famine, the efforts of rapid industrialization, the repression of those who opposed or who were believed to be opposed to him—especially the launching of the Great Proletarian Cultural Revolution (1966–1976)—may have caused the death of an estimated 15 million persons. See also: **Economic, Social and Cultural Rights.** *Further Reading:* J. Chen, *Mao Papers, Anthology and Bibliography* (1970); A. Lawrence, *Mao Zedong: A Biography* (1991).

MAORI. See AUSTRALIA; INDIGENOUS PEOPLES.

MARRIAGE AND THE FAMILY. The right to marry and found a family are two of the rights explicitly recognized in the **International Bill of Human Rights**. In the first human rights bill, the **Universal Declaration of Human Rights** (UDHR) makes provisions for marriage and founding a family in Article 16:

1. Men and women of full age, without any limitation due to race, nationality or religion, have the right to marry and to found a family. They are entitled to equal rights as to marriage, during marriage and at its dissolution.

2. Marriage shall be entered into only with the free and full consent of the intending spouses.

3. The family is the natural and fundamental group unit of society and is entitled to protection by society and the State.

The other instruments that make up the International Bill of Human Rights essentially replicate what the declaration provides, although there is greater emphasis on the protection of the **family** and children. The **International Convention on the Elimination of All Forms of Racial Discrimination** prohibits racial **discrimination** in the right to marry and choose a spouse; Article 16 of the **Convention on the Elimination of All Forms of Discrimination Against Women** (CEDAW) expands the rights of women in relation to marriage and the family. For example, men and women have the same rights to choose a spouse; the same rights and responsibilities during marriage and its dissolution; the same personal rights, including the right to choose a family name, a profession, and an occupation; the same rights and responsibilities as parents in matters relating to children; the same rights with respect to ownership, acquisition, management, administration, enjoyment and disposition of property; and the same rights to freely decide on the number of and intervals between children. See also: Convention on Consent to Marriage, Minimum Age for Marriage and Registration of Marriages; Family. *Further Reading:* C. Kagitcibasi, *Family and Human Development Across Cultures* (1996); F.-X. Kaufmann, et al., eds., *Family Life and Family Policies in Europe* (1997).

MEXICO. Mexico is a federal republic which, like the **United States**, is composed of constitutional subdivisions called states, of which there are thirty-one and a federal district. The country is the cultural product of three major influences that have shaped its social and political life and are likely to continue doing so. First, there are the indigenous civilizations formed out of Zapotec, Maya, and Aztec cultures, the last of which was in its ascendancy when the country was taken over by Spain in 1519. From 1519 to 1821, when Mexico gained its independence, the country was controlled by Spain, whose influence is the second cultural feature of Mexican society. The third is the English-speaking United States, which Mexico borders to its north. Mexico, Canada, and the United States formed the North American Free Trade Agreement (NAFTA) signed in 1992 and effective in 1994.

Although, on account of the Spanish influence, the country's estimated population of over 96 million people is overwhelmingly Christian (97 percent Roman Catholic and 2 percent Protestant), this religious homogeneity masks profound socioeconomic and political divisions. By the time Mexico gained its independence in 1821, its population had already divided into three dominant subdivisions, which continues today: (1) a Spanish-born and Mexican-born white elite, which have competed to control national power; (2) the **indigenous peoples**—Amerindians; and (3) the offspring of the mixture between Europeans and Amerindians, mestizos. The Amerindians and Mestizos have been fighting since 1821 what scholars describe as a losing battle for social **equality**, although leftist parties have recently increased their impact in this area.

The Institutional Revolutionary Party (PRI), through which the elite classes continue to control national life, has used radical rhetoric to appeal to the disadvantaged and win every presidential election in the past sixty-eight years. But its record in **human rights** is poor. While it preserves the appearance of protecting the principle of **democratic entitlement**, it undermines that principle through fraudulent elections. The norm of equality and nondiscrimination is routinely violated, especially in cases of women and Amerindians, and terror tactics are now used to control many of those who are opposed to the PRI or who seek fundamental socioeconomic reforms.

In the case of women, for instance, the government has turned its back on rising domestic violence and flagrant discriminatory practices in northern *maquiladoras* (assembly factories). There, to reduce the cost of pregnancy- and maternity-related benefits, major international corporations from the United States and other countries require women job applicants to take pregnancy tests. The objective is to eliminate those women whose tests are positive. Labor unions and their leaders, human rights groups, and **journalists** who want to improve, protest, or report on poor working conditions, are threatened, attacked, tortured, or killed. Even church-related human rights groups are subject to threats from other groups that are seen as links with the PRI.

Since 1994, two groups representing peasants have engaged in organized uprisings against the government. First is the Zapatista Army of National Liberation from the state of Chiapas, which in January 1994, began fighting the government in the name of economic justice and freedom. And then, in August 1996, the Popular Revolutionary Army launched a guerrilla attack against the government. The political challenges to the government continue, but its most notable response has been to invite negotiations and respond with violence, abductions, disappearances, and illegal detentions.

See also: Declaration on the Protection of All Persons from Enforced Disappearance; Economic, Social and Cultural Rights. *Further Reading*: S. D. Morris, *Political Reformism: An Overview of Contemporary Mexican Politics* (1995); B. Nolan, *Mexico Is People: Land of Three Cultures* (1973).

MIGRANT WORKERS. See INTERNATIONAL CONVENTION ON THE PROTECTION OF THE RIGHTS OF ALL MIGRANT WORKERS AND THEIR FAMILIES.

MILOSEVIC, SLOBODAN (1941–). Slobodan Milosevic is a Serb politician who assumed political leadership of the former Yugoslavia in 1980, after the death of Marshal Tito (Josip Broz, 1892–1980). The latter, who was the only national leader former Yugoslavia had known since 1945, used his war-hero stature and the force of his personality to induce the many nations that composed his country to live together. In addition, the ideology of communism and the centralized political machinery of the federal state helped to de-emphasize ethnic or national (Serbian, Slovenian, Croatian, Bosnia-Herzegovenian, for example) identities. By the time Milosevic consolidated his power in 1987–1988, however, he began to show clear preferences for his fellow Serbians, thus aggravating preexisting social and economic problems in the various nations (or republics, as they were constitutionally called). The republics, seeking answers to their respective economic and social conditions, began to pursue withdrawal from the federation and seek political independence. Milosevic, in an effort to ensure his place among the Serbs, began taking strong nationalist stands, including giving support to Serb militias in their fight for territories and to effect **ethnic cleansing** in Bosnia and Croatia.

Milosevic has been accused by many of **war crimes** as well as **crimes against humanity**. Thus far, however, no formal charges have been directed at him, and it is uncertain whether the UN-established International Criminal Tribunal for the Former Yugoslavia will indict him. See also: Bosnia-Herzegovina; War Crimes Tribunals. *Further Reading*: A. Djilas, "Serbia's Milosevic: A Profile," *For. Aff.*, vol. 72 no. 3 (1993); J.V.A. Fine and R. W. Donia, *Bosnia and Herzegovina: A Tradition Betrayed* (1995).

MINORITIES. The term minorities has never been satisfactorily defined in international **human rights** instruments. Article 27 of the **International Covenant on Civil and Political Rights** (ICCPR), for instance, simply provides that "In those States in which ethnic, religious or linguistic minorities exist, persons belonging to such minorities shall not be denied the right, in community with the other members of their group, to enjoy their own culture, to profess and practise their own religion, or to use their own language."

For years, apart from what regional instruments have sought to do, the global community has struggled to define the term minority and to elaborate the rights such minorities have. That definition is not yet forthcoming, but in 1993, the United Nations **General Assembly** succeeded in adopting a global instrument, the **Declaration on the Rights of Persons Belonging to National or Ethnic, Religious and Linguistic Minorities,** which elaborates the rights of those minorities. Under the declaration individuals and groups are left to engage in a process of self-definition.

There are groups, such as sexual minorities, on whose behalf the UN has not done much. Court cases, using the norms of equality and nondiscrimination, have on occasion protected the rights of such groups and their members, but they remain vulnerable, in the absence of specific instruments offering protection. See also: Framework Convention for the Protection of National Minorities. *Further Reading:* W. Kymlicka, *The Rights of Minority Culture* (1995); J. Spinner, *The Boundaries of Citizenship: Race, Ethnicity and Nationality in the Liberal State* (1994).

MORAL AND MATERIAL INTERESTS. Individuals are recognized to have cultural rights, including the right to participate freely in the cultural life of the community. Among these cultural rights are individual's rights to the moral and material interests resulting from their work. Article 27 (2) of the **Universal Declaration of Human Rights** (UDHR) provides that each person "has the right to the protection of the moral and material interests resulting from any scientific, literary or artistic production of which he [or she] is the author." Article 15 (1) (c) of the **International Covenant on Economic, Social and Cultural Rights** speaks of the right of everyone to "benefit from the protection of the moral and material interests resulting from any scientific, literary or artistic production of which he [or she] is the author." *Further Reading:* C. Lury, *Cultural Rights* (1993); R. Beddard and D. M. Hill, eds., *Economic, Social and Cultural Rights* (1992).

MOTHERHOOD AND CHILDHOOD. As part of the importance assigned to the **family** in global and regional human rights instruments, women and children are specifically recognized and accorded special protection. In the **Universal Declaration of Human Rights** (UDHR), there is particular recognition of the status of motherhood and childhood: Article 25 (2) proclaims that "Motherhood and childhood are entitled to special care and assistance. All children, whether born in or out of wedlock, shall enjoy the same social protection."

Because Article 25 (1) deals with the right of everyone to a "standard of living adequate for the health and well-being" of oneself and one's family, "including food, clothing, housing, and medical care and necessary social services," one may conclude that the protection to which motherhood and childhood are entitled includes an "adequate standard of living." But that entitlement embraces far more, as is evident in the rights associated with the family, and the rights recognized by the Convention on the Rights of the Child (CRC) and the **Convention on the Elimination of All Forms of Discrimination Against Women** (CEDAW). See also: Child, Rights of. *Further Reading*: S. Koven and S. Michel, *Mothers of a New World* (1993); G. Mink, *The Wages of Motherhood* (1995); G. Van Buren, "The International Protection of Family Members' Rights as the 21st Century Approaches," *HRQ*, vol. 17 no. 4 (1995).

MOSCOW MECHANISM. See HUMAN DIMENSION (MECHANISM).

MOTHERS OF THE PLAZA DE MAYO. The Mothers of the Plaza de Mayo (Las Madres de la Plaza de Mayo) is the name given to a group of Argentinean mothers, primarily housewives, who began demonstrating outside the presidential palace (plaza de Mayo) in 1977 in response to what has come to be called the "dirty war" in Argentina (1976–1982). During the dirty war, the military regime that had seized power, suspended political institutions, and engaged in an "anti-subversive campaign" to capture and interrogate all members of suspected organizations, their relatives, sympathizers, as well as anyone identified as likely to oppose its rule. The campaign was brutal, with **arbitrary arrest and detention, rape,** murder, and torture routinely practiced.

To mask its conduct and especially to avoid international censorship, the military junta began a systematic practice of numbing terror—forced disappearances. It was the disappearance of thousands of innocent citizens of all ages, especially idealistic young adults who vanished without a trace into what was later learned to be 300 secret concentration camps throughout Argentina, that brought the mothers into confrontation with the government. The demonstrations were initially a search for relief from the grief and pain of their "disappeared children," but these "madwomen of the Plaza de Mayo," as the military regime dismissively called them, risked their lives, when others, intimidated by state-sponsored terror, were silent.

As the mothers met daily in front of the presidential palace, the size of the demonstrations grew, mostly because other mothers came to discover that they all shared common experiences. The world began to take notice, and what had begun as the efforts of a few women to find personal consolation became a movement to get rid of the military junta. When the junta was removed from power in 1982, the movement not only made a profound contribution in the search for victims, but the evidence of what had taken place in Argentina confirmed the horrors the mothers had presented to the world for over half a decade. Further, the movement expanded the general commitment of mothers to the promotion of **human rights** and social justice in Argentina and the world.

The model of mothers in Argentina has found its way to many countries, including **Bosnia-Herzegovina**, Guatemala, Honduras, and Sri Lanka. From March 27–30, 1994, representatives of some fourteen organizations of mothers met in Paris, France, at the First International Meeting of Mothers and Women in Struggle, to discover ways to confront oppression and injustice, share family loss, and promote the cause of social justice, human rights, and human dignity. Among those gathered at the meeting were representatives from Bosnia-Herzegovina, **Serbia**, Ukraine, **Brazil**, and **Israel**. Since 1994, the movement has not been as visible to the international public, but its members have been working to build political and moral influence within their countries, including Argentina, as a way of securing greater global impact.

In 1980, the Mothers of the Plaza de Mayo received the Norwegian Prize of the People, which is awarded to those who qualify for the Nobel Prize for Peace but do not receive it; in 1992, the group received the Sakharov Prize for Freedom of Thought from the European Parliament. See also: *Nunca Mas*; Sakharov, Andrei. *Further Reading:* M. Agosin, *Mothers of the Plaza de Mayo: The Story of Renee Epelbaum, 1976–1985* (1989); M. G. Bouvard, *Revolutionizing Motherhood: The Mothers of the Plaza de Mayo* (1994); A. Malin, "Mothers Who Won't Disappear," *HRQ*, vol. 16 no. 1 (1994).

MOVEMENT AND RESIDENCE. The right to freedom of movement and residence is one that is fundamental to human dignity. It is also one that permits a person to escape or limit persecution, discrimination, and, sometimes, to protect life. The **Universal Declaration of Human Rights** (UDHR) provides in Article 13 that

1. Everyone has the right to freedom of movement and residence within the borders of each State.

2. Everyone has the right to leave any country, including his own, and to return to his country.

Article 14 (1) of the Universal Declaration Specifies the right "to seek and enjoy in other countries asylum from persecution." In similar fashion, the **International Covenant on Civil and Political Rights** (ICCPR) also deals with the right of movement and residence, and specifically indicates the degree of limitation that may be placed on it. Article 12 states:

1. Everyone lawfully within the territory of a State shall, within that territory, have the right to liberty of movement and freedom to choose his residence.

2. Everyone shall be free to leave any country, including his own.

3. The above-mentioned rights shall not be subject to any restrictions except those which are provided by law, are necessary to protect national security, public order . . . , public health or morals or the rights and freedoms of others, and are consistent with the other rights recognized in the present Covenant.

4. No one shall be arbitrarily deprived of the right to enter his own country.

The global community has also sought to give particular protection to certain groups that have historically been subject to **discrimination** in the right to movement and residence. Article 5 of the **International Convention on the Elimination of All Forms of Racial Discrimination**, for example, affirms the right of all races to freedom of movement and residence. And Article 15 (4) of the **Convention on the Elimination of Discrimination Against Women** (CEDAW) reads that: "States Parties shall accord to men and women the same right with regard to the law relating to movement of persons and freedom to choose their residence and domicile."

Regional human rights instruments, such as the **African Charter on Human and Peoples' Rights**, the **American Convention on Human Rights**, and the **European Convention on Human Rights**, also deal with this right. See also: Asylum. *Further Reading:* B. Cant, *Invented Identities* (1996); S. S. Juss, *Immigration, Nationality and Citizenship* (1994); C. McClain, ed., *Chinese Immigrants and American Law* (1994); M. L. Silver and M. Melkonian, eds., *Contested Terrain* (1995).

MYANMAR. See BURMA.

MY LAI MASSACRE. This incident is linked to the Vietnam War, which began as a war of independence by the Vietnamese from French colonial rule. Because the North Vietnamese, who had defeated the French in 1954 in the French Indochina War (1946–1954) had established a communist regime and were seeking to unite all of Vietnam under their control, the **United States** sought to prevent unification and control as part of its declared effort to contain the spread of communism. First, the United States sought containment by giving aid to the French, and when France was defeated, the United States became progressively more engaged in the war, and by 1968, had over 500,000 troops in South Vietnam.

On March 16, 1968, a battle-scarred American fighting unit, under Captain Ernest Medina, entered the South Vietnamese village of My Lai to search for members of the Viet Cong guerrilla group. The soldiers tortured the men of the village in order to gain information from them, and then massacred hundreds of unarmed civilians (the current estimate is 400), including women, children, and old men. Some twenty-five soldiers were charged, but only six were court-martialed and all were acquitted except for Lieutenant William Calley, who was found guilty of war crimes and sentenced to life imprisonment on March 29, 1971. In 1975 he was released on parole.

The trial and conviction are very important from a number of **human rights** perspectives. First is the link between *rights* and *responsibilities*. In the human rights regime, one speaks often of the **right to life**, for example. But that right has no legal or moral weight if others do not have a responsibility to respect it. Second, the human rights regime emphasizes the *priority of human rights*. Even in times of war, human rights are to be respected and unarmed civilians are not to be targets of military activities.

Third, *personal* responsibility is underscored. Before the development of the human rights movement, a soldier in the field could excuse or justify his or her behavior on the grounds that what he or she did was commanded by a superior officer, as Lieutenant Calley claimed at trial, and as some defendants at Nuremberg claimed as well. The decision in the Calley case stated that orders from superior officers cannot exempt a soldier from responsibility to adhere to the laws of war and the rights of individuals. See also: Geneva Conventions; Crimes Against Humanity; Superior Orders; War Crimes. *Further Reading:* M. Bilton and K. Sim, *Four Hours in My Lai* (1992); M. Gershen, *Destroy or Die: The True Story of Mylai* (1971); S. M. Hersh, *My Lai 4: A Report of the Massacre and Its Aftermath* (1970).

N _____

NAGORNO-KARABAKH. This is the name of a predominantly mountainous Armenian enclave in the southwestern area of the Republic of Azerbaijan. It occupies about 1,700 square miles, has an estimated population of about 195,000 people and represents one of the more important contemporary examples of the problems that tend to accompany the right to **self-determination**.

The modern history of the area began in 1918, immediately after the Russian Revolution, when the Russian territories of Christian Armenia and Muslim Azerbaijan became independent republics. In 1920, however, when both Armenia and Azerbaijan became republics within the Soviet Union, Karabakh, with its predominantly Armenian (about 78 percent) population, was transferred from Azerbaijan to Armenian control. In 1923, **Joseph V. Stalin,** then leader on nationality issues, retransferred Karabakh and its inhabitants back to Azerbaijan, providing for its "cultural autonomy."

While the 1923 transfer may have pleased the Muslims within and outside the USSR, it incited the smoldering resentment of Armenians—a resentment that finally exploded in 1988, when the ethnic Armenians of Karabakh began overt agitation for a transfer to Armenian jurisdiction. The demand for transfer was strongly opposed by both Azerbaijan and the Soviet Union. In 1989, the former Soviet Union assumed control of the disputed province but its intervention did not solve the problem, in part because Armenia suffered a great earthquake in 1988 and Azerbaijan, at war with the Armenia-supported Karabakh Armenians, cut off all land routes to Armenia and blocked oil, food, and other deliveries. After the dissolution of the Soviet Union in 1991 and the accompanying independence of Armenia and Azerbaijan that year, the inflamed antagonisms between ethnic Armenians and their Azerbaijan rulers burst into a full-blown civil war. By 1995, the Karabakh Armenian forces, overtly supported by the country of Armenia, had gained control of most of the area of south-western Azerbaijan, including Nagorno-Karabakh, as well as the territory linking the Karabakh enclave to Armenia.

The violence that accompanied the dispute over Nagorno-Karabakh has been brutal. Not only have there been **human rights** violations, including massacres on both sides, summary executions, and torture, but most Azeris have been expelled from the area, as Armenian forces consolidated their positions, and an estimated 900,000 (Azeris) have been made refugees. Charges of **ethnic cleansing** have been alleged against Armenia. See also: Russia. *Further Reading:* T. Swietochowski, *Russia and Azerbaijan: A Borderland in Transition* (1995); P. Verluise, *Armenia in Crisis* (1995).

NAIROBI FORWARD-LOOKING STRATEGIES FOR THE ADVANCEMENT OF WOMEN. See WORLD CONFERENCES ON WOMEN.

NATIONALITY. The terms refers to an individual's membership in a nation-state. The status of membership entitles an individual to claim and receive protection from the state of which she or he is a member, and the state, in turn, expects allegiance from that person and the acceptance of certain obligations. A person who has no such membership in any nation-state is said to be stateless.

The **Universal Declaration of Human Rights** (UDHR) proclaims the right to a nationality in Article 15 as follows:

1. Everyone has the right to a nationality.
2. No one shall be arbitrarily deprived of his nationality nor denied the right to change his nationality.

Dealing with the same right, but in this case focusing on children without a nationality who are most vulnerable, the **International Covenant on Civil and Political Rights** (ICCPR), in Article 24 (3) provides that "Every child has the right to acquire a nationality." And because race and sex have been used historically to deny nationality to people, the global community specifically sought to prevent this type of **discrimination** in the future. In Article 5 of the **International Convention on the Elimination of All Forms of Racial Discrimination,** states undertake to prohibit and eliminate racial discrimination and "to guarantee to everyone, without distinction as to race, colour or national origin . . . the right to [a] nationality." The **Convention on the Elimination of All Forms of Discrimination Against Women** (CEDAW) provides in Article 9:

1. States Parties shall grant to women equal rights with men to acquire, change or retain their nationality. They shall ensure in particular that neither marriage to an alien nor change of nationality of the husband during marriage shall automatically change the nationality of the wife, render her stateless or force upon her the nationality of the husband.

2. States Parties shall grant to women equal rights with men with respect to the nationality of their children.

The issue of nationality is also dealt with in regional human rights instruments, such as the **African Charter on Human and People's Rights**, the **American Convention on Human Rights**, and the **European Convention on Human Rights**. See also: Convention on the Nationality of Married Women; Genocide. *Further Reading:* Council of Europe, *Nationality of Spouses of Different Nationalities and Nationality of Children Born in Wedlock* (1977); W. Kymlicka, *Multicultural Citizenship* (1995); J. Spinner, *The Boundaries of Citizenship: Race, Ethnicity, and Nationality in the Liberal State* (1994).

NATION-BUILDING. The term nation refers to a group of people who, based on a claimed common cultural past, seek to have a common social and political future. The expression "common cultural past" has many complex meanings, but it is usually linked to an ethnic (racial), religious, or linguistic community and/or a community that has had its identity formed out of a shared history of suffering, triumph, or a combination of the preceding features. A "common social and political future" refers to a desire to forge a consciously organized future together (usually in the form of a state), grounded in the shared, cultural past. Nation-building, therefore, refers to the creation or recreation of a common past among the people of a given country, with a view toward shaping a common future together.

Because of imperial rivalries, colonial controls, and immigration patterns, among other factors, many states accommodate people of varying cultural backgrounds and identities—people who have little or nothing in common. Or, to the extent that there is a shared common past, it is overridden by cultural differences. When governments are faced with such differences as they seek to create a sense of unity and solidarity (common past and common future), they generally find opposition from groups that seek to maintain their own identities; that opposition is sometimes used to justify repression. Similarly, for those governments that seek to protect the cultural rights of **minorities** within their borders, nation-building means developing institutions—judicial, administrative, and executive—that can win the confidence of the people and consistently protect their rights as human beings. See also: Ethnic Cleansing. *Further Reading:* G. Gottlieb, *Nation Against State* (1993); T. R. Gurr, *Minorities at Risk: A Global View of Ethnopolitical Conflicts* (1993); W. Pfaff, *The Wrath of Nations* (1993); A. Smith, *National Identity* (1991).

NATURAL LAW. Natural law refers to a concept or theory that holds that there are principles or laws of nature that govern the physio-chemical, cultural, and social universe. These principles are part of human nature and are expressed through human beings *as they are* as well as *what they can become.* Laws of nature have certain attributes: (1) they are discoverable by reason, which itself is a product of nature; (2) they offer standards to judge moral rightness or wrongness and the faculties to recognize natural rights that are associated with those standards; (3) they transcend and are superior to human-made law; and (4) they are unchangeable, inalienable, and universal.

Since the principles are, for example, inalienable, it means that no political or other authority can take the rights associated with them away. Such authorities can refuse to recognize them and may in fact violate those rights. It also means that human beings have a natural claim to have those rights recognized. Natural law gained its greatest development in the West, chiefly through its Greco-Roman and Judeo-Christian traditions. It has been expressed in many other traditions, however, including Buddhist, Chinese, Egyptian, Hindu, Islamic, Mayan, and Taoist.

It is out of the tradition of the natural law concept that **human rights** have evolved. So, the preamble to the **Universal Declaration of Human Rights** (UDHR) begins with a call to nation-states to recognize "the *inherent* [author's emphasis] dignity and the equal and inalienable rights of all members of the human family." As well, as in the case of principles governing the physical universe—with no exception for time or place—the human rights norms contained in human rights instruments are universal. They refer to "all," "everyone," "members of the human family," and "no one." Finally, human rights instruments, to the extent that they express natural law, are superior to national legislation. Legislative enactments, in fact, gain their legitimacy only to the extent that they are in conformity with the norms of human rights. It follows, therefore, that the future legitimacy of social and political systems, including governments, will largely depend on how they embody the values of human rights. *Further Reading:* E. Bloch, *Natural Law and Human Dignity* (1986); R. Tuck, *Natural Rights Theories, Their Origin and Development* (1979).

NEW WORLD INFORMATION AND COMMUNICATIONS ORDER. The right to freedom of thought, opinion, and expression is one that is recognized by all major global and regional human rights instruments. In particular, Article 19 (2) of the **International Covenant on Civil and Political Rights** (ICCPR) provides that "Everyone shall have the right to freedom of expression; this right shall include freedom to seek, receive and impart information and ideas of all kinds, regardless of frontiers, either orally, in writing or in print, in the form of art, or through any other media of his choice." The expression "seek, receive and impart information" suggests that individuals have a right not simply to be passive recipients but active imparters of information and to impart and receive in all its forms without respect for national boundaries. Limitations are confined to measures designed to assure respect for the rights and reputation of others, protection of public order, public health, or morals, and the proscription against propaganda for war and the "advocacy of national, racial or religious hatred that constitutes incitement to discrimination, hostility or violence" (Article 20 (2) of the International Covenant or Civil and Political Rights).

During the 1970s, people throughout the world began to see information and communication as having a far more important bearing on **human rights** than they had earlier in the century. Indeed, it began to dawn on a considerable number of people and countries that the right to seek, receive, and impart information is a *fundamental* right for individuals, communities, and nations, that is to say, it is a right that is a prerequisite for other rights, including: (1) the right to assemble, discuss, participate, and related *association* rights; (2) to inquire, to be informed, to inform, and related *information* rights; and (3) to culture, education, health care, food, privacy, and related *development* rights. Likewise, it became clear that the full realization of the right to communicate would require that information and communication *resources* be made available to all (democratization of communication) at the individual, local, national, and international levels.

As individuals and countries became more aware of the importance of information and communication, they simultaneously realized that the ideal of the "free flow" of information was becoming a one-way flow, a vertical flow, and a flow defined by a market dominance in which individuals and communities, including countries, were only receivers of information and communication. That dominance governed the means of communication, including signs, words, language, reading, writing, mail, telephone, local and international media, satellites, and computers. Dominance also governed the expanding infrastructure of libraries and data banks, publishing companies, broadcasting bands, and amplifications of radio and telephone services by new technologies such as the Internet. Finally, realization extended to a recognition that the *content* of information and communication was often characterized by distortion, alienation, stereotyping, and even victimization. Because of the general awareness of the importance of information and communication to human rights, and the view that dominance is nonpromotive and not very protective of human rights, a number of states, led by the industrially less-developed and some socialist nations, called for a new world information and communications order (NWICO).

That call came as a result of a series of meetings in the mid-1970s. In 1978 at the General Conference of the **United Nations Educational, Scientific and Cultural Organization** (UNESCO) and the United Nations **General Assembly**, two resolutions were passed and adopted, and a consensus reached on the term "new more just and more efficient information and communication order," as well as the need to begin efforts to create such an order. In the meantime, as a result of the series of meetings mentioned above, the director-general of UNESCO was instructed, in 1976, to undertake a review of all problems of communication in and between societies, and Director-General Amadou-Mahtar M'Bow established the International Commission for the Study of Communication Problems. Called the MacBride Commission, after its chair, the late Sean MacBride of Ireland, the commission—composed of sixteen members largely representative of the world's ideological, political, economic, and geographical spectrum (the **United States**, U.S.S.R., Egypt, Indonesia, India, France, and Cambodia, for example)— reached a consensus that was published in 1980 in the form of a report entitled, *Many Voices, One World*.

The report called for a democratization of information and communication resources, for greater responsibility on the part of people in the professional fields of communication and information, and a greater effort on the part of governments to help employ, or encourage the employment of, information and communication resources to promote and protect human rights. During the discussion process concerning the manner by which the world might go about creating a "new more just and more efficient information and communication order," bitter differences developed between the Western and non-Western countries. The latter charged that the West was unwilling to support reforms that might threaten its dominance in the field of information and communication, and the West contended that the non-West was interested in using government to control the media. As a result of those differences, the United States and the **United Kingdom** withdrew from UNESCO in 1985 and 1986, respectively. The United Kingdom has since returned, and the United States is reviewing its position, with indications that it, too, will return. See also: Information; Journalists; Propaganda. *Further Reading:* International Commission for the Study of Communication Problems, *Many Voices, One World: Towards a New More Just and More Efficient World Information and Communication Order* (1981); P. Ball, M. Girouardi, and A. Chapman, "Information Technology, Information Management, and Human Rights," *HRQ*, vol. 19 no. 4 (1997).

NIGERIA. The Federal Republic of Nigeria is a country located in West Africa with a population estimated by the UN (1997) to be over 115 million people. It gained its independence from Britain in 1960, with powerful ethnic groups—especially the Hausa-Fulani to the north, the Yoruba to the southwest, and the Ibo to the southeast—vying for political ascendency. With over 100 smaller ethnic groups, several regional languages to rival English (the official language), and a religious identification of about 50 percent Muslim, 34 percent Christian, and 16 percent other, the country boasts considerable diversity. That diversity, coupled with external interference in its affairs, and the earlier-mentioned political rivalry, has been a source of much social and political instability.

Since 1970, the country has been struggling to recover from a bitter civil war (1966–1970), which began as a conflict between the Muslim Hausa and the predominantly Christian Ibo. Recovery has been undermined by a number of factors, chief among them a succession of military coups. The last of the coups took place in 1993, when General Sani Abacha annulled the results of a popular election in June 1993, and assumed executive power. He promised to return Nigeria to a democratically elected civilian government by October 1, 1998, but he died suddenly in June 1998 and was succeeded by General Abdulsalam Abubaker. General Abubaker begun to relax some of the political restrictions imposed on Nigerians by his predecessor and has also promised early elections.

Apart from violating the democratic rights to which the people of Nigeria are entitled, the various military governments of the country have been associated with a number of other human rights abuses, including the suspension of constitutional guarantees of **human rights** protections. Since 1993, **arbitrary arrests and detentions** have become routine, as have summary executions by security forces, and harassment of opposition activities, including the criminalizing of criticism of the government, has continued since 1996. The 1995 execution of Ken Saro-Wiwa, the leader of the Movement for the Survival of the Ogoni People—one of the smaller ethnic groups in Nigeria—has highlighted a major problem that Nigeria will continue to face: the problem of forging an inclusive national identity out of its ethnic, religious, and regional diversities and rivalries, and the challenge of affording human rights protection to all as it struggles to build that identity. See also: Democratic Entitlements; Nation-Building; Minorities. *Further Reading:* A. Adedeji and O. Otite, *Nigeria: Renewal from the Roots? The Struggle for Democratic Development* (1997); J. Peters, *The Nigerian Military and the State* (1997).

NON-DEROGATION. See DEROGATION.

NONGOVERNMENTAL ORGANIZATION. Many are the changes that have taken place in international relations over the past fifty years. Few, if any, of those changes have been as significant as the rise of what has come to be called a "global civil society," a society made up of a multitude of voluntary associations and networks: women's groups, farming and housing cooperatives, religion-based organizations, professional societies, business institutions, trade unions, to name a few. These groups are collectively called nongovernmental organizations (NGOs). These international NGOs, which have existed for a long time, have grown in size, diversity, and international influence since 1909, when there were almost 175 such groups, to today, when they number over 30,000, each of which operates in no fewer than three countries.

Among the factors that account for the rapid growth of NGOs in the last fifty years, are people's disenchantment with government and their increased awareness that popular participation at the international and global levels of governance is a compelling necessity if the values they cherish are to be protected. No area of values has invited more attention from the

NGO community than **human rights**. Indeed, it can be confidently asserted that were it not for NGOs, the norms of human rights would not have become as widely known as they are and few governments would respect the norms.

As harsh as the last statement may appear, experience and reflection demonstrate its accuracy. States, on the one hand, whose powers are regulated by the norms of human rights, are disinterested in promoting or protecting those rights when doing so limits their powers. On the other hand, NGOs, and individual human beings, to whom those rights belong, seek to nurture and preserve the values those rights advance and protect. So groups like **Amnesty International, (AI), Physicians for Human Rights** (PHR), and **Defense for Children International** (DFI), devote themselves to the promotion and protection of human rights.

Most NGOs are from Western industrialized countries, and some individuals from the less industrially developed areas have begun to question the independence of NGOs from Western influence. See also: Amnesty International; Physicians for Human Rights. *Further Reading:* D. Otto, "Nongovernmental Organizations and the United Nations System: The Emerging World of International Civil Society," *HRQ*, vol. 18 no. 1 (1996); J. Rosenberg, *The Empire of Civil Society* (1994); K. Wellard and J. G. Copestake. *Non-governmental Organizations and the State in Africa* (1993).

NON-INTERVENTION. See INTERVENTIONISM.

NORTHERN IRELAND. Northern Ireland, sometimes referred to as Ulster, is the product of the division of the country of Ireland, which the **United Kingdom** effected in 1920. The area, during Ireland's colonization by Britain, was the scene of land expropriated from Irish Catholic peasants and awarded to Protestants who had rendered service in Britain's wars. As Irish nationalists (predominantly Catholic) began to demand the right to **self-determination** (first, home rule, from 1829–1916, and then independence, from 1916–1921), Ulster Protestants organized against it. But the Irish War of Independence (1918–1921), a guerrilla campaign initiated largely on account of Britain's execution of Irish nationalists who had engaged in a 1916 uprising against Britain, produced political assassinations and killings of informers, attacks against the police and the military, and such intercommunal bitterness that the United Kingdom agreed to concede independence in 1920.

That agreement effected the partition of Ireland into two parts: one portion, predominantly Catholic and made up of the twenty-six southern countries, became the Irish Free State, now called the Republic of Ireland, and the other portion, the predominantly Protestant six northern countries, became Ulster or Northern Ireland. Many Irish nationalists have never accepted this partition, and when the politically carved out Protestant majority of Ulster, led by the pro-British Ulster Unionists, began to insist on perpetual union with Britain and coupled that insistence with housing, employment, and educational **discrimination** against Catholics, a new round of violence began in Northern Ireland in the 1960s. That violence, led by the nationalist Irish Republican Army (IRA), a paramilitary group that was organized in 1919, caused Britain to increase its military presence in Ulster—at first to protect the Catholic minority, but later to confront the IRA. On January 30, 1972, "Bloody Sunday," some thirteen peaceful protesters were killed by British troops—killing that Britain contended was caused by confusion, but which Irish nationalists saw as planned. The incident undermined the position of those who thought an American-type civil rights movement could succeed in Ulster, and excited rising levels of violence, led by the IRA, on one side, and British security forces and their allies, including the Ulster Defense Association (UDA), on the other.

In 1993 (and by that time some 3,000 lives were lost in the conflict that began in 1967), a Framework Agreement was signed between Britain and the Republic of Ireland. That agreement provides that the United Kingdom will not oppose an all-Ireland union. Ireland (along with the IRA, which secretly participated in the negotiations), in turn, agreed to respect the majority decision in Ulster and to alter its constitution to protect Protestant sensitivities concerning minority rights. Protestants, while a majority in Ulster, would be a minority in a united Ireland. Violence continued, however, because Protestants who wanted to retain their union with the United Kingdom continued their discrimination against Catholics, and the IRA continued its insistence on a united Ireland. A new round of negotiations, begun with the help of the United States, resulted in an historic agreement in April 1998 (called the Good Friday Agreement).

The agreement provides for the creation of new governmental institutions for Northern Ireland that will assure greater Catholic participation and remove Ulster from direct rule by the United Kingdom. Additionally, the new agreement provides for cross-border cooperation between Northern Ireland and the Republic of Ireland in the areas of transportation, agriculture, and the environment. The people of Northern Ireland may also democratically pursue ties with Ireland as well as the United Kingdom. This new agreement, were it to succeed (and voters in both the Republic of Ireland and Northern Ireland have overwhelmingly supported it), would end decades of human rights violations. *Further Reading:* "Honoring the Dead 'through a Fresh Start,' " *BG* (April 11, 1998); P. Catterall and S. McDougall, *The Northern Ireland Question in British Politics* (1996); "In Chapter and Verse, the New Relationships," *NYT* (April 11, 1998); P. O'Malley, *Biting at the Grave: The Irish Hunger Strikes and the Politics of Despair* (1990).

NUNCA MAS. This Spanish phrase that means "Never Again," is actually the title of a report by an Argentinean commission that was created to investigate and render an account of what took place there during what has come to be called the "dirty war." The war, replete with **death squads**, was engaged in from 1976 to 1982 by a brutal military dictatorship against leftist guerrillas and civilian opposition to its rule. The report, published in 1984, details blood-curdling torture practices (stripping of skin from people's bodies, introduction of pipes into the anus), **rape**, murder "for fun," and disappearances of those who protested the increasing tyranny of the regime. Many infants, belonging to women who were arrested, were kidnapped and made to "disappear"—some were sent to favored persons for adoption. Some of the other children were tortured and killed; others were sexually abused.

It was out of the conditions briefly described above that the **Mothers of the Plaza de Mayo**, a human rights organization composed of mothers whose children had disappeared, was born. See also: Convention Against Torture and Other Cruel, Inhuman or Degrading Treatment or Punishment; Declaration on the Protection of All Persons from Enforced Disappearance. *Further Reading:* The Argentine National Commission on the Disappeared, *Nunca Mas: The Report of the Argentine National Commission on the Disappeared* (1986); C. S. Nino, *Radical Evil on Trial* (1996); D. Rock, *Argentina, 1516–1987: From Spanish Colony to Alfonsin* (1987).

NUREMBERG WAR CRIMES TRIALS. This term refers to trials that took place in Nuremberg, Germany, after World War II, from 1945 to 1947. These trials were conducted by judges from the **United States**, Britain, France, and the USSR, before whom over 175 Austrians and Germans were accused of **crimes against peace, crimes against humanity**, and **war crimes** during World War II. The accused were alleged to have either participated in the planning, preparation, or prosecution of that war, or in the actual murder, torture, enslavement, deportation, or other activities falling under the crimes with which they were charged.

Some thirty-five of the accused were acquitted. The others convicted were given varying sentences, with the twenty-four major criminals (including W. Keitel, J. von Ribbenthrop, A. Rosenberg, and J. Streicher) sentenced to death. Both the trials and the executions have been criticized on a number of grounds, the most serious of which is that the judges and prosecutors were drawn from the victors and all those accused and tried were from countries that had lost the war. The trials were very important, however, not only because they gave some victims and survivors of victims of human rights abuses a sense of international moral response to their spiritual and moral plight, but also because they helped to establish the legal basis for *personal* accountability during war. See also: International Criminal Court; My Lai Massacre; Superior Orders; War Crimes. *Further Reading:* J. E. Persico, *Nuremberg: Infamy on Trial* (1994); B. F. Smith, *The Road to Nuremberg* (1981).

NYERERE, JULIUS (1922–). Julius Nyerere served as president of Tanzania from 1961 to 1985, when he retired from office. Admiration for him steadily grew internationally, as he championed the cause of African unity (Pan-Africanism), and "African Socialism," which he claimed supported the idea of communal patterns of property ownership, popular political participation, rural development, and a classless struggle approach to social development. The latter principle, which is one of the major differences between African and Marxian socialism, did not always endear him to the Soviet Union. When he laid out his thinking in the 1967 Arusha Declaration, he gained further international support, especially when he began to insist on a *basic needs* approach to the elimination of poverty and to focus on economic development in the least industrially advanced countries.

In the areas of **human rights**, he was a fierce supporter of the right to **self-determination**. So much so, that he supported the independence of Biafra, the former Ibo area of **Nigeria** that sought to secede from that country from 1966 to 1970, despite the disapproval of his fellow African leaders. He also led international efforts against **apartheid**, and when Idi Amin, the brutal Ugandan dictator, increased his human rights abuse in Uganda, Nyerere led an invasion of that country in 1979, toppled the dictator, and restored the constitutionally elected government to office. Finally, apart from his efforts to eliminate poverty, his support for **economic, social and cultural rights**, especially for children, was outstanding. On the issue of children, his position is aptly captured in his 1969 statement: "Giving birth is something in which mankind and animals are equal. . . . But rearing the young, especially educating them for many years, is something which is a unique gift and responsibility of humans."

After Nyerere left office, many of his policies were reversed, in some cases because they had, for a variety of reasons, failed. A more market friendly economy has been introduced in Tanzania, and few make much public mention of African socialism. *Further Reading:* C. J. Hatch, *Two African Statesman: Kaunda of Zambia and Nyerere of Tanzania* (1976); W. E. Smith, *Nyerere of Tanzania* (1983).

O _____

OBJECT OF INTERNATIONAL LAW. Before 1945, individuals were *objects* of international law. That is, like ships, petroleum, mud islands, and rivers, international law could apply to individuals as it applies to objects, but individuals had no rights they could claim and assert in their own name. They were not *subjects* of international law. After World War II, the human rights movement changed the status of individuals from objects and recognized them as subjects. Individuals now have claims (rights) under international law that they can assert not only independently *of* their own governments but *against* their governments as well. See also: European Court of Human Rights; Inter-American Court of Human Rights; Human Rights Commissions; Human Rights Committee. *Further Reading:* United Nations, *Human Rights: Questions and Answers* (1987); United Nations, *Status of the Individual and Contemporary International Law* (1992).

OBLIGATION TO IMPLEMENT HUMAN RIGHTS COVENANTS. **Human rights** are merely abstractions if they are not implemented. The institutions that have the principal obligation to implement human rights are states. In the **International Bill of Human Rights**, as well as other human rights instruments, states pledge to undertake domestic, legislative, judicial, and other measures to enforce the rights they have individually and collectively recognized. Article 2 of the **International Covenants on Human Rights** typifies the types of obligations assumed by states. The **International Covenant on Economic, Social and Cultural Rights** provides the following in Article 2:

1. Each State Party to the present Covenant undertakes to take steps, individually and through international assistance and co-operation, especially economic and technical . . . with a view to achieving progressively the full realization of the

rights recognized in the present Covenant by all appropriate means, including particularly the adoption of legislative measures.

2. The States Parties to the present Covenant undertake to guarantee that the rights enunciated in the present Covenant will be exercised without discrimination of any kind. . . .

The **International Covenant on Civil and Political Rights** (ICCPR) is even more elaborate and specific in its focus on the obligation of states to enforce human rights. Article 2 (1) and (2) of that covenant provide that each state that is a party to it "undertakes to respect and to ensure to all individuals within its territory and subject to its jurisdiction the rights recognized" in the Covenant "without distinction of any kind"; and that "Where not already provided for by existing legislative or other measures, each State Party to the present Covenant undertakes to take the necessary steps . . . to adopt such legislative or other measures as may be necessary to give effect to the rights recognized." Section 3 of the same article states:

Article 2 (3). Each State Party to the present Covenant undertakes:

a. To ensure that any person whose rights or freedoms as herein recognized are violated shall have an effective remedy, notwithstanding that the violation has been committed by persons acting in an official capacity;

b. To ensure that any person claiming such a remedy shall have his rights thereto determined by competent judicial, administrative or legislative authorities . . . ;

c. To ensure that the competent authorities shall enforce such remedies when granted. See also: Judiciary; Remedy. *Further Reading:* O. Schachter, "The Obligation to Implement the Covenant in Domestic Law," in *The International Bill of Rights: The Covenant on Civil and Political Rights*, ed. L. Henkin (1981).

OFFICE OF HIGH COMMISSIONER FOR HUMAN RIGHTS. For a number of years, especially during the 1980s and early 1990s, **human rights** advocates vainly sought the creation of a High Commissioner for Human Rights. Such a person, it was reasoned, could coordinate all the human rights activities of the UN, give them coherence, and be the needed, single global voice in the field of human rights. In June 1993, the **World Conference on Human Rights** adopted the Vienna Declaration and Programme of Action, in which it recommended that the United Nations **General Assembly** begin consideration of the question of the establishment of a High Commissioner for Human Rights. In accordance with that recommendation, the General Assembly in Resolution A/48/141 of December 20, 1993, created the post of High Commissioner for Human Rights.

The resolution requires that the person who fills the post must have a "high moral standing and personal integrity" and "shall possess expertise, including in the field of human rights, and the general knowledge and understanding of the diverse cultures necessary for the impartial, objective, non-selective and effective performance of the duties of High

Commissioner." The position of High Commissioner is appointed by the secretary-general of the UN, with the approval of the General Assembly. In making the appointment, the secretary-general is to take into consideration the principle of geographical rotation, meaning that if an existing High Commissioner were to have come from Latin America, for example, his or her successor should be chosen from another geographical region of the world. The appointment has a fixed term of four years, with the possibility of one renewal for another fixed term of four years. The resolution also stipulates that the High Commissioner for Human Rights be the United Nations official "with principal responsibility for the United Nations human rights activities under the direction and authority of the Secretary-General."

In pursuing the fulfillment of his or her responsibilities, the High Commissioner must play "an active role in removing the current obstacles and meet the challenges to the full realization of all human rights and in preventing the continuation of human rights violations throughout the world, as reflected in the Vienna Declaration and Programme of Action" (VDAPA). He or she is to be guided by

[T]he recognition that all human rights—civil, cultural, economic, political and social—are universal, indivisible, interdependent and interrelated and that, while the significance of national and regional particularities and various historical, cultural and religious backgrounds must be borne in mind, it is the duty of states, regardless of their political, economic and cultural systems, to promote and protect all human rights and fundamental freedoms.

The High Commissioner also has the duty to provide, through the **Center for Human Rights** and other appropriate institutions, advisory, technical, and financial assistance to states that request them; to coordinate the UN's education and public information program; and to supervise the Centre for Human Rights. All the work of the High Commissioner must be done within the "framework of the overall competence, authority and decisions of the General Assembly, the Economic and Social Council and the Commission on Human Rights." The High Commissioner must report annually to the UN **Commission on Human Rights** on his or her activities and, through the United Nations **Economic and Social Council** (ECOSOC), to the General Assembly.

Under the General Assembly resolution creating the post of High Commissioner, the Office of High Commissioner for Human Rights was to have been located in Geneva, Switzerland, with a liaison office in New York. However, in a report of July 14, 1997, from Secretary-General Kofi Annan to the General Assembly, a change was proposed. The report, "Renewing the United Nations: A Program for Reform," recommended the consolidation of the liaison office in New York and the Centre for Human Rights in Geneva. Annan believes that the consolidation arrangement will better achieve the goal assigned to the position of High Commissioner. The consolidation has not yet been truly implemented, but the consolidated entities will become the Office of High Commissioner for Human Rights. See also: Advisory Services in the Field of Human Rights. *Further Information:* Office of the High Commissioner for Human Rights/Centre for Human Rights, Palais des Nations, CH 1211 Geneva 10, Switzerland, Tel.: 011–41–22–9173–456.

OPINION AND EXPRESSION. Freedom of opinion and expression is one of the fundamental **human rights** recognized by the global community. The **Universal Declaration of Human Rights** (UDHR) in Article 19 proclaims that right as follows: "Everyone has the right to freedom of opinion and expression; this right includes freedom to hold opinions without interference and to seek, receive and impart information and ideas through any media and regardless of frontiers."

The **International Covenant on Civil and Political Rights** (ICCPR) elaborates this right and, in addition, indicates that its exercise is not without possible restrictions. The restrictions, as well as the conditions under which they may be properly applied, are specified. Those who believe in absolute freedom in this area find the provisions somewhat troubling because they fear issues of national security and public order may be used by governments to abuse the right to freedom of opinion and expression. The relevant portions of Article 19 of the ICCPR read as follows:

1. Everyone shall have the right to hold opinions without interference.

2. Everyone shall have the right to freedom of expression; this right shall include freedom to seek, receive and impart information and ideas of all kinds, regardless of frontiers, either orally, in writing or in print, in the form of art, or through any other media of his choice.

3. The exercise of the rights provided for in paragraph 2 of this article carries with it special duties and responsibilities. It may therefore be subject to certain restrictions, but these shall only be such as are provided by law and are necessary:

a. For respect of the rights or reputations of others;

b. For the protection of national security or of public order . . . or of public health or morals.

The protections that are provided for in Article 20 of the ICCPR are repeated, with some additions, in the International Covenant on the Elimination of All Forms of Racial Discrimination, and other human rights instruments, especially the regional ones, also create concerns for those who oppose limitations on the freedom of opinion and expression. Article 20 reads:

1. Any propaganda for war shall be prohibited by law.

2. Any advocacy of national, racial or religious hatred that constitutes an incitement to discrimination, hostility or violence shall be prohibited by law.

See also: Information; Thought, Conscience and Religion.

ORGANIZATION FOR SECURITY AND CO-OPERATION IN EU-ROPE. This international organization, OSCE, the successor to the former Conference on Security and Co-operation Europe (CSCE), came into being in January 1995. Unlike its predecessor, which was born during the Cold War to help reconcile differences between rival military and political blocs, the OSCE was created "in and for a new world," a world in which the preexisting political blocs are no more. And while matters of security are an important concern to its members, the broader areas of economic, social, cultural, and political cooperation are becoming far more significant. Similarly, the CSCE human rights agenda, which was seen by many of the countries of the former Soviet Union and Eastern Europe as somewhat secondary, has now become central to OSCE.

The participating members (initially CSCE had thirty-five), which include the **United States** and **Canada,** the countries of Western Europe, Eastern Europe, **Russia,** and other states that came out of the former Soviet Union, number fifty-four. There have been suggestions that OSCE replace the North Atlantic Treaty Organization (NATO) as the forum for cooperation and security concerns among its members. OSCE is the institution that now oversees the relevant portions of the **Helsinki Accords,** especially its human dimension. See also: Human Dimension Mechanism. *Further Reading:* J. Wright, "The OSCE of Europe and Minority Rights," *HRQ,* vol. 18 no. 1 (1996).

ORGANIZATION OF AFRICAN UNITY. This international organization representing Africa was created in 1963 by thirty-two African states. The OAU, which today has more than fifty members, focuses on issues affecting the African continent, including opposition to **apartheid,** support for decolonization of the continent, preservation of existing territorial borders of member states, and, to some extent, promotion of the Pan-African goal of continental political unity. The OAU also pursues efforts to create a united African stance in multilateral diplomacy in the United Nations and similar international institutions. The organization has experienced some divisions among its members, especially when **Julius Nyerere** intervened in Uganda to overthrow the human rights abusing government of Idi Amin; on the issue of **self-determination** for **Western Sahara** and Biafra; and on the military coups in **Nigeria.** The OAU has not been forceful, either, in condemning violations of **human rights** by member states, including the **genocide** in **Rwanda.**

It was the OAU, however, which authorized the drafting of the **African Charter on Human and Peoples' Rights,** and at a meeting in Nairobi, Kenya, June 24–27, 1981, the organization took the historic step of adopting that charter and passing it on to member states to begin the ratification process. *Further Reading:* C.O.C. Amate, *Inside the OAU: Pan-Africanism in Practice* (1986); G. Harris, *Organization of African Unity* (1994).

ORGANIZATION OF AMERICAN STATES. Founded in 1948 by twenty-one original members, the Organization of American States (OAS) is the regional international organization of the Americas or, more comprehensively, the Western Hemisphere, including the Caribbean. Today, it boasts thirty-five members, including **Cuba,** which has been suspended, but the OAS has become progressively less prominent in international political activities. The reduction in prominence bespeaks the ending of the Cold War, which in large measure was the international motivation for its creation—at the time, the **United States** sought regional solidarity against communism—and the emergence of international economic agendas as the principal focus of global diplomacy. The OAS Charter provides for such economic agendas, but member states have sought to pursue those agendas in other forums.

While regional security was the primary reason for the United States' push for the creation of the OAS, Latin American countries had another aim: to limit United States intervention in their affairs. So one of the central legal and moral principles of the organization is that of nonintervention. That principle was the basis for much division in the Inter-Americas when the United States intervened militarily in Grenada in 1983 and in the Dominican Republic in 1965; it also served as a basis for solidarity with the United States in 1962, when the USSR stationed missiles in Cuba.

In the field of **human rights,** the OAS has had a mixed record. On the one hand, it has created some very important and promising human rights institutions such as the **Inter-American Court of Human Rights** and the Inter-American Commission on Human Rights, two institutions that have begun to have an important impact on human rights in the Americas. Likewise, the OAS has adopted some far-reaching human rights instruments, such as the **American Declaration on the Rights and Duties of Man** (ADRDM) and the **American Convention on Human Rights.** Two of its specialized agencies, the **Inter-American Commission of Women** and the Inter-American Indian Institute have also made significant contributions to the promotion of human rights. On the other hand, the OAS has not been effective in ensuring the protection of the "dignity and freedom" for the people of the hemisphere. In some cases, as in Argentina during the 1970s and early 1980s, **Brazil** during the 1960s, and Guatemala from the middle 1960s to the 1990s, to use three instances, the OAS did little, although the violations of human rights in the instances cited had assumed epidemic proportions. See also: Chile; Human Rights Commissions; *Nunca Mas*; Truth Commissions. *Further Reading:* C. O. Stoetzer, *The Organization of American States* (1993).

OSLO ACCORDS. See ISRAEL.

P

PACT OF SAN JOSE. See AMERICAN CONVENTION ON HUMAN RIGHTS.

PAKISTAN. See BANGLADESH.

PALESTINE LIBERATION ORGANIZATION. The Palestine Liberation Organization (PLO) was founded in 1964 and is the officially recognized representative of the Palestinian people. Since the date of its founding, it has had as its goal—a goal fiercely advocated by its leader, Yasir Arafat— the establishment of a Palestinian state. The achievement of that goal, however, until 1993–1994, was linked to the destruction of the state of **Israel.** In 1974, the PLO gained observer status with the United Nations and it has since participated in the work of the United Nations **General Assembly.**

Much of the PLO's life, as an organization, has been outside Palestine. It was, for example, expelled from Jordan where it was headquartered, following a violent 1970 confrontation with that country's government. After leaving Jordan, it established headquarters in Lebanon, where it was attacked in 1982 by **Israel** and forced to flee to Tunisia. It was headquartered there until 1993–1994, when it returned to Palestine (Gaza and the West Bank), after concluding an agreement with Israel. That agreement was historic in three important senses: (1) it marks a change in Israel's policy not to negotiate with the PLO, which had carried out many violent attacks on Israel, in part to force it to withdraw from the occupied territories— primarily the West Bank and Gaza, which Israel had been occupying since the 1967 Arab–Israeli War; (2) it embodies the PLO's renunciation of its former goal to destroy the state of Israel; and (3) for both Israel and the PLO, it represents an effort to tame if not abort the feared rising influence of a more radical Palestinian group called Hamas.

In 1995, another agreement was concluded between the PLO and Israel. That agreement provides for a Palestinian Authority, led by the PLO, to assume local powers in the occupied territories; it also provides for additional negotiations to determine the future status of those territories and East Jerusalem. Some Palestinian and Israeli groups have opposed this agreement, and the consequences of that opposition have included suicide bombings against Israeli civilians by Hamas, increased arbitrary arrests and detentions by Israel, the assassination, by an Israeli (Yigal Amir), of Israel's prime minister, Yitzhak Rabin, and a delay in and even a threat to the process of **self-determination** for the Palestinians. In the West Bank and Gaza, the newly created Palestinian Authority has been secretive, guilty of **arbitrary arrest and detention** of Palestinians, and disinclined to accept criticism. There is also some evidence that the PLO has been using its base in the occupied territories to encourage attacks on Israel's civilian population. Despite all the differences with Israel, an October 1998 agreement guaranteed by the United States provided that Israel transfer 13 percent of the West Bank to PLO control and for the resumption of talks to further Israeli–Palestinian agreements about the final status of the West Bank and Gaza. See also: Intifadah. *Further Reading:* R. Khalidi, *Palestinian Identity* (1997); I. Gershoni and J. P. Jankowski, eds., *Rethinking Nationalism in the Arab Middle East* (1997).

PALME, OLAF (1927–1986). Olaf Palme was a Swedish political leader who served as prime minister of his country from 1969 to 1976 and again from 1982 to 1986. His death in 1986 by gunfire on his way home from a social engagement with his wife, remains an unsolved murder case.

His work in the area of **human rights** was always a part of his support for *social democracy*, which not only focuses on the **civil and political rights** associated with democracy under capitalism, but also emphasizes **economic, social and cultural rights**. He was also one of Europe's strongest opponents of **apartheid** and all forms of racial discrimination. He was, as well, a strong advocate of the human community's right to peace. Despite the fact that Sweden had been an important arms-exporting state, he championed arms control and, in 1980, chaired the Palme Commission (an international commission) on global disarmament. See also: Declaration on the Right of Peoples to Peace; International Convention on the Elimination of All Forms of Racial Discrimination. *Further Reading:* P. Alston, "Peace as a Human Right," *BPP*, vol. 11 (1980).

PARLIAMENT OF THE WORLD'S RELIGIONS. See RELIGION AND HUMAN RIGHTS.

PEACE. See DECLARATION ON THE RIGHT OF PEOPLES TO PEACE.

PEOPLES. The term *peoples* is an international concept that denotes human cultural groups, as distinct from individuals, in which certain **human rights** are said to be inherent. These rights include the right to **self-determination**, the right to enjoy "permanent sovereignty over their natural wealth and resources," and the right to preserve and promote their cultural heritage.

The precise meaning of peoples has never been fully established, but it generally refers to groups whose extended cultural heritage, unique historical experience, and expectations about a common future place on them the stamp of social and cultural distinctiveness that merits and justifies the rights mentioned above. In 1960, the United Nations **General Assembly** designated colonial countries and peoples as entitled to independence. In 1966, the two **international covenants on human rights** proclaimed that "all peoples have the right to self-determination. By virtue of that right they freely determine their political status and freely pursue their economic, social and cultural development." In 1981, the African states named their regional human rights instrument, the **African Charter on Human and Peoples' Rights**.

Because peoples are entitled to certain rights, it follows that the identity of peoples is very important. Hence, the long fight that began in the 1980s, to shift the designation of indigenous persons throughout the world from indigenous populations, aboriginals, and native and tribal groups to **indigenous peoples**. It also explains why the Basques in Spain and France, the Chechnyans in **Russia**, the Kashmiri in **India**, Kurds, Palestinians, and the people of Tibet and **Western Sahara** have sought and received recognition as peoples. The Kurds, Palestinians, and Saharawi have been recognized as peoples. See also: Chechnya; China; Kurdistan. *Further Reading:* A. Cassese, *Self-Determination of Peoples: A Legal Reappraisal* (1995); J. Crawford, *The Rights of Peoples* (1988).

PETITION. See HUMAN RIGHTS COMMISSIONS; HUMAN RIGHTS COMMITTEE.

PHILIPPINES. The Republic of the Philippines is an archipelago in the Pacific Ocean off the southeastern coast of Asia. It is comprised of over 7,000 islands; the two largest are Luzon and Mindanao. The country, with an estimated population of over 68 million people was colonized by Spain from 1565 to 1898. From 1898 to 1946, when it gained its independence, it was controlled by the **United States**, except for the period 1941–1945, when it was occupied by Japan. The population is overwhelmingly Christian (over 85 percent Roman Catholic and about 4 percent Protestant), with Islam, which is largely concentrated on Mindanao, representing about 6 percent. Languages include English, which is used in higher education and government, Tagalog, and Visayan.

Since independence, the country has had a mixed record on **human rights**, especially after 1965, when Ferdinand Marcos was elected president. He immediately began to entrench himself as a dictator, denying people their right to **democratic entitlement**. From 1972 to 1981, using left-wing insurgency as an excuse, Marcos held the country under martial law. During that time, his government routinely violated the **civil and political rights** of citizens, and when in 1983, opposition leader Benigno Aquino returned from exile in the United States, he was assassinated. A peaceful, grassroots rebellion, led by Corazon Aquino, widow of Benigno Aquino, overthrew Marcos in 1986, and a new constitution with a bill of rights was adopted in 1987.

Under Article 13 of the new constitution, a Philippine national Commission of Human Rights was created and vested with powers to investigate, on its own initiative or in response to complaints from any party, all forms of human rights violations. The Philippine Commission on Human Rights also has visitational and investigative powers over jails, prisons, and other detention facilities. In a 1988 report to the United Nations **Human Rights Committee** indicating what steps it had taken to protect human rights, the government of the Philippines indicated that enforcement of its commission's decisions was to be left entirely to the Philippine judiciary.

Despite improvements in human rights protections in certain areas of civil and political rights—freedom of speech and the press, independence of the judiciary, periodic elections, for example—major areas of human rights violations remain. **Discrimination** against women and **indigenous peoples** is rampant; women are exploited by unethical operators who use the poverty that women and girls face to promise employment abroad only to subject many of them to conditions under which sex and prostitution are the major attraction; domestic violence, especially marital **rape**, has been widespread. Additionally, disappearances still take place, and the government has not adequately responded to the use of private security forces maintained by local landowners, political figures, and criminal gangs to administer extrajudicial punishments, including killings. The latter course of conduct appears to be engaged in by government forces as well, especially in relation to Muslim separatists on Mindanao. Finally, education and health care for the poor, protection of land and mineral resources of indigenous peoples, especially on northern Luzon, and the protection of workers from intimidation by employers are areas of human rights that the government has largely neglected. See also: Convention for the Suppression of the Traffic in persons and the Exploitation of the Prostitution of Others; Public Emergency; Slavery, the Slave Trade, and Slavery-like Practices. *Further Reading:* G. Casper, *Fragile Democracies* (1995); B. Johnson, *The Four Days of Courage: The Untold Story of the People Who Brought Marcos Down* (1987).

PHYSICAL AND MENTAL HEALTH. The right to physical and mental health is among those **economic, social and cultural rights** recognized by the international community. The **International Covenant on Economic, Social and Cultural Rights** provides the following in Article 12:

1. The States Parties to the present Covenant recognize the right of everyone to the enjoyment of the highest attainable standard of physical and mental health.

2. The steps to be taken by the States Parties to the present Covenant to achieve the full realization of this right shall include those necessary for:

a. The provision for the reduction of stillbirth-rate and of infant mortality and for the healthy development of the child;

b. The improvement of all aspects of environmental and industrial hygiene;

c. The prevention, treatment and control of epidemic, endemic, occupational and other diseases;

d. The creation of conditions which would assure to all medical service and medical attention in the event of sickness.

On varying terms, regional human rights instruments also provide this right. The **International Covenant on Economic, Social and Cultural Rights,** in recognizing the right to the "highest attainable standard" of physical and mental health, however, provides the broadest scope for the exercise of this right. See also: Health. *Further Reading:* E. I. Pavalon, *Human Rights and Health Care Law* (1980); World Health Organization, *Promotion of the Rights of Patients in Europe* (1995).

PHYSICIANS FOR HUMAN RIGHTS. This is a **nongovernmental organization** (NGO) of health professionals, scientists, and concerned citizens that employs the knowledge, insights, and skills of medical and forensic scientists to investigate and prevent violations of **human rights.** The organization also works to provide assistance to victims and educate health professionals about the contribution they can make to protect human rights throughout the world.

Since its founding in 1986, Physicians for Human Rights (PHR) has conducted over seventy-six missions to many countries. Among its accomplishments are the exhumation of mass graves in the former Yugoslavia and **Rwanda,** in order to help provide medical and legal evidentiary assistance to the international criminal tribunals for the former Yugoslavia and Rwanda; DNA fingerprinting in El Salvador to help in family reunification of children abducted by the Salvadoran army over a decade earlier; and the study of medical response to political violence and government-sanctioned torture in **Turkey.** In addition, PHR collected soil samples in Iraqi **Kurdistan,** which provided physical evidence of **Iraq's** use of lethal nerve agents on Kurdish villages—a **crime against humanity.** It has been a leader in the campaign to inform and alarm the world about the medical disasters posed by **land mines;** has produced an important expose on cruel and inhuman treatment of prisoners in a **United States** county jail; and has developed a methodology to help document rape and war trauma.

The PHR has a significant publishing program, which includes the *Record*, an important newsletter; two of its recently published books are *War Crimes in the Balkans* (1996) and *Torture in Turkey* (1996). See also: Ethnic Cleansing; Milosevic, Slobodoa; Serbia; War Crimes Tribunals. *Further Information:* Physicians for Human Rights, 100 Boylston Street, Suite 702, Boston, Mass. 02116, Tel.: (617) 695–0041.

POLAND. Poland is a state located in north-central Europe. It has a population of about 41 million people, over 90 percent of whom are Roman Catholic. The remainder of the population are Eastern Orthodox (5 percent), followers of Protestant denominations (2 percent), or believers in Judaism and Islam who constitute less than one percent of the population.

Nazi Germany's invasion of Poland on September 1, 1939, signaled the beginning of World War II. When Russia invaded Poland on September 17, Poland was divided between Germany and Russia until 1941, when, after Germany's attack on Russia, the entire country came under Nazi rule. The Nazis exterminated millions of Polish citizens, most of them Jews. After the war, following its liberation by the armed forces of the USSR in 1945, the country came under the control of the United Workers (communist) Party. The party, taking direction from the USSR, denied the Polish people their right to **democratic entitlement** for over forty years. Likewise, the party-led government seized church property, denied legal status to the Catholic Church (and other religious groups as well), and often made pledged support for the party a precondition for the "free exercise" of the right to associate.

At different times, in 1956 and 1970, for example, Polish society unsuccessfully challenged the nondemocratic rule of the Communist Party. But after 1978, when Karol Wojtyla (1920–), a Polish cardinal, was elected Pope John Paul II, a new surge of nationalism, coupled with pent-up social and economic frustrations, gave birth to a powerful union-led and Catholic Church–supported national movement called *Solidarity*. The movement, led by Lech Walesa (1943–) erupted into open confrontation and violence in 1980, and culminated in the Polish military replacing the Communist Party in control of the government. With martial law declared (1981–1982), wholesale government violations of **civil and political rights**, including the criminalization of *Solidarity*, followed. But opponents of the government, encouraged by Lech Walesa's receipt of the Nobel Peace Prize (1983) and the United States' imposition of economic sanctions against Poland, continued their defiance with full vigor. By 1989, with declining legitimacy nationally and internationally, and democratic sentiments emerging in the USSR, the government of Poland legalized *Solidarity* and the Catholic Church and allowed multiparty elections. The elections resulted in a *Solidarity* leader becoming prime minister, and the following year, 1990, Lech Walesa was elected president.

After the events of 1989–1990, Polish society faced radical economic changes designed to shift it from a communist to a capitalist pattern of economic organization. One result has been a less-regulated economy and greater opportunities for private initiatives. Another result has been the undermining of **economic, social and cultural rights**, so much so, that following the results of a 1993 election, *Solidarity* was replaced by a coalition of parties, some of which had their roots in the former Communist Party. In 1997, that coalition had not done what it claimed it would, and was replaced by a new coalition government, which includes many supporters of *Solidarity*, but committed to a greater balance between the civil and political rights capitalism seeks and the **economic, social and cultural rights** socialism espouses. See also: Russia. *Further Reading:* G. Blazyca and R. Rapacki, *Poland into the 1990s* (1991); J. Hardy and A. Rainnie, *Restructuring Krakow* (1996); Human Rights Watch, *Hidden Victims: Women in Post-Communist Poland* (1992).

POLISARIO. See WESTERN SAHARA.

POLITICAL RIGHTS. See CIVIL AND POLITICAL RIGHTS; DEMOCRATIC ENTITLEMENT.

POL POT. See CAMBODIA.

POVERTY. Poverty, which today affects over 1 billion people, is an issue of great concern to the UN. Its concern has been particularly focused on the relationship between poverty and **human rights**.

In 1988, the UN secretary-general submitted to the UN **General Assembly** a report entitled *International Co-operation for the Eradication of Poverty* (UN Doc. A/44/467). That report noted: (1) the increase in the number of persons in poverty; (2) the links between the increase and the number of vulnerable persons, including refugees, migrant workers, disabled people, and women and children; and (3) the correlation between that number and war-related violence, as well as famines and trends in modernization that weaken traditional support and mutual obligation systems. In the last case, for example, privatization of natural resources, such as water and grazing lands, and the commercialization of economic activities, further the marginalization of the socially vulnerable.

Armed with the information from the report, in August 1992, the **Commission on Human Rights** authorized a study on human rights and extreme poverty, which was completed in 1996. A year before, however, from March 6–12, 1995, the global community met in Copenhagen, Denmark, at the UN-sponsored World Summit for Social Development. At the summit, countries adopted the Copenhagen Declaration and Programme of Action through which they pledged themselves to ten commitments. The second of those commitments deals specifically with poverty and reads as follows:

We commit ourselves to the goal of eradicating poverty in the world, through decisive national actions and international co-operation, as an ethical, social, political and economic imperative of humankind.

To this end . . . we will:

a. Formulate or strength, as a matter of urgency, and preferably by the year 1996, the International Year for the Eradication of Poverty, national policies and strategies geared to substantially reducing overall poverty in the shortest possible time, to reducing inequalities, and to eradicating absolute poverty by a target date to be specified by each country in its national context.

The declaration goes on to detail other aspects of the commitment, especially that of focusing on the "needs and rights of women and children" and the adoption of strategies designed to give effect to that commitment. The strategies include the "full implementation of the relevant human rights instruments such as the International Covenant on Economic, Social and Cultural Rights and the International Covenant on Civil and Political Rights." See also: International Covenant on Civil and Political Rights; International Covenant on Economic, Social and Cultural Rights; Standard of Living. *Further Reading:* J. D. Berrick, *The Faces of Poverty* (1995); World Summit for Social Development, *Copenhagen Declaration and Programme of Action* (1995).

PRINCIPLES OF INTERNATIONAL CO-OPERATION IN THE DETECTION, ARREST, EXTRADITION AND PUNISHMENT OF WAR CRIMES AND CRIMES AGAINST HUMANITY. On December 3, 1973, the United Nations General Assembly, in order to encourage and facilitate the prosecution and punishment of persons properly accused of war crimes and crimes against humanity, elaborated and proclaimed nine principles of international cooperation to which states have committed themselves. The first five principles are:

1. War crimes and crimes against humanity, wherever they are committed, shall be subject to investigation and the persons against whom there is evidence that they have committed such crimes shall be subject to tracing, arrest, trial and, if found guilty, to punishment.

2. Every State has the right to try its own nationals for war crimes or crimes against humanity.

3. States shall co-operate with each other . . . with a view to halting and preventing war crimes and crimes against humanity, and shall take the domestic and international measures necessary for that purpose.

4. States shall assist each other in detecting, arresting and bringing to trial persons suspected of having committed such crimes and, if they are found guilty, in punishing them.

5. Persons against whom there is evidence that they have committed war crimes and crimes against humanity shall be subject to trial and, if found guilty, to punishment, as a general rule in the countries in which they committed those crimes. In that connection States shall co-operate on questions of extraditing such persons.

The four other principles deal with cooperation in obtaining information and evidence, with not granting **asylum** to persons if there are serious grounds for suspecting that they have committed war crimes or crimes against humanity, with not taking any legislative or other measures that may impair international obligations and with ensuring punishment for those found guilty in conformity with the provisions of the UN Charter and other principles of international law.

PRINCIPLES OF INTERNATIONAL LAW RECOGNIZED IN THE CHARTER AND IN THE JUDGMENT OF THE NUREMBERG TRIBUNAL. These principles undergird the trials of Austrian and German criminals after World War II. To ensure that they would remain or become standards in future international relations, not simply rules of former wartime trials, the United Nations **General Assembly** requested its **International Law Commission** (ILC) to formulate and refine the principles. The body of principles, as formulated in 1950 by the ILC, is as follows:

1. Any person who commits an act which constitutes a crime under international law is responsible therefore and liable to punishment.

2. The fact that international law does not impose a penalty for an act which constitutes a crime under international law does not relieve the person who committed the act from responsibility under international law.

3. The fact that a person who committed an act which constitutes a crime under international law acted as Head of State or responsible government official does not relieve him from responsibility under international law.

4. The fact that a person acted pursuant to order of his government or of a superior does not relieve him from responsibility under international law, provided a moral choice was in fact possible to him.

5. Any person charged with a crime under international law has the right to a fair trial on the facts and the law.

6. The crimes hereinafter set out are punishable as crimes under international law:

   a. Crimes against peace: . . .

   b. War crimes: . . .

   c. Crimes against humanity: . . .

7. Complicity in the commission of a crime against peace, a war crime, or a crime against humanity as set forth in principle 6 is a crime under international law.

See also: Crimes Against Humanity; Crimes Against Peace; War Crimes.
Further Reading: J. F. Persico, *Nuremberg: Infamy on Trial* (1994); B. F. Smith, *The Road to Nuremberg* (1981); *UN Yearbook 1950* (852–57).

PRINCIPLES OF MEDICAL ETHICS RELEVANT TO THE ROLE OF HEALTH PROFESSIONALS, PARTICULARLY PHYSICIANS, IN THE PROTECTION OF PRISONERS AND DETAINEES AGAINST TORTURE AND OTHER CRUEL, INHUMAN OR DEGRADING TREATMENT OR PUNISHMENT.

Persons who are detained, imprisoned, or otherwise subject to the control of public authorities are no less human than those who are not subject to that control. As such, they are entitled to the protection of their **human rights**. In order to help in that protection, especially with respect to the conduct of health professionals, the United Nations **General Assembly**, on December 18, 1982, adopted the following six principles:

Principle 1. Health personnel, particularly physicians, charged with the medical care of prisoners and detainees have a duty to provide them with protection of their physical and mental health and treatment of disease of the same quality and standard as is afforded to those who are not imprisoned or detained.

Principle 2. It is a gross contravention of medical ethics, as well as an offense under applicable international instruments, for health personnel, particularly physicians, to engage, actively or passively, in acts which constitute participation in, complicity in, incitement to or attempts to commit torture or other cruel, inhuman or degrading treatment or punishment.

Principle 3. It is a contravention of medical ethics for health personnel, particularly physicians, to be involved in any professional relationship with prisoners or detainees the purpose of which is not solely to evaluate, protect or improve their physical and mental health.

Principle 4. It is a contravention of medical ethics for health personnel, particularly physicians:

a. To apply their knowledge and skills in order to assist in the interrogation of prisoners and detainees in a manner that may adversely affect the physical or mental health condition of such prisoners or detainees and which is not in accordance with the relevant international instruments;

b. To certify or to participate in the certification of, the fitness of prisoners or detainees for any form of treatment or punishment that may adversely affect their physical or mental health. . . .

Principle 5. It is a contravention of medical ethics for health personnel, particularly physicians, to participate in any procedure for restraining a prisoner or detainee unless such a procedure is determined in accordance with purely medical criteria as being necessary for the protection of the physical or mental health or safety of the prisoner or detainee himself, of his fellow prisoners or detainees, or of his guardians, and presents no hazard to his physical or mental health.

Principle 6. There may be no derogation from the forgoing principles on any grounds whatsoever, including public emergency.

See also: Health; Physical and Mental Health. *Further Reading:* G. J. Annas and M. A. Grodin, *The Nazi Doctors and the Nuremberg Code* (1992); E. I. Pavalon, *Human Rights and Health Care Law* (1980).

PRIVACY. The emergence of the age of communications, which is in part defined by computerized databases, makes the risk to individual privacy all the more threatening and real. The right of every individual to privacy, which is recognized by the global community, offers some protection. The **Universal Declaration of Human Rights** (UDHR) states in Article 12 that "No one shall be subjected to arbitrary interference with his privacy, family, home or correpondence, nor to attacks upon his honour and reputation. Everyone has the right to the protection of the law against such interference or attacks."

The **International Covenant on Civil and Political Rights** (ICCPR) provides the same protection as the UDHR. Indeed, the right to privacy is stated in almost identical wording and fashion. The relevant portion of Article 17 of the ICCPR reads:

1. No one shall be subjected to arbitrary or unlawful interference with his privacy, family, home or correspondence, nor to unlawful attacks on his honour and reputation.

2. Everyone has the right to the protection of the law against such interference or attacks.

The **European Convention on Human Rights** (Article 8) and the **American Convention on Human Rights** (Article 11) offer protection comparable to that of the global instruments. Equally important, the United Nations **Human Rights Committee** has interpreted the provisions of the ICCPR to include guarantees against all prohibited interference from the state as well as from persons or corporations, for example. See also: Declaration on the Use of Scientific and Technological Progress in the Interest of Peace and for the Benefit of Mankind. *Further Reading:* B. Kahin and C. Nesson, *Borders in Cyberspace* (1997); H. MacNeil, *Without Consent* (1992); J. F. Metzl, "Information Technology and Human Rights," *HRQ*, vol. 18 no. 4 (1996).

PROCEDURAL GUARANTEES, PROCESSES AND PROTECTIONS. International human rights instruments, at the global and regional levels, not only define and elaborate the substantive rights of individuals and groups, they also prescribe the manner in which the rights may be exercised, enforced, and, when deemed necessary, limited. Likewise, especially in cases of alleged criminal conduct, human rights instruments provide measures to ensure fairness in the protection of those rights and remedies when they are violated. What follows, combined with the provisions in **fair trial** is a partial listing of the globally recognized guarantees and protections.

The **Universal Declaration of Human Rights** (UDHR) provides the following principles:

Article 6. Everyone has the right to recognition everywhere as a person before the law.

Article 7. All are equal before the law and are entitled without discrimination to equal protection of the law. All are entitled to equal protection against any discrimination in violation of this Declaration and against any incitement to such discrimination.

Article 9. No one shall be subjected to arbitrary arrest, detention or exile.

Article 10. Everyone is entitled in full equality to a fair and public hearing by an independent and impartial tribunal, in the determination of his rights and obligations and of any criminal charge against him.

Article 11 (1). Everyone charged with a penal offence has the right to be presumed innocent until proved guilty according to law in a public trial at which he has had all the guarantees necessary for his defence.

(2). No one shall be held guilty of any penal offence on account of any act or omission which did not constitute a penal offence, under national or international law, at the time when it was committed. Nor shall a heavier penalty be imposed than the one that was applicable at the time the penal offence was committed.

In dealing with same subject, but in much greater detail, the **International Covenant on Civil and Political Rights** (ICCPR) provides:

Article 14 (1). All persons shall be equal before the courts and tribunals. In the determination of any criminal charge against him, or of his rights and obligations in a suit at law, everyone shall be entitled to a fair and public hearing by a competent, independent and impartial tribunal established by law. The Press and the public may be excluded from all or part of a trial for reasons of morals, public order . . . or national security in a democratic society, or when the interest of the private lives of the parties so requires, or to the extent strictly necessary in the opinion of the court in special circumstances where publicity would prejudice the interests of justice; but any judgement rendered in a criminal case or in a suit at law shall be made public except where the interest of juvenile persons otherwise requires or the proceedings concern matrimonial disputes of the guardianship of children.

Sections 2 and 3 of Article 14 deal with the right to be presumed innocent until proven guilty by law in cases where an individual is charged with a criminal offense; in criminal cases certain "minimum guarantees" to a fair trial are elaborated. Sections 4–7 of Article 14 provide further procedural protections, such as the right to have one's conviction and sentence reviewed by a higher tribunal; to be compensated in case of wrongful accusation; and the right not to be tried or punished twice for an offense for which one has been already convicted or acquitted. Articles 15 and 16 of the covenant, which deal with further protections and guarantees, merely repeat those mentioned in the Universal Declaration of Human Rights. The regional international instruments, especially those of the Americas and Western Europe, largely replicate the global instruments. See also: Derogation; Public Emergency.

PROCLAMATION OF TEHERAN. This proclamation was adopted by the International Conference on Human Rights, which took place in Teheran, Iran, from April 22 to May 13, 1968. Apart from being an important expression of international sentiments commemorating the twentieth anniversary of the **Universal Declaration of Human Rights** (UDHR), the proclamation is significant for three reasons: (1) it underlined the universality of **human rights**; (2) it linked peace, justice, and human rights, noting that the latter cannot be fully realized without the first two; (3) it affirmed that the Universal Declaration of Human Rights is not merely a body of standing ideals but an instrument of *international obligation*.

The first two paragraphs of the proclamation give a fair sense of the shared international understanding and commitments that came out of the conference, as states

Solemnly proclaim(ed) that:

1. It is imperative that the members of the international community fulfil their obligations to promote and encourage respect for human rights and fundamental freedoms for all without distinctions of any kind such as race, colour, sex, language, religion, political or other opinions;

2. The Universal Declaration of Human Rights states a common understanding of the peoples of the world concerning the alienable and inviolable rights of all members of the human family and constitutes an obligation for the members of the international community.

The proclamation also deals with the indivisible character of the different classes of human rights, the need to encourage the younger generation in their aspirations for a better world, and the need to pursue disarmament, since disarmament would release human and material resources to be used for the promotion of **human rights**.

The proclamation, in an affirmation of faith and encouragement, ends in the following manner:

The International Conference on Human Rights,

1. *Affirming* its faith in the principles of the Universal Declaration of Human Rights and other international instruments in the field,

2. *Urges* all peoples and governments to dedicate themselves to the principles enshrined in the Universal Declaration of Human Rights and to redouble their efforts to provide for all human beings a life consonant with freedom and dignity and conducive to physical, mental, social and spiritual welfare.

See also: Armed Conflict; International Bill of Human Rights;

PROPAGANDA. Among the **human rights** recognized by the world community is the freedom of thought, opinion, and expression. Article 19 of the **Universal Declaration of Human Rights** (UDHR) provides that "this right includes the freedom to hold opinions without interference and to seek, receive and impart information and ideas through any media and regardless of frontiers." Article 19 of the **International Covenant on Civil and Political Rights** (ICCPR) essentially repeats the provisions of the declaration, but Article 20 of the covenant, seeking to curb and even prevent certain types of propaganda, imposes two limitations on the freedom of opinion and expression:

1. Any propaganda for war shall be prohibited by law.
2. Any advocacy of national, racial or religious hatred that constitutes incitement to discrimination, hostility or violence shall be prohibited by law.

The 1965 **International Convention on the Elimination of All Forms of Racial Discrimination** elaborates and reinforces the limitations imposed by the ICCPR as follows:

Article 4. States Parties condemn all propaganda and all organizations which are based on ideas or theories of superiority of one race or group of persons of one colour or ethnic origin, or which attempt to justify or promote racial hatred and discrimination in any form, and undertake to adopt immediate and positive measures designed to eradicate all incitement . . . and, to this end . . . :

a. Shall declare an offence punishable by law all dissemination of ideas based on racial superiority or hatred, incitement to racial discrimination, as well as all acts of violence or incitement to such acts against any race or group of persons of another colour or ethnic origin, and also the provision of any assistance to racist activities, including financing thereof;

b. Shall declare illegal and prohibit organizations, and also organized and all other propaganda activities, which promote and incite racial discrimination, and shall recognize participation in such organizations or activities as an offence punishable by law.

In 1978, the **United Nations Educational, Scientific and Cultural Organization** (UNESCO), whose purposes include the removal of distrust, suspicion, and ignorance among people and helping prepare the "intellectual and moral solidarity" on which the dignity of human beings can be nurtured, adopted the Declaration on Race and Racial Prejudice. That declaration provides:

Article 7. In addition to political, economic and social measures, law is one of the principal means of ensuring equality in dignity and rights among individuals, and of curbing any propaganda, any form of organization or any practice which is based on ideas or theories referring to the alleged superiority of racial or ethnic groups or which seeks to justify or encourage racial hatred and discrimination in any forms.

Despite the curbs provided or called for by the human rights instruments mentioned above, states have been reluctant to impose them, in part due to fears that curbs of the kind recommended could lead to unacceptable limitations on the freedom of speech and the press. The 1994 **genocide** in **Rwanda,** during which radio broadcasts were used to incite hatred and violence against the Tutsi and, although less pronounced, a similar type of propaganda during the war in the former Yugoslavia, are likely to cause countries to pause and reflect on the need to impose the curbs suggested. See also: Ethnic Cleansing; Serbia.

PROPERTY. The right to own and enjoy property is recognized in a number of relevant global and regional human rights instruments. The **Universal Declaration of Human Rights** (UDHR) provides in Article 17 that

1. Everyone has the right to own property alone as well as in association with others.
2. No one shall be arbitrarily deprived of his property.

Article 5 of the **International Convention on the Elimination of All Forms of Racial Discrimination** includes the right, without distinction as to race, color or national origin, "to own property alone as well as in association with others." It also provides for the "right to inherit" property. The **Convention on the Elimination of All Forms of Discrimination Against Women** (CEDAW) states the following:

Article 16 (1). States Parties shall take appropriate measures to eliminate discrimination against women in all matters relating to marriage and family relations and in particular shall ensure, on the basis of equality of men and women: . . .

h. The same rights of both spouses in respect to ownership, acquisition, management, administration, enjoyment and disposition of property, whether free of charge or for a valuable consideration.

Other articles in CEDAW deal with rights facilitative of the right to ownership—rights such as that to bank loans, to mortgages, and other forms of financial credit, and the right to enter into contracts.

The regional human rights instruments, especially the **African Charter on Human and Peoples' Rights** and the **American Convention on Human Rights** explicitly or implicitly deal with the right to property. The American Convention, in addition, provides for just compensation to owners, when private property is taken for "public utility or social interests." It also prohibits using the right of ownership of property for the exploitation of one human being by another. And the African Charter provides:

Article 14. The right to property shall be guaranteed. It may only be encroached upon in the interest of public need or in the general interest of the community and in accordance with the provisions of appropriate laws.

See also: Bonded Labor. *Further Reading:* M. Cunliffe, *The Right to Property: A Theme in American History* (1974); T. Hodgskin, *The Natural and Artificial Right of Property Contrasted* (1981); D. Usher, *The Economic Prerequisite to Democracy* (1981).

PROSTITUTION. See CONVENTION FOR THE SUPPRESSION OF THE TRAFFIC IN PERSONS AND THE EXPLOITATION OF THE PROSTITUTION OF OTHERS; SLAVERY; THE SLAVE TRADE, AND SLAVERY-LIKE PRACTICES.

PUBLIC EMERGENCY. This expression refers to a specific condition during which limitations on or **derogation** from recognized norms of **human rights** are permissible. That condition arises when there are circumstances that "threaten the life of the nation." Article 4 (1) of the **International Covenant on Civil and Political Rights** deals with the condition as follows:

In time of public emergency which threatens the life of the nation and the existence of which is officially proclaimed, the States Parties to the present Covenant may take measures derogating from their obligations under the present Covenant to the extent strictly required by the exigencies of the situation, provided that such measures are not inconsistent with their other obligations under international law and do not involve discrimination solely on the ground of race, colour, sex, language, religion or social origin.

Article 4, as a careful reading in its entirety should disclose, *requires* that the existence of the public emergency be "publicly proclaimed" by states; that measures taken derogating from those states' obligations under the covenant be those that are and only to the extent "strictly required by the exigencies of the situation," and that when the right of derogation is exercised by any state, it should communicate immediately to the secretary general of the United Nations, indicating the provision(s) of the covenant from which it is derogating and the reasons for such derogation. The article also spells out the rights from which there can be no derogation, under any circumstances, including public emergencies.

Despite the requirements indicated above, the proclamation of public emergencies can be abused. To make that abuse more difficult to engage in, the European Commission of Human Rights has identified certain characteristics that should accompany any crisis that is defined as a public emergency:

1. It must be actual or imminent.
2. Its effects must involve the whole nation.

3. The continuance of the organized life of the community must be threatened.

4. The crisis or danger must be exceptional in that the normal measures or restrictions permitted by the Convention for the maintenance of public safety, health and order are plainly inadequate.

See also: Human Rights Commissions; Principles of Medical Ethics Relevant to the Role of Health Professionals, Particularly Physicians, in the Protection of Prisoners and Detainees Against Torture and Other Cruel, Inhuman and Degrading Treatment. *Further Reading:* T. Buergenthal, "To Respect and Ensure: State Obligations and Permissible Derogations" in *The International Bill of Rights: The Covenant on Civil and Political Rights*, ed. L. Henkin (1981).

PURGE. The expression is an international term that refers to the mass **expulsion** of political opponents from a political or social movement or political party. Purges have been engaged in by political leaders such as **Joseph V. Stalin, Mao Zedong,** and Pol Pot. Expulsions sometimes involve the extrajudicial killing of opponents, but whether or not they result in loss of life, purges entail gross violations of **human rights.** Those rights include the right of **thought, conscience, and religion,** the right to free association, the right to freedom of speech, to liberty and security of person, and the right to equal protection of the law. See also: Cambodia; China; Forced Labor. *Further Reading:* Asia Research Centre, *The Great Cultural Revolution* (1968); D. Bonavia, *Verdict in Peking: The Trial of the Gang of Four* (1993); M. McCauley, *Stalin and Stalinism* (1995).

Q

QUEBEC. See CANADA; SELF-DETERMINATION.

R

RACIAL DISCRIMINATION. See INTERNATIONAL CONVENTION ON THE ELIMINATION OF ALL FORMS OF RACIAL DISCRIMINATION.

RACISM. Racism or racialism is a term that expresses a belief or ideology that human beings are naturally divided into a biological category called race, which is the principal determinant of human traits, character, and capacities. Racial differences, according to this belief, express themselves in terms of skin color and other physical attributes; they also manifest themselves in what are viewed as inherent mental and moral capabilities that make one race (and a country, if it is racially defined) superior or inferior to another.

Racism gives rise to racial discrimination, and played a major role in the genocidal activities of Nazi Germany. It also fueled much of the war effort (in terms of how enemies were depicted and treated, including how Japanese Americans were treated) between Japan and the **United States** during World War II, and served as an important factor in shaping the constitution and formulating the functions of the **United Nations Educational, Scientific and Cultural Organization** (UNESCO). This organization has spent much of its more than fifty years of existence trying to eliminate racial and other stereotypes that people hold about one another. The international community has adopted important human rights instruments outlawing discrimination based on race. Despite these efforts, the belief in racial differences and the resulting discrimination have continued within and between countries. The Roma people (called Gypsies) who have fled the Czech Republic and Hungary to **Canada** and elsewhere complain about it; the Maori of New Zealand and **Australia** bitterly voice like complaints; the Ainu and Koreans in Japan see racism in the discriminatory treatment they face; blacks in the United States, North Africans in France, Turks in Germany, Palestinian Arabs in **Israel**, Chinese in Indonesia, and Jews almost everywhere view themselves as subjected to varying forms of **discrimination** based on the suppositions of race.

On November 27, 1978, UNESCO adopted the Declaration on Race and Racial Prejudice, a declaration that the international community hopes will help fight racism. Articles 1, 2, and 10 of the declaration deal with the theory of racism, define it, and indicate the assumed responsibilities of regional and global international organizations as follows:

Article (1). All human beings belong to a single species and are descended from a common stock. They are born equal in dignity and rights and all form an integral part of humanity.

(2). All individuals and groups have the right to be different, to consider themselves as different and to be regarded as such. However, the diversity of life styles and the right to be different may not, in any circumstances, serve as a pretext for racial prejudice; they many not justify in law or in fact any discriminatory practice whatsoever, nor provide a ground for the policy of *apartheid*, which is the extreme form of racism.

(3). Identity of origin in no way affects the fact that human beings can and may live differently, nor does it preclude the existence of differences based on cultural, environmental and historical diversity nor the right to maintain cultural identity.

(4). All peoples of the world possess equal faculties for attaining the highest level of intellectual, technical, social, economic, cultural and political development.

(5). The differences between achievements of the different peoples are entirely attributable to geographical, historical, political, economic, social and cultural factors. Such differences can in no case serve as a pretext for any rank-ordered classification of nations and peoples.

Article 2 (1). Any theory which involves the claim that racial or ethnic groups are inherently superior or inferior, thus implying that some would be entitled to dominate or eliminate others, presumed to be inferior, or which bases value judgements on racial differentiation, has no scientific foundation and is contrary to the moral and ethical principles of humanity.

(2). Racism includes racist ideologies, prejudiced attitudes, discriminatory behavior, structural arrangements and institutional practices resulting in racial inequality as well as the fallacious notion that discriminatory relations between groups are morally and scientifically justifiable . . . it hinders the development of its victims, perverts those who practice it, divides nations internally, impedes international cooperation and gives rise to political tensions between peoples; it is contrary to the fundamental principles of international law and, consequently, seriously disturbs international peace and security.

(3). Racial prejudice, historically linked with inequalities in power, reinforced by economic and social differences between individuals and groups, and still seeking today to justify such inequalities, is totally without justification.

Article 10. International organizations, whether universal or regional, governmental or non-governmental, are called upon to co-operate and assist, so far as their re-spective fields of competence and means allow, in the full and complete implemen-tation of the principles set forth in this Declaration, thus contributing to the legitimate struggle of all men, born equal in dignity and rights, against the tyranny and oppression of racism, racial segregation, *apartheid*, and genocide, so that all the peoples of the world may be forever delivered from these scourges.

See also: Apartheid; Ethnic Cleansing; Genocide. *Further Reading:* J. Dower, *War without Mercy* (1986); Report by Mr. Maurice Gle-Ahanhanzo, Special Rap-porteur on Contemporary Forms of Racial Discrimination, Xenophobia and Re-lated Intolerance, UN Doc. CN.4/1997/71 (January 16, 1997).

RAPE. The rape of women during warfare has had a long history. In the post-1945 world, there are many examples of it. German soldiers commit-ted rape against women, especially the Jewish women of defeated countries. Recent evidence indicates that in Korea, Japanese soldiers abducted and subjected an estimated 100,000 women to rape during World War II; and during the Vietnam War, American soldiers routinely raped Vietnamese women. In **Bangladesh**, an estimated 250,000 to 400,000 women were raped as that country fought for independence from Pakistan in 1971; and in Uganda in the 1980s and in Liberia during the civil war of the 1990s, large numbers of women were raped, sometimes as many as ten soldiers in a single episode of gang rape. Perhaps no recent example of wartime rape has been as morally outrageous as the war in the former Yugoslavia (1991–1995), during which systematic rape, including gang rape, of Croat, Mus-lim, and Serbian women and girls was pursued as an instrument of state policy.

The sources of the prevalence of rape during warfare are many. First, license to rape is considered an incentive for soldiers. Second, rape is re-garded as an attack on the *honor* of the enemy male population, and war **propaganda** continues the fear of dishonor as a "spur to the courage of troops" and uses it as a recruitment tool for male soldiers, who must pro-tect *their* women. Third, especially in the late 1990s when civilian casualty rates during war have grown from 5 percent in World War I to over 80 percent, rape is seen as a means to demoralize the enemy. Fourth, rape is used to disable the enemy by destroying the bonds of family and society at large—this is particularly true when rape is committed in "full view" of relatives and others. Fifth, it is used as an expression of ethnic, religious, or racial hatred and contempt. Sixth, it is used against women as an ex-pression of misogyny. Seventh, it is used as recreation ("comfort") for sol-diers. Eighth, it is used as an instrument to induce mass flight, as in **ethnic cleansing**.

Despite this cruel and often savage international criminal behavior to-ward women (there are some instances of rape against men, but very few as compared with women), little has been done until recently to deal with that behavior. Evidence of rape by soldiers was introduced at the **Nuremberg War Crimes Trials**, but it was not even mentioned in any of the final judgments. Indeed, while rape has been part of international humanitarian law, it was not mentioned as a specific category under **crimes against humanity**, although it was deemed to be included in the phrase "other inhuman acts." The post-1945 human rights instruments contain rights that any act of rape violates: the right to security of person, liberty, privacy, dignity, and to found a family; likewise, the right against torture, cruel, and degrading treatment, **arbitrary arrest and detention**, and the right to physical and psychological integrity. In more specific terms, in 1994 the United Nations **General Assembly** adopted the **Declaration on the Elimination of Violence Against Women**, which explicitly prohibits rape.

The terms of the International Criminal Tribunal for the Former Yugoslavia, established on May 25, 1993, by the UN, contain explicit provisions for the criminal charge of rape; so, too, does the International Criminal Tribunal for Rwanda, established on November 8, 1994. Rape is among the substantive crimes against humanity over which the proposed **International Criminal Court** (ICC) will have jurisdiction. See also: Geneva Conventions; War Crimes Tribunals. *Further Reading:* R. Gutman, *Witness to Genocide* (1993); T. Meron, "Rape as a Crime under International Humanitarian Law," *AJIL*, vol. 87 (1993); S. Swiss and J. E. Giller, "Rape as a Crime of War," *JAMA*, vol. 270 (1993); A. Stiglmayer, ed., *Mass Rape: The War Against Women in Bosnia-Herzegovina* (1994).

RATIFICATION. Ratification is an international term that refers to the act by which a modern international treaty (such as a convention) becomes binding on states. Although a treaty, including human rights instruments, is said to be concluded as soon as mutual consent is achieved and indicated by the signature of the parties that negotiated it, its binding obligatory force is generally deferred until ratification.

Each state has it own ratification process. In the **United States**, for example, it is the Senate that ratifies treaties. And it can prevent a treaty from taking effect in the United States by delaying ratification or by rejecting it, as it is currently doing with the **Convention on the Elimination of All Forms of Discrimination Against Women** (CEDAW). The Senate, as is the case for the process in other countries, can also vote to accept the treaty, thus making it binding on the United States. One of the major efforts of the human rights movement is to get states to ratify human rights treaties. See also: Adjudication; Standard-Setting.

RED CROSS CONVENTIONS. See GENEVA CONVENTIONS.

RED CROSS MOVEMENT. See INTERNATIONAL COMMITTEE OF THE RED CROSS.

REFUGEES. See CONVENTION RELATING TO THE STATUS OF REF-
UGEES.

RELATIVISM AND UNIVERSALISM. One of the more vexing themes in
the area of **human rights** is whether those rights are universal in character
or if they should be viewed in terms that are relative to cultural and other
differences among humans. This is of utmost significance because the concept of human rights that gave birth to the modern human rights movement
is based on the claim that all human beings share a common spiritual and
moral identity, regardless of cultural and other differences. It is this identity
that is said to distinguish humans from members of the animal kingdom,
and that which affixes on individuals the stamp of humanity. Those who
espouse a universalist point of view say that the moral and legal entitlements called human rights, do not derive from one's membership in a nation, social class, religious grouping, gender, racial category, or cultural
pattern or background, but from one's membership in the family of persons
called humans, and those rights must be recognized and enforced as such.

Relativistism, which is espoused most forcefully in non-Western countries
(although it has advocates in the West), has three major areas of focus: (1)
the origins of our contemporary focus on human rights; (2) the dominant
emphasis associated with the formulation and enforcement of those rights;
and (3) the attributed (or demonstrable) intent of those who espouse universalism. On the matter of origin, relativism argues that the West and the
culture that defines it are the principal source of human rights norms. Those
norms, in substance, not only reflect the bias of that culture, but even the
legalistic language in which they are couched bespeaks their Western orientation. Other countries, therefore, not only have the right but the duty
to recast those norms in ways reflective of their own cultures.

On the question of dominant emphasis, supporters of relativism contend
that the West, in the formulation and enforcement of human rights, has
shown a preference for **civil and political rights,** with a particular focus on
the individual to the neglect of the community and duties toward it. **Economic, social and cultural rights** tend to be either overlooked or de-
emphasized by the West. Other countries, relativism opines, historically
have either reversed the West's emphasis or sought to develop and protect
the indivisible links between both classes of rights. Relativists argue that
the West's emphasis also has a bearing on the selectivity with which it goes
about dealing with violations of human rights. It condones and supports
sanctions against violations of civil and political rights while doing little or
nothing about violations of economic, social and cultural rights. Indeed,
because of the dominance of the West in the area of international communication, not only its own citizens but citizens of other countries have
increasingly come to equate human rights with civil and political rights

only. This selectivity bears a relationship to a demonstrable intent on the part of the West, claim some relativists.

The West seeks to use its cultural values, although its army and technology will continue to play a back-up role, to dominate the world. This form of cultural imperialism, in the guise of human rights, follows the use to which Christianity was put as the West penetrated the rest of the world from the fifteenth to the nineteenth centuries, and seeks to deny that the cultural values of other societies have a valid bearing on the definition and implementation of human rights. Many universalists, somewhat sympathetic to the charge that the West emphasizes civil and political rights, contend that this criticism is confusing the universal nature of the rights with the particular emphasis that one or more governments may give to the promotion and protection of those rights. Many also view the arguments of some relativists as seeking to justify a de-emphasis on civil and political rights. See also: Bangkok Declaration; Proclamation of Tehran; World Conference on Human Rights. *Further Reading:* A. R. Renteln, *International Human Rights: Universalism versus Relativism (1990)*; U. Baxi, ed., *The Right To Be Human* (1987); S. Kothari and H. Sethi, eds., *Rethinking Human Rights: Challenges for Theory and Action* (1989).

RELIGION AND HUMAN RIGHTS. Religion and human rights have had a long and complex relationship that includes the association of religion with certain violations of **human rights**, with the promotion and protection of human rights, and with the sources of and inspiration for many of the cornerstones of the human rights movement.

Because of the first relationship, many human rights thinkers and advocates wrongly view and treat religion as if it were an obstacle to human rights promotion and protection. Such thinkers and activists, for example, point to the modern history of conflicts between and within states that are in whole or in part linked to religious identities. They also point to contemporary conflicts throughout the world to support their claim: for instance, between Protestants and Catholics in Northern Ireland, between Sikhs and Hindus in **India**, Muslims and Orthodox Serbs or Christian Croats in the former Yugoslavia, between Christian **Russia** and Muslim **Chechnya**, as well as between fundamentalist and secular groups within countries from Egypt, Iran, **Israel**, and France to Indonesia, Sri Lanka, **Turkey**, and the **United States**.

The link between religion and the above-mentioned conflicts cannot be denied; and the human rights abuses associated with those conflicts are many and grave. Yet, the suspicion that religion and human rights are incompatible is not factually supportable. First, most of the human rights abuses that take place in the name of religion result from political and other leaders who seek to use and often to distort religion and religion-based identities to gain and maintain power. Second, the supposed incompatibility overlooks the extent to which religious groups are at the forefront in influencing governments to act at national and global levels to support **economic, social and cultural rights**, including the right to food, shelter, clothing, and education. Third, an important basis for the suspected incompatibility is the perception that "secular nationalism" seeks to transcend identities of tribe, clan, ethnicity, class, and even race, and as such, is promotive of an expanded identity that human rights sponsor. Religion, the line of reasoning goes, tends to deal with "in" and "out" groups, those who are and are not believers. Grouping people into believers and nonbelievers perpetuates intolerance and **discrimination** toward nonbelievers in the same way that tribal and ethnic groups treat members and nonmembers. But secular nationalism does the same thing toward noncitizens or nonnationals, especially immigrants and "foreigners." Fourth, skepticism disregards the role of religion as both a conceptual source and an inspiration in the normative cornerstone of the human rights movement.

The world religions—Baha'ism, Buddhism, Christianity, Hinduism, Islam, Jainism, Judaism, Zoroastrianism (Confucianism and Taoism, also, if they are viewed as religions)—have manifested over the centuries that they are capable of serving as a source of common identity that transcends tribe, race, class, and nationality. They are beginning to show the potential for doing the same with respect to gender. Indeed, the very concept of human dignity, on which human rights are based, has it roots in the major religions. Buddhism, for example, is defined by the idea of an expanding and inclusive self. Within the United Nations, many religions have been strong supporters in the **standard-setting** process, which has shaped the many human rights instruments covered in this volume. In some cases, such as the adoption of the **Universal Declaration of Human Rights** (UDHR) (1948), the **Declaration on the Elimination of All Forms of Intolerance and of Discrimination Based on Religion or Belief** (1981), and the Convention on the Rights of the Child (CRC) (1989), the support of religion-based groups was crucial. And in 1993, respected leaders of the world's major faiths adopted the **Declaration of a Global Ethic** at a meeting of the Parliament of the World's Religions, held in Chicago, Illinois, from September 2–4. The declaration, which strongly supports human rights, takes the position that there can be no true global order and human rights cannot be fully realized without a global ethic. Finally, the Japanese scholar and Buddhist leader, Diasaku Ikeda, has called for religions to turn away from the remnants of exclusivity and competitiveness and assume the task of helping create global citizens. See also: Child, Rights of; East Timor; Fundamentalism; Holy See; Serbia; Sharia. *Further Reading:* Boston Research Center for the Twenty-First Century, *The United Nations and the World's Religions: Prospects for a Global Ethics* (1994); A. D. Hertzke, *Representing God in Washington* (1998); J. Kelsay and S. B. Twiss, eds., *Religion and Human Rights* (1994).

RELIGIOUS INTOLERANCE AND DISCRIMINATION. See DECLARATION ON THE ELIMINATION OF ALL FORMS OF INTOLER-

ANCE AND OF DISCRIMINATION BASED ON RELIGION OR BELIEF.

REMEDY. Remedy is the name given to the means by which individuals or groups may enforce a recognized right. Enforcement may take the form of action to prevent violation of a right, to stop ongoing violations, and/ or afford redress, including monetary compensation, for violations. The **Universal Declaration of Human Rights** (UDHR) provides for the right to appropriate remedy in Article 8: "Everyone has the right to an effective remedy by the competent national tribunals for acts violating the fundamental rights granted him by the constitution or by law."

The **International Covenant on Civil and Political Rights** (ICCPR) not only provides for the right to remedy, but for competent institutions and authorities to enforce it. The relevant provisions of the covenant state:

Article 2 (3). Each State Party to the present Covenant undertakes:

a. To ensure that any person whose rights or freedoms as herein recognized are violated shall have an effective remedy, notwithstanding that the violation has been committed by persons acting in an official capacity;

b. To ensure that any person claiming such remedy shall have his right thereto determined by competent judicial, administrative or legislative authorities, or by any other competent authority provided for by the legal system of the State, and to develop the possibilities for judicial remedy;

c. To ensure that the competent authorities shall enforce such remedies when granted.

Other human rights instruments, regional and global, also provide for the right to effective remedy. For example, the **American Convention on Human Rights** provides in Article 10 that "Every person has the right to be compensated in accordance with the law in the event he has been sentenced by a final judgment through the miscarriage of justice."

The **Europe Convention on Human Rights** in Article 13 provides a more expansive basis for remedy than its American counterpart, and calls for an "effective remedy before a national authority notwithstanding that the violation has been committed by persons acting in an official capacity," and in cases of violation of *any* of the rights and freedoms recognized, not simply in cases of miscarriages of justice. Article 14 of the **Convention Against Torture and Other Cruel, Inhuman or Degrading Treatment or Punishment** requires that each state provide victims of torture with an "enforceable right to fair and adequate compensation." In cases where the victim dies from torture, his or her dependents are "entitled to compensation." See also: Compensation for Victims of Human Rights Abuse. *Further Reading:* P. Schuck, *Suing Government: Citizen Remedies for Official Wrong* (1983).

REST, LEISURE AND REASONABLE LIMITATION ON WORKING HOURS. This right, which is sometimes only partially quoted by opponents of **human rights** as the right to leisure, is one of the most important rights recognized by the international community. This right seeks to protect individuals from exploitation in the form of numbers of hours worked and ensure rest and leisure for physical and spiritual health and renewal. The **Universal Declaration of Human Rights** (UDHR), focuses on this right in Article 24: "Everyone has the right to rest and leisure, including reasonable limitation of working hours and periodic holidays with pay."

Dealing with the same right, the **International Covenant on Economic, Social and Cultural Rights** provides what the UDHR allows and goes beyond to emphasize working conditions in general as well as on paid public holidays (not all holidays are public). The relevant portion of that covenant reads:

Article 7. The States Parties to the present Covenant recognize the right of everyone to the enjoyment of just and favourable conditions of work, which ensure, in particular:

d. Rest, leisure and reasonable limitation of working hours and periodic holidays with pay, as well as remuneration for public holidays.

See also: Physical and Mental Health.

RIGHT OF PETITION. At the time of the drafting of the **Universal Declaration of Human Rights** (UDHR), many countries, but especially **nongovernmental organizations** (NGOs), favored the inclusion of an article on the right of individuals or nonstage groups to petition national and international political authorities concerning the protection of **human rights**. The text of the Human Rights Drafting Committee included the following statement: "No state shall deny to any individual the right, either individually or in association with others, to petition or communicate with the Government of his state or of his residence or the United Nations."

The proposal for a specific article was ultimately defeated, primarily because states feared individuals and groups would most likely go directly to the UN, to seek protection of their rights against abusive governments. Such direct action by individuals was viewed by states as potentially embarrassing, undermining their legitimacy, and impairing their **sovereignty**. Today, only a very weak system of petition exists. See also: Human Rights Commissions; Human Rights Committee. *Further Reading:* J. P. Humphrey, *No Distant Millennium: The International Law of Human Rights* (1989); E. Asbjorn, et al., eds., *The Universal Declaration of Human Rights: A Commentary* (1992).

RIGHT TO DEVELOPMENT. See DECLARATION ON THE RIGHT TO DEVELOPMENT.

RIGHT TO LEAVE AND RETURN. One of the often overlooked **human rights**, but one that is critical to relieving human suffering, to effective international cooperation, to development of the human personality, and full enjoyment of all human rights, is the right of free movement and residence, especially the right to leave and return to countries. The **Universal Declaration of Human Rights** (UDHR) recognizes this right in Article 13 as follows:

1. Everyone has the right to freedom of movement and residence within the borders of each State.

2. Everyone has the right to leave any country, including his own, and to return to his country.

Likewise, the **International Covenant on Civil and Political Rights** (ICCPR) proclaims this right and, in addition, stipulates certain limited conditions under which its exercise may be restricted. The relevant portion of Article 12 that covenant provides:

2. Everyone shall be free to leave any country, including his own.

3. The above-mentioned rights shall not be subject to any restrictions except those which are provided by law, are necessary to protect national security, public order . . . public health or morals or the rights and freedoms of others, and are consistent with the other rights recognized in the present Covenant.

4. No one shall be arbitrarily deprived of the right to enter his own country.

The effective exercise of the right to leave and return to one's country bears with it other implied rights, such as the right to seek and obtain travel documents, to seek and obtain foreign exchange, and not to be denied one's nationality or citizenship, or one's legal residence. See also: Asylum; Convention on the Reduction of Statelessness; Expulsion; Movement and Residence.

RIGHT TO LIFE. This is a right whose absence makes it impossible to enjoy any other **human rights**. Because of the centrality of this right, issues concerning abortion and the death penalty have become very important in national and international public and private life. The **Universal Declaration of Human Rights** (UDHR) in Article 3 proclaims that "Everyone has the right to life, liberty and security of person." Article 6 of the **International Covenant on Civil and Political Rights** (ICCPR) not only recognizes the right to life, but in Article 6 deals with some of the legal and moral tensions that are associated with that right.

1. Every human being has the inherent right to life. This right shall be protected by law. No one shall be arbitrarily deprived of his life.

2. In countries which have not abolished the death penalty, sentence of death may be imposed only for the most serious crimes in accordance with the law in force

at the time of the commission of the crime and not contrary to the provisions of the present Covenant and to the Convention on the Prevention and Punishment of the Crime of Genocide. This penalty can only be carried out pursuant to a final judgment rendered by a competent court.

3. When deprivation of life constitutes the crime of genocide, it is understood that nothing in this article shall authorize any State Party to the present Covenant to derogate in any way from any obligation assumed under the provisions of the Convention on the Prevention and Punishment of the Crime of Genocide.

4. Anyone sentenced to death shall have the right to seek pardon or commutation of the sentence. Amnesty, pardon or commutation of the sentence of death may be granted in all cases.

5. Sentence of death shall not be imposed for crimes committed by persons below eighteen years of age and shall not be carried out on pregnant women.

6. Nothing in this article shall be invoked to delay or to prevent the abolition of capital punishment by any State Party to the present Covenant.

In 1989, the United Nations **General Assembly** adopted and opened for ratification the Second Optional Protocol to the International Covenant on Civil and Political Rights. Article 1 of this protocol expresses the view that the abolition of the death penalty will contribute to the "enhancement of human dignity and [the] progressive development of human rights." It reads:

1. No one within the jurisdiction of a State Party to the present Optional Protocol shall be executed.

2. Each state shall take all necessary measures to abolish the death penalty within its jurisdiction.

International developments between the time of the proclamation of the Universal Declaration of Human Rights and the Second Optional Protocol to the International Covenant on Civil and Political Rights have given the right to life a more weighty claim that it had fifty years ago. And, as should be seen by referring to **capital punishment**, the Second Optional Protocol merely mirrors the changes that have taken place in national life throughout the world.

The "right to life movement," in the United States, ought not to be confused with the general focus of the right to life, because although the inherent right to life advanced by the relevant human rights instruments is applicable to the concerns of the right to life movement, the movement itself has thus far not made it applicable. The reasons for not linking the movement to the human rights regime are many, but among them are two that are highlighted here. First, many leaders of the right to life movement harbor suspicions about certain areas of human rights, including the emerging prohibition against capital punishment, and second, the definition of "person" is something which, at the international level, could be even more problematic than at the domestic level. See also: Genocide; Holy See.

RIO DECLARATION. See ENVIRONMENT.

ROMANIA. Romania, which is presently a constitutional republic with a multiparty system that sponsors a directly elected head of state, was previously a Socialist republic within the former communist bloc. The Socialist republic was dominated by two dictators after the Romanian monarchy was overthrown in 1946: Gheorghe Gheorghiu-Dej, who served as head of the Communist Party from 1946 to 1963, when he died, and Nicolae Ceausescu (1918–1989), who controlled the party from 1965 to 1989. He was overthrown, sentenced to death, and executed by the National Salvation Front, a coalition of local and national groups, which led a popular uprising that began in mid-December 1989.

Romania is located in Eastern Europe and borders on Ukraine to the northeast, Hungary to the northwest, Yugoslavia (**Serbia**) to the southwest, Bulgaria to the south, and the Black Sea and Moldova to the east. It has a population of about 24 million people who are overwhelmingly ethnic Romanian (over 85 percent), with Hungarians, Roma, Germans, Ukrainians, Serbo-Croatians, and Jews in descending order of percentages, making up the remainder. Russians, Slovaks, and Turks are also found in small numbers. Over 70 percent of the population are members of the Romanian Orthodox Church, with 7–8 percent embracing Roman Catholicism (mostly Hungarians). The rest of the population are principally Protestants, including Lutherans, Jehovah's Witnesses, and Baptists.

During the dictatorships mentioned above, violations of **human rights**, especially during the later years of Ceauşescu's rule, became rampant. Religious and ethnic minorities were repressed, freedom of speech, press, association, and movement were largely nonexistent. Torture, extrajudicial killings, and arbitrary imprisonment were commonplace. The *Securitate* (state police) encouraged betrayal among citizens, and while newly born babies were denied registration for weeks and persons sixty years or older were denied needed aid, including medicine, the president and party leaders lived in palaces and sumptuous villas.

Since 1989, the new leaders have not dealt with all the human rights problems. Respect for minority rights has improved, as seen in the 1997 reopening of a high school (closed since 1968) for members of northern Romania's 300,000-strong Ukrainian minority. So, too, the 1996 Romania-Hungary "land for ethnic rights" treaty, which now guarantees Western European-type minority rights to some 2 million ethnic Hungarians in Romania, and the improvement in the rights associated with the principle of **democratic entitlement**. While there has been some improvement in respect for minority rights, anti-Semitism, as evidenced by the desecration of some 200 Jewish graves, continues; discrimination against the Roma people remains rampant; and violence against women, including **rape,** has not been addressed by the government. Further, the constitutional prohibition of "defamation of the country" unduly restricts free expression, and the denial of permission to Jehovah's Witnesses to hold an International Convention in Bucharest in July 1996 was an important setback for freedom of religion and association. The government, apparently responding to the Romanian Orthodox Church's efforts to limit the activities of certain competing religions, denied the requested permission from the Jehovah's Witnesses.

Of utmost importance in assessing the changes in the human rights record of Romania are its policies on minority rights and democratic entitlement, but a disturbing view of the policy on minority rights has emerged in international discussions. While Romania's reforms in the area of democratic entitlement (including changes toward a more market-oriented economy) are genuine, the reforms respecting minority rights have been induced more by its goal to join the European Union (EU) than by any fundamental change in its political culture. See also: Framework Convention for the Protection of National Minorities; Thought, Conscience and Religion; Racism. *Further Reading:* T. Gallagher, *Romania after Ceausescu* (1995); J. Held, ed., *Populism, Racism and Society in Eastern Europe* (1996); L. Stan, ed., *Romania in Transition* (1997).

ROOSEVELT, ELEANOR (1884–1962). One of the most outstanding leaders in the human rights movement, Eleanor Roosevelt was the wife of **Franklin D. Roosevelt,** thirty-second president of the **United States.** When he died in April 1945, she had already gained a public standing of her own in addition to her role as First Lady. She also used that position to effect a profound impact on the United States by serving as the "legs and eyes" of her physically impaired husband and by prodding him to influence national improvements in housing, education, and health care, as well as in the status of women and **minorities.**

In December 1945, Eleanor Roosevelt was appointed by President Harry S. Truman as a member of the United States delegation to the UN, where she became chairperson of the United Nations Commission on Human Rights. It was in her role as chair that she performed three crucial tasks in the drafting and adoption of the **Universal Declaration of Human Rights** (UDHR). First, she played a mediatory role in the commission, that is, she sought to reconcile differences that emerged among members of the commission. Second, she exercised a strong and effective mediatory role in the United States delegation, which was divided between those who sought to embrace a liberal-univeralist policy and those who espoused a conservative-nationalist outlook. Third, she had a leading role in the actual drafting of the Universal Declaration and in its adoption and support by the United States.

The significance of her work should be assessed not only in terms of the declaration itself, but also in terms of the spiritual and moral force that the declaration has had on all subsequent international human rights instruments. Likewise, her interest in and concern for the plight of refugees helped set the tone for international policy in this area. In 1946, during the United Nations **General Assembly**'s first session in London, she used her international standing to help win the fight against forcibly returning about 1 million refugees to Eastern Europe.

There are three other important areas in which Eleanor Roosevelt had a significant role in the international human rights movement. First, her arguments against the adoption of a minority article undermined the efforts of those who struggled with the issue and sought to include it in the declaration. While Eleanor Roosevelt saw some countries as having minority problems, she denied that the United States had one and argued against the inclusion of an article on minorities. Second, she expended considerable time and effort in seeking to educate the American and international public about **human rights**. Third, when President John F. Kennedy (1917–1963) appointed her as the first head of the National Commission on the Status of Women in 1961, she used that position to help further the women's movement for equal rights in the United States. See also: Commission on Human Rights; Convention Relating to the Status of Refugees. *Further Reading:* A. G. Mower, *The United States, the United Nations, and Human Rights: The Eleanor Roosevelt and Jimmy Carter Eras* (1979); E. Roosevelt, *On My Own, The Years Since the White House* (1958); E. Roosevelt, "The Promise of Human Rights," *For. Aff.*, no. 3 (1948).

ROOSEVELT, FRANKLIN D. (1882–1945). Franklin D. Roosevelt was the thirty-second president of the United States and served from 1933 to 1945, when he died. His contribution to the human rights movement and the substantive body of **human rights** derives from four areas. First, his strong support for the creation of the UN and the actual shaping of the United Nations **Charter**, which provides for the promotion of human rights and fundamental freedoms as one of the purposes of the world organization. Second, his proposal of "four essential human freedoms," Four Freedoms, in his annual message to Congress on January 6, 1941, defined the moral and political atmosphere that helped shape the **Universal Declaration of Human Rights** (UDHR). He presented those freedoms as follows:

- The First is freedom of speech and expression—everywhere in the world.
- The Second is freedom of every person to worship God in his own way—everywhere in the World.
- The Third is freedom from want—which, translated into world terms, means economic understandings which will secure to every nation a healthy peacetime life for its inhabitants—everywhere in the world.

- The Fourth is freedom from fear which, translated into world terms, means a world-wide reduction in armaments to such a point and in such a thorough fashion that no nation will be in a position to commit aggression against any neighbor—everywhere in the world.

That is no vision of a distant millennium. It is a definite basis for a kind of world attainable in our own time and generation.

Third, though in a restricted manner, Roosevelt supported the principle of **self-determination** against the imperial ambitions of Britain during World War II (to retain its empire intact). Fourth, although Roosevelt died before he had a chance to push for its implementation, his proposal for "a second Bill of Rights"—a body of **economic, social and cultural rights**—could have been the means by which a U.S.-led West could have had a greater moral weight in the scales of human rights and more fruitfully reconcile some of the bitter, emerging differences between itself and the Global South (or Third World). The United States, except during a brief period of President Jimmy Carter's tenure in office, has never supported economic, social, and cultural rights, the class of human rights that the Global South finds as important as, if not more important than **civil and political rights**. In 1944, President Roosevelt outlined a plan for a second Bill of Rights—the first being the civil and political rights found in the first ten amendments to the Constitution. The second Bill of Rights reads as follows:

- The right to a useful and remunerative job in the industries, or shops or farms or mines of the Nation;
- The right to earn enough to provide adequate food and clothing and recreation;
- The right of every farmer to raise and sell his product at a return that will give him and his family a decent living;
- The right of every businessman, large and small, to trade in an atmosphere of freedom from unfair competition and domination by monopolies at home or abroad;
- The right of every family to a decent home;
- The right of adequate medical care and the opportunity to achieve and enjoy good health;
- The right to adequate protection from economic fears of old age, sickness, accident, and unemployment; [and]
- The right to a good education.

After Roosevelt's death, no one touched his second Bill of Rights. Only lately have scholars such as Louis Sohn begun to discuss it. See also: European Social Charter. *Further Reading:* L. B. Sohn, *The Human Rights Movement: From Roosevelt's Four Freedoms to the Interdependence of Peace, Development and Human Rights* (1995).

RUSSIA. Contemporary Russia, which was born in 1991, is at once a country seeking a radical political departure from its past and a country that is the product of its past. That past includes the political form and social culture of the former Soviet Russia, which lasted from 1918 to its demise in 1991, and of Tzarist Russia, which existed from 1480 to 1917. Under the Tzarist regime, which was a semifeudal authoritarian structure coexisting with a communal peasantry and an emerging capitalist focus, Russia acquired a large empire. The empire, plus a few other areas, later acquired, were effectively incorporated into Soviet Russia, a Marxist state, composed of fifteen republics and officially known as the Union of Soviet Socialist Republics (USSR). The republics were Armenia, Azerbaijan, Byelorussia, Estonia, Georgia, Kazakhstan, Kyrgyzstan, Latvia, Lithuania, Moldavia (now Moldova), Russian Soviet Federated Socialist Republic (which dominated the union), Tajikistan, Turkmenistan, Ukraine, and Uzbekistan. At the dissolution of the Soviet Union in 1991, fourteen of the fifteen constituent republics gained their independence and the Russian Federation succeeded to the rights and responsibilities of the former USSR.

Despite its loss of control over its republics, the Russian Federation is still the largest country in the world (almost double the land area of the **United States**), with a population of about 150 million people. It is pursuing a transformation from a largely centralized, state-managed economy, and authoritarian political system, to a stable market economy and democratic government. But its approach to this transformation includes many of the authoritarian practices and violations of **human rights** that define its past and its efforts at creating a market economy have been characterized by wide spread failure.

Throughout its existence, the USSR—especially during the time of **Joseph V. Stalin**—systematically engaged in **forced labor**, torture, extrajudicial killings, limitations on freedom of speech, press, and religion, subjection of the judiciary to the political organs of the state, and violations of the right of association, freedom of **movement and residence**, and the right to privacy and to national **self-determination**. The USSR, however, did protect (although not without some discrimination) **economic, social and cultural rights** such as the right to education, health care, housing, food, and social security among others. In its march to transform itself, Russia has introduced a new constitutional system, which promises to honor human rights in general and the **Helsinki Accords**, in particular. But what has been its record?

Privatization has been accompanied by wholesale violations of economic, social, and cultural rights; **self-determination**, although largely accorded to the Baltic and Eastern European countries, has been denied to **Chechnya**, whose 1994–1996 attempted secession was brutally repressed, and religious freedom, although improved, is now restricted by a 1997 law, which protects the Russian Orthodox Church from competition from other Christian faiths. Under the new law, religious organizations, such as the Russian Orthodox Church, which authorities certify as having been active in Russia for fifteen or more years, will have the right to own property, control radio and television stations, operate schools, distribute religious literature, and have tax exempt status, as well as enjoy the right to conduct services in hospitals and cemeteries. Those organizations that do not satisfy the fifteen-year rule (such as the Roman Catholic Church and most Protestant organizations), will not have such rights and can only carry out financial transactions and charity work. Further, while freedom of the press has improved, the government has exercised careful control of the broadcast media in favor of President Yeltsin.

Other human rights problems include troublesome threats against states within whose borders there are significant Russian minorities (Latvia, Moldova, Tajikistan, Ukraine, for instance), the treatment of whom displeases Russia. There is also **discrimination** against dark-skinned people (Armenians, Chechens, Kurds, and Tajiks, for example), who are also often harassed, arrested, and deported from urban areas under the guise of fighting crime. Violence against women, including many thousands killed by their husbands, is prevalent. The Russian state has been particularly inattentive to the last two areas, and the broader **discrimination** against women as privatization has increased is not being addressed at all. Likewise, the right to freedom of **movement and residence** is impaired by residence permits (*propiskas*), which determine where people may live or work. The cost of those permits is beyond the financial means of many ethnic Russians (including citizens of former USSR republics), who seek to move from increasing conditions of poverty in the more rural areas to the larger cities. The children of persons denied such permits (and some refugees) are particularly vulnerable, because they are not eligible for social and health services and cannot attend school. Finally, while the systematic abuse of psychiatry as a form of punishment has decreased dramatically from the Soviet era, the practice continues. Cruel and degrading treatment of prisoners also continues, and the **arbitrary arrest and detention** of the poor in urban areas (and increasing poverty) as well as attacks and maltreatment of homosexuals raise questions about the degree of Russia's commitment to human rights. The practice of refusing to grant political **asylum** to dissidents from countries of the former USSR, and of extraditing such persons without the benefit of a court hearing, only adds to the questions about human rights in Russia.

Perhaps the greatest failure of the Russian government is that the economy has collapsed from great corruption and total disregard for economic, social, and cultural rights. The social security of the elderly has been undermined, the health care system largely destroyed, and people have begun to be seriously undernourished. The remaining democratic process has been threatened with a return of authoritarian rule, and, regardless of whatever help it may have, Russia will recover only after many years. *Further Reading:* N. Melvin, *Russians Beyond Russia's Borders* (1995); A. Aslund, ed., *Economic Transformation in Russia* (1994).

RWANDA. The Republic of Rwanda is an east African country that borders on Burundi, Congo (formerly Zaire), Tanzania, and Uganda. Before 1994, the country had a population of about 7.8 million people and a society dominated by two rival ethnic groups, the Tutsi, who make up 14 percent of the population, and the Hutu, who constitute 85 percent. The remaining 1 percent of the population is composed of the Batwa. Religions practiced include Animism 16 percent, Christianity (Roman Catholicism about 55 percent, Protestant denominations about 12 percent), and Islam, 14 percent.

The country's modern history began after World War I, when it was transferred by the League of Nations from defeated Germany, to which it belonged as a colony, to Belgium. Belgium administered it until 1962, when it gained its independence and became a member of the UN. During its administration, Belgium did little to prepare Rwanda for independence, and successive Belgian governments nurtured and reinforced the existing domination by the Tutsi aristocracy over the largely subservient, but increasingly socially and politically resentful, Hutu majority. Ethnic conflicts, which broke out in 1959, were serious enough to invite questions about whether independence should be deferred until a more stable interethnic relationship was established. Conflicts, however, continued after independence through the 1960s and 1970s, with varying levels of intensity and with the Hutu gaining the upper hand. In 1990, the exiled, Uganda-based Tutsi Rwandan Patriotic Front (RPF) attempted an invasion of Rwanda, but was repelled by the Rwandan government, with the help of Belgium and France. By 1992, however, fighting between the Hutu-led government and the RAF created an estimated 1 million refugees. A UN-sponsored agreement, the Arusha Accords, was negotiated the following year and signed by both the RAF and the government. It provided for power-sharing between the Hutu and the Tutsi, the integration of the rebel and government armies, an ease in interethnic tensions, and democratic elections.

The hopes invited by the Arusha Accords were quickly dashed, as the presidents of Rwanda and neighboring Burundi (both Hutu) were killed, when the aircraft in which they were both flying was shot down in April 1994. What followed, fueled by old suspicions, was nothing less than a frenzy of killing, as the Hutu (some urged and directed by the government) massacred hundreds of thousands of people, mostly Tutsi, but also some Hutu persons of the political opposition who were perceived as sympathetic to, or collaborators with, the Tutsi. Massacred, also, were a number of religious functionaries, especially priests and nuns. More than 1.8 million people fled to neighboring countries and some 2 million were displaced within Rwanda. In August 1995, the government of National Unity of Rwanda was organized and internationally recognized, but it is the RPF, which defeated the former Hutu-led government, that controls the political life of the country, along with the potential for considerable future social and political instability.

The new government has helped internally displaced persons return to their homes, thus offering them a degree of security. But there are over 1 million Rwanda refugees outside the country. And some members of the former Hutu government army, the Armed Forces of Rwanda now located in Congo, have been threatening to renew the civil war. During the above-described **genocide**, judicial and police systems, which are indispensable for human rights protection, were paralyzed. But new personnel, most of them Tutsis, are being recruited and trained. In September 1996, for example, some 280 newly trained judges and magistrates were sworn in, and in the same month and year, the government officially promulgated a law establishing procedures for trying and punishing persons charged with genocide and **crimes against humanity**. In March 1996, some 750 police persons graduated from a British-run training program, and they, along with others in training, began the process of reestablishing social and legal order.

In November 1994, the United Nations **Security Council** created an International Criminal Tribunal for Rwanda. By December 1995, it announced eight indictments of genocide suspects. Since then its work has been relatively slow, due in part to the social and political conditions in Rwanda, but also because of the tribunal's dependence on the cooperation of other countries, including Rwanda's neighbors. Some neighbors, including Congo and Burundi have their own domestic social and political problems that prevent cooperation. An increase in indictments and convictions occurred in 1998 including the conviction of Jean-Paul Akayesu, former mayor of Taba in central Rwanda, due to the crimes of genocide, in September. See also: Cambodia; Ethnic Cleansing; Rape; War Crimes Tribunals. *Further Reading:* P. Akhavan, "The International Tribunal for Rwanda: The Politics and Pragmatics of Punishment," *AJIL*, vol. 90 no. 3 (1996); R. Kushen and K. Harris, "Surrender of Refugees by the United States to the War Crimes Tribunals for Yugoslavia and Rwanda," *AJIL*, vol. 90 no. 3 (1996); G. Punier, *The Rwanda Crisis: History of a Genocide* (1997).

S

SAAMI. Formerly known as the Lapps, the Saami people are about 90,000 persons who lay claim to what they call Saamiland (formerly, Lapland), an area encompassing territories that today form much of the states of Finland, Norway, Sweden, and a part of **Russia**'s Kola Peninsula. About 34 percent of the Saami are located in Norway, with the others varyingly distributed within the borders of the other countries. In recent years, as has been the case of other **indigenous peoples** throughout the world, the Saami have been making claims on the states within which they live to recognize their right to **self-determination.**

Defining themselves as indigenous peoples who descend (their claims go back some 10,000 years) from the earliest populations of the area but do not control the governments of the territories in which they live, the Saami claim a distinctive culture, which has been empirically supported by linguistic evidence. From the standpoint of international relations and the impact of **human rights** on those relations, however, the matter of cultural distinctiveness is not the only important issue at stake. It is also the recognition of the Saami as *a people*, and the resulting implications of that recognition. The implications include the right to nurture and develop their culture, to protect themselves from the assimilationist policies of the states in which they live, the right to revitalize their cultural heritage, and, most important from the standpoint of the Saami and the Nordic countries (Finland, Norway, and Sweden), the right to **sovereignty** over the land and natural resources.

Sovereignty is characterized as most important for both sides, because to the Saami land is the basis on which survival and generational and *cultural continuity* are properly realized, nurtured, preserved, and developed. From the point of view of the Nordic countries, territory is that which defines the *state.*

If these lands are not present, the state does not exist. In the case of Norway, for example, territories claimed by the Saami represent over 50 percent of Norway's territory. Further, since the lands to which the Saami lay claim are rich in gold, diamonds, and timber resources, the country that controls those lands becomes equally important.

The right to sovereignty over the lands and its resources brings with it the right to control those lands and resources. Thus, the Nordic countries are faced with important decisions; so, too, are the Saami, who have organized themselves transnationally into the Nordic Saami Council. This body is, in turn, part of the World Council of Indigenous Peoples, a global **nongovernmental organization** (NGO) that seeks to represent and advance the interests and claims of indigenous peoples throughout the world on human rights issues. For the Saami, a major focus of their effort is to regain control of their traditional lands, which they claim the Nordic countries took from them over a number of centuries, using techniques such as the legal doctrine of *res nullius*, which claims that territories to which it is applied belong to no one, so anyone can claim it. Additionally, the requirement that people must speak a certain language as a precondition to own land or that they have "permanent settlement" of the land in order to claim it (the Saami were formerly a nomadic people) operated to the disadvantage of the Saami. For Nordic states, their emphasis is to make certain that sovereignty claims do not lead to calls for political independence, resulting in territorial losses and political disintegration. (Multinational corporations, which have interests in these lands and their resources are also concerned about what happens to the lands because they seek stability in the supply of resources—stability necessary for long-term planning).

Efforts are being made by the Nordic countries to offer greater cultural autonomy to the Saami, and to devise means by which mutual accommodations can be effected in relationship to the lands and the resources of those lands. Already, the Saami effort to move away from national courts and seek protection through international law has paid some dividends. The Nordic countries have become more active participants in the UN's activities to shape a human rights instrument that can deal with all indigenous peoples. A 1979 treaty between Finland and Norway was renegotiated in 1982 to give greater protection to the fishing rights of the Saami, and the former assimilationist policies of the governments are being reversed. The Saami, in turn, have indicted that they are not seeking political independence. In January 1997, the Norwegian government acknowledged many of the Saami claims to their lands and has created a joint Saami-Norwegian group to work out the type of adjustments that will accommodate the concerns of all. *Further Reading:* F. L. Korsmo, "Nordic Security and the Saami Minority," *HRQ,* vol. 10 no. 4 (1988); D. F. Saunders, *Formation of the World Council of Indigenous Peoples* (1977); J. Velin, "Norway's Northerners Dig in to Defend Land, Lifestyle, Language," *CSM* (January 29, 1997).

SAFEGUARDS GUARANTEEING THE PROTECTION OF THE RIGHTS OF THOSE FACING THE DEATH PENALTY. The human rights movement and the UN have been pursuing, since 1948, the abolition of the death penalty. The UN has also been concerned about the practice of arbitrary and sometimes summary executions in various countries throughout the world. Seeking to limit such executions and afford other protections to those facing the death penalty, the United Nations **Economic and Social Council** (ECOSOC) on May 25, 1984, approved a body of rules known as Safeguards Guaranteeing the Protection of the Rights of Those Facing the Death Penalty. The safeguards were adopted with the "understanding that they shall not be invoked to delay or prevent the abolition of capital punishment."

1. In countries which have not abolished the death penalty, capital punishment may be imposed only for the most serious crimes, it being understood that their scope should not go beyond intentional crimes with lethal or extremely grave consequences.

2. Capital punishment may be imposed only for a crime for which the death penalty is prescribed by law at the time of its commission, it being understood that if, subsequent to the commission of the crime, provision is made by law for the imposition of a lighter penalty, the offender shall benefit thereby.

3. Persons below 18 years of age at the time of the commission of the crime shall not be sentenced to death, nor shall the death sentence be carried out on pregnant women, or on new mothers, or on persons who have become insane.

4. Capital punishment may be imposed only when the guilt of the person charged is based upon clear and convincing evidence leaving no room for an alternative explanation of the facts.

5. Capital punishment may only be carried out pursuant to a final judgment rendered by a competent court after legal process which gives all possible safeguards to ensure a fair trial, at least equal to those contained in article 14 of the International Covenant on Civil and Political Rights, including the right of anyone suspected of or charged with a crime for which capital punishment may be imposed to adequate legal assistance at all stages of the proceedings.

6. Anyone sentenced to death shall have the right to appeal to a court of higher jurisdiction, and steps should be taken to ensure such appeals shall become mandatory.

7. Anyone subject to the death penalty shall have the right to seek pardon, or commutation of sentence; pardon or commutation of sentence may be granted in all cases of capital punishment.

8. Capital punishment shall not be carried out pending any appeal or other recourse procedure or other proceeding relating to pardon or commutation of the sentence.

9. Where capital punishment occurs, it shall be carried out so as to inflict the minimum possible suffering.

See also: Capital Punishment; Fair Trial; Procedural Guarantees, Processes and Protections. *Further Reading:* H. A. Bedau, ed., *The Death Penalty in America* (1997).

SAKHAROV, ANDREI D. (1921–1989). Andrei Sakharov was a citizen of the Soviet Union, a reknowned physicist who helped his country design and develop its hydrogen bomb, and a human rights activist. In the area of **human rights**, in part due to the influence of his wife, Yelena Bonner, he used his fame to champion the right to **self-determination** and **civil and political rights**, including freedom of **movement and residence** as well as the right to leave and return to one's country.

The principle of national self-determination became his concern after the Soviet Union crushed in 1968 a promising political movement in Czechoslovakia when it sought to gain greater autonomy within the Soviet-led socialist bloc. That concern remained with him throughout the rest of his life and kindled his opposition to the Soviet invasion of **Afghanistan** in 1979. In the wider field of civil and political rights, he became a dissident, challenging the totalitarian system of the Soviet Union. After 1975, when he won the Nobel Peace Prize, he used his increased international stature to help organize the Helsinki Watch group (now the **International Helsinki Federation [IHF]**) in 1976. That group, which sought to monitor the human rights area of the 1975 **Helsinki Accords**, has had an important effect on the slow but demonstrable improvement in human rights protection in the former Soviet Union and now **Russia** as well as Eastern Europe. Because of his challenge to the Soviet government, he and his wife were exiled in the late 1970s to the provincial city of Gorky but in 1986, he was released by Mikhail Gorbachev.

The true evidence of improved respect for human rights, to which Sakharov had contributed so much, became evident in 1989 when he was given a state funeral by the government. The European Parliament has established a human rights prize in his name, the Sakharov Prize for Freedom of Thought. See also: Organization for Security and Co-operation in Europe. *Further Reading:* E. Bonner, *Alone Together* (1986); A. Sakharov, *Memoirs* (1990).

SAUDI ARABIA. The Kingdom of Saudi Arabia is an Arab country located in the southwestern extemity of Asia and occupies most of the Arabian Peninsula. It has a population of about 14 million people (85 percent Sunni and 12 percent Shi'a Muslims), sits atop a major share of the world's known oil reserves, and houses the city of Mecca, the spiritual center of Islam. Islam boasts over a billion members and is one of the fastest growing religions in the world. The fact that Saudi Arabia is the seat of Islam's spiritual center is, by itself, important. But the country, closely associated with the West, is also very important by virtue of its strategic location and its command of oil resources, the secure and reliable access to which is so vital to the health of industrial and industrializing countries.

The oil industry has transformed the country from a pastoral, agricultural, and, to some degree, communal society in the 1930s and 1940s, to one that is now a rapidly urbanizing welfare state, in which agriculture accounts for about 8–9 percent of the total amount of locally produced goods and services. The modernization process has been unaccompanied by much respect for **human rights**. Indeed, the country did not abolish slavery until 1962, and has been a consistent violator of human rights.

Support for the latter assertion is not difficult. First, it is an absolute monarchy, ruled by the House of Saud. That dynasty, which has ruled the country since 1926, has never allowed the people of Saudi Arabia to exercise their **democratic entitlement**. Freedom of speech, press, assembly, and association are unprotected (political parties are not even allowed), and workers—many of whom are foreigners—cannot bargain collectively. Second, the country routinely engages in torture, as well as other cruel, inhuman and degrading treatment and punishment of people. For instance, it allows execution by beheading or stoning; it punishes some wrongdoers by amputation of hands or legs, sometimes hands *and* legs; and it administers **capital punishment** for offenses varying from murder and repeated theft to the use of alcohol, drug trafficking, and adultery. Third, it engages in **arbitrary arrest and detention**. In a few cases cited by the United Nations **Commission on Human Rights**, detainees were held for over two years without bail and then released without ever having been freed or officially charged with a crime. Equally significant, family members are often not told in a timely manner of such detentions. Fourth, there is no freedom of religion. The government recognizes Islam as the official religion of the country, citizens must be Muslims, and the open practice of other religions is prohibited. Further, public conversion of a Muslim to another religion is a crime punishable by death.

Discrimination is rampant in a number of areas. Women, for example, are not allowed to take public transportation between two points within the country, or travel abroad unless written permission is obtained from their husbands or the closest male relative. Similar types of discrimination continue against women in work, domestic violence, and other areas of life. The Shi'a minority is also discriminated against in access to social services and government jobs, especially those in "national security sectors." Crimes against Muslims tend to be punished more severely than those against non-Muslims. Finally, in the area of cultural rights, violations are almost structural in the sense that they now form a pattern. Authorities, for example, seriously limit participation of the population in the larger cultural community by prohibiting academic study of evolution, Freud, Marx, Western music, and, in general, Western philosophy.

Despite their human rights violations, the West has been loath to criticize

Saudi Arabia, primarily because of its strategic and economic importance. See also: Civil and Political Rights; Convention on the Elimination of All Forms of Discrimination Against Women. *Further Reading:* Arab Organization for Human Rights, "Human Rights in the Arab World: Saudi Arabia," *AOHR Newsletter,* no. 14–15 (1988); Z. Husain, *Global Islamic Politics* (1995); R. Lacey, *The Kingdom: Arabia and the House of Saud* (1981).

SCIENCE AND TECHNOLOGY. Science and its application, technology, are two areas of human culture that have always been important in the evolution and development of individuals and **peoples.** Relevant human rights instruments, which express concerns about the potential adverse impacts of these two cultural expressions, have also sought to ensure that individuals and groups benefit from them. Article 27 (1) of the **Universal Declaration of Human Rights** (UDHR) proclaims that "Everyone has the right . . . to enjoy the arts and to share in scientific advancement and its benefits." The **International Covenant on Economic, Social and Cultural Rights** details those rights as well as what states must do to ensure its full enjoyment in Article 15.

1. The States Parties to the present Covenant recognize the right of everyone:

   b. To enjoy the benefits of scientific progress and its applications;

2. The steps to be taken by the States Parties to the present Covenant to achieve the full realization of this right shall include those necessary for the conservation, the development and the diffusion of science and culture.

3. The States Parties to the present Covenant undertake to respect the freedom indispensable for scientific research and creative activity.

4. The States Parties to the present Covenant recognize the benefits to be derived from the encouragement and development of international contacts and co-operation in the scientific and cultural fields.

See also: Cloning and Biomedicine; Declaration on the Right to Development; Declaration on the Use of Scientific and Technological Progress in the Interest of Peace and for the Benefit of Mankind.

SECURITY COUNCIL. This is one of the six principal organs of the United Nations. Since 1945, it has been concerned primarily with peace and security *between* states, called international peace and security. In recent years, however, it has become increasingly involved in conflicts *within* states, domestic peace and security, as well as *human security.* The last two areas of security are intimately linked to **human rights,** whether they pertain to refugees, religious persecution, selected **democratic entitlement,** degradation of the **environment,** or to the protection against torture, **genocide,** or **crimes against humanity.** The recent creation of the International Criminal Tribunal for the Former Yugoslavia (1993), and The International

Criminal Tribunal for Rwanda (1994) are examples of the Security Council's recent involvement in the field of human rights.

The Security Council is composed of fifteen members, five of whom, China, France, Russia, the United Kingdom, and the United States, are permanent members; the other ten are elected for two-year terms by the United Nations General Assembly. The nonpermanent members, which by general understanding, are allotted to major geographical areas, facilitate representative collective action when the Security Council needs to act. Five seats are allotted to Africa and Asia; one to Eastern Europe; two to the Americas (including the Caribbean); and two to Western Europe. Under the United Nations Charter the Security Council is the organ with primary jurisdiction to preserve international peace and security. This role includes encouraging pacific settlements of disputes; determining whether a threat to peace, a breach of peace, or an act of aggression exists; and calling on members to undertake defined, collective action against peace-violators. Sometimes, as in the case of South Africa—on which the United Nations Security Council imposed economic sanctions—problems within a state threaten international peace and security, and many of those problems are often gross human rights violations. See also: International Criminal Court; War Crimes Tribunals. *Further Reading:* S. Bailey, *The UN Security Council and Human Rights* (1994); Commission on Global Governance, *Our Global Neighborhood* (1995).

SELF-DETERMINATION. Most of the **human rights** recognized by states under international human rights instruments, deal with the rights of individuals, as distinct from groups. One of the few areas in which group rights are recognized is the area of self-determination—an extension of individual self-determination. Both of the international human rights covenants, the **International Covenant on Economic, Social and Cultural Rights** and the **International Covenant on Civil and Political Rights** (ICCPR), are identical in Article 1:

1. All peoples have the right of self-determination. By virtue of that right they freely determine their political status and freely pursue their economic, social and cultural development.

2. All peoples may, for their own ends, freely dispose of their natural wealth and resources without prejudice to any obligations arising out of international economic co-operation, based upon the principle of mutual benefit, and international law. In no case may a people be deprived of its own means of subsistence.

3. The States Parties to the present Covenant, including those having responsibility for the administration of Non-Self-Governing and Trust Territories, shall promote the realization of the right of self-determination, and shall respect that right, in conformity with the provisions of the Charter of the United Nations.

When groups such as the Basques of Spain and France, Chechnyans, Kurds, Quebecers, Tamils of Sri Lanka, Tibetans, and other **indigenous** peoples seek to assert the right of self-determination, there is always an immediate concern and often a problem on the part of states within whose borders such peoples live: will self-determination mean territorial division? If so, will such a division weaken the national power of the country? Will it induce other **peoples** to seek equivalent status? What of the resources within the area to be divided? How, if practicable, may such resources be shared? How will the national debt be apportioned? Can a less drastic alternative be pursued?

Such questions and others often prompt states to refuse support for the right to self-determination, even when the exercise of that right entails only a search for cultural autonomy within an existing society. The results of such refusals are many, including wars (intranational and international); religious, ethnic, linguistic, and racial persecution; refugees; starvation; and **genocide**, among others. The exercise of this right and its international recognition have also caused the undermining of the legitimacy of empires—Soviet, British, French, Ottoman, for example—which collapsed under the passion of peoples' demand for political independence. See also: Declaration on the Granting of Independence to Colonial Countries and Peoples; Nation-building; Saami. *Further Reading:* J. Crawford, *The Rights of Peoples* (1988); M. H. Halperin, D. J. Scheffer, and P. L. Small, *Self-Determination in the New World Order* (1992); United Nations, *The Right of Self-Determination* (1981).

SERBIA. Serbia was the most powerful republic of the former Yugoslavia. It now seeks, along with Montenegro and **Kosovo**, to inherit the rights of the now dissolved Yugoslavia. Serbia, which was part of the former Ottoman Empire, gained its independence in 1878. After 1878, and especially during the first two decades of the twentieth century, it sought to form a "Greater Serbia" out of the ethnically Serbian areas then controlled by the Austro-Hungarian Empire. In part, this nationalist challenge to Austria-Hungary resulted in World War I. In 1918, Serbia joined Slovenia and Croatia to form the United Kingdom of Serbs, Croats, and Slovenes, renamed Yugoslavia in 1929, which the Serbs dominated until 1991.

During World War II, the country was invaded by Germany and a puppet fascist regime was created. But with determined fighting, led by Marshal Tito (Josip Broz [1892–1980]) and his communist supporters, the country was liberated, and Tito went on to control the public life of the country from 1945 to 1980, when he died. During the years of Tito's rule, the six republics that formed the Yugoslav federation, **Bosnia-Herzegovina**, Croatia, Macedonia, Montenegro, Serbia, and Slovenia, were not only held together by the force of Tito's personality and the country's relative economic prosperity, but by the political control of the Communist Party, which limited the expression of nationalist sentiments. The fact that the people within the federation also moved out of and into sister republics, established new lives, and formed new families across ethnic, religious, and linguistic backgrounds also created a considerable sense of unity. After 1980, a succession of crises developed, including conflicting maneuverings for coveted positions among leaders within the republics. Those crises, coupled with economic problems during the 1980s, resulted in the ascendancy of **Slobodan Milosevic,** whose rise to power was largely gained by the reassertion of Serbian nationalism that had as its ambition an even greater standing within the federation. Other nationalists, especially those in Slovenia and Croatia, rejected Serbian ambition and sought political independence. Each declared independence in 1991; Bosnia-Herzegovina followed later that year.

Serbia responded by vainly seeking to use military force to prevent the republics from leaving the federation. It also gave support to organized Serbian ethnic groups within the territories of the newly proclaimed independent states of Slovenia, Croatia, and Bosnia-Herzegovina, in their attacks on the newly formed governments and **peoples** as a means to retain and expand control over the land areas where ethnic Serbs lived. The struggle for independence and land resulted in the reemergence of old hatreds, systematic slaughter of human beings, **genocide,** interethnic **rape, expulsion** of people from areas where they had long lived, and millions of refugees and displaced persons. Much of the conduct that involved Bosnia, Croatia, and Serbia is called **ethnic cleansing** with over 100,000 persons killed.

On May 30, 1992, the UN imposed sanctions on Serbia. Since that date, a number of international peace plans, including the U.S.-sponsored Dayton Accords of November 1995, have been tried to bring peace to the former Yugoslavia, especially in the conflict affecting Bosnia-Herzegovina. A UN-created international criminal tribunal is also in the process of prosecuting individuals responsible for human rights violations, including **crimes against humanity** and **war crimes.** UN peacekeeping forces and a U.S.-led North Atlantic Treaty Organization (NATO) force have been seeking to maintain enough order to help promote reconciliation in the war-ravaged area. The Dayton Accords have thus far stopped the fighting, but its scheduled elections have not brought political order. In the meantime, over 2 million refugees from the war remain unsettled, over 60 percent of the housing units awaiting them are damaged, and an estimated 2.5 to 3 million **land mines** are still scattered across the former Yugoslavia. At the International Criminal Tribunal for the former Yugoslavia a number of individuals have been indicted, but others such as Radovan Karadzic, who was the political leader of the Bosnian Serbs, and General Ratko Mladic, the military commander accused of the worst atrocities committed in Europe since World War II, still remain in the Republika Srpska, the Serbian half of Bosnia.

Within Serbia there are reports of disappearances, torture, and extrajudical killings. Likewise, **discrimination** against Albanians in the province of

Kosovo, and more generally against Muslims and the Roma people has been flagrant. **Civil and political rights**, in general, have been seriously compromised. See also: Convention Relating to the Status of Refugees; War Crimes Tribunal. *Further Reading:* A. Bell-Fialkoff, *Ethnic Cleansing* (1996); Physicians for Human Rights, *War Crimes in the Balkans* (1996); L. Silber and A. Little, *Yugoslavia: Death of a Nation* (1996); A. Stiglmayer, ed., *Rape: The War Against Women in Bosnia-Herzegovina* (1994).

SEXUAL HARASSMENT. One of the areas of violence against human beings, especially against women, is sexual harassment. The practice, in earlier centuries, entailed unwelcome sexual advances by social superiors toward domestic servants and factory workers. In contemporary times, advances are made generally by men against women and girls. When advances are unwanted, the consequences, then as now, are the same: hostility, insults, job dismissals, job refusals, unfavorable references, demotion, non-promotions, transfers, ridicule, loss of status, and damaged self-esteem. For centuries nothing was done to deal with sexual harassment, but the human rights movement, especially the women's rights movement, has sponsored moral and legal action.

In 1985, at the World Conference on Women held in Nairobi, Kenya, sexual harassment became an important part of the agenda. The 1993 Vienna Declaration and Programme of Action (VDAPA), adopted by the **World Conference on Human Rights** held in Vienna, Austria, in June 1993, proclaims that "all forms of sexual harassment . . . are incompatible with the dignity and worth of the human person." In February 1994, the United Nations **General Assembly** adopted a **Declaration on the Elimination of Violence Against Women**. Article 2 of the declaration specifically forbids "sexual harassment and intimidation at work." The Beijing Declaration, dealing with violence against women was adopted by the Fourth World Conference on Women, held in Beijing, China, in 1995, affirms in identical language the prohibition of the Declaration on the Elimination of Violence Against Women.

In the United States, sexual harassment has assumed two dominant forms: "quid pro harassment," where employment or promotion decisions are affected by responses to sexual advances, and the "work environment variety," which entails conduct that creates an "intimidating, hostile or offensive" working environment or which unreasonably interferes with a person's work performance. In the Civil Rights Act of 1991, the **United States** provides compensatory and punitive damages for victims of sexual harassment. See also: World Conference on Women. *Further Reading:* N. D. Setin, L. Marshall, and C. R. Tropp, *Secrets in Public: Sexual Harassment in Our Schools* (1993); N. Wolfson, *Hate Speech, Sex Speech, Free Speech* (1997); U.S. Public Law No. 102–166, 105 State. 1071; S. G. Bingham, ed., *Conceptualizing Harassment as Discoursive Practice* (1994).

SHARIA. Sharia is an Arab term that literally means the way, the path, or the road of Islam, as shown or revealed through its founder, the Prophet Muhammad. The term also denotes the comprehensive and sacred body of Islamic law, based on the Qur'an and the sayings and deeds of the Prophet Muhammad, which governs all aspects of Muslim individual and community life. Because this body of law is viewed by most Muslims as eternal and immutable, attempts to change it (or its interpretation) have caused conflicts within and between Islamic societies, as well as between Islamic societies and non-Islamic countries.

Within Islamic societies, the source of the conflict centers around efforts on the part of secularists, who seek to reform Islam, including the Sharia, and those who seek to preserve or return society to the strict codes of the Sharia. The last group are Islamic fundamentalists, who often see the modernization process (sometimes called secularization or Westernization), which seeks to de-emphasize religious values, as an evil that must be confronted, fought against, and defeated.

One area of conflict that is generating much bitterness is **human rights**, which are universal, and another is espousing freedom of religion and promotion of the norm of equality, regardless of race, sex, class, or national identity. As regards universality, if the prohibition against cruel, inhuman and degrading treatment or punishment is to be regarded as universal, it would mean that the Sharia's apparent call for stoning (in cases of adultery, for instance) and physical amputation of feet or hands (in cases of theft, for example) would have to be rejected—a course of action that many fundamentalists would not accept. Secularists, however, not only take the position that rules concerning adultery, for example, are part of a guide offered over 1,250 years ago to less morally refined societies, but that the Sharia ought no longer to have comprehensive application to all phases of social life. With respect to the norm of equality, Islam recognizes racial, national, and social equality. On the matter of sexual **equality**, however, it has been generally unwilling to accord women equality with men. The qualifying term "generally" is used because in Islamic societies such as Tunisia, the rights of women are undergoing considerable changes, and in a number of other Islamic societies, women have become heads of government or state as in the case of Benazir Bhutto who served as Prime Minister of Pakistan. Also, while in countries like the **United Kingdom** women were granted the right to own property independent of their husbands only in 1870, Muslim women have always had that right, and while a country like Switzerland did not recognize the right of women to vote until 1971, Muslim women in countries like **Turkey, Iraq**, and Pakistan were casting ballots long before then. In general, however, the Sharia—as interpreted—does not provide for sexual equality, and so, in countries where fundamentalists have succeeded in imposing the full weight of the Sharia (Afghanistan under the Taliban, for example), women have lost many of the rights that more secular regimes have promoted. Under conservative regimes like that in Saudi Arabia, few rights are recognized for women.

In the area of religious freedom, while Islam has always accorded general equality to "religions of the book"—Christianity and Judaism—and provided **asylum** to Jews and others fleeing religious persecution in Europe from the fifteenth to the eighteenth centuries, it frowns on conversion of Muslims to other religions. In **Saudi Arabia**, conversion or attempted conversion is a crime, and some religious communities such as the Bahai, in Iran, have often been persecuted. See also: Afghanistan; Bahai International Community; Declaration on the Elimination of All Forms of Intolerance and of Discrimination Based on Religion or Belief; Fundamentalism; Relativism and Universalism; Religion and Human Rights. *Further Reading:* E. Artzt, "The Application of International Human Rights in Islamic States," *HRQ,* vol. 12 no. 2 (1990); M. Z. Husain, *Global Islamic Politics* (1995); A. A. Mazrui, "Islamic and Western Values," *For. Aff.,* vol. 76 no. 5 (1997); A. Gauhar, ed., *The Challenge of Islam* (1978).

SHARPEVILLE MASSACRE. See SOUTH AFRICA.

SIKHS. Sikhs are a cultural group that, worldwide, constitute more than 17 million people, about 15 million of whom live in **India**. This group takes its identity from Sikhism, a religion founded in India in the fifteenth century that combines elements of Hinduism and Islam, although it claims to stand independent of them.

Sikhs, Hindus, and Muslims lived under the control of British India, which lasted from 1857, when the Mongul regime that had ruled India fell, until 1947. But when Pakistan and India gained their independence in 1947, the area known as Punjab—having been created out of the former British India—where Sikhism was founded and flourished, was divided into two parts: Western Punjab, went to form much of today's Pakistan, while eastern Punjab was allocated to India. The Sikhs, many of whom feared or harbored suspicions about the predominantly Muslim Pakistan, fled from western Punjab (an estimated 2.5 million) and moved to India (primarily eastern Punjab). In turn, they expelled Muslims from eastern Punjab. This mass movement and expulsion of people did not only create many refugees but incited intense violence and caused heavy loss of life.

Despite the violence and displacement caused by partition, Sikhs quickly restored social order to their lives and helped make eastern Punjab what is today considered the "breadbasket of India." Beginning in the mid-1960s, through their political party, the Akali Dal, they agitated for cultural autonomy within India, with some leaders actually calling for a separate nation. The call for independence caused the Indian government of Prime Minister Indira Gandhi to take measures, including efforts to remove arms that Sikh nationalists had stored in their most sacred shrine, the Golden

Temple of Amritsar. An assault on the temple by the Indian army in 1984 resulted in the death of J. S. Bhindranwale, leader of the Akali Dal, and a similar fate for hundreds of his followers, along with significant damage to the temple.

In October 1984, five months after the attack on the temple, Sikh nationalists exacted revenge by assassinating Prime Minister Gandhi. The social and political uncertainty and turmoil caused by her assassination invited calls for further violence against the Sikhs, many more of whom were killed. Today, an uneasy relationship exists between the Punjab and the federal government of India, as Sikh nationalists accuse the federal government of illegal arrests and detentions and continue to demand greater autonomy. Even more important than the **ethnic cleansing** that took place in 1947, the clamor for **self-determination** by the Sikhs, and the charges of illegal detention against the Indian government, is the fact that the disaffection of the Sikhs in recent years contributes significantly to political instability in India, and the rise of communal conflicts within the country. See also: Bangladesh. *Further Reading:* R. A. Kapur, *Sikh Separatism: The Politics of Faith* (1986); W. H. McLeod, *The Sikhs: History, Religion, and Society* (1989).

SINGAPORE. The Republic of Singapore gained its independence in 1965, when it withdrew from the Federation of Malaysia. It occupies Singapore Island, which is located in Southeast Asia, off the southernmost tip of the Malay Peninsula. The country has a population of approximately 2.8 million people, ethnically composed as follows: 78 percent Chinese, 14 percent Malays, 7 percent Indians, and 2 percent others, including Indonesians and Japanese. Linguistically and religiously the country is equally diverse. Official languages include English (the language of higher education and government), Chinese, Malay, and Tamil; religions practiced include Buddhism, Christianity, Confucianism, Islam, and Taoism.

Despite its ethnic, religious, and linguistic diversity, Singapore has been able, since independence, to shape a politically stable and economically successful society. Under the able leadership of the Action Party, which has governed the country since 1965, Singapore has achieved one of the highest literacy rates in the world and a material standard of living that exceeds that of its former colonial master, the **United Kingdom**, and all but few of the other industrial societies.

Singapore has been been involved in a number of issues the area of **human rights**. First, along with a number of other Asian countries such as Malaysia, it has accused the West of seeking to impose its version of **human rights** on the rest of the world. In particular, its leaders argue that Confucian values emphasize the norm of the group—the community—over the more atomistic individualism, to which the West gives preference. Second, **economic, social and cultural rights** are as important, if not more important, than **civil and political rights**. Singapore has also accused the West of selectively emphasizing certain civil and political rights (freedom of the press, religion, and association) to regain control of non-Western areas of the globe, including Asia. The West, for its part, accuses Singapore of being authoritarian, of not allowing enough freedom of speech and the press, and exercising undue control over economic life. Singapore, in return, contends that the results of its approach to economic development, which entails considerable government involvement, planning, and regulation, speak for themselves. That approach, it argues, proves that the "free market" model of the West has no empirical claim to superiority, and that that model bears no correlation with the greater protection and promotion of human rights, when economic, social and cultural rights are given equal weight with civil and political rights. See also: Bangkok Declaration; Relativism and Universalism. *Further Reading:* B. H. Chi, *Communitarian Ideology in Democracy in Singapore* (1995); W. G. Huff, *The Economic Growth of Singapore* (1994).

SLAVERY, THE SLAVE TRADE, AND SLAVERY-LIKE PRACTICES. In July 1997, Americans were shocked to learn that servitude and slavery-like practices still existed within their borders, this time in the form of deaf Mexicans who, under the threat of severe punishment by their "bosses" (smugglers), had to work as trinket vendors in New York and elsewhere. In the **United Kingdom**, the Anti-Slavery Society in 1993 exposed that country's "secret slaves"—workers who were brought in from overseas to do domestic work in Britain. Quite frequently, the world learns that slavery and the slave trade in children and women forced into prostitution and **forced labor**, are found among the powerless in Africa, Asia, Europe, the Americas, and elsewhere. The conditions of poverty, illiteracy, and **discrimination** that make slavery prevalent point to the indivisible character of **human rights**.

Although countries had entered into agreements over many years to abolish slavery and the slave trade, the United Nations **Economic and Social Council** (ECOSOC) found it necessary to adopt in 1956 a Supplementary Convention on the Abolition of Slavery, the Slave Trade, and Institutions and Practices Similar to Slavery (in 1926, states had considered and adopted the Slavery Convention, which sought to abolish slavery in all its forms). The Supplementary Convention was deemed necessary because of the need to reinforce the prohibition against slavery and eliminate slavery-like practices, which were becoming increasingly pervasive. The convention defines slavery, persons in servile status, and the slave trade, as follows:

Article 7. For the purposes of the present Convention:

a. "Slavery" means . . . the status or condition of a person over whom any or all of the powers attaching to the right of ownership are exercised, and the "slave" means a person in such a condition or status;

b. "A person of servile status" means a person in the condition or status resulting from any of the institutions or practices mentioned in article 1 of this Convention;

c. "Slave trade" means and includes all acts involved in the capture, acquisition or disposal of a person with intent to reduce him to slavery; all acts involved in the acquisition of a slave with a view to selling or exchanging him; all acts of disposal by sale or exchange of a person acquired with a view to being sold or exchanged; and, in general, every act of trade or transport in slaves by whatever means of conveyance.

Article 1 of the Supplementary Convention deals with and defines slavery-like practices, as referred to in Article 7, as follows:

Article 1. Each of the States Parties to this Convention shall take all practicable and necessary legislative and other measures to bring about progressively and as soon as possible the complete abolition of the following institutions and practices . . . :

a. Debt Bondage, that is to say, the status or condition arising from a pledge by a debtor of his personal services or those of a person under his control as security for a debt, if the value of those services as reasonably assessed is not applied towards the liquidation of the debt or the length and nature of those services are not respectively limited and defined;

b. Serfdom, that is to say, the condition or status of a tenant who is by law, custom or agreement bound to live and labour on land belonging to another person and to render some determinative service to such other person, whether for reward or not, and is not free to change his status;

c. Any institution or practice whereby:

(1) A woman, without the right to refuse, is promised or given in marriage on payment of a consideration in money or in kind to her parents, guardian, family or any other person or group; or

(2) The husband of a woman, his family, or his clan, has the right to transfer her to another person for value received or otherwise; or

(3) A woman, on the death of her husband is liable to be inherited by another person;

d. Any institution or practice whereby a child or young person under the age of 18 years, is delivered by either or both his natural parents or by his guardian to another person, whether for reward or not, with a view to the exploitation of the child or young person or his labour.

The human rights regime further provides for the elimination of slavery, the slave trade and slavery-like practices. Article 4 of the **Universal Declaration of Human Rights** (UDHR), for example, proclaims that "No one shall be held in slavery or servitude; slavery and the slave trade shall be prohibited in all their forms." And the **International Covenant on Civil and Political Rights provides** (ICCPR) in Article 8 that

1. No one shall be held in slavery; slavery and the slave-trade in all their forms shall be prohibited.

2. No one shall be held in servitude.

3. (a). No one shall be required to perform forced or compulsory labor.

The rest of Article 8 goes on to indicate what is excluded from the term "forced or compulsory labour": military service, service exacted by the state during periods of emergency or calamity threatening the life of the community, and work imposed as punishment for criminal activities, if the person were properly charged, tried, and convicted. See also: Bonded Labor; Child Labor; Convention for the suppression of the Traffic in Persons and the Exploitation of the Prostitution of Others. *Further Reading:* B. Anderson, *Britain's Secret Slaves* (1993); C. Goldberg, "Sex Slavery, Thailand to New York," *NYT* (September 11, 1995); Human Rights Watch (Asia), *Contemporary Forms of Slavery in Pakistan* (1996); L. Tucker, "Child Slavery in Modern India: The Bonded Labor Problem," *HRQ*, vol. 19 no. 3 (1997).

SOCIAL SECURITY. The right to social security in the **United States** and, to an extent in Western Europe, has become an important issue, the extent to which, if any, governments are responsible to promote and protect this right and whether resources will be available to fulfill this right for future generations. The **Universal Declaration of Human Rights** (UDHR) proclaims this right as follows:

Article 25 (1). Everyone has the right to a standard of living adequate for the health and well-being of himself and his family, including . . . the right to security in the event of unemployment, sickness, disability, widowhood, old age or other lack of livelihood in circumstances beyond his control.

The **International Covenant on Economic, Social and Cultural Rights** also provides for this right in Article 9 in the following manner: "The States Parties to the present Covenant recognize the right of everyone to social security, including social insurance." The **International Convention on the Elimination of All Forms of Racial Discrimination** explicitly states in Article 5 what is implied in the Universal Declaration of Human Rights and in the International Covenant on Economic, Social and Cultural Rights: the right to social security is one that is tied to the norm of equality and nondiscrimination, so one is entitled to Social Security regardless of one's race, nationality, social status, religion, sex, or other identity. The 1979 **Convention on the Elimination of All Forms of Discrimination Against Women** (CEDAW) provides as follows:

Article 11 (1). States Parties shall take all appropriate measures to eliminate discrimination against women in the field of employment in order to ensure, on the basis of equality of men and women, the same rights, in particular . . .

e. The right to social security, particularly in cases of retirement, unemployment, sickness, invalidity and old age and other incapacity to work, as well as the right to paid leave.

One of the strategies of those who want to eliminate social security is to link it with the hated (at least in the **United States** and, to an extent, in the **United Kingdom**) "welfare state." When linked with the welfare state, social security is not presented as a human right but as a social entitlement. But groups such as European labor unions that are committed to its protection as a human right, are organizing to fight for that protection. In the Global South, where economies are not as well developed and more of the population are young (under 20 years of age), the issues of social security are not as prominent, although more and more references to social security are found in Latin America, whose Charter of Social Guarantees offers, to a degree, some of the same protections as social security. See also: European Social Charter; Inter-American Charter of Social Guarantees. *Further Reading:* International Labor Organization, *Into the Twenty-First Century: The Development of Social Security* (1984); J. Myles and J. Quadagno, *States, Labor Markets, and the Future of Old Age Policy* (1991); J. Dixon and R. P. Scheurell, eds., *Social Security Programs: A Cross Cultural Comparative Perspective* (1995).

SOKA GAKKAI INTERNATIONAL. This is a Buddhist **nongovernmental organization** (NGO) based in Japan, with 76 constituent organizations and membership in 128 countries. Founded in 1975 by philosopher and educator Diasaku Ikeda, Soko Gakkai International (SGI) is rooted in Nichiren Buddhism, which places its highest emphasis on the sanctity of life, a commitment to education and a culture of peace, and a belief in the process of "human revolution": the self-directed transformation of the individual who, through transformation, overcomes the inner impulse toward hatred and violence. To Nichiren Buddhists, violence is "the fundamental darkness of life."

Soko Gakkai are two Japanese words that mean "create value" and "society." SGI is, therefore, an international institution committed to the creation of values. Basic to that view is the concept of self-realization, the progressive process of permanent autocreation (a form of self-creation)—the working out of individual fulfillment and capacity to shape a "new" person out of the "old." It is from the same person that institutional and other values emanate and develop.

In the area of **human rights**, SGI believes it is not enough to elaborate abstract norms in the form of treaties, though they are important and are likely to continue to be important. To realize the fulfillment of human rights norms, there must be people who embody the values those rights express and who will create a culture that respects and enforces those rights. Persons and cultures cannot be created by the existing international system that emphasizes selfishness on the part of the individual and the group, including the nation-state. The process of autocreation entails the change of persons who are hinged to the "self" and the "other" to the progressive elimination of the separation between "self and other." Goodness is in fact defined in terms of conduct that aspires toward the union of selves, toward human solidarity, whose expected conduct is in the motto of SGI: "Be the heart of a network of global citizens. Be a bridge for dialogue between civilizations. Be a beacon lighting the way to a century of life."

SGI takes the position that peace and human rights need human solidarity, which will come about through education (including education for global citizenship), intercultural and other forms of dialogue, and autocreation. Two institutions that SGI created in the **United States** are particularly important from the standpoint of human rights: Soka University of America, which is located in Aliso Viejo, California, is dedicated to education for global citizenship and the collective future of humankind, and the Boston Research Center for the Twenty-First Century, located in Cambridge, Massachusetts, that is dedicated to the promotion of intercultural dialogue, including the intercultural elements of human rights promotion and protection, the **environment**, and nurturing a culture of peace. See also: Declaration of a Global Ethic; Religion and Human Rights. *Further Reading:* D. Ikeda, *Creating a Century without War Through Human Solidarity* (1995); D. Ikeda, *New Horizons of a Global Civilization* (1997). *Further Information:* Boston Research Center for the Twenty-First Century, 396 Harvard Street, Cambridge, Mass. 02138, Tel.: 617–491–1090; Soka University of America, 101 Columbia, Aliso Viejo, Calif., 92656, Tel.: 714–448–4137.

SOUTH AFRICA. The Republic of South Africa (called Azania by some nationalists) is located in southern Africa and shares borders with Botswana, Mozambique, Swaziland, and Zimbabwe and has a population of about 40 million people. That population is approximately 77 percent black, 11 percent white, 19 percent mixed, and 3 percent Indian. The percentage of blacks is, in turn, divided into several national and ethnic groups, including the Zulu, the Xhosa, the Sotho, and the Tswana, each of whom had its own distinct history before being incorporated into South Africa. A similar subdivision can be made in the percentages of white persons, since English-speaking and Afrikaans-speaking (former Dutch settlers) groups have retained some of their cultural differences. Christianity is the predominant religion (about 70 percent), with Hinduism, Islam, and Animism sharing the remaining 30 percent.

European settlement in South Africa began in 1652, as Dutch members of the Dutch East India Company established themselves in an area now called Cape Town. The settlers, called Afrikaners or Boers, defeated and expelled the local inhabitants from the land, and then organized an economy based on the enslavement of the **indigenous people**. After the Napoleonic Wars, during which the French and their Dutch allies were defeated,

Britain took over the former Dutch colony and brought in English-speaking settlers and, in the early 1930s, abolished slavery in areas under its jurisdiction. Reacting to the abolition policy, the Boers moved inland from the Cape Colony (now Cape Town) and established "three republics": Transvaal, Orange Free State, and Natal. Natal was quickly annexed by Britain, and as the Boers took steps to limit or exclude the influx of persons who sought to move into Transvaal and Orange Free State to partake in the rich diamond resources found there, war ensued (1899–1902) between Britain and Boers. The Boers were defeated and in 1910 the Union of South Africa was formed from the Cape Colony (Capetown), Transvaal, Orange Free State, and Natal. Today, this union is the Republic of South Africa.

South Africa participated in World Wars I and II, although not without bitter disagreements between English-speaking and Afrikaans-speaking whites. The Afrikaners, organized around the Nationalist Party, wanted a society based on white supremacy; the English-speaking group, while largely accepting the idea of white supremacy, wanted to integrate nonwhites into society at large. In 1948, the Nationalist Party won and imposed apartheid, a policy of enforced racial separation, on South Africa. At first, the black majority sought to use the tactic of nonviolence to destroy apartheid, but following the Sharpeville Massacre of 1960, when South African police fired on a crowd of peaceful demonstrators, mostly school children, killing dozens and wounding hundreds, blacks made a decision to resist the government with force. What followed was the systematic violation of the **human rights** of nonwhites in South Africa. Violations by the government included torture, disappearances, **arbitrary arrest and detention,** murder, poor or no education, impairment of the right to speak and associate, to security of person, to found a family, and the freedom of movement, including the right to leave one's country and return to it.

As local and international pressure grew, including UN economic sanctions and an international treaty that made apartheid one of the **crimes against humanity,** the country became increasingly ungovernable, due to violence, civil disobedience in cities and townships, and the rise of fascist movements among "extremist whites." In addition, South Africa, in part reacting to its isolation, had secretly developed nuclear weapons and begun to intervene in the affairs of neighboring countries, Angola and Mozambique in particular. These two courses of conduct created international tensions not only because they were frowned on by most of the international community, but because they placed great strains on the South African economy and incited more domestic and international anxieties. It was in the midst of this potential social and political explosion that **Nelson Mandela,** leader of the most important black political organization, the African National Congress (ANC), was released from jail in 1990 after twenty-eight years of imprisonment. Mandela, along with Nationalist Party leader, F. W. DeKlerk, led the drafting of a new constitution, under which free multiracial elections took place in 1994. The ANC won an overwhelming majority and Nelson Mandela was elected president.

The constitution of South Africa seeks to create one nation out of many racial and ethnic groups, a society free of racial **discrimination,** but also one in which all the norms of human rights will be respected and protected. Indeed, the constitution adopted one of the world's broadest guarantees of human rights, including freedom of speech, movement, and **democratic entitlement;** the right to a speedy and public trial; freedom of **thought, conscience and religion;** and privacy. It also enshrines the right to adequate housing, food, water, health care, and education, as well as "the right to an environment which is not detrimental to . . . health and well-being." In addition, the constitution prohibits discrimination based on race, gender, nationality, sexual orientation, pregnancy, or marital status. Of utmost importance, it provides for an independent judiciary.

Despite the promise of human rights promotion and protection by the constitution, the task of fulfilling that promise is not an easy one. First, there are deep divisions in the black community, including differences with the Zulu nation, which seeks greater autonomy within South Africa and is overwhelmingly represented by the Ikatha Party. Second, some black leaders, including those from the Pan-African Congress, a former rival of the ANC, are troubled by the ANC's policy that grants pardons to Nationalist leaders who help establish the truth of human rights violations during the apartheid regime. Third, angry white groups, which resent their loss of political power, are challenging the legitimacy of the government. Finally, whites have control of about 70 percent of the country's material wealth, while 50 percent of the blacks live below the poverty line. See also: Expulsion; Racism; Truth Commissions. *Further Reading:* S. Daley, "A New Charter Wins Adoption in South Africa," *NYT* (May 9, 1996); A. Handley and J. Herbst, "South Africa: The Perils of Normalcy," *CH,* vol. 96 no. 610 (1997); A. J. Steenkamp, *The South African Constitution of 1993 and the Bill of Rights: An Evaluation in Light of International Human Rights Norms,"* *HRQ,* vol. 17 no. 1 (1995).

SOVEREIGNTY. Sovereignty refers to a fundamental concept of international law. It defines the supreme authority of the state to make and enforce laws with respect to all property, events, institutions, and persons within its borders. According to the concept, what a state does or does not do within its borders is its own business and other states have no right to comment on or interfere in another state's affairs. Because of the attribute of sovereignty, all states are said to be equal, regardless of how they differ in size, power, and influence.

Human rights imposes limits on sovereignty. A state is no longer free to make and enforce laws relating to human beings—including its own citizens—as it sees fit, without accountability to the international community.

Thus, there is tension between sovereignty and the norms of human rights, a fact that is often attested to by the protests of countries like **China** and Sudan, when they have been accused by other states of violating human rights. Protests of that kind, generally, are wrongly made on the grounds that such accusations constitute an impermissible interference in the internal affairs of the protesting country, but such protests have no validity in international law, since every state is obligated to promote and protect the human rights of everyone. See also: Interventionism; South Africa; War Crimes Tribunals. *Further Reading:* M. Heiberg, *Subduing Sovereignty* (1994); D. Jacobson, *Rights Across Borders* (1997).

STALIN, JOSEPH V. (1879–1953). Born in the Republic of Georgia, Stalin was among the leaders of the revolutionary group that successfully inaugurated the Russian Revolution in 1917. Through a series of well-calculated steps, he not only gained control of the Communist Party machinery in 1922, but used that control to purge and otherwise destroy actual or supposed rivals and enemies, and thereby assure absolute control of the USSR between 1925 and 1953, when he died.

During his tenure as leader, he launched and implemented a number of Five-Year Plans to effect rapid industrialization and agricultural collectivization, provided the overwhelming majority of citizens with the right to education, employment, health care, social security, and housing, among other **economic, social and cultural rights**, and played a major role in the defeat of Nazi Germany during World War II. The good associated with his regime, however, is outstripped by the wanton violations of **human rights**.

First, Stalin's regime violated the right to **self-determination**, when it forcibly annexed the Baltic States (Estonia, Latvia, and Lithuania) in 1940. After World War II it created puppet regimes in the countries of Eastern Europe, and used them to shape undemocratic societies in the region, a condition that lasted until 1989–1990. Second, Stalin's government violated freedom of **thought, conscience and religion** not only in its uncompromising limits on freedom of expression and the free exercise of religion but in its efforts at *thought* control. Third, Stalin's government, in its pursuit of totalitarian control, engaged in **purges** that chilled debate and dissent—undermining any semblance of **democratic entitlement**—and engaged in mass killings of people, violating their very **right to life**. The purges, the worst expressions of which occured during the 1920s and 1930s, took place without the benefit of the right to a fair trial.

Stalin also instituted forced agricultural collectivization, which caused (deliberately, in some instances) the starvation and death of over 1 million people. His **forced labor** policy blatantly violated the right of everyone to "free choice of employment" and "just and favorable conditions of work." The total number of Stalin's non-war victims is estimated to be above 20 million. Even the revolutionary ideals which, among other goals, sought the solidarity of workers throughout the world and the progressive reduction or "withering away" of the state's role in social life, were cynically compromised in favor of authoritarian rule. See also: Collectivization; Gulag Archipelago; Nagorno-Karabakh; Russia. *Further Reading:* A. S. Adams, *Stalin and His Times* (1972); R. Conquest, *The Great Terror: A Reassessment* (1990); M. McCauley, *Stalin and Stalinism* (1995).

STANDARD MINIMUM RULES FOR THE TREATMENT OF PRISONERS. Throughout the world, humanists have always been concerned about the treatment given to prisoners, and prison reform movements, with few exceptions, included efforts to improve the treatment accorded prisoners. Since 1945, the world community, through the UN, has sought ways by which inhumane treatment could be reduced, if not eliminated. In 1955, the First United Nations Congress on the Prevention of Crime and the Treatment of Offenders was held in Geneva, Switzerland, where it adopted a body of some ninety-five rules, which was approved by the United Nations **Economic and Social Council** (ECOSOC) on July 31, 1957, and is today known as the Standard Minimum Rules for the Treatment of Prisoners. These rules, a summary of which follows, are not "intended to describe in detail a model system of penal institutions," but the essential elements of an adequate system.

The rules include the requirement of proper registration of prisoners, including information about their identity, reasons for commitment, the authority for that commitment, and the day and hour of admission and release. Rule 7 (2) reads: "No persons shall be received in an institution without a valid commitment order of which the details shall have been previously entered in the register." The rules also include a requirement for the separation of different categories of prisoners.

Rule 8. The different categories of prisoners shall be kept in separate institutions or part of institutions taking account of their sex, age, criminal record, the legal reason for their detention and the necessities of their treatment. Thus,

a. Men and women shall as far as possible be detained in separate institutions; in an institution which receives both men and women the whole of the premises allocated to women shall be entirely separate;

b. Untried prisoners shall be kept separate from convicted prisoners;

c. Persons imprisoned for debt and other civil prisoners shall be kept separate from persons imprisoned by reason of a criminal offence;

d. Young prisoners shall be kept separate from adults.

Some rules deal with adequate physical accommodation, proper lighting, and appropriate clothing and bedding for prisoners. Likewise, provisions are made for "food of nutritional value adequate for health," water, exercise, and medical services. Prisoners are also entitled to written and/or oral (if illiterate) information about regulations governing the treatment of prisoners of their category, to make requests and complaints, and to have contact with the outside world. They are entitled, also, to access to recreational and instructional books, to have their religious needs met, as far as possible, to have their property placed in safe custody, and to have relatives or spouses notified of illness, transfer, death, or other changes in their status or condition. In instances where prisoners must work, that work must "not be of an afflictive nature."

Protection is also provided for two special classes of prisoners, those under arrest and awaiting trial, and the "mentally abnormal," the former to be treated as if they are innocent, the latter to be placed into institutions appropriate to their condition. See also: Procedural Guarantees, Processes, and Protections; Safeguards Guaranteeing the Protection of the Rights of Those Facing the Death Penalty; United Nations Standard Minimum Rules for the Administration of Juvenile Justice. *Further Reading:* R. S. Clarke, *The United Nations Crime Prevention and Criminal Justice Program* (1994); H. Franke, *The Emancipation of Prisons* (1995); P. Van Voorhis, *Psychological Classification of Adult Male Prison Inmates* (1994).

STANDARD OF LIVING. Concern about people's standard of living, especially what has come to be known as the "minimum standard," has been part of the United Nations' focus since its founding. Today, whether measured in terms of minimum wages, the "poverty line," or "basic needs," that concern is more and more an international one, as the economic and social welfare of people is less and less determined by local and even national institutions and practices, and more by what has become the global economy. International human rights instruments recognize the right of everyone to a certain standard of living, and the **Universal Declaration of Human Rights** (UDHR), dealing with that right, proclaims in Article 25 that

1. Everyone has the right to a standard of living adequate for the health and well-being of himself and his family, including food, clothing, housing and medical care and necessary social services. . . .
2. Motherhood and childhood are entitled to special care and assistance. All children, whether born in or out of wedlock, shall enjoy the same social protection.

The **International Covenant on Economic, Social and Cultural Rights**, in dealing with the same right, repeats much of what the Universal Declaration of Human Rights states, but goes beyond its provisions, to indicate in part that the right is not confined to that which is "adequate for health and well-being," especially in a world of expanding social and economic possibilities. Article 11 (1) of the covenant states:

The States Parties to the present Covenant recognize the right of everyone to an adequate standard of living for himself and his family, including adequate food, clothing and housing, and to the continuous improvement of living conditions. The

States Parties will take appropriate steps to ensure the realization of this right, recognizing to this effect the essential importance of international co-operation. . . .

See also: Economic, Social and Cultural Rights; Universal Declaration on the Eradication of Hunger and Malnutrition. *Further Reading:* R. Beddard and D. M. Hill, eds., *Economic, Social and Cultural Rights* (1992); A. Eide, C. Krause, and A. Rosas, eds., *Economic, Social and Cultural Rights: A Textbook* (1995).

STANDARD-SETTING. The human rights movement is said to have had three stages or phases: (1) the phase by which the principles and norms of **human rights** were formulated; (2) the phase entailing the ratification of the norms or standards, thus making them binding on states; and (3) the phase involving the enforcement of the standards. The first of the three stages is called the standard-setting stage. That phase has been very successful, thus far. The second phase has been progressing, although not without some disappointments, such as the reluctance of some important countries like the United States to ratify some human rights treaties. The third stage represents the greatest current challenge, as individuals, nonstate groups, and some countries struggle to create institutions that will ensure the reliable and just enforcement of the universal norms of human rights. See also: Adjudication; European Court of Human Rights; Inter-American Court of Human Rights; International Criminal Court; Ratification. *Further Reading:* J.T.P. Humphrey, *Human Rights and the United Nations: The Great Adventure* (1984); A. Samnoy, *Human Rights as International Consensus: The Making of the Universal Declaration of Human Rights, 1945–1948* (1993).

STATELESSNESS. See CONVENTION ON THE REDUCTION OF STA-TELESSNESS; CONVENTION RELATING TO THE STATUS OF STATELESS PERSONS.

STATE OF EMERGENCY. See PUBLIC EMERGENCY.

STERILIZATION. Forced sterilization is the process or act by which a person is involuntarily deprived of the power of reproduction. The practice, which was used by Nazi Germany against Jews, the Roma people, and others, and by Japanese against Chinese and Koreans, among others, has been condemned as a moral outrage. Since World War II, a number of countries, including **China** and **India,** have employed sterilization as a means of curbing their respective rates of population growth. Both countries characterize their programs as voluntary, although China's voluntary policy, which centers around the official encouragement of families to observe a one-child policy, is sometimes met with some skepticism.

In August 1997, reports from Sweden revealed that successive governments of that country had engaged in the practice of forced sterilization from 1935 to 1976, with an estimated 60,000 women who were deemed to be either "inferior," "poor," or of "mixed racial quality" (from non-Nordic stock) undergoing the process. The reports also indicated that Belgium and Finland followed a similar practice after World War II.

Forced sterilization invites outrage because people intuitively view it as morally wrong and because it clearly violates many elementary **human rights**. For instance, the practice violates the right of everyone "to found a family," to the integrity of his or her person, to **equality** and nondiscrimination, and to be treated with respect for his or her inherent dignity, the last right correlating with, among others, the prohibition against cruel, inhuman and degrading treatment.

Much of the support for forced sterilization comes from ideas that have their sources in the science of eugenics, an area of enquiry that deals with the improvement (or cleansing) of the genetic or hereditary quality of a racial, ethnic, or national group. In Sweden and the **United States,** for instance, discussions about eugenics extend to possible sterilization of families or persons who, generation after generation, burden institutional care centers, or what may be broadly called the social welfare system.

Forced sterilization against the Jews during World War II was one of the instruments used by the Nazis in acts of **genocide** against them, and the **Convention on the Prevention and Punishment of the Crime of Genocide** has sterilization in mind, when it provides for and criminalizes the following acts:

Article 2. In the present Convention, genocide means any of the following acts committed with the intent to destroy, in whole or in part, a national, ethnical, racial or religious group, as such: . . .

    c. Deliberately inflicting on the group conditions of life calculated to bring about its physical destruction in whole or in part;

    d. Imposing measures intended to prevent birth within the group; . . .

See also: Apartheid; Ethnic Cleansing. *Further Reading: Chan v. Minister of Employment and Immigration, et al., ILM,* vol. 35 no. 1 (1995); S. Haydon, "Sweden Faces Claims over Sterilization," *BG* (August 25, 1997).

STOCKHOLM DECLARATION OF THE UNITED NATIONS CONFERENCE ON THE HUMAN ENVIRONMENT. See ENVIRONMENT.

STRUCTURAL ADJUSTMENT LOANS. See CONDITIONALITY.

SUB-COMMISSION ON THE PREVENTION OF DISCRIMINATION AND PROTECTION OF MINORITIES.

This body was established by the United Nations **Commission on Human Rights** (CHR) in 1947, under the authority of the United Nations **Economic and Social Council** (ECOSOC). It is a group of experts in the field of **human rights** drawn from every region of the world, which meets annually for a period of four or more weeks in Geneva, Switzerland. It makes reports to the Commission on Human Rights and, through that Commission, to the UN Economic and Social Council and the United Nations **General Assembly** on all matters under its jurisdiction. Its jurisdiction, as defined in 1947 and later updated, is: (1) to undertake studies and make recommendations to the Commission on Human Rights concerning the prevention of **discrimination** on the basis of race, sex, nationality, language, religion, or in any other area relating to human rights and fundamental freedoms; and (2) to perform any other functions or tasks that may be assigned to it by the United Nations Economic and Social Council or the Commission on Human Rights.

Although the sub-commission meets only once a year, its functions are discharged on a continuing basis through **working groups**, special rapporteurs, and studies. In May 1970, by Resolution 1503, the Economic and Social Council authorized the sub-commission to establish the Working Group on Communications to consider all complaints "which appear to reveal a consistent pattern of gross and reliably attested violations of human rights and fundamental freedoms" within the sub-commission's jurisdiction. The sub-commission has the authority to examine those communications (complaints) that are identified by the working group as satisfying the terms of Resolution 1503, along with whatever information is supplied by the complained-about government, and to decide whether or not to forward the cases to the Commission on Human Rights. When such cases are so forwarded, the commission decides on what further steps it should take. The entire process of receipt, examination, and disposition of the communication or complaint is confidential.

There are other working groups associated with the sub-commission, including those dealing with detention, **indigenous peoples**, contemporary forms of slavery, and **minorities**. Special rapporteurs and studies cover areas varying from compensation to victims of gross violations of human rights, discrimination against HIV or AIDS victims, states of emergency, and the right to a fair trial, to human rights and the **environment**, privatization of prisons, human rights and population transfers, and treaties and indigenous peoples. In the latter regard, the sub-commission played a major role in the preparation and drafting of the 1993 UN Declaration on the Rights of Persons Belonging to National or Ethnic, Religious or Linguistic Minorities. So, too, has been the character of its role in the preparation of the 1994 Draft Declaration on the Rights of Indigenous Peoples. *Further Reading:* D. Weissbrodt, P. L. Parker, A. Z. Kayal, "The Forty-Fourth Session of the UN Sub-Commission on Prevention of Discrimination and Protection of Minorities and the Special Session of the Commission on Human Rights on the Situation in the former Yugoslavia," *HRQ*, vol. 15 no. 2 (1993).

SUBJECT OF INTERNATIONAL LAW. See OBJECT OF INTERNATIONAL LAW.

SUDAN. See HOLY SEE.

SUPERIOR ORDERS. This is an international term that refers to a long and, until recently, widely followed international practice, wherein soldiers who engaged in a course of wartime conduct that was legally and morally wrong could have their conduct excused or justified on the grounds that it was ordered by a superior officer. This defense was rejected at the **Nuremberg War Crimes Trials** and Tokyo War Crimes Trials, as well as in the trial of Lieutenant William L. Calley in the case of the **My Lai Massacre**.

With the evolution of human rights law, such a defense is no longer available, since states and their representatives, including military officers and their soldiers, are not free to violate **human rights**, even when circumstances permit limitations on the exercise of some of those rights. See also: Derogation; Principles of International Law Recognized in the Charter and in the Judgment of the Nuremberg Tribunal; Public Emergency. *Further Reading:* J. Bodley, *Anthropology and Contemporary Human Rights Problems* (1985); N. Roht-Arriaza, ed., *Impunity and Human Rights in International Law Practice* (1995).

T

THIRD GENERATION RIGHTS. See GENERATIONS OF RIGHTS.

THOUGHT, CONSCIENCE AND RELIGION. Few **human rights** in the civil and political class of rights are as important as the one under discussion. And few have been more abused, because of fear, intolerance, ignorance and suspicion. It is through thought, conscience, and religion, some thinkers claim, that individuals truly become conscious of themselves, capable of transcending their circumstances, and morally and spiritually involved with other human beings, including the process of constructing communities. The right to freedom of thought, conscience, and religion is proclaimed in Article 18 of the **Universal Declaration of Human Rights** (UDHR): "Everyone has the right to freedom of thought, conscience and religion; this right includes freedom to change his religion or belief, and freedom, either alone or in community with others in public or private, to manifest his religion or belief in teaching, practice, worship and observance."

The **International Covenant on Civil and Political Rights** (ICCPR) also provides for this right. The covenant, however, elaborates the right to freedom of thought, conscience, and religion and indicates the conditions under which its exercise may be limited. Article 18 reads as follows:

1. Everyone shall have the right to freedom of thought, conscience and religion. This right shall include freedom to have or to adopt a religion or belief of his choice, and freedom, either individually or in community with others and in public or private, to manifest his religion or belief in worship, observance, practice and teaching.

2. No one shall be subject to coercion which would impair his freedom to have or to adopt a religion or belief of his choice.

3. Freedom to manifest one's religion or beliefs may be subject only to such limitations as are prescribed by law and are necessary to protect public safety, order, health, or morals or the fundamental rights and freedoms of others.

4. The States Parties to the present Covenant undertake to have respect for the liberty of parents and, when applicable, legal guardians to ensure the religious and moral education of their children in conformity with their own convictions.

Other global human rights instruments, such as the **International Convention on the Elimination of All Forms of Racial Discrimination** (Article 5) and the Convention on the Rights of the Child (CRC) (Article 14), also deal with the right to freedom of thought, conscience, and religion. At the regional level, the **African Charter on Human and Peoples' Rights** (Article 8), the **American Convention on Human Rights** (Article 12), and the **European Convention on Human Rights** (Article 9) recognize this right, too. See also: Charter 77; Declaration of a Global Ethic; Declaration on the Elimination of All Forms of Intolerance and Discrimination Based on Religion or Belief; Havel, Václav; Religion and Human Rights; Saudi Arabia; Sharia. *Further Reading:* Council for a Parliament of the World's Religions, *Towards a Global Ethic* (1993); M. Juergensmeyer, *The Cold War: Religious Nationalism Confronts the Secular State* (1993); L. Kurtz, *Gods in the Global Village* (1995); K. J. Partsch, "Freedom of Conscience and Expression and Political Freedoms" in *The International Bill of Rights: The Covenant on Civil and Political Rights*, ed. L. Henkin (1981).

TIBET. See CHINA.

TIENANMEN SQUARE. See CHINA.

TOKYO WAR CRIMES TRIALS. After much of the work of Nuremberg War Crimes Trials was completed, an International Military Tribunal for the Far East was established in Tokyo on January 19, 1946, to try Japanese war criminals. The tribunal completed its work on November 4, 1948, sentencing twenty-five defendants, including seven of them to death.

The trials were very controversial, especially with respect to their impartiality. First, because the procedures followed in the Tokyo trials were different from those applied at Nuremberg. For example, while it took a "moral certainty" to convict alleged wrongdoers at Nuremberg, it required only a preponderance of evidence (a simple majority, which is a much lower standard) for conviction in Tokyo. Second, the eleven judges, the main prosecutor, and the ten attorneys associated with the prosecution were appointed by the American Supreme Commander in the Far East, General Douglas MacArthur. And third, controversial in the view that the trials were tainted by racial considerations and violative of the norm against nondiscrimination, in general, and racial discrimination in particular. See also: Yamashita, Tomoyuki; Yellow Peril. *Further Reading:* A. C. Brackman,

The Other Nuremberg: The Untold Story of the Tokyo War Crimes Trials (1987); P. R. Piccigallo, *The Japanese on Trial* (1979); J. N. Shklar, *Legalism: Law, Morals and Political Trials* (1986); B.V.A. Rolling and G. F. Rutter, eds., *The Tokyo Judgement* (1977).

TORTURE. See CONVENTION AGAINST TORTURE AND OTHER CRUEL, INHUMAN OR DEGRADING TREATMENT OR PUNISHMENT.

TOXIC AND DANGEROUS PRODUCTS AND WASTES. See ENVIRONMENT.

TRAFFIC IN PERSONS AND THE EXPLOITATION OF THE PROSTITUTION OF OTHERS. The phenomenon of the traffic in persons concerns the use of human beings as sexual merchandise, transferred or exchanged from one person or place to another. It is more specifically captured in the words of Special Rapporteur Jean Fernand-Laurent, in his report to the United Nations **Commission on Human Rights**, which requested his study and report. Updated by the work of Special Rapporteur Benjamin Whitaker and Abdelwahab Bouhdiba, a few selected paragraphs, numbered in accordance with the report, follow:

16. Contrary to an opinion too widespread, prostitution is not the oldest profession. (It was and still is unknown in many so-called "primitive" societies.) But it is true that it is found today in varying degrees in all organized States, in all cultures and in all parts of the world, especially where the population is very dense and where money changes hands frequently.

17. In an analysis of the problem, it can be approached from several angles. . . . One approach is from the angle of ethnology, sociology or cultural history . . . or again, from the point of view of political economy. . . . Prostitution can also be judged by the standards of public health, religion or morality. We ourselves . . . shall take the human rights approach . . . and from that point of view we, like the Commission on Human Rights, consider prostitution to be a form of slavery.

A. A three-way trade

18. Like slavery in the usual sense, prostitution has an economic aspect. While being a cultural phenomenon rooted in masculine and feminine images given currency by society, it is a market and indeed a lucrative one. The merchandise involved is men's pleasure, or their image of pleasure. The merchandise is unfortunately supplied by physical intimacy with women or children. Thus the alienation of the person is more far-reaching than in slavery in its usual sense, where what is alienated is working strength, not intimacy.

19. The market is created by demand, which is met by supply. The demand comes from the client, who could be called the "prostitutor," the supply is provided by the prostitute. This is the simplest but also the rarest example. In most cases

(8 or 9 times out of 10 . . .), a third person comes into the picture, perhaps the most important: this is the organizer and exploiter of the market—in other words, the procurer in his various guises: go-between or recruiter, pimp, owner of a house of prostitution, "massage parlour" or bar, or provider of a hotel room or studio. The procurer is usually a professional, involved to some extent with the world of crime . . .

20. In industrialized market-economy States, a concern not to hamper trade allows an overt market for eroticism, and pornography to develop alongside the discreet prostitution market. The two complement and reinforce each other. The streets on which the sex shops are located are those where prostitution is heaviest.

30. In some industrialized countries, child prostitution has recently been organized to benefit the pornographic industry, which produces photo albums, films and video cassettes. Children are photographed or filmed in indecent positions, and those pictures are sold for high prices through a clandestine network of persons interested in such things. The trade may be national or international.

32. Certain intelligence services and . . . firms act as procurers when, in order to corrupt or compromise a statesman or businessman, they arrange for him to meet women, styled as hostesses or secretaries, who are trained in this particular form of "high-class" prostitution.

33. Procurers usually conduct their activities with impunity. Perhaps because the police or investigating official are not sufficiently zealous . . . or because it is sometimes difficult to obtain proof of such offenses . . .

Related to the issue of prostitution as a form of slavery is the exploitation of child labor, as elaborated in the previously mentioned study by Mr. Adbelwahab Bouhdiba, Special Rapporteur of the Sub-Commission on the Prevention of Discrimination and Protection of Minorities. Continuing the use of selected numbered paragraphs, the report states that

118. Child prostitution is, together with the sale of children, the most distressing part of the story. There has always been a demand for children for sexual purposes because of their freshness and simplicity. Our age which is "permissive" and at the same time surfeited and sexually vulgarized in the extreme, seeks all kinds of erotic refinements. There is a great demand among our contemporaries for the sexuality of the child, through which they seek to renew their jaded sensuality. Hence the universal flourishing of child prostitution. "S.O.S. Enfants" estimates that some 5,000 boys and 3,000 girls below the age of 18 are involved in prostitution in Paris. The prostitutes most in demand in Latin America are between the ages of 10 and 14 . . .

119. The picture is the same in Hong Kong, and in Bangkok, where girls scarcely weaned are handed over for the equivalent of a few United States dollars to pimps and very soon find themselves shut up in some brothel for life. In Macao girls can be bought for $100 to $200. When they land on the American coast they are "worth" 40 times as much.

120. A complete account of the "escort" service system ought to be given here. Barcelona, Bombay, Macao, Singapore, Amsterdam, Hamburg, Paris, Mar-

seilles, New York, Mexico City, and so on. The market for pornography, with the help of video techniques, has provided very extensive scope for the expansion in the exploitation of the sexuality of children, which is finding increasing outlets in Europe and North America, and more recently in the oil-producing countries.

122. The effect of tourism on child prostitution should be mentioned because the extraordinary advance of tourism has led to dangerous developments. The presence of children of both sexes ready to satisfy the sexual appetites of organized bodies of tourists is very often an additional attraction. Young boys lured into prostitution may be said to be part of the "decor" of . . . Rio de Janeiro, Abijan, Dakar, Colombo, Istanbul etc. . . .

See also: Bonded Labor; Child Labor; Convention for the Suppression of the Traffic in Persons and the Exploitation of the Prostitution of Others; Slavery, the Slave Trade, and Slavery-like Practices. *Further Reading: Report of Mr. Jean-Laurent, Special Rapporteur on the Suppression of the Traffic in Persons and the Exploitation of the Prostitution of Others,* delivered to the First Regular Session of the Economic and Social Council of 1983, No. 12 of the Provisional Agenda. (Activities for the Advancement of Women: Equality, Development and Peace.) UN Doc. E./1983/7 (17 March 1983).

TRUSTEESHIP COUNCIL. This institution, one of the six principal organs of the United Nations, is vested with the task of supervising the administration of trust territories, colonial areas that were taken from certain defeated states during World Wars I and II, such as Germany, Italy, and Japan, and placed under UN control. Supervision of the territories was to be pursued with the understanding that the **peoples** who populated these areas were to be helped in their social, economic, and political development. With such development realized, the population of the trust territories were to be allowed to exercise their right to **self-determination** "without any condition or reservation, in accordance with their freely expressed will and desire."

Of the eleven territories placed under supervision, all (including Rwanda, Tanzania, Somalia, Nauru, and Samoa) except the Trust Territory of the Pacific Islands (TTPI), have achieved independence. In case of TTPI, it has elected to have a special "associated" relationship with the United States.

Since the Trusteeship Council has completed its assigned task, international discussions at the state level and with **nongovernmental organizations** (NGOS) have taken place about the future of this UN body. Views vary widely, including the position taken by some political leaders that this body should be allowed to just "self-destruct." But the weight of opinion has been that it should be assigned one of two very important tasks: (1) that of managing the "global commons," those regions of the globe such as outer space and the areas of the oceans beyond national jurisdictions that belong to all people, or (2) that of dealing with the global environment. In either case, it will be involved in matters critical to the future of **human rights**. See also: Declaration on the Granting of Independence to Colonial Countries and Peoples; Environment; Self-Determination. *Further Reading:* Commission on Global Governance, *Our Global Neighborhood* (1995); W. C. Gordon, *The United Nations at the Crossroads of Reform* (1994).

TRUTH COMMISSIONS. In many countries where the more brutal violations of **human rights** have taken place, neither the society undergoing the actual violations nor the world at large has full knowledge of the nature and scope of the human rights violations, because most abuses take place in secrecy and/or are accompanied by denials. In most cases, what is known to the general public is the disappearances of persons, examples of murder, torture, illegal detention, and thousands of relatives and associates left in emotional pain and shock. In some countries, the resulting ethnic, religious, linguistic, and social divisions, as well as civilian suspicion of and alienation from political institutions (including the military, police, and judicial system), make governance all but impossible.

A relatively recent and somewhat popular institution offers an important promise: it claims that a transition from regimes linked to gross human rights abuses to one with governance structures, procedures, and processes protective of human rights can be effected, if the truth of human rights abuses are uncovered and made known. This institution is called a truth commission, and the idea that supports the claim for such an institution includes the importance of establishing an accurate record of a country's past, and, by so doing, providing a true account of its government's disputed past. Such accounts prevent "history from being lost or rewritten" and help societies learn from its past and avoid future abuses. Truth commissions, which are fact-finding institutions, also permit the state to acknowledge its behavior and induce catharsis to society, especially among the survivors of violence or their relatives and associates, for whom the silence or the dispute about what took place is often as brutal as the abuse itself. There are those who disapprove of truth commissions on the grounds that digging up the past or offering official acknowledgement only serves to aggravate existing suspicions, hatreds, and social divisions.

Since the 1970s, there have been more than fifteen truth commissions, including ongoing ones in Guatemala and **South Africa**. In South Africa, the Truth and Reconciliation Commission—headed by human rights activist and Nobel Laureate, Archbishop Desmond Tutu—is particularly important, given the duration and intensity of the bitter racial divisions engendered by the human rights abuses in **apartheid** South Africa. The aftermath especially where the results have been published, has been mixed, although weighted on the side of the promise its supporters have advanced. In countries such as Argentina, **Chile,** and El Salvador, the process of healing, however slow, appears to have begun, although potential for social explosion, including the spirit of revenge, still exists in all three societies. In Ethiopia and South Africa, divisions continue, and the verdict, unknown at present. See also: Amnesty Laws; *Nunca Mas:* Mandela, Nelson. *Further Reading:* M. Gevisser, "The Witness," *NYT Magazine* (June 22, 1997); P. B. Haynor, "Fifteen Truth Commissions—1974–1994: A Comparative Study," *HRQ*, vol. 16 no. 4 (1994); D. Weissbrodt and P. W. Fraser, "Report of the Chilean National Commission on Truth and Reconciliation," *HRQ*, vol. 14 no. 4 (1992).

TURKEY. Turkey is a constitutional republic with a multiparty parliament, the Grand National Assembly. Its parliamentary body elects the president, and the political party (the Motherland Party or the Welfare Party, for example) which can command a majority in parliament, leads the government through a prime minister. The country is located between western Asia and southeastern Europe, and shares borders with the Black and Aegean Seas, Bulgaria, Greece, Syria, Iraq, Iran, Azerbaijan, Armenia, and Georgia. It has a population of about 60 million people, 90 percent of whom are Muslims (Sunni), and the rest are made up primarily of Christians and Jews. Kurds, a linguistic minority, constitute about 19 percent of the population.

Since 1923, when the country became a republic under the founding leadership of Mustafa Kemal (Kemal Atatürk, or father of Turkey), it has sought to create a modern secular and democratic society. At first, it appeared that Turkey would easily succeed, as Atatürk (1924–1926) abolished the caliphate, introduced universal suffrage for men and women, proclaimed equality before the law and inviolability of life and property, prohibited polygamy, permitted divorce, and made civil marriage compulsory. In addition, some **economic, social and cultural rights** were supported: primary education was made free and compulsory, and social insurance, public health services, maternity clinics and nurseries as well as community cultural centers were introduced. Problems developed, however, centering around four major issues: (1) **self-determination** for the Kurds, (2) secularization, (3) social democracy, and (4) cultural, as well as political, identity.

With respect to self-determination, the Kurds, led by the Kurdistan Workers Party (PKK), seek independence for the Kurds and have been fighting the government of Turkey for over thirty years. The government, which until 1996 forbade even the teaching of the Kurdish language—a violation of their **human rights**—has refused to entertain the idea of Kurdish independence. The result has been a vicious ongoing war between the PKK and the Turkish government. On the matter of secularization, the Muslims of Turkey are divided. Many claim, very much like some of their Christian counterparts in the United States, Hindu counterparts in **India**, and Orthodox Jewish counterparts in **Israel**, that their society should more closely mirror their religious values. They have used their religious schools to advance those values, creating problems between the army, which has seen itself as the guardian of secularism, and the Islamists (Muslims who insist on promoting Islamic values). The issue of secularization came to a head in 1997, when the first Islamist government since 1923 had to resign under pressure from the military, and with the introduction of measures in parliament to limit, perhaps even abolish, religious education. The matter of social democracy has faced problems also, because Turkey has not only alternated between military dictatorship and political democracy since 1945, but the egalitarian promise of the republic is increasingly being undermined by an augmented free-market economic emphasis. Finally, the question of Turkey's close link with the West since 1945 and its relationship to the world of Islam has begun to cause great stress in its society. Islamists want the country to forge greater political and cultural ties with other Muslim nations, while the secularists—including the leadership of the army—want greater ties with the West, including the European Union (EU) and the North Atlantic Treaty Organization (NATO), the West's military alliance.

Given its problems, the Turkish government often feels besieged and responds with torture (especially for the Kurds), extrajudicial killings, arbitrary detentions, disappearances, "mystery killings," harassments, police brutality, and general intimidation of the civilian population. In addition, freedom of speech, the press, and religion, as well as unaddressed violence against women and **child labor**, trouble the country. Even members of the Turkish Medical Association, who seek to minister to the widespread practice of torture, have been persecuted. To compound matters, forced prostitution is rife in the country.

Western Europe, for a number of political and cultural reasons, including fear of religious conflict and the influx of cheaper labour, has been reluctant to forge greater ties with Turkey. The country's human rights record, especially with respect to the Kurds—many of whom are now fleeing to Western Europe as refugees—has caused the European Union (EU) to turn down Turkey's request for membership. The United States, which sees Turkey as a vital ally, has been reluctant to criticize the country too publicly or too harshly. It has also expressed concern about the European Union's rejection of Turkey's efforts to have greater ties with it, knowing that such a stance on the part of Western Europe could feed the interests of the Turkish Islamists who want greater ties with Muslim countries. See also: Kurdistan; Thought, Conscience and Religion. *Further Reading:* Anti-Slavery International, *Forced Prostitution in Turkey* (1993); R. Hutchings and J. Rugman, *Ataturk's Children: Turkey and the Kurds* (1996); Physicians for Human Rights, *Torture in Turkey and Its Accomplices* (1996).

TUTU, DESMOND. See TRUTH COMMISSIONS.

U

UNITED KINGDOM. Comprised of England, **Northern Ireland**, Scotland, and Wales, the United Kingdom is located off the northwest coast of Europe in the North Atlantic Ocean. It is a constitutional monarchy with a long tradition of democratic parliamentary government, elected periodically through a multiparty system. The United Kingdom has a population of about 59 million people, composed primarily of English, Scots, Irish, and Welsh ethnic or national groupings. Since the 1960s, it has added substantial numbers of persons from its former, far-flung empire, which in 1945 was home to one-quarter of the world's population spread over a third of the globe. The citizens and residents of the former British empire, though united in speaking English, are overwhelmingly nonwhite; most are from religious backgrounds—Buddhist, Confucian, Hindu, or Islamic, among others—that are neither Christian nor Judaic, the two religious traditions that had formerly, almost exclusively, defined the United Kingdom.

The country has a record of fairly strong support for **human rights** as a concept and in practice, especially **civil and political rights**. There are some areas, however, in which its record is less strong: **self-determination**, non-discrimination, **fair trial**, and social **equality**.

On the matter of the right to self-determination, the United Kingdom has an inconsistent record. On the one hand, since 1945 it has supported—but not without political confrontation—the independence of former colonial territories, from Ghana, Guyana, and **India** to Cyprus, Kenya, and Malaysia; more recently it has supported greater cultural and political autonomy for Scotland and Wales. On the other hand, it has stubbornly supported its 1921 gerrymandered Protestant majority in Northern Ireland (it separated six of the nine counties of Ulster to form Northern Ireland, adding the other three to the mostly southern counties, twenty-six in all, to form the Republic of Ireland, to which it later conceded independence). Britain's support has come with a protracted conflict with the Irish Republican Army (IRA), which has opposed the gerrymandered splitting of Ireland. The issue concerning human rights protection against **discrimination** is also related, although not exclusively, to Northern Ireland.

Catholics, who compose about a third of the population in Northern Ireland suffer from discrimination in employment, education, housing, and social services. Likewise, the nonwhite population of the United Kingdom has been the victim of racial and, sometimes, religious discrimination. A 1970 Race Relations Act makes racial discrimination unlawful in fields of employment, education, and social services; it also makes the publication and distribution of verbal or written materials, which are racially insulting, abusive or otherwise likely to stir up racial hatred, a punishable offense. A 1976 (amended in 1989) Fair Employment Act also outlaws discrimination in Northern Ireland on grounds of religion. These laws, however, are not always enforced, so discrimination continues.

Tied to the issue of discrimination is the right to physical integrity and a fair trial. The last two rights, plus the freedom from torture, are also independently implied. Racial minorities are disproportionately stopped and searched by police, and they are seriously underrepresented in criminal justice system professions. And, faced with the tragic crisis in Northern Ireland, the United Kingdom has used emergency legislation against violent opposition from the IRA, legislation that compromises human rights standards of arrest, detention, interrogation, and the right to counsel. In 1978, the **European Court of Human Rights** found that the United Kingdom had not only engaged in practices deemed to be cruel, inhuman, and degrading to IRA prisoners, but had engaged in torture as well. In 1995, the UN **Human Rights Committee** and the UN **Committee Against Torture** (CAT) vainly appealed to the United Kingdom to repeal the emergency legislation. In April 1998, the United Kingdom, with the mediatory help of the **United States**, concluded an agreement (called the Good Friday Agreement) on Northern Ireland—one that holds promise for a solution to a centuries-old problem. In August 1998 some nationalist opponents of the Good Friday Agreement set off a car bomb in Omagh, Northern Ireland, which killed 28 people. But the response by all sides to the agreement, including emergency legislation by the United Kingdom, suggests a determination to pursue reconciliation and peace.

On the issue of social equality, the United Kingdom, until the Labor Government came to power in 1997, refused to support the **economic, social and cultural rights** provided by the **European Social Charter**. The Labor Government has indicated that it will support those rights in the United Kingdom. The government has also been taking steps to work out an agreement on Northern Ireland; it has publicly committed itself to realign its laws in accordance with the **European Convention on Human Rights,** in order to deal more effectively with human rights issues, including those of equality and nondiscrimination. See also: Framework Convention for the Protection of National Minorities; International Convention on the Elimination of All Forms of Racial Discrimination; Propaganda. *Further Reading:* P. Hewitt, *The Abuse of Power: Civil Liberties in the United Kingdom* (1982); P. S. Hodge, *Scotland and the Union* (1996); R. Gordon and R. Wilmot-Smith, eds., *Human Rights in the United Kingdom* (1997).

UNITED NATIONS CHARTER. The charter of the United Nations is the nearest thing to a world constitution. It was signed on June 26, 1945, at the conclusion of the United Nations Conference on International Organization in San Francisco, California. The charter, which entered into force on October 24, 1945, defines the ends, powers, purposes, and principles of the United Nations as well as the limitations and commitments accepted by member states. Among those ends is that of promoting "social progress and better standards of life in greater freedom." The first article of the charter, which specifies the purposes and principles of the global organization, states the following with respect to **human rights:**

Article 1 (3). To achieve international co-operation in solving international problems of an economic, social, cultural, or humanitarian character, and in promoting and encouraging respect for human rights and for fundamental freedoms for all without distinction as to race, sex, language, or religion.

Promoting and encouraging human rights and fundamental freedoms are, therefore, among the purposes for which the UN was created. The particular nature of international economic and social cooperation on which Article 1 of the charter touches, and the character of the commitment made by member states in relationship to that cooperation and the promotion of human rights, are elaborated in Article 55 and 56 of the charter.

Article 55. With a view to the creation of conditions of stability and well-being which are necessary for peaceful and friendly relations among nations based on respect for the principle of equal rights and and self-determination of peoples, the United Nations shall promote:

a. higher standards of living, full employment, and conditions of economic and social progress and development;

b. solutions of international economic, social, health, and related problems; and international cultural and educational co-operation;

c. universal respect for, and observance of, human rights and fundamental freedoms for all without distinction as to race, sex, language, or religion.

Article 56. All Members pledge themselves to take joint and separate action in co-operation with the Organization for the achievement of the purposes set forth in Article 55.

See also: Declaration on the Right to Development; Economic, Social and Cultural Rights. *Further Reading:* L. M. Goodrich, *Charter of the United Nations:*

Commentary and Documents (1969); B. Simma, ed., *The Charter of the United Nations: A Commentary* (1994).

UNITED NATIONS CHILDREN FUND. This organization was created in 1946 by the United Nations **General Assembly** to provide emergency supplies of food, medicine, clothing and housing to children rendered destitute, especially in Europe, by the ravages of World War II. Originally called the United Nations International Children's Emergency Fund (UNICEF), the organization was made permanent in 1953 by the General Assembly, and its name changed to the United Nations Children's Fund. Its well-known acronym, UNICEF, has nevertheless been retained.

Today UNICEF's activities extend throughout the world, especially in industrially less-developed states and the countries of Eastern Europe. Its activities include projects to improve education, health care, and housing for children. UNICEF also cares for refugees and works with other UN agencies such as the **United Nations Educational, Scientific and Cultural Organization** (UNESCO), and interested nongovernmental organizations (NGOs), to coordinate international action on behalf of children. Two of its most important areas of activities have been its critical support for the 1989 Convention on the Rights of the Child (CRC), followed by the push to have that convention ratified by states, and the 1997 support for the treaty banning **land mines.**

UNICEF reports to the United Nations **Economic and Social Council** (ECOSOC) and, through its reports, to the United Nations General Assembly. It is governed by an executive board, with members elected by ECOSOC from every region of the world. In 1994, UNICEF received the Nobel Peace Prize. It is headquartered in Geneva, Switzerland, and is supported by states, contributions from individuals, and the profits from the sale of materials like greeting cards. See also: Child, Rights of; Defense for Children International. *Further Reading:* M. Black, *Children First: The Story of UNICEF, Past and Present* (1996); C. Bellamy, ed., *State of the World's Children 1997* (1997).

UNITED NATIONS COMMISSION ON HUMAN RIGHTS. See COMMISSION ON HUMAN RIGHTS.

UNITED NATIONS COMMISSION ON THE STATUS OF WOMEN. See COMMISSION ON THE STATUS OF WOMEN.

UNITED NATIONS CONFERENCE ON THE HUMAN ENVIRONMENT. See ENVIRONMENT.

UNITED NATIONS DECADE FOR WOMEN. See COMMISSION OF THE STATUS OF WOMEN.

UNITED NATIONS DRAFT DECLARATION ON THE RIGHTS OF INDIGENOUS PEOPLES. See INDIGENOUS PEOPLES.

UNITED NATIONS ECONOMIC AND SOCIAL COUNCIL. See ECONOMIC AND SOCIAL COUNCIL.

UNITED NATIONS EDUCATIONAL, SCIENTIFIC AND CULTURAL ORGANIZATION. This institution, UNESCO, is a specialized agency of the UN, which was established by a separate constitution on November 16, 1945, and came into force on November 4, 1946.

The organization is the product of an inspired principle, enshrined in the preamble to its constitution, which claims that "since wars begin in the minds of men [humans], it is in the minds of men (humans) that the defences of peace must be constructed." Among its specific purposes and functions is that of contributing to international peace and security "by promoting collaboration among . . . nations through education, science and culture in order to further universal respect for justice, for the rule of law and for human rights and fundamental freedoms which are affirmed for the peoples of the world, without distinction of race, language or religion by the Charter of the United Nations."

In pursuing the fulfillment of its purposes, UNESCO has been involved at the forefront of activities ranging from standard-setting to eliminate **discrimination in education,** promoting sharing the fruits of scientific research, and ensuring the protection of cultural artifacts and the means by which the free-flow of information is pursued, to furthering intercultural exchanges, removing the "ignorance and prejudice" that invite hostility and stereotyping, and advancing a sense of solidarity among the **peoples** of the world. In the field of education, for example, UNESCO participates at all levels—public and private—of schools, universities, cultural and scientific institutions, libraries and museums, mass media (press, radio, television), voluntary associations, trade unions, cooperatives, and even families. Further, it often provides the content of that education, and a variety of means, including technical, to facilitate learning.

The work of the organization has, at times, been controversial. Its support in the 1980s for the initiative of less industrially developed countries to create what is called a **New World Information Order** provoked **United States** withdrawal from the organization in 1985 and the **United Kingdom** in 1986. The United Kingdom has returned and the United States is considering doing so. UNESCO is located in Paris, France. See also: Propaganda; Racism. *Further Reading:* H. Huxley, *UNESCO: Its Purposes and Its Philosophy* (1947); UNESCO, *UNESCO: Why the S?* (1985); C. Wells, *The UN, UNESCO, and the Politics of Knowledge* (1987).

UNITED NATIONS GENERAL ASSEMBLY. See GENERAL ASSEMBLY.

UNITED NATIONS HIGH COMMISSIONER FOR HUMAN RIGHTS. See OFFICE OF HIGH COMMISSIONER FOR HUMAN RIGHTS.

UNITED NATIONS HIGH COMMISSIONER FOR REFUGEES. The office of High Commissioner for Refugees (UNHCR) was authorized by a statute adopted by the United Nations **General Assembly** on December 14, 1950, but it officially came into existence on January 1, 1951, replacing the International Refugee Organization (1947–1951), which itself was a successor to the United Nations Relief and Rehabilitation Administration that had been established in 1943 to help persons displaced by World War II, many of whom were unable to be returned to their countries of origin. By the time the International Refugee Organization ceased operating, it had resettled more than 1 million refugees, but the UN had already recognized that the issue of refugees was likely to be of extended duration.

Established to deal with persons who fled their countries because of a well-founded fear of persecution for reasons of race, religion, nationality, political opinion, or membership in a particular social group, the UNHCR was faced with an increase from 17 to 27 million refugees between 1991 and 1995. Since 1995, the number is said to have declined to about 22 million, but could rise again. There is now one refugee for every 255 persons on earth.

The UNHCR acts under the authority of the General Assembly, and takes direction from it or the United Nations **Economic and Social Council**. The work of the high commissioner must be of "an entirely non-political character," and "shall be humanitarian and social." In more specific terms, the functions of the high commissioner include giving legal protection to stateless persons, providing repatriation or resettlement to refugees, serving as coordinator of refugee-related activities among governments and between governments and international organizations, providing publicity for refugees problems, offering **advisory services in the field of human rights**, and keeping in close contact with and supporting the efforts of private organizations concerned with the welfare of refugees.

The office of High Commissioner for Refugees was awarded the Nobel Peace Prize in 1954 and 1981. See also: Convention Relating to the Status of Refugees, Convention Relating to the Status of Stateless Persons. *Further Reading:* L. A. Camino and R. M. Krulfeld, *Reconstructing Lives, Recapturing Meaning: Refugee Identity, Gender, and Culture Change* (1994); UNHCR, *The State of the World's Refugees 1995* (1995).

UNITED NATIONS HUMAN RIGHTS COMMISSION. See COMMISSION ON HUMAN RIGHTS.

UNITED NATIONS HUMAN RIGHTS COMMITTEE. See HUMAN RIGHTS COMMITTEE.

UNITED NATIONS SECRETARIAT. The Secretariat is one of the six principal organs of the United Nations and the chief administrative arm of the UN system. It consists of a secretary-general and a staff, which functions as an international civil service. The staff is a full-time bureaucracy and provides not only the technical machinery to serve member states more effectively, but most important, it imparts a sense of identity and continuity to the UN. Apart from discharging housekeeping functions such as that of paying UN workers and preparing the agendas for the meetings of bodies such as the United Nations **General Assembly** and the United Nations **Security Council**, the Secretariat is responsible for implementing the decisions of the other organs of the UN, especially the Security Council and the General Assembly. Its chief administrative officer, the secretary-general, also has the legal capacity for political initiative: he or she may bring to the attention of the Security Council issues that may threaten international peace and security. In the required annual report to the General Assembly, the secretary-general has the opportunity not only to summarize the work of the organization, but to focus on important issues, express opinions, and to make recommendations. Finally, the secretary-general proposes items for inclusion in the agenda of the meetings of the Security Council, General Assembly, Economic and Social Council (ECOSOC) and the **Trusteeship Council.**

In the field of **human rights**, the Secretariat's responsibilities are now discharged through the **Office of High Commissioner for Human Rights.** Formerly, some of those functions were carried out by the **Centre for Human Rights,** which had offices in New York and Geneva, Switzerland. Now the work of the Centre, under an implemented proposal from the current Secretary-General Kofi Annan, has been consolidated into one office, Office of the High Commissioner for Human Rights. Those responsibilities, which extend to the work of the Office of the **United Nations Children's Fund** (UNICEF) and the Office of High Commissioner for Refugees, entail the entire range of the UN's responsibility to ensure the promotion and protection of human rights.

Former secretaries-general of the UN are Trygve Lie, Norway (1946–1953); Dag Hammarskjold, Sweden (1953–1961); U Thant, Burma (1962–1971); Kurt Waldheim, Austria (1972–1981); Javier Perez de Quellar, Peru (1982–1991); Boutros Boutros-Ghali, Egypt (1992–1997); and Kofi Annan, Ghana (1997–   ). See also: Commission on Human Rights; Human Rights Committee; United Nations High Commissioner for Refugees.

UNITED NATIONS SECURITY COUNCIL. See SECURITY COUNCIL.

UNITED NATIONS STANDARD MINIMUM RULES FOR THE ADMINISTRATION OF JUVENILE JUSTICE. Also known as The Beijing Rules because it is a body of standards drafted at a 1984 preparatory meeting held in Beijing, China, it has the aim of promoting the welfare of juveniles throughout the world and represents a comprehensive international social policy. The rules were recommended by the Seventh United Nations Congress on the Prevention of Crime and the Treatment of Offenders, held in Milan, Italy, from August 26 to September 6, 1985, and adopted by the United Nations **General Assembly** on November 29, 1985.

With that adoption, member states were invited to shape their respective national legislative policies and practices to the Beijing Rules. These rules reflect the general view that because of the early state of their human development, juveniles must be given particular care and support. The rules include the requirement that a carefully designed system of juvenile justice be developed and integrated into an overall social policy for juveniles; that all procedural safeguards, including the presumption of innocence, notification of charges, the right to remain silent, and the right to the presence of a lawyer or guardian, be protected during criminal proceedings; that criminal responsibility should be coextensive with the *individual's* moral development and psychological capacity for responsibility; that *discretion* be allowed at all stages of the proceedings of juvenile justice; that the right to privacy be respected, especially to protect the child from permanent identification as a "delinquent" or "criminal"; and that specially trained police persons be used in the juvenile justice system.

Other rules deal with detention and trial, principles of **adjudication**, disposition measures such as probation, community service, financial penalties, record keeping, and institutional and noninstitutional treatment. All such measures are required to be pursued with the objective of finding the means of dealing with juveniles that correspond to their level of moral development and capacity for social responsibility. See also: Child, Rights of; Procedural Guarantees Processes and Protections; Standard Minimum Rules for the Protection of Prisoners. *Further Reading:* S. Ghazzi-Guarino, *Balancing Juvenile Justice* (1995); I. M. Schwartz, *Juvenile Justice and Public Policy* (1992); K. Tomasevski, ed., *Children in Adult Prisons* (1986).

UNITED NATIONS SUB-COMMISSION ON PREVENTION OF DISCRIMINATION AND PROTECTION OF MINORITIES. See SUB-COMMISSION ON PREVENTION OF DISCRIMINATION AND PROTECTION OF MINORITIES.

UNITED NATIONS UNIVERSITY. This is a system of academic institutions, headquartered in Tokyo, Japan, which was established by the United Nations **General Assembly** on December 11, 1972. It is a decentralized system that is still evolving, but whose aims are (1) the pursuit of research that is oriented to more effective responses to the demanding problems that confront the global community, and (2) the post-graduate education and training of young scholars and research workers who will have as their central outlook, not the concerns of individual nation-states, but human survival, development, and welfare.

The system, coordinated through its center in Japan, is governed by a University Council whose members are appointed jointly by the UN secretary-general and director-general of the United Nations **Educational, Scientific and Cultural Organization** (UNESCO). The rector of the University, a member of the council, is appointed by the UN secretary-general in consultation with the director-general of UNESCO. The University is materially supported by voluntary contributions from states and by nongovernmental entities. Currently, it is seeking an endowment fund of sufficient amounts that would ensure less future dependence on contributors, but it has not yet achieved that goal.

Since its inception, the university has devoted its attention to a number of issues that are global in reach and significance, including: (1) hunger, poverty, and the global environment; (2) **science and technology** and their social, ethical, and **human rights** implications; (3) the global economy and social and economic transformation; (4) human development and the co-existence of **peoples**, social systems, and cultures, especially as those cultures are informed by religious, racial, and ethnic differences as well as value preferences; (5) international and human security, conflict resolution, and global transformation; and (6) communications and global change. In most, if not all these areas of focus, the university has emphasized, at least implicitly, some aspect of human rights, and in its examination of issue areas such as religion and ethical systems, migration, scientific and technological development, and human and social development, its emphasis on human rights has been explicit. See also: University for Peace.

UNITED NATIONS VOLUNTARY FUND FOR ADVISORY SERVICES AND TECHNICAL ASSISTANCE IN THE FIELD OF HUMAN RIGHTS. This fund was established by the secretary-general of the UN in 1987, responding to requests from the United Nations **Commission on Human Rights** (CHR). Since then, the importance of the fund and securing support for it, have been repeatedly emphasized at international forums, including the 1993 **World Conferences on Human Rights.**

The fund can receive contributions from governments, intergovernmental and **nongovernmental organizations** (NGOs), and from individuals. The principal purpose the receipts are designed to serve is that of helping in the international implementation of human rights instruments, through the offering of advisory services and technical assistance. Such assistance and services have been in part furnished over the years by the **Centre for Human Rights,** which is now a part of the **Office of High Commissioner for Human Rights.** Such services include the training of lawyers, police persons, and social workers, disseminating information, advising governments in the organization of judicial systems, and the research and collection of data. Governments have not been forthcoming in their support of the fund, in part because they are likely to be the objects of scrutiny, as the fund is more able to finance the needed activities in the field of advisory and technical services. The future of the fund, therefore, could well depend on individuals and nongovernmental organizations. See also: Advisory Services in the Field of Human Rights.

UNITED STATES. By 1945, at the conclusion of World War II, the United States had become the most powerful nation in the world—a status it has since held, although its economic advantages have eroded over the years. The United States has a population of over 268 million people, composed of a majority of people who trace their ancestry to Europe, but also has significant percentages of its population from Africa, Latin American and the Caribbean, Asia (including **Cambodia, China,** Japan, **India,** Korea, Pakistan, and Vietnam, **Israel,** American Indians, and others). The population is overwhelmingly Christian, but increasingly, other religions are significantly represented: the Baha'i, Buddhism, Confucianism, Hinduism, and Islam. The official language is English, but Spanish has become a first or second language for 15 to 18 percent of the population, although there is a developing "English first" and "English only" movement. One may defensibly say that the United States boasts one of the most ethnically diverse populations in the world and one that is becoming more religiously diverse.

In the field of **human rights,** the United States has had a mixed history. On the one hand, at its very birth, the Declaration of Independence had its moral and philosophical foundations in the concept of human rights, and some of its leaders, President **Franklin D. Roosevelt** and his wife, **Eleanor Roosevelt,** for example, played unarguably indispensable roles in the formulation and development of the early human rights agenda of the United Nations. Likewise, since 1948, the United States has been commendably forceful in publicly censuring many governments for their human rights violations. It even led the 1991 Gulf War against **Iraq** to support **Kuwait's** right to **self-determination,** although economic and military security motives were uppermost considerations. At present, the United States is confronting **China** and **Cuba** (it continues to maintain trade sanctions against Cuba) over their respective human rights record in the area of **civil and political rights,** especially freedom of speech, press, and religion. In the case of China, the additional issue of self-determination for Tibet and, though less so, for Taiwan, are also important. Additionally, United States courts have been receptive to human rights claims brought by individuals such as Cubans against their governments. Internationally, it has sought, though not consistently, to help trace, identify, and prosecute persons guilty of

crimes against humanity, including **genocide**. United States support for UN creation of international criminal tribunals for **Rwanda** and the former Yugoslavia was pivotal.

On the other hand, since the 1950s, despite claiming to support human rights, including those associated with **democratic entitlement**, the United States has supported a number of dictatorial regimes—in Argentina, **Brazil, Chile,** the Dominican Republic, Guatemala, **Haiti,** Indonesia, Iran, Nicaragua, the **Philippines, Saudi Arabia, South Africa,** and Zaire—that have been among the worst abusers of human rights. Further, the country has not ratified—and therefore cannot be held legally accountable under them—some of the most important human rights instruments, including the **International Covenant on Economic, Social and Cultural Rights,** the **Convention on the Elimination of All Forms of Discrimination Against Women** (CEDAW), the Convention on the Rights of the Child (CRC), and even the **American Convention on Human Rights.** Also, the United States has been found, by some human rights groups, including **Human Rights Watch** (HRW), to engage in unequal enforcement of its criminal laws and to house prisoners in conditions that are sometimes degrading, often exposing many—including women and children—to **rape, sexual harassment,** and intimidation by prison officials. Internationally, the United States has been subjected to five major criticisms: First, that it has been very selective in its regard for and support of human rights, usually disregarding **economic, social and cultural rights.** Hence, large numbers of people, including children, go hungry, many are homeless (almost 3 percent of New York City in the 1990s), and even larger numbers are without health care. And to the extent the federal government intervenes to help in these areas, it is not responding to a *right* that individuals can claim. Second, that in the area of **civil and political rights,** it has been one of the strongest opponents of the abolition of the death penalty, as well as the effort to make the age of eighteen the minimum age for entering the army. Third, that the United States views its own laws as superior to the norms of human rights (a view that accounts in part for the limited number of human rights instruments it has ratified), although its laws fall very short of international human rights standards. Fourth, that the United States has been seeking to emphasize and use some selected human rights as a means to impose its own social and economic model on the rest of the world. Fifth, that the United States has been reluctant to support collective rights, including the right of **peoples** to an **environment** sustaining of human health, life, and nonhuman life-forms.

The emphasis in criticism number five is on the word *right*. The United States, it is argued, is willing to make certain adjustments in its environmental standards, but is not enthusiastic about elaborating rights that people may use to assert claims on behalf of themselves and the human and nonhuman environment. See also: Atlantic Charter; Capital Punishment; Carter, Jimmy (James Earl, Jr.); Ethnic Cleansing; Right to Life; Serbia. *Further Reading:* I. Cohn and G. S. Goodwin-Gill, *Child Soldiers: The Role of Children in Armed Conflict* (1994); S. D. Collins, *Let Them Eat Ketchup: The Politics of Poverty and Inequality*; D. P. Forsythe, *Human Rights and U.S. Foreign Policy* (1988); Human Rights Watch, *Crossing the Line* (1995); Human Rights Watch, *Modern Capital of Human Rights? Abuses in the State of Georgia* (1996); National Center on Homelessness and Poverty, http://www.n1chp.org/index.htm; D. D. Newsom, *The Diplomacy of Human Rights* (1986).

UNIVERSAL DECLARATION OF HUMAN RESPONSIBILITIES. As the world has become more like a global village where problems in one area increasingly affect people, places, and things in other areas (and thus the globe as a whole), human beings have come to recognize the need for global solutions to global problems. Such would-be global solutions, if they are to be effective and long-lasting, and if they are to be expressions of the interests and concerns of all, must be based on the ideas, values, and standards that emanate from and are respected by all cultures and societies. Many of those ideas, values, and standards are present today in the form of the rights with which this book deals. The inalienable rights of all peoples are likely to be respected and better promoted, however, if people accept responsibilities to respect and promote those rights.

The recognition of the need to fashion international standards of human responsibilities that are co-equal to the international standards of human rights that developed after 1945 has been voiced often and strongly by individuals and groups, especially since 1948, the date on which the UN proclaimed the **Universal Declaration of Human Rights.** In 1997, the InterAction Council, a global nongovernmental organization that boasts among its members 24 former chiefs of state or heads of government from countries throughout the world, including Brazil, Canada, Germany, Japan, Singapore, and the United States, began to draft a set of universal ethical standards. That draft, largely building on the wisdom of religious leaders and other thinkers throughout the ages, was completed in 1997 and was submitted to the UN **General Assembly** in 1998 for consideration and adoption.

Entitled the Universal Declaration of Human Responsibilities, the draft is divided into a preamble and five thematic sections that observe the following order: Fundamental Principles for Humanity, Non-Violence and Respect for Life, Justice and Solidarity, Truthfulness and Tolerance, and Mutual Respect and Partnership.

In the case of the preamble, it takes the position that "recognition of the inherent dignity and of the equal and inalienable rights of all members of the human family [as] the foundation of freedom, justice and peace in the world . . . implies obligations or responsibilities;" that the "exclusive insistence on rights can result in conflict, division, and endless dispute;" and that "the neglect of human responsibilities can lead to lawlessness and chaos." It further contends that "the rule of law and the promotion of human rights depend on the readiness of men and women to act justly;" and that "human aspirations for progress and improvement can only be realized by agreed values and standards applying to all people and institutions at all times."

The first theme covers the first four articles of the declaration. The first and the third of those articles capture the responsibilities covered.

Article 1. *Every person*, regardless of gender, ethnic origin, social status, political opinion, language, age, nationality, or religion, *has a responsibility to treat all people in a humane way.*

Article 3. No person, no group or organization, no state, no army or police stands above good and evil; all are subject to ethical standards. Everyone has a responsibility to promote good and avoid evil in all things.

The second theme, non-violence and respect for life, covers Articles 5 to 7, which follow:

Article 5. Everyone has a responsibility to **respect life**. No one has the right to injure, to torture or to kill another human person. This does not exclude the right of justified self-defense of individuals or communities.

Article 6. Disputes between states, groups or individuals should not be resolved with violence. No government should tolerate or participate in acts of genocide or terrorism, nor should it abuse women, children, or any other civilian as instruments of war. Every citizen and public official has a responsibility to act in a peaceful, non-violent way.

Article 7. Every person is infinitely precious and must be protected unconditionally. The animals and the natural environment also demand protection. All people have a responsibility to protect the air, water and soil of the earth for the sake of present inhabitants and future generations.

The theme of justice and solidarity runs through Articles 8 to 11, and it deals with the responsibility of every person "to behave with *integrity, honesty and fairness.*" As such, "no person or group should arbitrarily deprive any other person or group of their property." Likewise, all people, providing they are given the necessary tools, have a responsibility to make serious efforts to overcome poverty, malnutrition, ignorance and inequality. They should also "promote sustainable development all over the world in order to assure dignity, freedom, security and justice for all people." Article 10 specifically provides for "equal access to education and to meaningful work," and urges everyone to lend "support to the needy, the disadvantaged, the disabled and to victims of discrimination. Article 11 reads:

All property and wealth must be used responsibly in accordance with justice and for the advancement of the human race. Economic and political power must not be handled as an instrument of domination, but in the service of economic justice and of the social order.

With respect to the theme truthfulness and tolerance, it is covered in Articles 12 to 15. And Article 12 provides that, "Every person has the responsibility to *speak and act truthfully*." Since the "right to privacy and to personal and professional confidentiality is to be respected," according to the same article, a balance had to be struck, especially in cases where speaking the truth could impair that confidentiality and seriously endanger privacy. So Article 12 also provides that, "No one is obliged to tell the truth to everyone [agents of a political regime who are seeking to find dissidents, for example] all the time." Article 13 provides that, "No politicians, public servants, business leaders, scientists, writers are exempt from general ethical standards, nor are physicians, lawyers and other professionals who have special duties to clients. . . ." Articles 14 and 15 read as follows:

Article 14. The freedom of the media to inform the public and to criticize institutions of society and governmental actions, which is essential for a just society, must be used with responsibility and discretion. Freedom of the media carries special responsibility for accurate and truthful reporting. Sensational reporting that degrades the human person or dignity must at all times be avoided.

Article 15. While religious freedom must be guaranteed, the representatives of religions have special responsibility to avoid expressions of prejudice and acts of discrimination toward those of different beliefs. They should not incite or legitimize hatred, fanaticism and religious wars, but should foster tolerance and mutual respect between all people.

Journalists, especially in the United States and the United Kingdom, who find any hint of limitation on their freedom disturbing are likely to find Article 14 troubling. But the content of that article captures very well the emerging global consensus on issues of media responsibility. The final theme, which deals with mutual respect and partnership, is encompassed in Articles 16 to 18. The first and the last of those articles provide the essence of the theme.

Article 16. *All men and all women have a responsibility to show respect* to one another *and understanding* in their partnership. No one should subject another person to sexual exploitation or dependence. Rather, sexual partners should accept the responsibility of caring for each other's well-being.

Article 18. Sensible family planning is the responsibility of every couple. The relationship between parents and children should reflect mutual love, respect, appreciation and concern. No parents or other adults should exploit, abuse or maltreat children.

Article 19, the last article, focuses on the complementarity between the Universal Declaration of Human Rights and the Universal Declaration of Human Responsibilities. See also: Asian Values; Duties; International Criminal Court; Declaration of a Global Ethic; World Charter for Nature.

UNIVERSAL DECLARATION OF HUMAN RIGHTS. This is the name given to a proclamation intended to establish a "common standard of achievement for all peoples and all nations" in the observance of civil, economic, political, social, and cultural rights. The Universal Declaration of Human Rights (UDHR), which was prepared by the United Nations **Economic and Social Council** (ECOSOC), was adopted by the United Nations **General Assembly** on December 10, 1948. In 1954, the UN began working on two draft covenants, intended to make the rights proclaimed in the declaration legally binding on countries. Those covenants, known as the **International Covenant on Economic, Social and Cultural Rights** and the **International Covenant on Civil and Political Rights** (ICCPR) together with the declaration and Optional Protocol to the Covenant on Civil and Political Rights, are known as the **International Bill of Human Rights**.

Although some of the rights proclaimed in the declaration have not yet been adopted as international legislation, that is to say, have not yet been ratified by states, they remain alive in the spirit of the other treaties, such as that on genocide, racial discrimination, and the two international covenants, that have gained international legislative standing. Equally important, individuals and nonstate groups have been using those proclaimed rights to pressure states into adopting the legislation necessary to put these rights into effect, and some countries, moved by the moral and spiritual power of the declaration have used it as a standard for crafting or upgrading their own national constitutions. Today, the declaration is the single most often cited international human rights instrument and the one which, by far, has had the most moral force in international relations. See also: Human Rights Day. *Further Reading:* J. H. Burgers, "The Road to San Francisco: The Revival of the Human Rights Idea in the Twentieth Century," *HRQ*, vol. 14 no. 4 (1992); A. Samnoy, *Human Rights as International Consensus: The Making of the Universal Declaration of Human Rights, 1945–1948* (1993).

UNIVERSAL DECLARATION ON THE ERADICATION OF HUNGER AND MALNUTRITION. Hunger and malnutrition affect large numbers of persons throughout the world, despite the right to **food** that is proclaimed in the **Universal Declaration of Human Rights** (UDHR) and recognized in Article 11 of the **International Covenant on Economic, Social and Cultural Rights**. To give greater emphasis to the right to food and focus on the urgent need to adopt policies geared to its fulfillment, a World Food Conference was convened under United Nations **General Assembly** Resolution 3180 (XXVII) of December 17, 1973. On November 16, 1974, the conference adopted the Universal Declaration on the Eradication of Hunger and Malnutrition, and on December 17, 1974, the UN General Assembly endorsed the declaration; paragraphs, 1, 2, and 4 of which read as follows:

1. Every man, woman and child has an inalienable right to be free from hunger and malnutrition in order to develop fully and maintain their physical and men-

tal faculties. Society today already possesses sufficient resources, organizational ability and technology and hence the competence to achieve this objective. Accordingly, the eradication of hunger is a common objective of all countries of the international community.

2. It is a fundamental responsibility of Governments to work together for higher food production and a more equitable and efficient distribution of food between countries and within countries. Governments should initiate immediately a greater concerted attack on chronic malnutrition and deficiency diseases among the vulnerable and lower income groups. In order to ensure adequate nutrition for all, Governments should formulate appropriate food and nutrition policies integrated in overall socio-economic and agricultural development plans based on adequate knowledge of available as well as potential food resources.

4. It is the responsibility of each State concerned . . . to remove the obstacles to food production and provide proper incentives to agricultural producers. . . . Moreover, it is necessary to recognize the key role of women in agricultural production and rural economy in many countries, and to ensure that appropriate education, extension programmes and financial facilities are made available to women on equal terms with men.

Since 1974, the number of hungry and malnourished persons have not substantially decreased, and in some areas of the world, such as Eastern Europe, and especially **Russia**, that number has skyrocketed because of increased poverty and the de-emphasis on **economic, social and cultural rights**. At the 1995 World Summit for Social Development, held in Copenhagen, Denmark, March 6–12, nation-states committed themselves to the elimination of poverty, which is viewed as the cause of hunger and malnutrition.

It should be observed that individuals who are hungry are not free; they are as subject to the demands of their stomachs as anyone might be to a military dictator, perhaps even more so. States do not always act with an awareness of this subjection. See also: Poverty; Standard of Living. *Further Reading:* J. Dreze, A. Sen, and A. Hussain, eds., *The Political Economy of Hunger* (1995); P. Uvin, *The International Organization of Hunger* (1994).

UNIVERSALISM AND RELATIVISM. See RELATIVISM AND UNIVERSALISM.

UNIVERSITY FOR PEACE. On September 7, 1978, the president of the Republic of Costa Rica, Rodrigo Carazo, in a speech to the United Nations **General Assembly**, proposed the creation of a University for Peace (UFP). His proposal was later adopted, and on December 5, 1980, the General Assembly authorized its establishment. Today, that institution boasts a 700-acre site near San Jose, the capital of Costa Rica, with a student body and faculty drawn from throughout the world, and a governing council composed of representatives designated by the secretary-general of the

United Nations, the rector of the **United Nations University**—headquartered in Tokyo—and the director-general of the **United Nations Educational, Scientific and Cultural Organization** (UNESCO).

The university is grounded in the view that "peace cannot continue to be, together with war, just an object of conferences and research;" it should also "penetrate into the study plans and programs for the survival of humanity." The UFP seeks to help achieve that penetration by pursuing the following instrumental objectives:

1. To study the effects of mass communications on the aggressive and violent behavior of people.

2. To study the relations of the press in social conflict, particularly wars.

3. To study the influence of language in bellicose and pacific behavior.

4. To study the impact of communications at all levels in world political activity.

5. To find effective dissemination techniques in order to create a peaceful social consciousness.

From the achieved consciousness sought in objective number five, the supporters of the University for Peace hope to create the basis for the construction of a world in which the human right to peace can be fully realized. See also: Crimes Against Peace; Declaration on the Rights of People to Peace. *Further Reading:* Government of Costa Rica, *Charter of the University for Peace Together with the International Agreement for the Establishment of the University for Peace* (1983); W. E. Langley, "Irenology and the University for Peace," *SJDA*, vol. 5 no. 3 (1986).

USSR (SOVIET UNION). See RUSSIA.

UNTOUCHABLES. See INDIA.

V

VIENNA CONFERENCE ON HUMAN RIGHTS. See WORLD CONFERENCES ON HUMAN RIGHTS.

VIENNA DECLARATION AND PROGRAMME OF ACTION. See ADVISORY SERVICES IN THE FIELD OF HUMAN RIGHTS; OFFICE OF HIGH COMMISSIONER FOR HUMAN RIGHTS; SEXUAL HARASSMENT; WORLD CONFERENCES ON HUMAN RIGHTS.

VIENNA MECHANISM. See HUMAN RIGHTS DIMENSION MECHANISM.

VIETNAM WAR. See KENT STATE TRAGEDY; MY LAI MASSACRE.

VISA. Everyone has the right to leave any country, including one's own, and return. The right to leave and return, however, is often linked to access to travel documents. One of the most important travel documents is a passport—an official document issued to private citizens (although it is usually regarded as the property of the issuing government) authenticating the identity of the bearer, offering diplomatic protection, and requesting would-be receiving states to extend to the bearer respect and protection of rights. A visa, however, is an endorsement permit or a pass that is stamped or written in the passport of one state, by officials of another country, allowing the the bearer to enter or exit that country. Visas may be for short or long periods of time, and without them, the right of movement may remain unfulfilled.

Some countries, like the **United States** and **Canada**, as well as members of the European Union (EU), have eliminated the need for passports by their respective citizens. Travel documents are among the most important needs of stateless persons and refugees. See also: Convention Relating to the Status of Refugees; Movement and Residence. *Further Reading:* U.S. Congress, House Committee on the Judiciary (Ninety Fourth Congress, Second Session, April 7 and 8, 1976), *Nonimmigrant Visas: Requirements and Procedures* (1976).

W

WALESA, LECH. See POLAND.

WAR CRIMES. This is to one of the three categories of criminal acts concerning war. The other two are **crimes against peace** and **crimes against humanity**. In all three categories, individuals may be held accountable, nationally or internationally.

Before 1945, the crimes mentioned below were often justified on the basis of "superior orders" and what is known as the "act of state" principle, which states that the executive, legislative, and judicial acts of a country, having effect within its borders, are not subject to the judicial scrutiny of other states. Since 1945, such justifications are no longer acceptable, in large measure due to the human rights movement.

War crimes include, but are not limited to, killing and wounding combatants who have surrendered or who have asked to surrender; hiding military targets under the emblem of the Red Cross or Red Crescent or otherwise abusing privileges attached to such emblems; killing, wounding, or engaging in the ill-treatment of prisoners of war, such as using them for medical or other experiments; plundering or pillaging of public or private property; killing hostages; deportation of the civilian population of occupied territories for slave labor or any other purpose; abusing the dead; and wanton destruction of cities, towns, or villages. See also: Forced Labor; International Committee of the Red Cross; Superior Orders. *Further Reading:* R. Goldstone, *Prosecuting War Criminals* (1996); J. W. Baird, ed., *From Nuremberg to My Lai* (1972).

WAR CRIMES TRIBUNALS. Except for the **Nuremburg War Crimes Trials** and the **Tokyo War Crimes Trials** following World War II, the international community has been reluctant to establish war crimes tribunals.

But faced in **Rwanda** and the former Yugoslavia with deliberate and systematic violations of **human rights** and the atrocious character of the violations committed—torture, **genocide,** mass internment, deportation, **rape,** and indiscriminate destruction of towns and villages as well as general inhumane treatment of the civilian population—the United Nations **Security Council** established two tribunals to try and punish wrongdoers. An International Criminal Tribunal for the Former Yugoslavia was established on May 25, 1993, and the International Criminal Tribunal for Rwanda was established on November 8, 1994.

Although these are *ad hoc* tribunals, the affirmative significance of their creation is considerable. First, unlike the Nuremberg and Tokyo War Crimes Trials, the tribunals were not created by the victors after a war, so there can be no defensible charge of "victor's justice." Second, the tribunals for Rwanda and the former Yugoslavia were established while the wars were going on, and their establishment had an intended deterrent effect on the violators of **human rights** and humanitarian law. Third, for the first time, **crimes against humanity,** for which wrongdoers were formerly prosecuted only in cases of international wars, are now—especially in the case of Rwanda—prosecuted in cases of internal conflicts. For example, Jean-Paul Akayesu, former Mayor of Taba, Rwanda, was found guilty on nine charges of genocide after the massacre of about 1 million Tutsis in 1994. Fourth, as a result of prosecutions in internal conflicts, "systematic attacks against. . . . civilian populations on national, political, ethnic, racial or religious grounds"—a basis for criminal prosecution under the rules of the tribunal for Rwanda—should be somewhat deterred in the future. If the deterrent effect were to develop, as hoped, minorities under human rights instruments should be more secure. Fifth, rape is no longer one of the "lesser" or "other" crimes committed during warfare. Under the rules of the tribunal for the former Yugoslavia, rape is explicitly criminalized as a major crime. Sixth, the establishment of criminal tribunals for Rwanda and the former Yugoslavia is an immense push in the direction of implementing human rights norms. Yet, not all is positive about the creation of the two tribunals.

First, because they were not created by victors in a war with global authority, there is little power to gather evidence and gain custody of alleged wrongdoers, and there is no power to secure the necessary budgetary support for the prosecution of criminals. Likewise, because of these weaknesses there is the possibility that the tribunals could fail to achieve some the goal for which they were created. For example, as of this writing, authorities in Rwanda and the former Yugoslavia have not been as supportive of the tribunals as had been hoped and expected; other important members of the international community have behaved similarly. Of the approximately 80 persons indicted in the former Yugoslavia, not a single top political or military leader is included in that number. Were the tribunals to fail, it will constitute an invitation to would-be violators of human rights to pursue contemplated abuses. Worse, victims and potential witnesses will be less likely to come forward to press or support claims of human rights violations. Finally, because these tribunals are *ad hoc*, a political leader, including an alleged wrongdoer, can outlast the life of such tribunals. There can be no more persuasive testimony for the need of a permanent **international criminal court**. See also: War Crimes. *Further Reading:* T. Meron, "International Criminalization of Internal Atrocities," *AJIL* vol. 89 no. 3, (1995); Security Council, *International Criminal Tribunal for the Former Yugoslavia, ILM,* vol. 32 no. 4 (1993); Security Council, *International Criminal Tribunal for Rwanda, ILM,* vol. 33 no. 6 (1994).

WESTERN SAHARA. Western Sahara, formerly Spanish Sahara, and also known as the Saharawi Arab Democratic Republic, is a phosphate and petroleum-rich territory located in northwest Africa bounded by the Atlantic Ocean in the west, Morocco in the north, Mauritania to the south, and with eastern frontiers adjacent to Algeria and Mauritania. The territory, with a population of about 180,000 people, was a Spanish colony until January 12, 1976, when Spain vacated it after signing a November 4, 1975, agreement transferring the area to Morocco and Mauritania, both of which claimed the territory as an historic part of their respective territories.

Since the mid-1970s, the UN has taken the position (reaffirmed by its **Commission on Human Rights** [CHR] in 1997), that the people of Western Sahara should have the right to **self-determination**. A 1975 Visiting Mission of the UN's Special Committee on Decolonization found the people of the area desirous of political independence, and not wanting to be part of Morocco or Mauritania. In an advisory opinion concerning Western Sahara, the **International Court of Justice** in 1975 dealt with the question of the relationship between a state's "historic claim of title" to a given territory (in this case, Morocco and Mauritania), and the claim of a people within that territory to enjoy their right to self-determination. The court ruled that in such cases the informed and freely expressed wishes of the adult population of such territories must be the determining factor.

Notwithstanding the court's ruling and the conclusion of the Committee on Decolonization, Morocco and Mauritania continued to claim the territory as an integral part of their respective countries. An independence and guerrilla movement in Western Sahara, led by a group called the *Polisario,* forced Mauritania to abandon its claim in 1979, but Morocco continues to assert its claim, with an army of over 100,000 troops engaged in military confrontation with the *Polisario.* A number of uneasy cease-fires have been called; and the UN, since 1990, has called for the organization and supervision by the UN, in cooperation with the Organization of African Unity (OAU), of a free, fair, and impartial referendum for self-determination. In August 1997, former U.S. Secretary of State, James Baker, was appointed by the UN secretary-general to mediate a solution between Morocco and the *Polisario* on behalf of the Saharawi people. See also: Declaration on the Granting of Independence to Colonial Countries and Peoples. *Further Reading:* T. M. Frank, "The Stealing of the Sahara," *AJIL*, vol. 70 no. 3 (1976); S. Peterson, "James Baker Steps into the N. African Sandstorm," *CSM* (August 1997); *Report of the United Nations Visiting Mission to Spanish Sahara*, UN Doc. A/110023, add. 5, Annex (November 7, 1975).

WILLIAMS, JODY. See LAND MINES.

WOMEN. See CONVENTION ON THE ELIMINATION OF ALL FORMS OF DISCRIMINATION AGAINST WOMEN; DECLARATION ON THE ELIMINATION OF VIOLENCE AGAINST WOMEN; WORLD CONFERENCES ON WOMEN.

WOMEN'S INTERNATIONAL LEAGUE FOR PEACE AND FREEDOM. This is a **nongovernmental organization** (NGO) that has consultative status with the United Nations **Economic and Social Council** (ECOSOC). It was founded in 1915 at The Hague, Holland, at the International Women's Congress held that year, to unite women throughout the world to oppose war, exploitation, and oppression of all kinds. The Women's International League for Peace and Freedom (WILFP) has stood for the norm of equality against racism and sexism, and for the promotion of **human rights** as an instrument of human needs. Their contribution is particularly significant in their work on behalf of **indigenous peoples, minorities,** migrant workers, the elimination of slavery and **capital punishment.** Among its important publications is *International Peace Update*, a magazine that is published bimonthly. See also: Declaration on the Rights of Peoples to Peace. *Further Information:* Women's International League for Peace and Freedom, 28 Case Postale 28, 1 rue de Varembe, CH 1211, Geneva 20, Switzerland. Tel.: 011–41–22–33–61–75.

WORK. The right of every person to work or employment is one that is recognized by states through many of the global human rights instruments, which also include associated rights, that is, other rights that are necessary to bring about to the right to work. Most states, however, perhaps because of the powerful influence of corporations, have not emphasized this right, although those very governments make good-faith efforts to ensure a sufficient degree of general employment in order to avoid the social and political problems that are the universal results of substantial unemployment. If the *right* to employment were emphasized, the amount of unemployment now facing the world—including many people in the most industrially advanced countries—would have to dealt with, as is done with the right to freedom of expression or practicing one's religion. See also: Employment.

WORKERS WITH FAMILY RESPONSIBILITIES. See CONVENTION CONCERNING EQUAL OPPORTUNITIES AND EQUAL TREATMENT FOR MEN AND WOMEN WORKERS: WORKERS WITH FAMILY RESPONSIBILITIES.

WORKING GROUPS. These are subgroups into which the United Nations **Commission on Human Rights** (CHR) is functionally subdivided. Working groups engage in detailed studies of specific issue areas of **human rights** such as those concerning slavery, **indigenous peoples, detention,** disappearances, and the optional protocol to torture. In addition, working groups sometimes develop and draft human rights instruments, which are later recommended to the Commission on Human Rights. If the commission accepts the recommendations, it will pass them to the United Nations **General Assembly** where they are debated and voted on. See also: Sub-Commission on the Prevention of Discrimination and Protection of Minorities.

WORLD CHARTER FOR NATURE. In part as a response to the growing environmental movement, which gained considerable momentum during the 1970s and 1980s, but also in clear recognition of the need to take a more forceful moral and legal position on the issue of the **environment,** the United Nations **General Assembly,** on October 28, 1982, adopted the World Charter for Nature. The charter is a "common standard by which all human conduct affecting nature is to be guided and judged," and recognizes that human beings are a part of nature and that life depends on the "uninterrupted functioning of natural systems." It also recognizes that civilization itself is "rooted in nature, which has shaped human culture and influenced all artistic and scientific achievement," and that "living in harmony with nature gives [one] the best opportunities" for the development of creativity, rest, and recreation.

The charter's content is defined by a number of principles, numbers 1–5, 23, and 24 of which give a fairly representative sense of the rights and responsibilities that it either explicitly states or implies.

I. GENERAL PRINCIPLES

1. Nature shall be respected and its essential processes shall not be impaired.

2. The genetic viability on the earth shall not be compromised; the population levels of all life forms, wild and domesticated, must be at least sufficient for their survival, and to this end necessary habitats shall be safeguarded.

3. All areas of the earth, both land and sea, shall be subject to these principles of conservation; special protection shall be given to unique areas, to representative samples of all the different types of ecosystems and to the habitats of rare or endangered species.

4. Ecosystems and organisms, as well as the land, marine and atmospheric resources that are utilized by man, shall be managed to achieve and maintain

optimum sustainable productivity, but not in such a way as to endanger the integrity of those other ecosystems or species with which they co-exist.

5. Nature shall be secured against degradation caused by warfare or other hostile activities.

III. IMPLEMENTATION

23. All persons, in accordance with their national legislation, shall have the opportunity to participate, individually or with others, in the formulation of decisions of direct concern to their environment, and shall have access to means of redress when their environment has suffered damage or degradation.

24. Each person has the duty to act in accordance with the provisions of the present Charter; acting individually, in association with others or through participation in the political process, each person shall strive to ensure that the objectives and requirements of the present Charter are met.

WORLD CONFERENCES ON HUMAN RIGHTS. In 1968, the first world conference on **human rights** was held in Teheran, Iran, from April 22 to May 13, to commemorate the twentieth anniversary of the **Universal Declaration of Human Rights** (UDHR) and to assess the progress of human rights promotion and protection throughout the world. In Vienna, Austria, a second conference was held June 14–25, 1993. It was the largest gathering of its kind in history, with grassroots human rights groups and special representatives from 171 countries. That conference had five main objectives: (1) to review and assess the progress made in the field of human rights since 1948, the year of the Universal Declaration of Human Rights; (2) to identify obstacles to the promotion and enjoyment of human rights and ways the obstacles might be overcome; (3) to examine the/links between the development and the enjoyment of economic, social, cultural, civil, and political rights; (4) to evaluate the effectiveness of the UN human rights mechanisms; and (5) to recommend ways to ensure adequate financial and other resources for human rights activities.

The objectives were particularly apt in light of the controversies preceding the 1993 conference, including those dealing with **relativism and universalism,** selectivity in the emphasis on certain groups of human rights, the indivisibility of all human rights, women's rights as human rights, and the weaknesses of the implementation mechanisms. Despite the areas of controversy, a consensus was arrived at the conference in the form of the Vienna Declaration and Programme of Action (VDAPA).

VDAPA affirmed that "all human rights are universal, indivisible and interdependent and interrelated." As such, the Vienna Declaration provides that the promotion and protection of **economic, social and cultural rights** must become subject to the same scrutiny and enforcement as that applied to **civil and political rights.** Further, the right to development and achievement of that development must be based on **democratic entitlement,** and that the *process* of development must include the eradication of extreme poverty. The VDAPA also calls for the elimination of **discrimination** in all its forms, the protection of the rights of women, including those dealing with all forms of violence such as **sexual harassment** and exploitation, and the promotion of the rights of the child as the fundamental building blocks in the promotion of the fundamental rights of people everywhere. Likewise, it proclaims the centrality of third generation rights, including the right to a healthful **environment,** calls for the treatment of the right to education as essential to the development of a global human rights culture, and provides that the mechanisms for protecting human rights at the national, regional, and global levels must be strengthened and better coordinated. In particular, it called for the creation of a United Nations Human Rights High Commissioner. See also: Bangkok Declaration; Child, Rights of; Declaration on the Right to Development; Generations of Rights; Office of High Commissioner for Human Rights; Proclamation of Teheran. *Further Reading:* Vienna Declaration and Programme of Action, UN Doc./A/CONF. 157.23 (1993).

WORLD CONFERENCES ON WOMEN. There have been four world conferences on women, each sponsored by the UN, with much of the planning done by the UN **Commission on the Status of Women** (CSW). Each of the conferences, in large measure influenced by the women's movement, played an important role in the promotion of **human rights,** especially the rights of women.

The first conference was held in Mexico City in 1975. Entitled the World Conference of the International Women's Year (1975 was declared International Women's Year by the UN), it raised the international consciousness about the profound nature and complexity of **discrimination** against women and adopted a set of objectives—a World Plan of Action—designed to relieve the deeply embedded cultural discrimination against women. The United Nations **General Assembly** endorsed the plan and, in addition, proclaimed 1976–1985 the United Nations Decade for Women, with the theme of **equality,** development, and peace.

The second conference was held in 1980, in Copenhagen, Denmark. By the time the conference convened, the **Convention on the Elimination of All Forms of Discrimination Against Women** (CEDAW) had been adopted by the UN and was in the process of being ratified by states. This second conference, in addition to reinforcing the use of the women's movement to marshal efforts on a worldwide scale to ensure gender equality, adopted a Programme of Action for the second half of the UN Decade for Women, especially elaborating on the existing obstacles to gender equality and expressing the international consensus on measures to be taken for the advancement of women. The third conference was held in Nairobi, Kenya, in

1985. Entitled the World Conference to Review and Appraise the Achievements of the UN Decade for Women and using the theme of equality, development, and peace as goals, the 1985 conference concluded that the World Plan of Action and the Programme of Action had contributed to the improvement of gender equality and had enlarged the perspective about the meaning of equality. In addition, it identified further objectives to the achievement of full equality and adopted Forward-Looking Strategies for the Advancement of Women that provide that by the year 2000 "all governments should have adequate, comprehensive and coherent national policies to abolish all obstacles to full and equal participation of women in all spheres of society."

Ten years after Nairobi, the fourth world conference was held in Beijing, China, September 4–15, 1995. This conference looked at how the themes of equality, development, and peace had fared since 1985, especially in the areas of women's rights to health care, **education, employment,** as well as women's status as agents in all spheres of social and political life. The conference also addressed what must be done to eliminate remaining obstacles to gender equality and promote a new women–men partnership for the twenty-first century.

From the deliberations of the fourth world conference came the Beijing Declaration and Platform for Action (BDPA). The BDPA endorsed the positions taken on women's rights at the 1993 World Conference on Human Rights: women's rights are human rights; affirmed the universality and indivisibility of human rights; called for women to control all aspects of their health; greater access of women, especially girls, to education; the adoption of economic policies designed to eliminate **poverty**—the "feminization of poverty" was a significant issue at the conference—and the pursuit of legal and social policies aimed at eliminating all forms of violence against women. The BDPA also focused on the rights of girl children, as a central concern. See also: Bangkok Declaration; Declaration on the Elimination of Violence Against Women; Economic, Social and Cultural Rights. *Further Reading:* Beijing Declaration and Platform for Action, UN Doc. A/CONF. 177/20 (October 17, 1995) and A/CONF. 177/20. Add.1. and see *ILM*, vol. 35 no. 2 (1966); R. Coomaraswamy, *Reinventing International Law: Women's Rights as Human Rights in the International Community* (1997); W. E. Langley, ed., *Women's Rights in International Documents* (1991).

WORLD COURT. See INTERNATIONAL COURT OF JUSTICE.

WORLD FEDERALIST MOVEMENT. The World Federalist Movement (WFM) exists as an organized movement and as an aspiring one. As an organized movement, it began in 1947 in the **United States** as the World Movement for World Government, but after 1956, the movement became the World Association of World Federalists, with associated groups throughout the world. Membership in the organized movement, however, estimated to have reached over 150,000 (47,000 in the United States alone) in 1949 has been on the decline since.

As an aspiring movement it is broad, rich, and expanding, as people come to recognize that the nation-state is a woefully inadequate political vehicle for the pursuit of certain social and political goals. The relative success of the European Union (EU), thus far, in taking steps toward possible political union has also given support to the aspiring movement.

The federalist movement's objective is the creation of a world federation, the government of which would have jurisdiction to deal with global issues through legislative, executive, and judicial institutions. Executive power sufficient to enforce the law—including the norms of **human rights**—would, supporters of the movement argue, ensure world peace. (At national and local levels, separate governments would remain to deal with issues of national and local character.) Today, many federalists would be satisfied if there were a revision of the **United Nations Charter**, allowing for the creation of such a federation. *Further Reading:* J. P. Baratta, "The International History of the World Federalist Movement," in *Peace and Change*, Vol. 14 no. 4 (1980); G. Clarke and L. B. Sohn, *World Peace Through World Law* (1958); A. Bosco, ed., *The Federal Idea: The History of Federalism from the Enlightenment to 1945* (1991). *Further Information*: World Federalist Association, 418 7th Street, S.E., Washington, D.C. 20003; World Association of World Federalists, Leliegracht 21, 1016 G R Amsterdam, The Netherlands. Tel.: 011–31–20–227502.

WORLD HEALTH ORGANIZATION. This international institution is a specialized agency of the United Nations. Its constitution, which was adopted in 1946, came into force in 1948. The organization, headquartered in Geneva, Switzerland, has the objective of fulfilling the right of all people to the "highest possible level of health." In order to successfully pursue that objective, the World Health Organization (WHO) engages in a wide range of functions, including serving as the coordinating and directing authority on international health work; establishing and maintaining effective collaboration with the UN and its other specialized organs such as the **International Labor Organization** (ILO) and the **United Nations Educational, Scientific and Cultural Organization** (UNESCO), as well as national health care organizations and related professional groups; and assisting governments to strengthen their health services and in furnishing technical assistance and ensuring aid, when requested, to countries.

Committed to the idea that health is a state of complete physical, mental, and social well-being and not merely the absence of disease or infirmity, WHO has sponsored research and conducted educational programs that have helped eradicate several epidemic diseases and control others. By 1977, it eradicated smallpox worldwide and targeted diphtheria, measles, polio, tetanus, and whooping cough for eradication. By 1995, over 90 percent of the world's children had been vaccinated and the organization had become deeply involved in a number of programs to deal with AIDS. It has also by itself or in cooperation with other international organizations, engaged in efforts to improve nutrition, housing, sanitation, drinking water, recreation, working conditions, and other areas of environmental hygiene. It works with the **United Nations Children's Fund** (UNICEF) and UNESCO in the areas of **education** and maternal and children's health. In 1993, WHO decided to cooperate with a number of groups, as well as states, to petition the **International Court of Justice** (ICJ) for an advisory opinion on the legality of using nuclear weapons. The focus of its involvement was that the use of such weapons would have a degrading effect on the condition of world health and the right to health. See also: Child, Rights of; Health. *Further Reading:* K. Cust, *A Just Minimum of Health Care* (1997); G. Milkes, *The Riches of the Poor* (1987); United Nations, *ACCIS Guide to United Nations Information Sources on Health* (1992).

X

XHOSA. See SOUTH AFRICA.

Y

YAMASHITA, TOMOYUKI (1885–1946). Tomoyuki Yamashita was the Japanese commander in charge of the Philippines during World War II, specifically from 1944 to 1945. He was tried, convicted, and hanged in Manila, the Philippines, after having been charged with **war crimes** under the principle known today as *commander responsibility*. Under that principle, he was not accused of having committed the atrocities charged, or having commanded that they be committed, or of even failing to take action to prevent them. He was accused of having "failed to exercise proper control over his troops and [thus] permitted the sacking of Manila."

The trial itself was controversial, with charges of "victors justice" and **racism**, especially when Yamashita's lawyers were not given adequate time to prepare for some of the charges. And when an appeal to the United States Supreme Court failed, the questions about the appropriateness of the trial became even more widespread. The importance of this case is the extent to which the Yamashita precedent is potentially helpful in enforcing **human rights** norms.

If commanding officers and their superiors, who do not have minute-to-minute or even day-to-day operational control over what their soldiers do in the field, can be charged with criminal responsibility for war crimes, then few political or military leaders are potentially shielded from wartime atrocities. And if the principle of commander responsibility were enforced, the atrocities of warfare would be substantially reduced, if not eliminated. No longer could soldiers in the field and junior officers (the "little fish") be the primary targets of war crimes trials. See also: *Superior Orders*. *Further Reading*: J. W. Dower, *War Without Mercy: Race and Power in the Pacific* (1986); A. M. Prevost, "Race and War Crimes Trial of General Tomoyuki Yamashita," *HRQ*, vol. 14 no. 3 (1992).

YEAR OF THE CHILD. See DEFENSE FOR CHILDREN INTERNATIONAL.

YELLOW PERIL. This is a term used before, during, and after World War II to denote a fear and concern that Asians (especially Japanese) might overrun areas populated by, or seen as important for the settlement of, whites. Deeply imbedded in racial attitudes and overtones, the term gained much currency after the Japanese (part of what has been called the Mongoloid race, which includes Chinese, Koreans, and Mongols) surprisingly defeated the Russians (a member of the white or Caucasian race) in the 1905 Russo-Japanese War. Until then, it was not though likely or even possible that a nonwhite country could defeat one populated and controlled by whites.

The fear of the Yellow Peril prevented the League of Nations from adopting a position in favor of racial equality, as Australia, Britain, and the **United States** strongly objected. Fear also played a major role in Western propaganda against Japan during World War II. Today, the expression is used to indicate the fear that Asian (particularly Japanese and Chinese) economic power could subdue the West and induce almost irrational responses to certain forms of investments by Japanese in the West, particularly the United States, such as the purchase of Rockefeller Center in New York City. Even the involvement of monies from Asian countries in the United States' 1996 presidential elections became problematic, as the initial focus was not so much on the illegalities of foreign campaign contributions but Asian contributions to the political process and its assumed threat to national security. Finally, it was racial attitudes, groomed on the fear of the Yellow Peril that largely caused widespread **discrimination** against Asians in the United States and led to the relocation by the United States of its own citizens of Japanese ancestry during World War II. See also: Propaganda; Racism. *Further Reading:* R. Daniels, *The Decision to Relocate Japanese Americans* (1975); J. W. Dower, *War Without Mercy: Race and Power in the Pacific War* (1986); W. F. Wu, *The Yellow Peril: Chinese Americans in American Fiction, 1850–1940* (1982).

YUGOSLAVIA. See ETHNIC CLEANSING; MILOSEVIC, SLOBODAN; SERBIA.

Z

ZIONISM. This is an international term that is used to describe a cultural and political movement which began in the nineteenth century and symbolized by the work of Theodore Herzl (1860–1904) for the establishment of a homeland for the Jewish people. This movement was launched primarily because Jews, regardless of how good a citizen they may have been in any given country, could never feel at home; they were always subject to persecution and broad discrimination.

A number of areas were considered as a possible homeland, including Argentina, Madagascar, and Uganda. But most Jewish people—people as understood and elaborated in the International Bill of Rights—sought their homeland in a place where they had historic ties, where they had previously had a homeland—Palestine. The movement, with the aid of the 1917 Balfour Declaration, named after the then British foreign minister and promising British support for the establishment of a national home in Palestine for the Jewish people, culminated in the establishment of the state of Israel in 1948.

In 1977, the UN General Assembly, influenced by the bitter Israeli–Arab conflict, passed a resolution declaring Zionism a "form of racism." This resolution was repealed in 1991, but not before it had generated much international accusation, distorted the terms of debate in many international forums, and invited moral outrage, especially in the West. See also: Self-Determination. *Further Reading:* M. Buber, *On Zion: The History of an Idea* (1973); J. E. Heller, *The Zionist Idea* (1949); A. Shalem, *Why the Jews Need a Land of Their Own* (1984).

APPENDIX A
SELECTED HUMAN RIGHTS GROUPS

For names and addresses of human rights groups that are the subject of entries in this work, see the entry under the name of the group. Additional groups are:

Asia Watch
485 Fifth Avenue
New York, N.Y. 10017 USA
Tel.: (212) 972–8400
Fax: (212) 972–0905

Centre for Constitutional Rights
666 Broadway 7th Floor
New York, N.Y. 10012 USA
Tel.: (212) 614–6464
Fax: (212) 614–6499

Cultural Survival
46 Brattle Street
Cambridge, Mass. 02138 USA
Tel.: (617) 441–5400
Fax: (617) 441–5417

Harvard Law School
   Human Rights Program
Pound Hall 401,
   Harvard Law School
Cambridge, Mass. 02138 USA
Tel.: (617) 495–9362
Fax: (617) 495–1110

International Commission of Jurists
PO Box 120
109 Route de Chene, CH-1224
Geneva, Switzerland
Tel.: 011–41–22–49–35–45

Lawyers Committee for Human Rights
333 Seventh Avenue 13th Floor
New York, N.Y. 10001–5004
Tel.: (212) 845–5200
Fax: (212) 845–5299

The Salvation Army
Public Relations Department
101 Queen Victoria Street
London EC4P 4EP
United Kingdom
Tel.: 011–44–171–236–5222

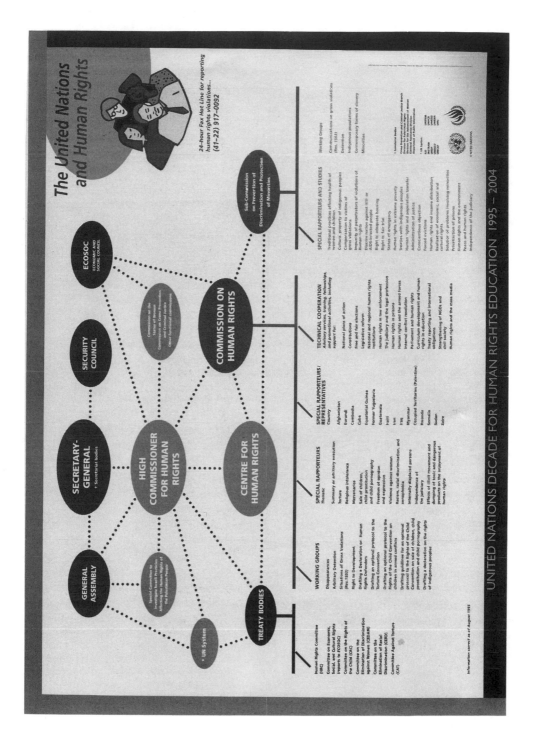

The United Nations and Human Rights

24-hour Fax Hot Line for reporting human rights violations...
(41-22) 917-0092

SECRETARY-GENERAL
† Secretarial bodies

SECURITY COUNCIL

ECOSOC
ECONOMIC AND SOCIAL COUNCIL

GENERAL ASSEMBLY

Special Committee to Investigate Israeli Practices Affecting the Human Rights of the Palestinian People

HIGH COMMISSIONER FOR HUMAN RIGHTS

Commission on the Status of Women
Commission on Crime Prevention and Criminal Justice
Other functional commissions

CENTRE FOR HUMAN RIGHTS

TREATY BODIES

COMMISSION ON HUMAN RIGHTS

Sub-Commission on Prevention of Discrimination and Protection of Minorities

* UN System

Treaty Bodies

Human Rights Committee (HRC)
Committee on Economic, Social, and Cultural Rights (reports to ECOSOC)
Committee on the Rights of the Child (CRC)
Committee on the Elimination of Discrimination against Women (CEDAW)
Committee on the Elimination of Racial Discrimination (CERD)
Committee Against Torture (CAT)

WORKING GROUPS

Disappearances
Arbitrary Detention
Situations of Gross Violations (Res. 1503)
Right to Development
Drafting a Declaration on Human Rights Defenders
Drafting an optional protocol to the Torture Convention
Drafting an optional protocol to the Rights of the Child Convention on children in armed conflicts
Drafting guidelines for an optional protocol to the Rights of the Child Convention on sale of children, child prostitution and child pornography
Drafting a declaration on the rights of indigenous peoples

SPECIAL RAPPORTEURS
Thematic

Summary or arbitrary execution
Torture
Religious Intolerance
Mercenaries
Sale of children, child prostitution and child pornography
Freedom of opinion and expression
Violence against women
Racism, racial discrimination, and xenophobia
Internally displaced persons
Independence of the judiciary
Effects of illicit movement and dumping of toxic and dangerous products on the enjoyment of human rights

SPECIAL RAPPORTEURS/ REPRESENTATIVES
Country

Afghanistan
Burundi
Cambodia
Cuba
Equatorial Guinea
Former Yugoslavia
Guatemala
Haiti
Iran
Iraq
Myanmar
Occupied Territories (Palestine)
Rwanda
Somalia
Sudan
Zaire

TECHNICAL COOPERATION
Advisory services, training, fellowships, and promotional activities, including support for:

National plans of action
Constitutions
Free and fair elections
Legislative reform
National and regional human rights institutions
Human rights in law enforcement
The judiciary and the legal profession
Human rights in prisons
Human rights and the armed forces
Internal conflict resolution
Parliament and human rights
Curriculum development and human rights in education
Treaty reporting and international obligations
Strengthening of NGOs and civil society
Human rights and the mass media

SPECIAL RAPPORTEURS AND STUDIES

Traditional practices affecting the health of women and children
Cultural property of indigenous peoples
Compensation to victims of gross violations
Impunity of perpetrators of violations of human rights
Discrimination against HIV or AIDS-infected people
Right to adequate housing
Right to fair trial
States of emergency
Human rights in extreme poverty
Treaties with indigenous peoples
Human rights and population transfer
Administration of justice
Conscientious objection
Forced evictions
Human rights and income distribution
Realization of economic, social and cultural rights
Scope of problems involving minorities
Privatization of prisons
Human rights and the environment
Peace and human rights
Independence of the judiciary

Working Groups

Communications on gross violations (Res. 1503)
Detention
Indigenous populations
Contemporary forms of slavery
Minorities

† *Secretariat bodies*

Crime Prevention and Criminal Justice Branch
Division for Palestinian Rights
Division for the Advancement of Women
Division for Economic and Social Information
Department of Public Information

Information correct as of August 1995

UNITED NATIONS

UNITED NATIONS DECADE FOR HUMAN RIGHTS EDUCATION 1995 – 2004

APPENDIX B
THE INTERNATIONAL BILL OF HUMAN RIGHTS

The Universal Declaration of Human Rights

[U.N.G.A. Res. 217 A(III) of Dec. 10, 1948, U.N. Doc. A/810, at 71 (1948).]

PREAMBLE

Whereas recognition of the inherent dignity and of the equal and inalienable rights of all members of the human family is the foundation of freedom, justice and peace in the world,

Whereas disregard and contempt for human rights have resulted in barbarous acts which have outraged the conscience of mankind, and the advent of a world in which human beings shall enjoy freedom of speech and belief and freedom from fear and want has been proclaimed as the highest aspiration of the common people,

Whereas it is essential, if man is not to be compelled to have recourse, as a last resort, to rebellion against tyranny and oppression, that human rights should be protected by the rule of law,

Whereas it is essential to promote the development of friendly relations between nations,

Whereas the peoples of the United Nations have in the Charter reaffirmed their faith in fundamental human rights, in the dignity and worth of the human person and in the equal rights of men and women and have determined to promote social progress and better standards of life in larger freedom,

Whereas Member States have pledged themselves to achieve, in co-operation with the United Nations, the promotion of universal respect for and observance of human rights and fundamental freedoms,

Whereas a common understanding of these rights and freedoms is of the greatest importance for the full realization of this pledge,

Now, therefore,

The General Assembly

Proclaims this Universal Declaration of Human Rights as a common standard of achievement for all peoples and all nations, to the end that every individual and every organ of society, keeping this Declaration constantly in mind, shall strive by teaching and education to promote respect for these rights and freedoms and by progressive measures, national and international, to secure their universal and effective recognition and observance, both among the peoples of Member States themselves and among the peoples of territories under their jurisdiction.

ARTICLE I

All human beings are born free and equal in dignity and rights. They are endowed with reason and conscience and should act towards one another in a spirit of brotherhood.

ARTICLE 2

Everyone is entitled to all the rights and freedoms set forth in this Declaration, without distinction of any kind, such as race, colour, sex, language, religion, political or other opinion, national or social origin, property, birth or other status.

Furthermore, no distinction shall be made on the basis of the political, jurisdictional or international status of the country or territory to which a person belongs, whether it be independent, trust, non-self-governing or under any other limitation of sovereignty.

ARTICLE 3

Everyone has the right to life, liberty and the security of person.

ARTICLE 4

No one shall be held in slavery or servitude; slavery and the slave trade shall be prohibited in all their forms.

ARTICLE 5

No one shall be subjected to torture or to cruel, inhuman or degrading treatment or punishment.

ARTICLE 6

Everyone has the right to recognition everywhere as a person before the law.

ARTICLE 7

All are equal before the law and are entitled without any discrimination to equal protection of the law. All are entitled to equal protection against any discrimination in violation of this Declaration and against any incitement to such discrimination.

ARTICLE 8

Everyone has the right to an effective remedy by the competent national tribunals for acts violating the fundamental rights granted him by the constitution or by law.

ARTICLE 9

No one shall be subjected to arbitrary arrest, detention or exile.

ARTICLE 10

Everyone is entitled in full equality to a fair and public hearing by an independent and impartial tribunal, in the determination of his rights and obligations and of any criminal charge against him.

ARTICLE 11

1. Everyone charged with a penal offence has the right to be presumed innocent until proved guilty according to law in a public trial at which he has had all the guarantees necessary for his defence.

2. No one shall be held guilty of any penal offence on account of any act or omission which did not constitute a penal offence, under national or international law, at the time when it was committed. Nor shall a heavier penalty be imposed than the one that was applicable at the time the penal offence was committed.

ARTICLE 12

No one shall be subjected to arbitrary interference with his privacy, family, home or correspondence, nor to attacks upon his honour and reputation. Everyone has the right to the protection of the law against such interference or attacks.

ARTICLE 13

1. Everyone has the right to freedom of movement and residence within the borders of each State.

2. Everyone has the right to leave any country, including his own, and to return to his country.

ARTICLE 14

1. Everyone has the right to seek and to enjoy in other countries asylum from persecution.

2. This right may not be invoked in the case of prosecutions genuinely arising from nonpolitical crimes or from acts contrary to the purposes and principles of the United Nations.

ARTICLE 15

1. Everyone has the right to a nationality.

2. No one shall be arbitrarily deprived of his nationality nor denied the right to change his nationality.

ARTICLE 16

1. Men and women of full age, without any limitation due to race, nationality or religion, have the right to marry and to found a family. They are entitled to equal rights as to marriage, during marriage and at its dissolution.

2. Marriage shall be entered into only with the free and full consent of the intending spouses.

3. The family is the natural and fundamental group unit of society and is entitled to protection by society and the State.

ARTICLE 17

1. Everyone has the right to own property alone as well as in association with others.

2. No one shall be arbitrarily deprived of his property.

ARTICLE 18

Everyone has the right to freedom of thought, conscience and religion; this right includes freedom to change his religion or belief, and freedom, either alone or in community with others and in public or private, to manifest his religion or belief in teaching, practice, worship and observance.

ARTICLE 19

Everyone has the right to freedom of opinion and expression; this right includes freedom to hold opinions without interference and to seek, receive and impart information and ideas through any media and regardless of frontiers.

ARTICLE 20

1. Everyone has the right to freedom of peaceful assembly and association.

2. No one may be compelled to belong to an association.

ARTICLE 21

1. Everyone has the right to take part in the government of his country, directly or through freely chosen representatives.

2. Everyone has the right of equal access to public service in his country.

3. The will of the people shall be the basis of the authority of government; this will shall be expressed in periodic and genuine elections which shall be by universal and equal suffrage and shall be held by secret vote or by equivalent free voting procedures.

ARTICLE 22

Everyone, as a member of society, has the right to social security and is entitled to realization, through national effort and international co-operation and in accordance with the organization and resources of each State, of the economic, social and cultural rights indispensable for his dignity and the free development of his personality.

ARTICLE 23

1. Everyone has the right to work, to free choice of employment, to just and favourable conditions of work and to protection against unemployment.

2. Everyone, without any discrimination, has the right to equal pay for equal work.

3. Everyone who works has the right to just and favourable remuneration ensuring for himself and his family an existence worthy of human dignity, and supplemented, if necessary, by other means of social protection.

4. Everyone has the right to form and to join trade unions for the protection of his interests.

ARTICLE 24

Everyone has the right to rest and leisure, including reasonable limitation of working hours and periodic holidays with pay.

ARTICLE 25

1. Everyone has the right to a standard of living adequate for the health and well-being of himself and of his family, including food, clothing, housing and medical care and necessary social services, and the right to security in the event of unemployment, sickness, disability, widowhood, old age or other lack of livelihood in circumstances beyond his control.

International Covenant
on Economic, Social and Cultural Rights

[Adopted by General Assembly resolution 2200 A(XXI) of December 16, 1966. 21 UNGOAR Supp. (No. 16) 49, U.N. Doc. A/6316(1966). Entry into Force: January 3, 1976.]

PREAMBLE

The States Parties to the present Covenant,

Considering that, in accordance with the principles proclaimed in the Charter of the United Nations, recognition of the inherent dignity and of the equal and inalienable rights of all members of the human family is the foundation of freedom, justice and peace in the world,

Recognizing that these rights derive from the inherent dignity of the human person,

Recognizing that, in accordance with the Universal Declaration of Human Rights, the ideal of free human beings enjoying freedom from fear and want can only be achieved if conditions are created whereby everyone may enjoy his economic, social and cultural rights, as well as his civil and political rights,

Considering the obligation of States under the Charter of the United Nations to promote universal respect for, and observance of, human rights and freedoms,

Realizing that the individual, having duties to other individuals and to the community to which he belongs, is under a responsibility to strive for the promotion and observance of the rights recognized in the present Covenant,

Agree upon the following articles:

PART I

Article 1

1. All peoples have the right of self-determination. By virtue of that right they freely determine their political status and freely pursue their economic, social and cultural development.

2. All peoples may, for their own ends, freely dispose of their natural wealth and resources without prejudice to any obligations arising out of international economic co-operation, based upon the principle of mutual benefit, and international law. In no case may a people be deprived of its own means of subsistence.

3. The States Parties to the present Covenant, including those having responsibility for the administration of Non-Self-Governing and Trust Territories, shall promote the realization of the right of self-determination, and shall respect that right, in conformity with the provisions of the Charter of the United Nations.

PART II

Article 2

1. Each State Party to the present Covenant undertakes to take steps,

---

2. Motherhood and childhood are entitled to special care and assistance. All children, whether born in or out of wedlock, shall enjoy the same social protection.

ARTICLE 26

1. Everyone has the right to education. Education shall be free, at least in the elementary and fundamental stages. Elementary education shall be compulsory. Technical and professional education shall be made generally available and higher education shall be equally accessible to all on the basis of merit.

2. Education shall be directed to the full development of the human personality and to the strengthening of respect for human rights and fundamental freedoms. It shall promote understanding, tolerance and friendship among all nations, racial or religious groups, and shall further the activities of the United Nations for the maintenance of peace.

3. Parents have a prior right to choose the kind of education that shall be given to their children.

ARTICLE 27

1. Everyone has the right freely to participate in the cultural life of the community, to enjoy the arts and to share in scientific advancement and its benefits.

2. Everyone has the right to the protection of the moral and material interests resulting from any scientific, literary or artistic production of which he is the author.

ARTICLE 28

Everyone is entitled to a social and international order in which the rights and freedoms set forth in this Declaration can be fully realized.

ARTICLE 29

1. Everyone has duties to the community in which alone the free and full development of his personality is possible.

2. In the exercise of his rights and freedoms, everyone shall be subject only to such limitations as are determined by law solely for the purpose of securing due recognition and respect for the rights and freedoms of others and of meeting the just requirements of morality, public order and the general welfare in a democratic society.

3. These rights and freedoms may in no case be exercised contrary to the purposes and principles of the United Nations.

ARTICLE 30

Nothing in this Declaration may be interpreted as implying for any State, group or person any right to engage in any activity or to perform any act aimed at the destruction of any of the rights and freedoms set forth herein.

Hundred and eighty-third plenary meeting.
10 December 1948.

individually and through international assistance and co-operation, especially economic and technical, to the maximum of its available resources, with a view to achieving progressively the full realization of the rights recognized in the present Covenant by all appropriate means, including particularly the adoption of legislative measures.

2. The States Parties to the present Covenant undertake to guarantee that the rights enunciated in the present Covenant will be exercised without discrimination of any kind as to race, colour, sex, language, religion, political or other opinion, national or social origin, property, birth or other status.

3. Developing countries, with due regard to human rights and their national economy, may determine to what extent they would guarantee the economic rights recognized in the present Covenant to non-nationals.

Article 3

The States Parties to the present Covenant undertake to ensure the equal right of men and women to the enjoyment of all economic, social and cultural rights set forth in the present Covenant.

Article 4

The States Parties to the present Covenant recognize that, in the enjoyment of those rights provided by the State in conformity with the present Covenant, the State may subject such rights only to such limitations as are determined by law only in so far as this may be compatible with the nature of these rights and solely for the purpose of promoting the general welfare in a democratic society.

Article 5

1. Nothing in the present Covenant may be interpreted as implying for any State, group or person any right to engage in any activity or to perform any act aimed at the destruction of any of the rights or freedoms recognized herein, or at their limitation to a greater extent than is provided for in the present Covenant.

2. No restriction upon or derogation from any of the fundamental human rights recognized or existing in any country in virtue of law, conventions, regulations or custom shall be admitted on the pretext that the present Covenant does not recognize such rights or that it recognizes them to a lesser extent.

PART III

Article 6

1. The States Parties to the present Covenant recognize the right to work, which includes the right of everyone to the opportunity to gain his living by work which he freely chooses or accepts, and will take appropriate steps to safeguard this right.

2. The steps to be taken by a State Party to the present Covenant to achieve the full realization of this right shall include technical and vocational guidance and training programmes, policies and techniques to achieve steady economic, social and cultural development and full and productive employment under conditions safeguarding fundamental political and economic freedoms to the individual.

Article 7

The States Parties to the present Covenant recognize the right of everyone to the enjoyment of just and favourable conditions of work which ensure, in particular:

(a) Remuneration which provides all workers, as a minimum, with:
(i) Fair wages and equal remuneration for work of equal value without distinction of any kind, in particular women being guaranteed conditions of work not inferior to those enjoyed by men, with equal pay for equal work;
(ii) A decent living for themselves and their families in accordance with the provisions of the present Covenant;
(b) Safe and healthy working conditions;
(c) Equal opportunity for everyone to be promoted in his employment to an appropriate higher level, subject to no considerations other than those of seniority and competence;
(d) Rest, leisure and reasonable limitation of working hours and periodic holidays with pay, as well as remuneration for public holidays.

Article 8

1. The States Parties to the present Covenant undertake to ensure:
(a) The right of everyone to form trade unions and join the trade union of his choice, subject only to the rules of the organization concerned, for the promotion and protection of his economic and social interests. No restrictions may be placed on the exercise of this right other than those prescribed by law and which are necessary in a democratic society in the interests of national security or public order or for the protection of the rights and freedoms of others;
(b) The right of trade unions to establish national federations or confederations and the right of the latter to form or join international trade-union organizations;
(c) The right of trade unions to function freely subject to no limitations other than those prescribed by law and which are necessary in a democratic society in the interests of national security or public order or for the protection of the rights and freedoms of others;
(d) The right to strike, provided that it is exercised in conformity with the laws of the particular country.

2. This article shall not prevent the imposition of lawful restrictions on the exercise of these rights by members of the armed forces or of the police or of the administration of the State.

3. Nothing in this article shall authorize States Parties to the International Labour Organisation Convention of 1948 concerning Freedom of Association and Protection of the Right to Organize to take legislative measures which would prejudice, or apply the law in such a manner as would prejudice, the guarantees provided for in that Convention.

Article 9

The States Parties to the present Covenant recognize the right of everyone to social security, including social insurance.

Article 10

The States Parties to the present Covenant recognize that:

1. The widest possible protection and assistance should be accorded to the family, which is the natural and fundamental group unit of society, particularly for its establishment and while it is responsible for the care and education of dependent children. Marriage must be entered into with the free consent of the intending spouses.

2. Special protection should be accorded to mothers during a reasonable period before and after childbirth. During such period working mothers should be accorded paid leave or leave with adequate social security benefits.

3. Special measures of protection and assistance should be taken on behalf of all children and young persons without any discrimination for reasons of parentage or other conditions. Children and young persons should be protected from economic and social exploitation. Their employment in work harmful to their morals or health or dangerous to life or likely to hamper their normal development should be punishable by law. States should also set age limits below which the paid employment of child labour should be prohibited and punishable by law.

Article 11

1. The States Parties to the present Covenant recognize the right of everyone to an adequate standard of living for himself and his family, including adequate food, clothing and housing, and to the continuous improvement of living conditions. The States Parties will take appropriate steps to ensure the realization of this right, recognizing to this effect the essential importance of international co-operation based on free consent.

2. The States Parties to the present Covenant, recognizing the fundamental right of everyone to be free from hunger, shall take, individually and through international co-operation, the measures, including specific programmes, which are needed:

(a) To improve methods of production, conservation and distribution of food by making full use of technical and scientific knowledge, by disseminating knowledge of the principles of nutrition and by developing or reforming agrarian systems in such a way as to achieve the most efficient development and utilization of natural resources;

(b) Taking into account the problems of both food-importing and food-exporting countries, to ensure an equitable distribution of world food supplies in relation to need.

Article 12

1. The States Parties to the present Covenant recognize the right of everyone to the enjoyment of the highest attainable standard of physical and mental health.

2. The steps to be taken by the States Parties to the present Covenant to achieve the full realization of this right shall include those necessary for:

(a) The provision for the reduction of the stillbirth-rate and of infant mortality and for the healthy development of the child;

(b) The improvement of all aspects of environmental and industrial hygiene;

(c) The prevention, treatment and control of epidemic, endemic, occupational and other diseases;

(d) The creation of conditions which would assure to all medical service and medical attention in the event of sickness.

Article 13

1. The States Parties to the present Covenant recognize the right of everyone to education. They agree that education shall be directed to the full development of the human personality and the sense of its dignity, and shall strengthen the respect for human rights and fundamental freedoms. They further agree that education shall enable all persons to participate effectively in a free society, promote understanding, tolerance and friendship among all nations and all racial, ethnic or religious groups, and further the activities of the United Nations for the maintenance of peace.

2. The States Parties to the present Covenant recognize that, with a view to achieving the full realization of this right:

(a) Primary education shall be compulsory and available free to all;

(b) Secondary education in its different forms, including technical and vocational secondary education, shall be made generally available and accessible to all by every appropriate means, and in particular by the progressive introduction of free education;

(c) Higher education shall be made equally accessible to all, on the basis of capacity, by every appropriate means, and in particular by the progressive introduction of free education;

(d) Fundamental education shall be encouraged or intensified as far as possible for those persons who have not received or completed the whole period of their primary education;

(e) The development of a system of schools at all levels shall be actively pursued, an adequate fellowship system shall be established, and the material conditions of teaching staff shall be continuously improved.

3. The States Parties to the present Covenant undertake to have respect for the liberty of parents and, when applicable, legal guardians to choose for their children schools, other than those established by the public authorities, which conform to such minimum educational standards as may be laid down or approved by the State and to ensure the religious and moral education of their children in conformity with their own convictions.

4. No part of this article shall be construed so as to interfere with the liberty of individuals and bodies to establish and direct educational institutions, subject always to the observance of the principles set forth in paragraph 1 of this article and to the requirement that the education given in such institutions shall conform to such minimum standards as may be laid down by the State.

Article 14

Each State Party to the present Covenant which, at the time of becoming a Party, has not been able to secure in its metropolitan territory or other territories under its jurisdiction compulsory primary education, free of charge, undertakes, within two years, to work out and adopt a detailed plan of action for the progressive implementation, within a reasonable number of years, to be fixed in the plan, of the principle of compulsory education free of charge for all.

Article 15

1. The States Parties to the present Covenant recognize the right of everyone:

(a) To take part in cultural life;

(b) To enjoy the benefits of scientific progress and its applications;

(c) To benefit from the protection of the moral and material interests resulting from any scientific, literary or artistic production of which he is the author.

2. The steps to be taken by the States Parties to the present Covenant to achieve the full realization of this right shall include those necessary for the conservation, the development and the diffusion of science and culture.

3. The States Parties to the present Covenant undertake to respect the freedom indispensable for scientific research and creative activity.

4. The States Parties to the present Covenant recognize the benefits to be derived from the encouragement and development of international contacts and co-operation in the scientific and cultural fields.

PART IV

Article 16

1. The States Parties to the present Covenant undertake to submit in conformity with this part of the Covenant reports on the measures which they have adopted and the progress made in achieving the observance of the rights recognized herein.

2. (a) All reports shall be submitted to the Secretary-General of the United Nations, who shall transmit copies to the Economic and Social Council for consideration in accordance with the provisions of the present Covenant;

(b) The Secretary-General of the United Nations shall also transmit to the specialized agencies copies of the reports, or any relevant parts therefrom, from States Parties to the present Covenant which are also members of these specialized agencies in so far as these reports, or parts therefrom, relate to any matters which fall within the responsibilities of the said agencies in accordance with their constitutional instruments.

Article 17

1. The States Parties to the present Covenant shall furnish their reports in stages, in accordance with a programme to be established by the Economic and Social Council within one year of entry into force of the present Covenant after consultation with the States Parties and the specialized agencies concerned.

2. Reports may indicate factors and difficulties affecting the degree of fulfillment of obligations under the present Covenant.

3. Where relevant information has previously been furnished to the United Nations or to any specialized agency by any State Party to the present Covenant, it will not be necessary to reproduce that information, but a precise reference to the information so furnished will suffice.

Article 18

Pursuant to its responsibilities under the Charter of the United Nations in the field of human rights and fundamental freedoms, the Economic and Social Council may make arrangements with the specialized agencies in respect of their reporting to it on the progress made in achieving the observance of the provisions of the present Covenant falling within the scope of their activities. These reports may include particulars of decisions and recommendations on such implementation adopted by their competent organs.

Article 19

The Economic and Social Council may transmit to the Commission on Human Rights for study and general recommendation or, as appropriate, for information the reports concerning human rights submitted by States in accordance with articles 16 and 17, and those concerning human rights submitted by the specialized agencies in accordance with article 18.

Article 20

The States Parties to the present Covenant and the specialized agencies concerned may submit comments to the Economic and Social Council on any general recommendation under article 19 or reference to such general recommendation in any report of the Commission on Human Rights or any documentation referred to therein.

Article 21

The Economic and Social Council may submit from time to time to the General Assembly reports with recommendations of a general nature and a summary of the information received from the States Parties to the present Covenant and the specialized agencies on the measures taken and the progress made in achieving general observance of the rights recognized in the present Covenant.

Article 22

The Economic and Social Council may bring to the attention of other organs of the United Nations, their subsidiary organs and specialized agencies concerned with furnishing technical assistance any matters arising out of the reports referred to in this part of the present Covenant which may assist such bodies in deciding, each within its field of competence, on the advisability of international measures likely to contribute to the effective progressive implementation of the present Covenant.

Article 23

The States Parties to the present Covenant agree that international action for the achievement of the rights recognized in the present Covenant includes such methods as the conclusion of conventions, the adoption of recommendations, the furnishing of technical assistance and the holding of regional meetings and technical meetings for the purpose of consultation and study organized in conjunction with the Governments concerned.

Article 24

Nothing in the present Covenant shall be interpreted as impairing the provisions of the Charter of the United Nations and of the constitutions of the specialized agencies which define the respective responsibilities of the various organs of the United Nations and of the specialized agencies in regard to the matters dealt with in the present Covenant.

Article 25

Nothing in the present Covenant shall be interpreted as impairing the inherent right of all peoples to enjoy and utilize fully and freely their natural wealth and resources.

PART V

Article 26

1. The present Covenant is open for signature by any State Member of the United Nations or member of any of its specialized agencies, by any State Party to the Statute of the International Court of Justice, and by any other State which has been invited by the General Assembly of the United Nations to become a party to the present Covenant.

2. The present Covenant is subject to ratification. Instruments of ratification shall be deposited with the Secretary-General of the United Nations.

3. The present Covenant shall be open to accession by any State referred to in paragraph 1 of this article.

4. Accession shall be effected by the deposit of an instrument of accession with the Secretary-General of the United Nations.

5. The Secretary-General of the United Nations shall inform all States which have signed the present Covenant or acceded to it of the deposit of each instrument of ratification or accession.

Article 27

1. The present Covenant shall enter into force three months after the date of the deposit with the Secretary-General of the United Nations of the thirty-fifth instrument of ratification or instrument of accession.

2. For each State ratifying the present Covenant or acceding to it after the deposit of the thirty-fifth instrument of ratification or instrument of accession, the present Covenant shall enter into force three months after the date of the deposit of its own instrument of ratification or instrument of accession.

Article 28

The provisions of the present Covenant shall extend to all parts of federal States without any limitations or exceptions.

Article 29

1. Any State Party to the present Covenant may propose an amendment and file it with the Secretary-General of the United Nations. The Secretary-General shall thereupon communicate any proposed amendments to the States Parties to the present Covenant with a request that they notify him whether they favour a conference of States Parties for the purpose of considering and voting upon the proposals. In the event that at least one third of the States Parties favours such a conference, the Secretary-General shall convene the conference under the auspices of the United Nations. Any amendment adopted by a majority of the States Parties present and voting at the conference shall be submitted to the General Assembly of the United Nations for approval.

2. Amendments shall come into force when they have been approved by the General Assembly of the United Nations and accepted by a two-thirds majority of the States Parties to the present Covenant in accordance with their respective constitutional processes.

3. When amendments come into force they shall be binding on those States Parties which have accepted them, other States Parties still being bound by the provisions of the present Covenant and any earlier amendment which they have accepted.

Article 30

Irrespective of the notifications made under article 26, paragraph 5, the Secretary-General of the United Nations shall inform all States referred to in paragraph 1 of the same article of the following particulars:

(a) Signatures, ratifications and accessions under article 26;
(b) The date of the entry into force of the present Covenant under article 27 and the date of the entry into force of any amendments under article 29.

Article 31

1. The present Covenant, of which the Chinese, English, French, Russian and Spanish texts are equally authentic, shall be deposited in the archives of the United Nations.

2. The Secretary-General of the United Nations shall transmit certified copies of the present Covenant to all States referred to in article 26.

International Covenant on Civil and Political Rights

[Adopted by General Assembly resolution 2200 A (XXI) of December 16, 1966, 21 GAOR Supp.(No. 16) 52, U.N. Doc. A/6316(1966). Entry into Force: March 23, 1976.]

PREAMBLE

The States Parties to the present Covenant,

Considering that, in accordance with the principles proclaimed in the Charter of the United Nations, recognition of the inherent dignity and of the equal and inalienable rights of all members of the human family is the foundation of freedom, justice and peace in the world,

Recognizing that these rights derive from the inherent dignity of the human person,

Recognizing that, in accordance with the Universal Declaration of Human Rights, the ideal of free human beings enjoying civil and political freedom and freedom from fear and want can only be achieved if conditions are created whereby everyone may enjoy his civil and political rights, as well as his economic, social and cultural rights,

Considering the obligation of States under the Charter of the United Nations to promote universal respect for, and observance of, human rights and freedoms,

Realizing that the individual, having duties to other individuals and to the community to which he belongs, is under a responsibility to strive for the promotion and observance of the rights recognized in the present Covenant,

Agree upon the following articles:

PART I

Article 1

1. All peoples have the right of self-determination. By virtue of that right they freely determine their political status and freely pursue their economic, social and cultural development.

2. All peoples may, for their own ends, freely dispose of their natural wealth and resources without prejudice to any obligations arising out of international economic co-operation, based upon the principle of mutual benefit, and international law. In no case may a people be deprived of its own means of subsistence.

3. The States Parties to the present Covenant, including those having responsibility for the administration of Non-Self-Governing and Trust Territories, shall promote the realization of the right of self-determination, and shall respect that right, in conformity with the provisions of the Charter of the United Nations.

PART II

Article 2

1. Each State Party to the present Covenant undertakes to respect and to ensure to all individuals within its territory and subject to its jurisdiction the rights recognized in the present Covenant, without distinction of any kind, such as race, colour, sex, language, religion, political or other opinion, national or social origin, property, birth or other status.

2. Where not already provided for by existing legislative or other measures, each State Party to the present Covenant undertakes to take the necessary steps, in accordance with its constitutional processes and with the provisions of the present Covenant, to adopt such legislative or other measures as may be necessary to give effect to the rights recognized in the present Covenant.

3. Each State Party to the present Covenant undertakes:

(a) To ensure that any person whose rights or freedoms as herein recognized are violated shall have an effective remedy, notwithstanding that the violation has been committed by persons acting in an official capacity;

(b) To ensure that any person claiming such a remedy shall have his right thereto determined by competent judicial, administrative or legislative authorities, or by any other competent authority provided for by the legal system of the State, and to develop the possibilities of judicial remedy;

(c) To ensure that the competent authorities shall enforce such remedies when granted.

Article 3

The States Parties to the present Covenant undertake to ensure the equal right of men and women to the enjoyment of all civil and political rights set forth in the present Covenant.

Article 4

1. In time of public emergency which threatens the life of the nation and the existence of which is officially proclaimed, the States Parties to the present Covenant may take measures derogating from their obligations under the present Covenant to the extent strictly required by the exigencies of the situation, provided that such measures are not inconsistent with their other obligations under international law and do not involve discrimination solely on the ground of race, colour, sex, language, religion or social origin.

2. No derogation from articles 6, 7, 8 (paragraphs 1 and 2), 11, 15, 16 and 18 may be made under this provision.

3. Any State Party to the present Covenant availing itself of the right of derogation shall immediately inform the other States Parties to the present Covenant, through the intermediary of the Secretary-General of the United Nations, of the provisions from which it has derogated and of the reasons by which it was actuated. A further communication shall be made, through the same intermediary, on the date on which it terminates such derogation.

Article 5

1. Nothing in the present Covenant may be interpreted as implying for any State, group or person any right to engage in any activity or perform any act aimed at the destruction of any of the rights and freedoms recognized herein or at their limitation to a greater extent than is provided for in the present Covenant.

2. There shall be no restriction upon or derogation from any of the funda-

mental human rights recognized or existing in any State Party to the present Covenant pursuant to law, conventions, regulations or custom on the pretext that the present Covenant does not recognize such rights or that it recognizes them to a lesser extent.

PART III

Article 6

1. Every human being has the inherent right to life. This right shall be protected by law. No one shall be arbitrarily deprived of his life.

2. In countries which have not abolished the death penalty, sentence of death may be imposed only for the most serious crimes in accordance with the law in force at the time of the commission of the crime and not contrary to the provisions of the present Covenant and to the Convention on the Prevention and Punishment of the Crime of Genocide. This penalty can only be carried out pursuant to a final judgement rendered by a competent court.

3. When deprivation of life constitutes the crime of genocide, it is understood that nothing in this article shall authorize any State Party to the present Covenant to derogate in any way from any obligation assumed under the provisions of the Convention on the Prevention and Punishment of the Crime of Genocide.

4. Anyone sentenced to death shall have the right to seek pardon or commutation of the sentence. Amnesty, pardon or commutation of the sentence of death may be granted in all cases.

5. Sentence of death shall not be imposed for crimes committed by persons below eighteen years of age and shall not be carried out on pregnant women.

6. Nothing in this article shall be invoked to delay or to prevent the abolition of capital punishment by any State Party to the present Covenant.

Article 7

No one shall be subjected to torture or to cruel, inhuman or degrading treatment or punishment. In particular, no one shall be subjected without his free consent to medical or scientific experimentation.

Article 8

1. No one shall be held in slavery; slavery and the slave-trade in all their forms shall be prohibited.

2. No one shall be held in servitude.

3. (a) No one shall be required to perform forced or compulsory labour;

(b) Paragraph 3 (a) shall not be held to preclude, in countries where imprisonment with hard labour may be imposed as a punishment for a crime, the performance of hard labour in pursuance of a sentence to such punishment by a competent court;

(c) For the purpose of this paragraph the term "forced or compulsory labour" shall not include:

(i) Any work or service, not referred to in sub-paragraph (b), normally required of a person who is under detention in consequence of a lawful order of a court, or of a person during conditional release from such detention;

(ii) Any service of a military character and, in countries where conscientious objection is recognized, any national service required by law of conscientious objectors;

(iii) Any service exacted in cases of emergency or calamity threatening the life or well-being of the community;

(iv) Any work or service which forms part of normal civil obligations.

Article 9

1. Everyone has the right to liberty and security of person. No one shall be subjected to arbitrary arrest or detention. No one shall be deprived of his liberty except on such grounds and in accordance with such procedures as are established by law.

2. Anyone who is arrested shall be informed, at the time of arrest, of the reason for his arrest and shall be promptly informed of any charges against him.

3. Anyone arrested or detained on a criminal charge shall be brought promptly before a judge or other officer authorized by law to exercise judicial power and shall be entitled to trial within a reasonable time or to release. It shall not be the general rule that persons awaiting trial shall be detained in custody, but release may be subject to guarantees to appear for trial, at any other stage of the judicial proceedings, and, should occasion arise, for execution of the judgement.

4. Anyone who is deprived of his liberty by arrest or detention shall be entitled to take proceedings before a court, in order that that court may decide without delay on the lawfulness of his detention and order his release if the detention is not lawful.

5. Anyone who has been the victim of unlawful arrest or detention shall have an enforceable right to compensation.

Article 10

1. All persons deprived of their liberty shall be treated with humanity and with respect for the inherent dignity of the human person.

2. (a) Accused persons shall, save in exceptional circumstances, be segregated from convicted persons and shall be subject to separate treatment appropriate to their status as unconvicted persons;

(b) Accused juvenile persons shall be separated from adults and brought as speedily as possible for adjudication.

3. The penitentiary system shall comprise treatment of prisoners the essential aim of which shall be their reformation and social rehabilitation. Juvenile offenders shall be segregated from adults and be accorded treatment appropriate to their age and legal status.

Article 11

No one shall be imprisoned merely on the ground of inability to fulfil a contractual obligation.

Article 12

1. Everyone lawfully within the territory of a State shall, within that

territory, have the right to liberty of movement and freedom to choose his residence.

2. Everyone shall be free to leave any country, including his own.

3. The above-mentioned rights shall not be subject to any restrictions except those which are provided by law, are necessary to protect national security, public order (*ordre public*), public health or morals or the rights and freedoms of others, and are consistent with the other rights recognized in the present Covenant.

4. No one shall be arbitrarily deprived of the right to enter his own country.

Article 13

An alien lawfully in the territory of a State Party to the present Covenant may be expelled therefrom only in pursuance of a decision reached in accordance with law and shall, except where compelling reasons of national security otherwise require, be allowed to submit the reasons against his expulsion and to have his case reviewed by, and be represented for the purpose before, the competent authority or a person or persons especially designated by the competent authority.

Article 14

1. All persons shall be equal before the courts and tribunals. In the determination of any criminal charge against him, or of his rights and obligations in a suit at law, everyone shall be entitled to a fair and public hearing by a competent, independent and impartial tribunal established by law. The Press and the public may be excluded from all or part of a trial for reasons of morals, public order (*ordre public*) or national security in a democratic society, or when the interest of the private lives of the parties so requires, or to the extent strictly necessary in the opinion of the court in special circumstances where publicity would prejudice the interests of justice; but any judgement rendered in a criminal case or in a suit at law shall be made public except where the interest of juvenile persons otherwise requires or the proceedings concern matrimonial disputes or the guardianship of children.

2. Everyone charged with a criminal offence shall have the right to be presumed innocent until proved guilty according to law.

3. In the determination of any criminal charge against him, everyone shall be entitled to the following minimum guarantees, in full equality:

(a) To be informed promptly and in detail in a language which he understands of the nature and cause of the charge against him;

(b) To have adequate time and facilities for the preparation of his defence and to communicate with counsel of his own choosing;

(c) To be tried without undue delay;

(d) To be tried in his presence, and to defend himself in person or through legal assistance of his own choosing; to be informed, if he does not have legal assistance, of this right; and to have legal assistance assigned to him, in any case where the interests of justice so require, and without payment by him in any such case if he does not have sufficient means to pay for it;

(e) To examine, or have examined, the witnesses against him and to obtain the attendance and examination of witnesses on his behalf under the same conditions as witnesses against him;

(f) To have the free assistance of an interpreter if he cannot understand or speak the language used in court;

(g) Not to be compelled to testify against himself or to confess guilt.

4. In the case of juvenile persons, the procedure shall be such as will take account of their age and the desirability of promoting their rehabilitation.

5. Everyone convicted of a crime shall have the right to his conviction and sentence being reviewed by a higher tribunal according to law.

6. When a person has by a final decision been convicted of a criminal offence and when subsequently his conviction has been reversed or he has been pardoned on the ground that a new or newly discovered fact shows conclusively that there has been a miscarriage of justice, the person who has suffered punishment as a result of such conviction shall be compensated according to law, unless it is proved that the non-disclosure of the unknown fact in time is wholly or partly attributable to him.

7. No one shall be liable to be tried or punished again for an offence for which he has already been finally convicted or acquitted in accordance with the law and penal procedure of each country.

Article 15

1. No one shall be held guilty of any criminal offence on account of any act or omission which did not constitute a criminal offence, under national or international law, at the time when it was committed. Nor shall a heavier penalty be imposed than the one that was applicable at the time when the criminal offence was committed. If, subsequent to the commission of the offence, provision is made by law for the imposition of a lighter penalty, the offender shall benefit thereby.

2. Nothing in this article shall prejudice the trial and punishment of any person for any act or omission which, at the time when it was committed, was criminal according to the general principles of law recognized by the community of nations.

Article 16

Everyone shall have the right to recognition everywhere as a person before the law.

Article 17

1. No one shall be subjected to arbitrary or unlawful interference with his privacy, family, home or correspondence, nor to unlawful attacks on his honour and reputation.

2. Everyone has the right to the protection of the law against such interference or attacks.

Article 18

1. Everyone shall have the right to freedom of thought, conscience and religion. This right shall include freedom to have or to adopt a religion or belief of his choice, and freedom, either individually or in community with others and in public or private, to manifest his religion or belief in worship, observance, practice and teaching.

2. No one shall be subject to coercion which would impair his freedom to have or to adopt a religion or belief of his choice.

3. Freedom to manifest one's religion or beliefs may be subject only to such limitations as are prescribed by law and are necessary to protect public safety, order, health, or morals or the fundamental rights and freedoms of others.

4. The States Parties to the present Covenant undertake to have respect for the liberty of parents and, when applicable, legal guardians to ensure the religious and moral education of their children in conformity with their own convictions.

Article 19

1. Everyone shall have the right to hold opinions without interference.

2. Everyone shall have the right to freedom of expression; this right shall include freedom to seek, receive and impart information and ideas of all kinds, regardless of frontiers, either orally, in writing or in print, in the form of art, or through any other media of his choice.

3. The exercise of the rights provided for in paragraph 2 of this article carries with it special duties and responsibilities. It may therefore be subject to certain restrictions, but these shall only be such as are provided by law and are necessary:

(a) For respect of the rights or reputations of others;

(b) For the protection of national security or of public order (*ordre public*), or of public health or morals.

Article 20

1. Any propaganda for war shall be prohibited by law.

2. Any advocacy of national, racial or religious hatred that constitutes incitement to discrimination, hostility or violence shall be prohibited by law.

Article 21

The right of peaceful assembly shall be recognized. No restrictions may be placed on the exercise of this right other than those imposed in conformity with the law and which are necessary in a democratic society in the interests of national security or public safety, public order (*ordre public*), the protection of public health or morals or the protection of the rights and freedoms of others.

Article 22

1. Everyone shall have the right to freedom of association with others, including the right to form and join trade unions for the protection of his interests.

2. No restrictions may be placed on the exercise of this right other than those which are prescribed by law and which are necessary in a democratic society in the interests of national security or public safety, public order (*ordre public*), the protection of public health or morals or the protection of the rights and freedoms of others. This article shall not prevent the imposition of lawful restrictions on members of the armed forces and of the police in their exercise of this right.

3. Nothing in this article shall authorize States Parties to the International Labour Organisation Convention of 1948 concerning Freedom of Association and Protection of the Right to Organize to take legislative measures which would prejudice, or to apply the law in such a manner as to prejudice, the guarantees provided for in that Convention.

Article 23

1. The family is the natural and fundamental group unit of society and is entitled to protection by society and the State.

2. The right of men and women of marriageable age to marry and to found a family shall be recognized.

3. No marriage shall be entered into without the free and full consent of the intending spouses.

4. States Parties to the present Covenant shall take appropriate steps to ensure equality of rights and responsibilities of spouses as to marriage, during marriage and at its dissolution. In the case of dissolution, provision shall be made for the necessary protection of any children.

Article 24

1. Every child shall have, without any discrimination as to race, colour, sex, language, religion, national or social origin, property or birth, the right to such measures of protection as are required by his status as a minor, on the part of his family, society and the State.

2. Every child shall be registered immediately after birth and shall have a name.

3. Every child has the right to acquire a nationality.

Article 25

Every citizen shall have the right and the opportunity, without any of the distinctions mentioned in article 2 and without unreasonable restrictions:

(a) To take part in the conduct of public affairs, directly or through freely chosen representatives;

(b) To vote and to be elected at genuine periodic elections which shall be by universal and equal suffrage and shall be held by secret ballot, guaranteeing the free expression of the will of the electors;

(c) To have access, on general terms of equality, to public service in his country.

Article 26

All persons are equal before the law and are entitled without any discrimination to the equal protection of the law. In this respect, the law shall prohibit any discrimination and guarantee to all persons equal and effective protection against discrimination on any ground such as race, colour, sex, language, religion, political or other opinion, national or social origin, property, birth or other status.

Article 27

In those States in which ethnic, religious or linguistic minorities exist, persons belonging to such minorities shall not be denied the right, in community with the other members of their group, to enjoy their own culture, to profess and practice their own religion, or to use their own language.

PART IV

Article 28

1. There shall be established a Human Rights Committee (hereafter referred to in the present Covenant as the Committee). It shall consist of eighteen members and shall carry out the functions hereinafter provided.

2. The Committee shall be composed of nationals of the States Parties to the present Covenant who shall be persons of high moral character and recognized competence in the field of human rights, consideration being given to the usefulness of the participation of some persons having legal experience.

3. The members of the Committee shall be elected and shall serve in their personal capacity.

Article 29

1. The members of the Committee shall be elected by secret ballot from a list of persons possessing the qualifications prescribed in article 28 and nominated for the purpose by the State Parties to the present Covenant.

2. Each State Party to the present Covenant may nominate not more than two persons. These persons shall be nationals of the nominating State.

3. A person shall be eligible for renomination.

Article 30

1. The initial election shall be held no later than six months after the date of the entry into force of the present Covenant.

2. At least four months before the date of each election to the Committee, other than an election to fill a vacancy declared in accordance with article 34, the Secretary-General of the United Nations shall address a written invitation to the States Parties to the present Covenant to submit their nominations for membership of the Committee within three months.

3. The Secretary-General of the United Nations shall prepare a list in alphabetical order of all the persons thus nominated, with an indication of the States Parties which have nominated them, and shall submit it to the States Parties to the present Covenant no later than one month before the date of each election.

4. Elections of the members of the Committee shall be held at a meeting of the States Parties to the present Covenant convened by the Secretary-General of the United Nations at the Headquarters of the United Nations. At that meeting, for which two thirds of the States Parties to the present Covenant shall constitute a quorum, the persons elected to the Committee shall be those nominees who obtain the largest number of votes and an absolute majority of the votes of the representatives of States Parties present and voting.

Article 31

1. The Committee may not include more than one national of the same State.

2. In the election of the Committee, consideration shall be given to equitable geographical distribution of membership and to the representation of the different forms of civilization and of the principal legal systems.

Article 32

1. The members of the Committee shall be elected for a term of four years. They shall be eligible for re-election if renominated. However, the terms of nine of the members elected at the first election shall expire at the end of two years; immediately after the first election, the names of these nine members shall be chosen by lot by the Chairman of the meeting referred to in article 30, paragraph 4.

2. Elections at the expiry of office shall be held in accordance with the preceding articles of this part of the present Covenant.

Article 33

1. If, in the unanimous opinion of the other members, a member of the Committee has ceased to carry out his functions for any cause other than absence of a temporary character, the Chairman of the Committee shall notify the Secretary-General of the United Nations, who shall then declare the seat of that member to be vacant.

2. In the event of the death or the resignation of a member to the Committee, the Chairman shall immediately notify the Secretary-General of the United Nations, who shall declare the seat vacant from the date of death or the date on which the resignation takes effect.

Article 34

1. When a vacancy is declared in accordance with article 33 and if the term of office of the member to be replaced does not expire within six months of the declaration of the vacancy, the Secretary-General of the United Nations shall notify each of the States Parties to the present Covenant, which may within two months submit nominations in accordance with article 29 for the purpose of filling the vacancy.

2. The Secretary-General of the United Nations shall prepare a list in alphabetical order of the persons thus nominated and shall submit it to the States Parties to the present Covenant. The election to fill the vacancy shall then take place in accordance with the relevant provisions of this part of the present Covenant.

3. A member of the Committee elected to fill a vacancy declared in accordance with article 33 shall hold office for the remainder of the term of the member who vacated the seat on the Committee under the provisions of that article.

Article 35

The members of the Committee shall, with the approval of the General Assembly of the United Nations, receive emoluments from United Nations resources on such terms and conditions as the General Assembly may decide, having regard to the importance of the Committee's responsibilities.

Article 36

The Secretary-General of the United Nations shall provide the necessary staff and facilities for the effective performance of the functions of the Committee under the present Covenant.

Article 37

1. The Secretary-General of the United Nations shall convene the initial meeting of the Committee at the Headquarters of the United Nations.

2. After its initial meeting, the Committee shall meet at such times as shall be provided in its rules of procedure.

3. The Committee shall normally meet at the Headquarters of the United Nations or at the United Nations Office at Geneva.

Article 38

Every member of the Committee shall, before taking up his duties, make a solemn declaration in open committee that he will perform his functions impartially and conscientiously.

Article 39

1. The Committee shall elect its officers for a term of two years. They may be re-elected.

2. The Committee shall establish its own rules of procedure, but these rules shall provide, *inter alia*, that:

(a) Twelve members shall constitute a quorum;

(b) Decisions of the Committee shall be made by a majority vote of the members present.

Article 40

1. The States Parties to the present Covenant undertake to submit reports on the measures they have adopted which give effect to the rights recognized herein and on the progress made in the enjoyment of those rights:

(a) Within one year of the entry into force of the present Covenant for the States Parties concerned;

(b) Thereafter whenever the Committee so requests.

2. All reports shall be submitted to the Secretary-General of the United Nations, who shall transmit them to the Committee for consideration. Reports shall indicate the factors and difficulties, if any, affecting the implementation of the present Covenant.

3. The Secretary-General of the United Nations may, after consultation with the Committee, transmit to the specialized agencies concerned copies of such parts of the reports as may fall within their field of competence.

4. The Committee shall study the reports submitted by the States Parties to the present Covenant. It shall transmit its reports, and such general comments as it may consider appropriate, to the States Parties. The Committee may also transmit to the Economic and Social Council these comments along with the copies of the reports it has received from States Parties to the present Covenant.

5. The States Parties to the present Covenant may submit to the Committee observations on any comments that may be made in accordance with paragraph 4 of this article.

Article 41

1. A State Party to the present Covenant may at any time declare under this article that it recognizes the competence of the Committee to receive and consider communications to the effect that a State Party claims that another State Party is not fulfilling its obligations under the present Covenant. Communications under this article may be received and considered only if submitted by a State Party which has made a declaration recognizing in regard to itself the competence of the Committee. No communication shall be received by the Committee if it concerns a State Party which has not made such a declaration. Communications received under this article shall be dealt with in accordance with the following procedure:

(a) If a State Party to the present Covenant considers that another State Party is not giving effect to the provisions of the present Covenant, it may, by written communication, bring the matter to the attention of that State Party. Within three months after the receipt of the communication, the receiving State shall afford the State which sent the communication an explanation or any other statement in writing clarifying the matter, which should include, to the extent possible and pertinent, reference to domestic procedures and remedies taken, pending, or available in the matter.

(b) If the matter is not adjusted to the satisfaction of both States Parties concerned within six months after the receipt by the receiving State of the initial communication, either State shall have the right to refer the matter to the Committee, by notice given to the Committee and to the other State.

(c) The Committee shall deal with a matter referred to it only after it has ascertained that all available domestic remedies have been invoked and exhausted in the matter, in conformity with the generally recognized principles of international law. This shall not be the rule where the application of the remedies is unreasonably prolonged.

(d) The Committee shall hold closed meetings when examining communications under this article.

(e) Subject to the provisions of sub-paragraph (c), the Committee shall make available its good offices to the States Parties concerned with a view to a friendly solution of the matter on the basis of respect for human rights and fundamental freedoms as recognized in the present Covenant.

(f) In any matter referred to it, the Committee may call upon the States Parties concerned, referred to in sub-paragraph (b), to supply any relevant information.

(g) The States Parties concerned, referred to in sub-paragraph (b), shall have the right to be represented when the matter is being considered in the Committee and to make submissions orally and/or in writing.

(h) The Committee shall, within twelve months after the date of receipt of notice under sub-paragraph (b), submit a report:

(i) If a solution within the terms of sub-paragraph (e) is reached, the Committee shall confine its report to a brief statement of the facts and of the solution reached;

(ii) If a solution within the terms of sub-paragraph (e) is not reached, the Committee shall confine its report to a brief statement of the facts; the written submissions and record of the oral submissions made by the States Parties concerned shall be attached to the report.

In every matter, the report shall be communicated to the States Parties concerned.

2. The provisions of this article shall come into force when ten States Parties to the present Covenant have made declarations under paragraph 1 of this article. Such declarations shall be deposited by the States Parties with the Secretary-General of the United Nations, who shall transmit copies thereof to the other States Parties. A declaration may be withdrawn at any time by notification to the Secretary-General. Such a withdrawal shall not prejudice the consideration of any matter which is the subject of a communication already transmitted under this article; no further communication by any State Party shall be received after the notification of withdrawal of the declaration has been received by the Secretary-General, unless the State Party concerned has made a new declaration.

Article 42

1. (*a*) If a matter referred to the Committee in accordance with article 41 is not resolved to the satisfaction of the States Parties concerned, the Committee may, with the prior consent of the States Parties concerned, appoint an *ad hoc* Conciliation Commission (hereinafter referred to as the Commission). The good offices of the Commission shall be made available to the States Parties concerned with a view to an amicable solution of the matter on the basis of respect for the present Covenant;

(*b*) The Commission shall consist of five persons acceptable to the States Parties concerned. If the States Parties concerned fail to reach agreement within three months on all or part of the composition of the Commission, the members of the Commission concerning whom no agreement has been reached shall be elected by secret ballot by a two-thirds majority vote of the Committee from among its members.

2. The members of the Commission shall serve in their personal capacity. They shall not be nationals of the States Parties concerned, or of a State not party to the present Covenant, or of a State Party which has not made a declaration under article 41.

3. The Commission shall elect its own Chairman and adopt its own rules of procedure.

4. The meetings of the Commission shall normally be held at the Headquarters of the United Nations or at the United Nations Office at Geneva. However, they may be held at such other convenient places as the Commission may determine in consultation with the Secretary-General of the United Nations and the States Parties concerned.

5. The secretariat provided in accordance with article 36 shall also service the commissions appointed under this article.

6. The information received and collated by the Committee shall be made available to the Commission and the Commission may call upon the States Parties concerned to supply any other relevant information.

7. When the Commission has fully considered the matter, but in any event not later than twelve months after having been seized of the matter, it shall submit to the Chairman of the Committee a report for communication to the States Parties concerned:

(*a*) If the Commission is unable to complete its consideration of the matter within twelve months, it shall confine its report to a brief statement of the status of its consideration of the matter;

(*b*) If an amicable solution to the matter on the basis of respect for human rights as recognized in the present Covenant is reached, the Commission shall confine its report to a brief statement of the facts and of the solution reached;

(*c*) If a solution within the terms of sub-paragraph (*b*) is not reached, the Commission's report shall embody its findings on all questions of fact relevant to the issues between the States Parties concerned, and its views on the possibilities of an amicable solution of the matter. This report shall also contain the written submissions and a record of the oral submissions made by the States Parties concerned;

(*d*) If the Commission's report is submitted under sub-paragraph (*c*), the States Parties concerned shall, within three months of the receipt of the report, notify the Chairman of the Committee whether or not they accept the contents of the report of the Commission.

8. The provisions of this article are without prejudice to the responsibilities of the Committee under article 41.

9. The States Parties concerned shall share equally all the expenses of the members of the Commission in accordance with estimates to be provided by the Secretary-General of the United Nations.

10. The Secretary-General of the United Nations shall be empowered to pay the expenses of the members of the Commission, if necessary, before reimbursement by the States Parties concerned, in accordance with paragraph 9 of this article.

Article 43

The members of the Committee, and of the *ad hoc* conciliation commissions which may be appointed under article 42, shall be entitled to the facilities, privileges and immunities of experts on mission for the United Nations as laid down in the relevant sections of the Convention on the Privileges and Immunities of the United Nations.

Article 44

The provisions for the implementation of the present Covenant shall apply without prejudice to the procedures prescribed in the field of human rights by or under the constituent instruments and the conventions of the United Nations and of the specialized agencies and shall not prevent the States Parties to the present Covenant from having recourse to other procedures for settling a dispute in accordance with general or special international agreements in force between them.

Article 45

The Committee shall submit to the General Assembly of the United Nations, through the Economic and Social Council, an annual report on its activities.

PART V

Article 46

Nothing in the present Covenant shall be interpreted as impairing the provisions of the Charter of the United Nations and of the constitutions of the specialized agencies which define the respective responsibilities of the various organs of the United Nations and of the specialized agencies in regard to the matters dealt within the present Covenant.

Article 47

Nothing in the present Covenant shall be interpreted as impairing the inherent right of all peoples to enjoy and utilize fully and freely their natural wealth and resources.

PART VI

Article 48

1. The present Covenant is open for signature by any State Member of the United Nations or member of any of its specialized agencies, by any State Party to the Statute of the International Court of Justice, and by any other State which has been invited by the General Assembly of the United Nations to become a party to the present Covenant.

2. The present Covenant is subject to ratification. Instruments of ratification shall be deposited with the Secretary-General of the United Nations.

3. The present Covenant shall be open to accession by any State referred to in paragraph 1 of this article.

4. Accession shall be effected by the deposit of an instrument of accession with the Secretary-General of the United Nations.

5. The Secretary-General of the United Nations shall inform all States which have signed this Covenant or acceded to it of the deposit of each instrument of ratification or accession.

Article 49

1. The present Covenant shall enter into force three months after the date of the deposit with the Secretary-General of the United Nations of the thirty-fifth instrument of ratification or instrument of accession.

2. For each State ratifying the present Covenant or acceding to it after the deposit of the thirty-fifth instrument of ratification or instrument of accession, the present Covenant shall enter into force three months after the date of the deposit of its own instrument of ratification or instrument of accession.

Article 50

The provisions of the present Covenant shall extend to all parts of federal States without any limitations or exceptions.

Article 51

1. Any State Party to the present Covenant may propose an amendment and file it with the Secretary-General of the United Nations. The Secretary-General of the United Nations shall thereupon communicate any proposed amendments to the States Parties to the present Covenant with a request that they notify him whether they favour a conference of States Parties for the purpose of considering and voting upon the proposals. In the event that at least one third of the States Parties favours such a conference, the Secretary-General shall convene the conference under the auspices of the United Nations. Any amendment adopted by a majority of the States Parties present and voting at the conference shall be submitted to the General Assembly of the United Nations for approval.

2. Amendments shall come into force when they have been approved by the General Assembly of the United Nations and accepted by a two-thirds majority of the States Parties to the present Covenant in accordance with their respective constitutional processes.

3. When amendments come into force, they shall be binding on those States Parties which have accepted them, other States Parties still being bound by the provisions of the present Covenant and any earlier amendment which they have accepted.

Article 52

Irrespective of the notifications made under article 48, paragraph 5, the Secretary-General of the United Nations shall inform all States referred to in paragraph 1 of the same article of the following particulars:

(a) Signatures, ratifications and accessions under article 48;

(b) The date of the entry into force of the present Covenant under article 49 and the date of the entry into force of any amendments under article 51.

Article 53

1. The present Covenant, of which the Chinese, English, French, Russian and Spanish texts are equally authentic, shall be deposited in the archives of the United Nations.

2. The Secretary-General of the United Nations shall transmit certified copies of the present Covenant to all States referred to in article 48.

Optional Protocol to the International Covenant on Civil and Political Rights

[Adopted by General Assembly resolution 2200 A (XXI) of December 16, 1966. 21 GOAR Supp. (No. 16) 59, U.N. Doc. 6316 (1966). Entry into Force: March 23, 1976.]

The States Parties to the present Protocol,

Considering that in order further to achieve the purposes of the Covenant on Civil and Political Rights (hereinafter referred to as the Covenant) and the implementation of its provisions it would be appropriate to enable the Human Rights Committee set up in part IV of the Covenant (hereinafter referred to as the Committee) to receive and consider, as provided in the present Protocol, communications from individuals claiming to be victims of violations of any of the rights set forth in the Covenant,

Have agreed as follows:

Article 1

A State Party to the Covenant that becomes a party to the present Protocol recognizes the competence of the Committee to receive and consider communications from individuals subject to its jurisdiction who claim to be victims of a violation by that State Party of any of the rights set forth in the Covenant. No communication shall be received by the Committee if it concerns a State Party to the Covenant which is not a party to the present Protocol.

Article 2

Subject to the provisions of article 1, individuals who claim that any of their rights enumerated in the Covenant have been violated and who have exhausted all available domestic remedies may submit a written communication to the Committee for consideration.

Article 3

The Committee shall consider inadmissible any communication under the present Protocol which is anonymous, or which it considers to be an abuse of the right of submission of such communications or to be incompatible with the provisions of the Covenant.

Article 4

1. Subject to the provisions of article 3, the Committee shall bring any communications submitted to it under the present Protocol to the attention of the State Party to the present Protocol alleged to be violating any provision of the Covenant.

2. Within six months, the receiving State shall submit to the Committee written explanations or statements clarifying the matter and the remedy, if any, that may have been taken by that State.

Article 5

1. The Committee shall consider communications received under the present Protocol in the light of all written information made available to it by the individual and by the State Party concerned.

2. The Committee shall not consider any communication from an individual unless it has ascertained that:

(*a*) The same matter is not being examined under another procedure of international investigation or settlement;

(*b*) The individual has exhausted all available domestic remedies. This shall not be the rule where the application of the remedies is unreasonably prolonged.

3. The Committee shall hold closed meetings when examining communications under the present Protocol.

4. The Committee shall forward its views to the State Party concerned and to the individual.

Article 6

The Committee shall include in its annual report under article 45 of the Covenant a summary of its activities under the present Protocol.

Article 7

Pending the achievement of the objectives of resolution 1514 (XV) adopted by the General Assembly of the United Nations on 14 December 1960 concerning the Declaration on the Granting of Independence to Colonial Countries and Peoples, the provisions of the present Protocol shall in no way limit the right of petition granted to these peoples by the Charter of the United Nations and other international conventions and instruments under the United Nations and its specialized agencies.

Article 8

1. The present Protocol is open for signature by any State which has signed the Covenant.

2. The present Protocol is subject to ratification by any State which has ratified or acceded to the Covenant. Instruments of ratification shall be deposited with the Secretary-General of the United Nations.

3. The present Protocol shall be open to accession by any State which has ratified or acceded to the Covenant.

4. Accession shall be effected by the deposit of an instrument of accession with the Secretary-General of the United Nations.

5. The Secretary-General of the United Nations shall inform all States which have signed the present Protocol or acceded to it of the deposit of each instrument of ratification or accession.

Article 9

1. Subject to the entry into force of the Covenant, the present Protocol shall enter into force three months after the date of the deposit with the Secretary-General of the United Nations of the tenth instrument of ratification or instrument of accession.

2. For each State ratifying the present Protocol or acceding to it after the deposit of the tenth instrument of ratification or instrument of accession, the present Protocol shall enter into force three months after the date of the deposit of its own instrument of ratification or instrument of accession.

Article 10

The provisions of the present Protocol shall extend to all parts of federal States without any limitations or exceptions.

Article 11

1. Any State Party to the present Protocol may propose an amendment and file it with the Secretary-General of the United Nations. The Secretary-General shall thereupon communicate any proposed amendments to the States Parties to the present Protocol with a request that they notify him whether they favour a conference of States Parties for the purpose of considering and voting upon the proposal. In the event that at least one third of the States Parties favours such a conference, the Secretary-General shall convene the conference under the auspices of the United Nations. Any amendment adopted by a majority of the States Parties present and voting at the conference shall be submitted to the General Assembly of the United Nations for approval.

2. Amendments shall come into force when they have been approved by the General Assembly of the United Nations and accepted by a two-thirds majority of the States Parties to the present Protocol in accordance with their respective constitutional processes.

3. When amendments come into force, they shall be binding on those States Parties which have accepted them, other States Parties still being bound by the provisions of the present Protocol and any earlier amendment which they have accepted.

Article 12

1. Any State Party may denounce the present Protocol at any time by written notification addressed to the Secretary-General of the United Nations. Denunciation shall take effect three months after the date of receipt of the notification by the Secretary-General.

2. Denunciation shall be without prejudice to the continued application of the provisions of the present Protocol to any communication submitted under article 2 before the effective date of denunciation.

Article 13

Irrespective of the notifications made under article 8, paragraph 5, of the present Protocol, the Secretary-General of the United Nations shall inform all States referred to in article 48, paragraph 1, of the Covenant of the following particulars:

(a) Signatures, ratifications and accessions under article 8;
(b) The date of the entry into force of the present Protocol under article 9 and the date of the entry into force of any amendments under article 11;
(c) Denunciations under article 12.

Article 14

1. The present Protocol, of which the Chinese, English, French, Russian and Spanish texts are equally authentic, shall be deposited in the archives of the United Nations.

2. The Secretary-General of the United Nations shall transmit certified copies of the present Protocol to all States referred to in article 48 of the Covenant.

342

APPENDIX C
CONVENTION ON THE RIGHTS OF THE CHILD

Convention on the Rights of the Child

[Adopted by General Assembly resolution 44/25 on November 20, 1989.
28 I. L. M. 1448. 44 U.N. GAOR Supp. (no. 49), 165 U.N. Doc. A/44/736(1989).]

PREAMBLE

The States Parties to the present Convention,

Considering that, in accordance with the principles proclaimed in the Charter of the United Nations, recognition of the inherent dignity and of the equal and inalienable rights of all members of the human family is the foundation of freedom, justice and peace in the world,

Bearing in mind that the peoples of the United Nations have, in the Charter, reaffirmed their faith in fundamental human rights and in the dignity and worth of the human person, and have determined to promote social progress and better standards of life in larger freedom,

Recognizing that the United Nations has, in the Universal Declaration of Human Rights and in the International Covenants on Human Rights, proclaimed and agreed that everyone is entitled to all the rights and freedoms set forth therein, without distinction of any kind, such as race, colour, sex, language, religion, political or other opinion, national or social origin, property, birth or other status,

Recalling that, in the Universal Declaration of Human Rights, the United Nations has proclaimed that childhood is entitled to special care and assistance,

Convinced that the family, as the fundamental group of society and the natural environment for the growth and well-being of all its members and particularly children, should be afforded the necessary protection and assistance so that it can fully assume its responsibilities within the community,

Recognizing that the child, for the full and harmonious development of his or her personality, should grow up in a family environment, in an atmosphere of happiness, love and understanding,

Considering that the child should be fully prepared to live in an individual life in society, and brought up in the spirit of the ideals proclaimed in the Charter of the United Nations, and in particular in the spirit of peace, dignity, tolerance, freedom, equality and solidarity.

Bearing in mind that the need to extend particular care to the child has been stated in the Geneva Declaration of the Rights of the Child of 1924 and in the Declaration of the Rights of the Child adopted by the General Assembly on 20 November 1959 and recognized in the Universal Declaration of Human Rights, in the International Covenant on Civil and Political Rights (in particular in articles 23 and 24), in the International Covenant on Economic, Social and Cultural Rights (in particular in article 10) and in the statutes and relevant instruments of specialized agencies and international organizations concerned with the welfare of children,

Bearing in mind that, as indicated in the Declaration of the Rights of the Child, "the child, by reason of his physical and mental immaturity, needs special safeguards and care, including appropriate legal protection, before as well as after birth,"

Recalling the provisions of the Declaration on Social and Legal Principles relating to the Protection and Welfare of Children, with Special Reference to Foster Placement and Adoption Nationally and Internationally; the United Nations Standard Minimum Rules for the Administration of Juvenile Justice (The Beijing Rules); 8/ and the Declaration on the Protection of Women and Children in Emergency and Armed Conflict,

Recognizing that, in all countries in the world, there are children living in exceptionally difficult conditions, and that such children need special consideration,

Taking due account of the importance of the traditions and cultural values of each people for the protection and harmonious development of the child,

Recognizing the importance of international co-operation for improving the living conditions of children in every country, in particular in the developing countries,

Have agreed as follows:

PART I

Article 1

For the purposes of the present Convention, a child means every human being below the age of eighteen years unless, under the law applicable to the child, majority is attained earlier.

Article 2

1. States Parties shall respect and ensure the rights set forth in the present Convention to each child within their jurisdiction without discrimination of any kind, irrespective of the child's or his or her parent's or legal guardian's race, colour, sex, language, religion, political or other opinion, national, ethnic or social origin, property, disability, birth or other status.

2. States Parties shall take all appropriate measures to ensure that the child is protected against all forms of discrimination or punishment on the basis of the status, activities, expressed opinions, or beliefs of the child's parents, legal guardians, or family members.

Article 3

1. In all actions concerning children, whether undertaken by public or private social welfare institutions, courts of law, administrative authorities or legislative bodies, the best interests of the child shall be a primary consideration.

2. States Parties undertake to ensure the child such protection and care as is necessary for his or her well-being, taking into account the rights and duties of his or her parents, legal guardians, or other individuals legally responsible for him or her, and, to this end, shall take all appropriate legislative and administrative measures.

3. States Parties shall ensure that the institutions, services and facilities responsible for the care or protection of children shall conform with the standards

established by competent authorities, particularly in the areas of safety, health, in the number and suitability of their staff, as well as competent supervision.

Article 4

States Parties shall undertake all appropriate legislative, administrative, and other measures for the implementation of the rights recognized in the present Convention. With regard to economic, social and cultural rights, States Parties shall undertake such measures to the maximum extent of their available resources and, where needed, within the framework of international co-operation.

Article 5

States Parties shall respect the responsibilities, rights and duties of parents or, where applicable, the members of the extended family or community as provided for by local custom, legal guardians or other persons legally responsible for the child, to provide, in a manner consistent with the evolving capacities of the child, appropriate direction and guidance in the exercise by the child of the rights recognized in the present Convention.

Article 6

1. States Parties recognize that every child has the inherent right to life.

2. States Parties shall ensure to the maximum extent possible the survival and development of the child.

Article 7

1. The child shall be registered immediately after birth and shall have the right from birth to a name, the right to acquire a nationality and, as far as possible, the right to know and be cared for by his or her parents.

2. States Parties shall ensure the implementation of these rights in accordance with their national law and their obligations under the relevant international instruments in this field, in particular where the child would otherwise be stateless.

Article 8

1. States Parties undertake to respect the right of the child to preserve his or her identity, including nationality, name and family relations as recognized by law without unlawful interference.

2. Where a child is illegally deprived of some or all of the elements of his or her identity, States Parties shall provide appropriate assistance and protection, with a view to speedily re-establishing his or her identity.

Article 9

1. States Parties shall ensure that a child shall not be separated from his or her parents against their will, except when competent authorities subject to judicial review determine, in accordance with applicable law and procedures, that such separation is necessary for the best interests of the child. Such determination may be necessary in a particular case such as one involving abuse or

neglect of the child by the parents, or one where the parents are living separately and a decision must be made as to the child's place of residence.

2. In any proceedings pursuant to paragraph 1 of the present article, all interested parties shall be given an opportunity to participate in the proceedings and make their views known.

3. States Parties shall respect the right of the child who is separated from one or both parents to maintain personal relations and direct contact with both parents on a regular basis, except if it is contrary to the child's best interests.

4. Where such separation results from any action initiated by a State Party, such as the detention, imprisonment, exile, deportation or death (including death arising from any cause while the person is in the custody of the State) of one or both parents or of the child, that State Party shall, upon request, provide the parents, the child or, if appropriate, another member of the family with the essential information concerning the whereabouts of the absent member(s) of the family unless the provision of the information would be detrimental to the well-being of the child. States Parties shall further ensure that the submission of such a request shall of itself entail no adverse consequences for the person(s) concerned.

Article 10

1. In accordance with the obligation of the States Parties under article 9, paragraph 1, applications by a child or his or her parents to enter or leave a State Party for the purpose of family reunification shall be dealt with by States Parties in a positive, humane and expeditious manner. States Parties shall further ensure that the submission of such a request shall entail no adverse consequences for the applicants and for the members of their family.

2. A child whose parents reside in different States shall have the right to maintain on a regular basis, save in exceptional circumstances, personal relations and direct contacts with both parents. Towards that end and in accordance with the obligation of States Parties under article 9, paragraph 2, States Parties shall respect the right of the child and his or her parents to leave any country, including their own, and to enter their own country. The right to leave any country shall be subject only to such restrictions as are prescribed by law and which are necessary to protect the national security, public order (*ordre public*), public health or morals or the rights and freedoms of others and are consistent with the other rights recognized in the present Convention.

Article 11

1. States Parties shall take measures to combat the illicit transfer and non-return of children abroad.

2. To this end, States Parties shall promote the conclusion of bilateral or multilateral agreements or accession to existing agreements.

Article 12

1. States Parties shall assure to the child who is capable of forming his or her own views the right to express those views freely in all matters affecting the child, the views of the child being given due weight in accordance with the age and maturity of the child.

2. For this purpose, the child shall in particular be provided the opportunity to be heard in any judicial and administrative proceedings affecting the child, either directly, or through a representative or an appropriate body, in a manner consistent with the procedural rules of national law.

Article 13

1. The child shall have the right to freedom of expression; this right shall include freedom to seek, receive and impart information and ideas of all kinds, regardless of frontiers, either orally, in writing or in print, in the form of art, or through any other media of the child's choice.

2. The exercise of this right may be subject to certain restrictions, but these shall only be such as are provided by law and are necessary:

(a) For respect of the rights or reputations of others; or

(b) For the protection of national security or of public order (ordre public), or of public health or morals.

Article 14

1. States Parties shall respect the right of the child to freedom of thought, conscience and religion.

2. States Parties shall respect the rights and duties of the parents and, when applicable, legal guardians, to provide direction to the child in the exercise of his or her right in a manner consistent with the evolving capacities of the child.

3. Freedom to manifest one's religion or beliefs may be subject only to such limitations as are prescribed by law and are necessary to protect public safety, order, health or morals, or the fundamental rights and freedoms of others.

Article 15

1. States Parties recognize the rights of the child to freedom of association and to freedom of peaceful assembly.

2. No restrictions may be placed on the exercise of these rights other than those imposed in conformity with the law and which are necessary in a democratic society in the interests of national security or public safety, public order (ordre public), the protection of public health or morals or the protection of the rights and freedoms of others.

Article 16

1. No child shall be subjected to arbitrary or unlawful interference with his or her privacy, family, home or correspondence, nor to unlawful attacks on his or her honour and reputation.

2. The child has the right to the protection of the law against such interference or attacks.

Article 17

States Parties recognize the important function performed by the mass media and shall ensure that the child has access to information and material from a diversity of national and international sources, especially those aimed at the promotion of his or her social, spiritual and moral well-being and physical and mental health. To this end, States Parties shall:

(a) Encourage the mass media to disseminate information and material of social and cultural benefit to the child and in accordance with the spirit of article 29;

(b) Encourage international co-operation in the production, exchange and dissemination of such information and material from a diversity of cultural, national and international sources;

(c) Encourage the production and dissemination of children's books;

(d) Encourage the mass media to have particular regard to the linguistic needs of the child who belongs to a minority group or who is indigenous;

(e) Encourage the development of appropriate guidelines for the protection of the child from information and material injurious to his or her well-being, bearing in mind the provisions of articles 13 and 18.

Article 18

1. States Parties shall use their best efforts to ensure recognition of the principle that both parents have common responsibilities for the upbringing and development of the child. Parents or, as the case may be, legal guardians, have the primary responsibility for the upbringing and development of the child. The best interests of the child will be their basic concern.

2. For the purpose of guaranteeing and promoting the rights set forth in the present Convention, States Parties shall render appropriate assistance to parents and legal guardians in the performance of their child-rearing responsibilities and shall ensure the development of institutions, facilities and services for the care of children.

3. States Parties shall take all appropriate measures to ensure that children of working parents have the right to benefit from child-care services and facilities for which they are eligible.

Article 19

1. States Parties shall take all appropriate legislative, administrative, social and educational measures to protect the child from all forms of physical or mental violence, injury or abuse, neglect or negligent treatment, maltreatment or exploitation, including sexual abuse, while in the care of parent(s), legal guardian(s) or any other person who has the care of the child.

2. Such protective measures should, as appropriate, include effective procedures for the establishment of social programmes to provide necessary support for the child and for those who have the care of the child, as well as for other forms of prevention and for identification, reporting, referral, investigation, treatment and follow-up of instances of child maltreatment described heretofore, and, as appropriate, for judicial involvement.

Article 20

1. A child temporarily or permanently deprived of his or her family environment, or in whose own best interests cannot be allowed to remain in that environment, shall be entitled to special protection and assistance provided by the State.

2. States Parties shall in accordance with their national laws ensure alternative care for such a child.

3. Such care could include, *inter alia*, foster placement, *kafalah* of Islamic law, adoption or if necessary placement in suitable institutions for the care of children. When considering solutions, due regard shall be paid to the desirability of continuity in a child's upbringing and to the child's ethnic, religious, cultural and linguistic background.

Article 21

States Parties that recognize and/or permit the system of adoption shall ensure that the best interests of the child shall be the paramount consideration and they shall:

(*a*) Ensure that the adoption of a child is authorized only by competent authorities who determine, in accordance with applicable law and procedures and on the basis of all pertinent and reliable information, that the adoption is permissible in view of the child's status concerning parents, relatives and legal guardians and that, if required, the persons concerned have given their informed consent to the adoption on the basis of such counselling as may be necessary;

(*b*) Recognize that inter-country adoption may be considered as an alternative means of child's care, if the child cannot be placed in a foster or an adoptive family or cannot in any suitable manner be cared for in the child's country of origin;

(*c*) Ensure that the child concerned by inter-country adoption enjoys safeguards and standards equivalent to those existing in the case of national adoption;

(*d*) Take all appropriate measures to ensure that, in inter-country adoption, the placement does not result in improper financial gain for those involved in it;

(*e*) Promote, where appropriate, the objectives of the present article by concluding bilateral or multilateral arrangements or agreements, and endeavour, within this framework, to ensure that the placement of the child in another country is carried out by competent authorities or organs.

Article 22

1. States Parties shall take appropriate measures to ensure that a child who is seeking refugee status or who is considered a refugee in accordance with applicable international or domestic law and procedures shall, whether unaccompanied or accompanied by his or her parents or by any other person, receive appropriate protection and humanitarian assistance in the enjoyment of applicable rights set forth in the present Convention and in other international human rights or humanitarian instruments to which the said States are Parties.

2. For this purpose States Parties shall provide, as they consider appropriate, co-operation in any efforts by the United Nations and other competent intergovernmental organizations or non-governmental organizations co-operating with the United Nations to protect and assist such a child and to trace the parents or other members of the family of any refugee child in order to obtain information necessary for reunification with his or her family. In cases where no parents or other members of the family can be found, the child shall be accorded the same

protection as any other child permanently or temporarily deprived of his or her family environment for any reason, as set forth in the present Convention.

Article 23

1. States Parties recognize that a mentally or physically disabled child should enjoy a full and decent life, in conditions which ensure dignity, promote self-reliance and facilitate the child's active participation in the community.

2. States Parties recognize the right of the disabled child to special care and shall encourage and ensure the extension, subject to available resources, to the eligible child and those responsible for his or her care, of assistance for which application is made and which is appropriate to the child's condition and to the circumstances of the parents or others caring for the child.

3. Recognizing the special needs of a disabled child, assistance extended in accordance with paragraph 2 of the present article shall be provided free of charge, whenever possible, taking into account the financial resources of the parents or others caring for the child, and shall be designed to ensure that the disabled child has effective access to and receives education, training, health care services, rehabilitation services, preparation for employment and recreation opportunities in a manner conducive to the child's achieving the fullest possible social integration and individual development, including his or her cultural and spiritual development.

4. States Parties shall promote, in the spirit of international co-operation, the exchange of appropriate information in the field of preventive health care and of medical, psychological and functional treatment of disabled children, including dissemination of and access to information concerning methods of rehabilitation, education and vocational services, with the aim of enabling States Parties to improve their capabilities and skills and to widen their experience in these areas. In this regard, particular account shall be taken of the needs of developing countries.

Article 24

1. States Parties recognize the right of the child to the enjoyment of the highest attainable standard of health and to facilities for the treatment of illness and rehabilitation of health. States Parties shall strive to ensure that no child is deprived of his or her right of access to such health care services.

2. States Parties shall pursue full implementation of this right and, in particular, shall take appropriate measures:

(a) To diminish infant and child mortality;

(b) To ensure the provision of necessary medical assistance and health care to all children with emphasis on the development of primary health care;

(c) To combat disease and malnutrition, including within the framework of primary health care, through, *inter alia*, the application of readily available technology and through the provision of adequate nutritious foods and clean drinking-water, taking into consideration the dangers and risks of environmental pollution;

(d) To ensure appropriate pre-natal and post-natal health care for mothers;

(*e*) To ensure that all segments of society, in particular parents and children, are informed, have access to education and are supported in the use of basic knowledge of child health and nutrition, the advantages of breast-feeding, hygiene and environmental sanitation and the prevention of accidents;

(*f*) To develop preventive health care, guidance for parents and family planning education and services.

3. States Parties shall take all effective and appropriate measures with a view to abolishing traditional practices prejudicial to the health of children.

4. States Parties undertake to promote and encourage international co-operation with a view to achieving progressively the full realization of the right recognized in the present article. In this regard, particular account shall be taken of the needs of developing countries.

Article 25

States Parties recognize the right of a child who has been placed by the competent authorities for the purposes of care, protection or treatment of his or her physical or mental health, to a periodic review of the treatment provided to the child and all other circumstances relevant to his or her placement.

Article 26

1. States Parties shall recognize for every child the right to benefit from social security, including social insurance, and shall take the necessary measures to achieve the full realization of this right in accordance with their national law.

2. The benefits should, where appropriate, be granted, taking into account the resources and the circumstances of the child and persons having responsibility for the maintenance of the child, as well as any other consideration relevant to an application for benefits made by or on behalf of the child.

Article 27

1. States Parties recognize the right of every child to a standard of living adequate for the child's physical, mental, spiritual, moral and social development.

2. The parent(s) or others responsible for the child have the primary responsibility to secure, within their abilities and financial capacities, the conditions of living necessary for the child's development.

3. States Parties, in accordance with national conditions and within their means, shall take appropriate measures to assist parents and others responsible for the child to implement this right and shall in case of need provide material assistance and support programmes, particularly with regard to nutrition, clothing and housing.

4. States Parties shall take all appropriate measures to secure the recovery of maintenance for the child from the parents or other persons having financial responsibility for the child, both within the State Party and from abroad. In particular, where the person having financial responsibility for the child lives in a State different from that of the child, States Parties shall promote the accession to international agreements or the conclusion of such agreements, as well as the making of other appropriate arrangements.

Article 28

1. States Parties recognize the right of the child to education, and with a view to achieving this right progressively and on the basis of equal opportunity, they shall, in particular:

(a) Make primary education compulsory and available free to all;

(b) Encourage the development of different forms of secondary education, including general and vocational education, make them available and accessible to every child, and take appropriate measures such as the introduction of free education and offering financial assistance in case of need;

(c) Make higher education accessible to all on the basis of capacity by every appropriate means;

(d) Make educational and vocational information and guidance available and accessible to all children;

(e) Take measures to encourage regular attendance at schools and the reduction of drop-out rates.

2. States Parties shall take all appropriate measures to ensure that school discipline is administered in a manner consistent with the child's human dignity and in conformity with the present Convention.

3. States Parties shall promote and encourage international co-operation in matters relating to education, in particular with a view to contributing to the elimination of ignorance and illiteracy throughout the world and facilitating access to scientific and technical knowledge and modern teaching methods. In this regard, particular account shall be taken of the needs of developing countries.

Article 29

1. States Parties agree that the education of the child shall be directed to:

(a) The development of the child's personality, talents and mental and physical abilities to their fullest potential;

(b) The development of respect for human rights and fundamental freedoms, and for the principles enshrined in the Charter of the United Nations;

(c) The development of respect for the child's parents, his or her own cultural identity, language and values, for the national values of the country in which the child is living, the country from which he or she may originate, and for civilizations different from his or her own;

(d) The preparation of the child for responsible life in a free society, in the spirit of understanding, peace, tolerance, equality of sexes, and friendship among all peoples, ethnic, national and religious groups and persons of indigenous origin;

(e) The development of respect for the natural environment.

2. No part of the present article or article 28 shall be construed so as to interfere with the liberty of individuals and bodies to establish and direct educational institutions, subject always to the observance of the principles set forth in paragraph 1 of the present article and to the requirements that the education given in such institutions shall conform to such minimum standards as may be laid down by the State.

Article 30

In those States in which ethnic, religious or linguistic minorities or persons of indigenous origin exist, a child belonging to such a minority or who is indigenous shall not be denied the right, in community with other members of his or her group, to enjoy his or her own culture, to profess and practise his or her own religion, or to use his or her own language.

Article 31

1. States Parties recognize the right of the child to rest and leisure, to engage in play and recreational activities appropriate to the age of the child and to participate freely in cultural life and the arts.

2. States Parties shall respect and promote the right of the child to participate fully in cultural and artistic life and shall encourage the provision of appropriate and equal opportunities for cultural, artistic, recreational and leisure activity.

Article 32

1. States Parties recognize the right of the child to be protected from economic exploitation and from performing any work that is likely to be hazardous or to interfere with the child's education, or to be harmful to the child's health or physical, mental, spiritual, moral or social development.

2. States Parties shall take legislative, administrative, social and educational measures to ensure the implementation of the present article. To this end, and having regard to the relevant provisions of other international instruments, States Parties shall in particular:

(*a*) Provide for a minimum age or minimum ages for admission to employment;

(*b*) Provide for appropriate regulation of the hours and conditions of employment;

(*c*) Provide for appropriate penalties or other sanctions to ensure the effective enforcement of the present article.

Article 33

States Parties shall take all appropriate measures, including legislative, administrative, social and educational measures, to protect children from the illicit use of narcotic drugs and psychotropic substances as defined in the relevant international treaties, and to prevent the use of children in the illicit production and trafficking of such substances.

Article 34

States Parties undertake to protect the child from all forms of sexual exploitation and sexual abuse. For these purposes, States Parties shall in particular take all appropriate national, bilateral and multilateral measures to prevent:

(*a*) The inducement or coercion of a child to engage in any unlawful sexual activity;

(*b*) The exploitative use of children in prostitution or other unlawful sexual practices;

(*c*) The exploitative use of children in pornographic performances and materials.

Article 35

States Parties shall take all appropriate national, bilateral and multilateral measures to prevent the abduction of, the sale of or traffic in children for any purpose or in any form.

Article 36

States Parties shall protect the child against all other forms of exploitation prejudicial to any aspects of the child's welfare.

Article 37

States Parties shall ensure that:

(*a*) No child shall be subjected to torture or other cruel, inhuman or degrading treatment or punishment. Neither capital punishment nor life imprisonment without possibility of release shall be imposed for offences committed by persons below eighteen years of age;

(*b*) No child shall be deprived of his or her liberty unlawfully or arbitrarily. The arrest, detention or imprisonment of a child shall be in conformity with the law and shall be used only as a measure of last resort and for the shortest appropriate period of time;

(*c*) Every child deprived of liberty shall be treated with humanity and respect for the inherent dignity of the human person, and in a manner which takes into account the needs of persons of his or her age. In particular, every child deprived of liberty shall be separated from adults unless it is considered in the child's best interest not to do so and shall have the right to maintain contact with his or her family through correspondence and visits, save in exceptional circumstances;

(*d*) Every child deprived of his of her liberty shall have the right to prompt access to legal and other appropriate assistance, as well as the right to challenge the legality of the deprivation of his or her liberty before a court or other competent, independent and impartial authority, and to a prompt decision on any such action.

Article 38

1. States Parties undertake to respect and to ensure respect for rules of international humanitarian law applicable to them in armed conflicts which are relevant to the child.

2. States Parties shall take all feasible measures to ensure that persons who have not attained the age of fifteen years do not take a direct part in hostilities.

3. States Parties shall refrain form recruiting any person who has not attained the age of fifteen years into their armed forces. In recruiting among those persons who have attained the age of fifteen years but who have not attained the

age of eighteen years, States Parties shall endeavour to give priority to those who are oldest.

4. In accordance with their obligations under international humanitarian law to protect the civilian population in armed conflicts, States Parties shall take all feasible measures to ensure protection and care of children who are affected by an armed conflict.

Article 39

States Parties shall take all appropriate measures to promote physical and psychological recovery and social reintegration of a child victim of: any form of neglect, exploitation, or abuse; torture or any other form of cruel, inhuman or degrading treatment or punishment; or armed conflicts. Such recovery and reintegration shall take place in an environment which fosters the health, self-respect and dignity of the child.

Article 40

1. States Parties recognize the right of every child alleged as, accused of, or recognized as having infringed the penal law to be treated in a manner consistent with the promotion of the child's sense of dignity and worth, which reinforces the child's respect for the human rights and fundamental freedoms of others and which takes into account the child's age and the desirability of promoting the child's reintegration and the child's assuming a constructive role in society.

2. To this end, and having regard to the relevant provisions of international instruments, States Parties shall, in particular, ensure that:

(*a*) No child shall be alleged as, be accused of, or recognized as having infringed the penal law by reason of acts or omissions that were not prohibited by national or international law at the time they were committed;

(*b*) Every child alleged as or accused of having infringed the penal law has at least the following guarantees:

(i) To be presumed innocent until proven guilty according to law;

(ii) To be informed promptly and directly of the charges against him or her, and, if appropriate, through his or her parents or legal guardians, and to have legal or other appropriate assistance in the preparation and presentation of his or her defence;

(iii) To have the matter determined without delay by a competent, independent and impartial authority or judicial body in a fair hearing according to law, in the presence of legal or other appropriate assistance and, unless it is considered not to be in the best interest of the child, in particular, taking into account his or her age or situation, his or her parents or legal guardians;

(iv) Not to be compelled to give testimony or to confess guilt; to examine or have examined adverse witnesses and to obtain the participation and examination of witnesses on his or her behalf under conditions of equality;

(v) If considered to have infringed the penal law, to have this decision and any measures imposed in consequence thereof reviewed by a higher competent, independent and impartial authority or judicial body according to law;

(vi) To have the free assistance of an interpreter if the child cannot understand or speak the language used;

(vii) To have his or her privacy fully respected at all stages of the proceedings.

3. States Parties shall seek to promote the establishment of laws, procedures, authorities and institutions specifically applicable to children alleged as, accused of, or recognized as having infringed the penal law, and, in particular:

(a) The establishment of a minimum age below which children shall be presumed not to have the capacity to infringe the penal law;

(b) Whenever appropriate and desirable, measures for dealing with such children without resorting to judicial proceedings, providing that human rights and legal safeguards are fully respected.

4. A variety of dispositions, such as care, guidance and supervision orders; counselling; probation; foster care; education and vocational training programmes and other alternatives to institutional care shall be available to ensure that children are dealt with in a manner appropriate to their well-being and proportionate both to their circumstances and the offence.

Article 41

Nothing in the present Convention shall affect any provisions which are more conducive to the realization of the rights of the child and which may be contained in:

(a) The law of a State Party; or

(b) International law in force for that State.

PART II

Article 42

States Parties undertake to make the principles and provisions of the Convention widely known, by appropriate and active means, to adults and children alike.

Article 43

1. For the purpose of examining the progress made by States Parties in achieving the realization of the obligations undertaken in the present Convention, there shall be established a Committee on the Rights of the Child, which shall carry out the functions hereinafter provided.

2. The Committee shall consist of ten experts of high moral standing and recognized competence in the field covered by this Convention. The Members of the Committee shall be elected by States Parties from among their nationals and shall serve in their personal capacity, consideration being given to equitable geographical distribution, as well as to the principal legal systems.

3. The members of the Committee shall be elected by secret ballot from a list of persons nominated by States Parties. Each State Party may nominate one person from among its own nationals.

4. The initial election to the Committee shall be held no later than six months after the date of the entry into force of the present Convention and thereafter every second year. At least four months before the date of each election, the

Secretary-General of the United Nations shall address a letter to States Parties inviting them to submit their nominations within two months. The Secretary-General shall subsequently prepare a list in alphabetical order of all persons thus nominated, indicating States Parties which have nominated them, and shall submit it to the States Parties to the present Convention.

5. The elections shall be held at meetings of States Parties convened by the Secretary-General at United Nations Headquarters. At those meetings, for which two thirds of States Parties shall constitute a quorum, the persons elected to the Committee shall be those who obtain the largest number of votes and an absolute majority of the votes of the representatives of States Parties present and voting.

6. The members of the Committee shall be elected for a term of four years. They shall be eligible for re-election if renominated. The term of five of the members elected at the first election shall expire at the end of two years; immediately after the first election, the names of these five members shall be chosen by lot by the Chairman of the meeting.

7. If a member of the Committee dies or resigns or declares that for any other cause he or she can no longer perform the duties of the Committee, the State Party which nominated the member shall appoint another expert from among its nationals to serve for the remainder of the term, subject to the approval of the Committee.

8. The Committee shall establish its own rules of procedure.

9. The Committee shall elect its officers for a period of two years.

10. The meetings of the Committee shall normally be held at United Nations Headquarters or at any other convenient place as determined by the Committee. The Committee shall normally meet annually. The duration of the meetings of the Committee shall be determined, and reviewed, if necessary, by a meeting of the States Parties to the present Convention, subject to the approval of the General Assembly.

11. The Secretary-General of the United Nations shall provide the necessary staff and facilities for the effective performance of the functions of the Committee under the present Convention.

12. With the approval of the General Assembly, the members of the Committee established under the present Convention shall receive emoluments from United Nations resources on such terms and conditions as the Assembly may decide.

Article 44

1. States Parties undertake to submit to the Committee, through the Secretary-General of the United Nations, reports on the measures they have adopted which give effect to the rights recognized herein and on the progress made on the enjoyment of those rights:

(a) Within two years of the entry into force of the Convention for the State Party concerned;

(b) Thereafter every five years.

2. Reports made under the present article shall indicate factors and difficulties, if any, affecting the degree of fulfilment of the obligations under the present Convention. Reports shall also contain sufficient information to provide

the Committee with a comprehensive understanding of the implementation of the Convention in the country concerned.

3. A State Party which has submitted a comprehensive initial report to the Committee need not, in its subsequent reports submitted in accordance with paragraph 1 (*b*) of the present article, repeat basic information previously provided.

4. The Committee may request from States Parties further information relevant to the implementation of the Convention.

5. The Committee shall submit to the General Assembly, through the Economic and Social Council, every two years, reports on its activities.

6. States Parties shall make their reports widely available to the public in their own countries.

Article 45

In order to foster the effective implementation of the Convention and to encourage international co-operation in the field covered by the Convention:

(*a*) The specialized agencies, the United Nations Children's Fund, and other United Nations organs shall be entitled to be represented at the consideration of the implementation of such provisions of the present Convention as fall within the scope of their mandate. The Committee may invite the specialized agencies, the United Nations Children's Fund and other competent bodies as it may consider appropriate to provide expert advice on the implementation of the Convention in areas falling within the scope of their respective mandates. The Committee may invite the specialized agencies, the United Nations Children's Fund, and other United Nations organs to submit reports on the implementation of the Convention in areas falling within the scope of their activities;

(*b*) The Committee shall transmit, as it may consider appropriate, to the specialized agencies, the United Nations Children's Fund and other competent bodies, any reports from States Parties that contain a request, or indicate a need, for technical advice or assistance, along with the Committee's observations and suggestions, if any, on these requests or indications;

(*c*) The Committee may recommend to the General Assembly to request the Secretary-General to undertake on its behalf studies on specific issues relating to the rights of the child;

(*d*) The Committee may make suggestions and general recommendations based on information received pursuant to articles 44 and 45 of the present Convention. Such suggestions and general recommendations shall be transmitted to any State Party concerned and reported to the General Assembly, together with comments, if any, from States Parties.

PART III

Article 46

The present Convention shall be open for signature by all States.

Article 47

The present Convention is subject to ratification. Instruments of ratification shall be deposited with the Secretary-General of the United Nations.

Article 48

The present Convention shall remain open for accession by any State. The instruments of accession shall be deposited with the Secretary-General of the United Nations.

Article 49

1. The present Convention shall enter into force on the thirtieth day following the date of deposit with the Secretary-General of the United Nations of the twentieth instrument of ratification or accession.

2. For each State ratifying or acceding to the Convention after the deposit of the twentieth instrument of ratification or accession, the Convention shall enter into force on the thirtieth day after the deposit by such State of its instrument of ratification or accession.

Article 50

1. Any State Party may propose an amendment and file it with the Secretary-General of the United Nations. The Secretary-General shall thereupon communicate the proposed amendment to States Parties, with a request that they indicate wheter they favour a conference of States Parties for the purpose of considering and voting upon the proposals. In the event that, within four months from the date of such communication, at least one third of the States Parties favour such a conference, the Secretary-General shall convene the conference under the auspices of the United Nations. Any amendment adopted by a majority of States Parties present and voting at the conference shall be submitted to the General Assembly for approval.

2. An amendment adopted in accordance with paragraph 1 of the present article shall enter into force when it has been approved by the General Assembly of the United Nations and accepted by a two-thirds majority of States Parties.

3. When an amendment enters into force, it shall be binding on those States Parties which have accepted it, other States Parties still being bound by the provisions of the present Convention and any earlier amendments which they have accepted.

Article 51

1. The Secretary-General of the United Nations shall receive and circulate to all States the text of reservations made by States at the time of ratification or accession.

2. A reservation incompatible with the object and purpose of the present Convention shall not be permitted.

3. Reservations may be withdrawn at any time by notification to that effect addressed to the Secretary-General of the United Nations, who shall then inform all States. Such notification shall take effect on the date on whch it is received by the Secretary-General.

Article 52

A State Party may denounce the present Convention by written notification to the Secretary-General of the United Nations. Denunciation becomes effective one year after the date of receipt of the notification by the Secretary-General.

Article 53

The Secretary-General of the United Nations is designated as the depositary of the present Convention.

Article 54

The original of the present Convention, of which the Arabic, Chinese, English, French, Russian and Spanish texts are equally authentic, shall be deposited with the Secretary-General of the United Nations.

In witness thereof the undersigned plenipotentiaries, being duly authorized thereto by their respective Governments, have signed the present Convention.

Glossary

AD HOC. This is a French term that means "for a special purpose or occasion." In international relations, an *ad hoc* body (committee, commission, court, or tribunal) is one established to perform a single or specific task, and its life ceases upon the completion of its assigned task.

ADOPTION. The formal act by which states that have negotiated a treaty accept the text of that treaty, as distinct from the obligations of its terms. In international instruments that are not formal treaties, adoption sometimes can mean acceptance of the terms of the instrument. The process of adoption varies, but if a treaty were negotiated at an international conference, for example, its text may be adopted by a two-thirds vote or by any percentage that may have been agreed upon.

AMNESTY. It is the forgetting or overlooking of an offense by a government, so that the alleged offender (individual or group) can become a full participant in society. Offers of amnesty are usually defined by certain limits of events and time.

COMPETENCE. This term refers to the legal fitness or capacity of a court to exercise jurisdiction over issues brought before it. (The term may also refer to the quality of evidence offered to a court.)

CONCILIATION. This refers to the process by which disputes are settled in a friendly manner, usually though the use of someone not involved in the dispute (a third party) as a mediator.

CONVENTION. The name given to certain written agreements concluded between states. A more general term is treaty, but other expressions such as covenant, compact, accord, and charter are used from time to time. Conventions are legally binding on the states that ratify them.

COUP D'ETAT. A French term, which means the use of force, by a group or groups, to effect the sudden change of government by unconstitutional means. Participants in such changes are usually led by members of the security forces of a state, including the military and/or the police.

COVENANT. This is a treaty that is said to be of exceptional moral importance, one whose obligations are seen as sacred.

CULTURAL IMPERIALISM. Imperialism is classically defined as the policy, practice, or advocacy of extending the power, control, and domination of one country over another country. Domination is usually effected through economic and military power. Cultural imperialism refers to the use of culture to effect a similar domination.

DECLARATION. A formal statement of agreement between or among states. Because declarations do not generally require ratification and to that extent do not correspond to treaties in the orthodox sense, commentators and some states argue that they do not have obligatory force. Such is not always the case, however, because declarations often contain statements of existing international law. And, in cases such as the Universal Declaration of Human Rights, they sometimes acquire an obligatory force of their own.

DRAFT DECLARATION. A formal statement of agreement between or among states that has not yet received final approval and may be subject to revisions. Draft treaties and draft statutes also do not have final approval.

ENTRY INTO FORCE. The date on which treaties or other international agreements begin to have legal application or take legal effect. Usually, a treaty enters into force in a manner and on a date stipulated by its terms, and it takes legal effect on those states that have accepted (through ratification) its obligations.

EQUALITY OF STATES. This term refers to the *sovereign* equality of independent countries. Although countries differ in size and power, by virtue of being sovereign they have the right to go to war, to coin their own money, to determine who becomes citizens, to become members of international organizations and negotiate treaties, for example. It is in this sense that they are said to be equal.

EXTRADITION. The delivery of a person suspected or convicted of an alleged wrong (usually a crime) by the state in whose borders he or she is located, to a state that has jurisdiction to try, convict and punish the suspect. In human rights law, an alleged wrongdoer may be the victim of persecution and, if so, the individual should not be extradited. The crime may also be of a political nature—treason and sedition, for example—that do not allow extradition. In cases of crimes against humanity, extradition is obligatory.

HUMAN RIGHTS INSTRUMENTS. This is a term that refers to any and all of the formal legal documents that together embody the ideals, principles, and norms of human rights.

INTERGOVERNMENTAL ORGANIZATIONS. The term refers to those organizations that operate across two or more states and whose members are themselves states. These organizations include the United Nations, the Organization of American States, and the Organization of African Unity.

LIMITATIONS. The term denotes restrictions on the full exercise of one's human rights and fundamental freedoms.

PARTY. Any state that accepts the obligations of an international agreement or other transaction. Sometimes, references are made to State Party or States Parties to a covenant.

PROTOCOL. A treaty that revises or adds to the terms of an earlier treaty. An optional protocol gives countries the choice to determine whether they wish to be bound to its additional terms.

RATIFICATION. An international term that denotes the act by which a state consents to be bound by the terms of a treaty.

RECOMMENDATION. The term refers to a means by which certain international organizations, especially the International Labor Organization, lay down international standards to regulate international life. Usually such recommendations, which are not ratifiable, are not legally binding. They represent international consensus, however, and as such have moral force, and can serve as guidelines for national policies.

RESOLUTION. As used in this volume, resolution is an international term for the formal expression of a consensus by an intergovernmental organization. Like declarations and recommendations, resolutions do not require ratification and create binding international obligations only when they are *accepted in practice* or other treaties by states.

SIGNATORY. Generally, the term refers to a state that signs an international agreement. Signing, for agreements that require ratification or other forms of acceptance, only indicates that the agreement has been authenticated and will be referred to the governments of the signing states. If the treaty does not need ratification or other forms of acceptance, then the act of signing (becoming a signatory) is the equivalent of consenting to be bound by the terms of the agreement. In many cases, signatories to an agreement that must be ratified promise not to engage in any course of conduct, during the period between signing and ratification, which might defeat the aim of the agreement.

SPECIAL RAPPORTEUR. The term, as used in this volume, refers to someone appointed by the UN Commission on Human Rights (or other UN organization) to investigate incidents of alleged governmental actions or omissions that are inconsistent with such government's human rights obligations.

STATE. The term state is used interchangeably with nation and nation-state to mean political and social collectivities that have sovereign independence. In one instance, described in the entry Nation-Building, the term nation is used in a cultural sense, along with its ideology, nationalism.

STATUTORY LIMITATION. This refers to a time period within which a lawsuit or other legal proceedings must be initiated. After the lapse of the time provided by law (statute), no suit can commence. In the case of some crimes, such as crimes against humanity, there is no statutory limitation.

TREATY. A generic term for written international agreements, whether they are called conventions, covenants, charters, concordats, or pacts.

Index

Italic page numbers indicate location of main entries.

About the Author

WINSTON E. LANGLEY is Professor of Political Science and International Relations at the University of Massachusetts, Boston. He specializes in human rights and is the co-author with Vivian C. Fox of *Women's Rights in the United States: A Documentary History* (Greenwood, 1994), which received the Gustavus Myers Center for the Study of Human Rights in North America award for the Outstanding Book on the Subject of Human Rights in North America. He is also author of *Human Rights: The Major Global Instrument* (1992) and *Women's Rights in International Documents* (1991).